C0-ABG-017

SHORTENED CPA LAW REVIEW

Third Edition

GEORGE C. THOMPSON

GERALD P. BRADY

Graduate School of Business
Columbia University

WADSWORTH PUBLISHING COMPANY, INC.

Belmont, California

L.C. CAT. CARD NO.: 70-155899

ISBN-0-534-00099-1

PRINTED IN THE UNITED STATES OF AMERICA

7 8 9 10 75 74

DEDICATION

To the late Professor James L. Dohr, who taught and inspired innumerable students in accounting and business law at the School of Business at Columbia University.

PREFACE

Once again, significant changes in the CPA commercial law examination have made a revision of *Shortened CPA Law Review* imperative. First, the Board of Examiners of the American Institute of CPAs has made some major changes in the subject areas included in the Business Law examination. Starting with the November 1972 exam, Antitrust, Federal Securities Regulation, and Regulation of the Employer and Employee Relationship are included as new and separate topics. Previously they had been collectively included as a minor area under the heading of Administrative Law and questions thereon appeared infrequently during the past decade. Another topic which is not indicated as a new topic but which certainly has changed drastically is Secured Transactions. The area had previously been fragmented, with part of it covered in a minor area called Liens. Conditional sales financing was covered in Sales and pledges and other collateralized loans were included in Bailments. Article 9 of the Uniform Commercial Code has synthesized and replaced all the above subject matter. Questions on Secured Transactions under the Code first appeared in the May 1967 exam. We have added entirely new sections covering Antitrust, Federal Securities Regulation, Secured Transactions, and Regulation of the Employer and Employee Relationship.

Second, the Board of Examiners eliminated their previous practice of grouping the topics into what amounted to major and minor areas of subject coverage. Instead, fourteen topics are listed in alphabetical order. The exact import of this change is difficult to assess. However, it is the opinion of the authors that the Board will continue to draw more frequently from topics such as Accountant's Legal Responsibility and Contracts than from topics such as Wills, Estates and Trusts and Property. To this end, we have tried to arrange the topics of the book on the basis of greatest importance to the candidate in preparing for the examination.

Finally, because of the near-unanimous adoption of the Uniform Commercial Code, the Board of Examiners decided that, beginning with the November 1966 CPA exam, candidates would be expected to apply only their knowledge of the Code in answering questions on subject areas of law covered by the Code (Sales, Commercial Paper, Secured Transactions, and Banking). Previously, candidates were also expected to have a knowledge of the older, separate Uniform Acts. Since the laws contained in these Acts are no longer applicable, we have deleted them. Sales, Commercial Paper (formerly

Negotiable Instruments), Secured transactions, and Banking are based exclusively on the Code. In addition, the major Code changes in the law relating to contracts for the sale of goods have been incorporated into the Contracts chapter. Other areas have also been changed to reflect the impact of the Code. Many areas, of course, were unaffected by the Code (e.g., Accountant's Legal Responsibility, Agency, Partnership, Corporations, and others). These areas have been revised to improve their scope and their effectiveness. Finally, we have added examination questions given in the six years since our last revision.

In spite of all these changes and the revisions we have made to keep pace with them, the purposes of this book remain basically the same:

1. To present a brief but nonetheless comprehensive review of business law.
2. To enable the CPA candidate to prepare more effectively for the business law examination. The outline form shortens the time necessary for review; it is logical and relatively easy to remember.
3. To build up the candidate's confidence. Questions from at least the last twenty CPA business law examinations are coordinated with each substantive area so the student may test and prove himself as he reviews.
4. To indicate an approach to the examination. The introduction shows common pitfalls and the proper mechanics and method of writing the examination.

The outline format has been designed especially for individual review and for use in CPA business law review courses. It may also be used as supplemental material in a business law course.

Our experience with the first and second editions of the book has, we feel, been highly satisfactory. A survey shows that this book covered over 95 percent of the questions included in exams given after our publication dates. No other book presents such a compact, comprehensive review for the law part of the CPA examination.

We again extend our special appreciation to Louis A. Sigaud, Esq., for his valuable aid on the original work in reviewing the entire outline for accuracy and scope of content and in contributing the Introduction. Professor Walter Werner, of the Columbia University School of Law and the Graduate School of Business, was kind enough to provide us with an incisive review of the Federal Securities Regulation topic; Professor Henry Reiling, of the Graduate School of Business, Columbia University, performed a similar review of Antitrust and Accountant's Legal Responsibility. We are indebted to them both for their aid and counsel. We are grateful to the American Institute of Certified Public Accountants for permission to use problems that have appeared on previous CPA examinations.

CONTENTS

INTRODUCTION

PREPARATION FOR THE BUSINESS LAW EXAMINATION

INTRODUCTION

PREPARATION FOR THE BUSINESS LAW EXAMINATION

*by Louis A. Sigaud**

Mr. Sigaud was, until his retirement in 1958, the Assistant Director of Education of the American Institute of Certified Public Accountants specializing in legal education. Mr. Sigaud is a well-known author in addition to being a practicing attorney. Recently Mr. Sigaud wrote the AICPA Manual and other material currently being used in the Institute's Seminar on Accountant's Legal Responsibility.

Adequate knowledge is necessary to pass any examination. Mere acquisition of knowledge, however, is not enough. The acquired knowledge must be qualitative and selective—yet comprehensive. It must have a realistic relation to the specific subject as well as to the scope, content, and depth of past examinations.

When an examination is intended to test not only the existence of adequate knowledge but also the ability to make effective use of it at a professional level, several other requirements must be met. These are: ability to recall quickly and accurately the principles applicable to specific problems and situations; ability to apply these principles with good judgment; and consequently, the ability to express logical decisions and solutions clearly.

The outlines in this work were purposely designed to meet all of these needs. A student who has used one of the standard textbooks in a course in business law will find these outlines extremely effective for essential review. The vital importance of intensive and effective review is dramatically illustrated by the fact that inadequate review is a major cause of failure in the CPA examination.

There are various methods of reviewing fundamentals and insuring their effective retention. Students compile and consult their own notes. Textbook writers include well-organized and useful digests and other review material in their works. And special review

* Author's Note: This excellent introduction by Louis Sigaud has been edited to reflect the changes indicated in the preface.

courses and books are also available. Each of these methods has its distinct advantages and limitations. The outlines in this book have a particular merit which makes them especially effective. They are based not on the particular organization, content, and treatment of a single textbook, but upon the topic descriptions of the AICPA *Information for CPA Candidates* and the over-all content of the standard textbooks on business law. They are also related to past examinations and are based on the general nature and relative frequency of questions in different areas.

COVERAGE OF THE EXAMINATION

Need for review is imperative, but there are other significant matters that should not be overlooked in taking CPA examinations. The nature of the examination must be clearly understood in advance. More particularly, the most effective answers must be given to the questions. Papers cannot be graded on the basis of the knowledge candidates may actually possess. They must be graded on the knowledge the candidates express in their examination papers. Clarity, definiteness, and responsiveness are potent aids in expressing that knowledge.

The CPA examination is meant to test over-all competence to practice at a particular level. The level is that of competence required for a medium-sized engagement anywhere or for a general practice consistent with the normal requirements of a medium-sized community. Specifically, as to knowledge of business law, the CPA examination is meant to have particular application to points of law that are apt to present themselves in such an accounting practice and in situations generally encountered in auditing. The basic purpose of requiring such knowledge is to enable accountants dealing with accounting matters to recognize readily the existence of legal problems and possible need for solution or action by competent and appropriate authority.

Business is organized and functions with due regard to principles of law applicable to its organization and operation. Ignorance of the law is no excuse, and the lack of knowledge can cause economic disaster. Accountants, in view of the special nature of the professional services they render their clients, must have an adequate knowledge of law. They must be able to see that a legal question or situation may exist under specific circumstances which might require preventive, remedial, or other action.

The law part of the examination seeks to test, through essay and objective questions, the ability of candidates (1) to recognize the existence of a legal problem from consideration of certain indicated facts, the general nature of the problem, and the basic legal principles applicable, and (2) to grasp, in a general way, the possible outcome of applying these legal principles to the situation. Accountants need an adequate knowledge of *business law,* and examination questions consequently fall within the scope of standard textbooks on this subject.

It is impossible, of course, to learn in advance what general topics are going to be covered in any CPA examination. But those who are intelligently and thoroughly prepared to deal with any topic that could reasonably be expected in the future are as well equipped as though gifted with foresight. The basic subject, business law, consists of a definitely limited number of topics, each of which is composed of a limited number of subdivisions. Each primary subdivision can be broken down into several subordinate parts with legal principles or rules which may be concisely stated. Such a breakdown constitutes a compact summary of the area in a systematic outline form. When an accountant masters and retains the more important principles in each, he can relate them effectively to most situations whether they occur in actual experience or in examination questions.

Because the major areas are broader and more significant, they play a proportionately larger role in the examinations. Although it is impossible to foresee the particular pattern of the forthcoming test, two very helpful clues are available. Past examinations reveal a general pattern. The areas in which most questions have been asked are likely to be equivalent in the future. At the very least, this analysis furnishes a guide to the relative amount of review that each subject may warrant.

Unfortunately, candidates who have the requisite knowledge often fail to communicate it. It is essential to organize one's ideas at the beginning of the examination in order to state them clearly and concisely.

Although it takes a little more time, some candidates read all the questions at the beginning of the examination in order to obtain an over-all picture. This results in a clearer understanding of each question. Others prefer to read one question at a time and then answer it. All candidates, of course, should read the rules and suggestions preceding the questions, noting how much time is allowed.

Regardless of approach, the candidate should fully understand the facts given in each question before he attempts to answer it. He should then apply his knowledge of legal principles to the facts and reach an appropriate conclusion. Only after such careful analysis is he prepared to support his answer with a clear, orderly, and definite expression of his reasons. Answers that do not conform to this pattern indicate to the grader that the candidate has failed to grasp the question or its factual content, or that he has answered without adequate preliminary organization, or that he does not know the related principles of law.

Answers that offer alternative possibilities but fail to state a conclusion on the validity of either are unresponsive. Intentionally or not, they reveal the candidate's unwillingness or inability to make a decision. Many answers ramble on, contain contradictory statements, and ultimately limp to a conclusion. This reflects an attempt to think through the conclusion and supporting reasons while writing, rather than deciding on an answer before writing. Obviously, such rambling and hesitant answers deserve less credit than a concise and well-organized statement.

A "responsive" answer is of paramount importance. "Responsiveness" demands that the answer be relevant, and in the particular form required. If a conclusion is asked for, it should be expressly stated; when an explanation is required, an unsupported conclusion clearly has no merit.

It is unnecessary to theorize further. The characteristics of responsiveness are shown by the model answers, published regularly in a supplement to the *Journal of Accountancy* a few months after each examination. These answers are prepared not only to give the correct and adequate solutions and explanations, but also to be directly responsive to the specific requirements of each question. The candidate who reviews the questions and answers of several past examinations will benefit in various ways. First, he trains himself to answer responsively and to make his answers brief, explicit, and comprehensive. Second, he learns to allocate his time properly and to apply his general knowledge of principles to specific facts and conditions. Third, he broadens his general knowledge of law in strategic areas.

Since CPA examinations are given semiannually and cover a limited number of general topics in business law, general problems presented in the past may recur in other forms. The same ideas can be made the subject of questions posed in significantly different ways. On the other hand, a change in the factual content of a question can transform it into a new problem requiring the application of completely different principles.

The ever-increasing number of candidates and the growing cost of grading have brought about a greater emphasis on objective questions. It is logical to use the type of objective question so successfully developed in business schools, law schools, and in bar examinations. The questions since 1958 have contained three or four objective questions out of a total number of eight questions.

Many problem-type questions have several parts. These should be initially read as a whole and their interrelationship weighed carefully so that each part can be answered clearly and precisely. There are bound to be unfortunate results when parts of questions are answered without reference to those that follow. Answers to an early part may contain material that is irrelevant there but partly or fully responsive to some later part. When a candidate goes on to answer a later part, he may have to refer to an earlier statement; or he may try to repeat it and apply it more precisely, thus losing valuable time. Neither method is satisfactory. Moreover, since the candidate failed to consider the entire question, answers to various parts may be contradictory.

Though all parts of a question should be read and considered in relation to the entire question, each part should be considered separately. A single all-inclusive answer for several parts is neither in line with stated requirements nor properly informative. This often presents an insoluble grading problem, since the grader cannot sort out the statements relating to the various parts from the general problem. If there are four parts to a question, there should be answers to all four. If one part is further subdivided, the answer should also be subdivided. When each answer is completed, the candidate should make sure that he has answered all the parts. This checking should be included in the time allowed for each question.

Accuracy, thoroughness, and awareness are particularly valuable for accountants. It is therefore puzzling to find a definite lack of these requisites among an appreciable number of candidates in every examination. This is shown by the many failures to comply with clearly expressed instructions. When such instructions are ignored, the consequences are usually disastrous.

ANXIETIES AND ATTITUDES

Tension is at the root of many of these problems and difficulties. Some temporary nervousness is understandable, but those who are adequately prepared should not be inordinately distraught.

The normal attitude should be one of justifiable assurance. A candidate should be sure that he has adequately prepared for the examination by an appropriate course of study backed by recent review. He should have both the aptitudes and inclination which lead to dedication for the profession of accounting. He should have full confidence in those who have established the requirements for admission to the profession and in those who enforce them.

Accounting is not a closed profession. It is constantly broadening its range of activities and is seriously under-manned in relation to both current and future needs. These two facts impose specific responsibilities. One is to bring the profession up to appropriate numerical strength to meet fully the increasing demands society is making upon it. The other is to establish and maintain standards of competence so as to insure that services required of professional accountants will be performed with requisite professional skill, judgment, and care. The consequence is that the profession and those who establish the requirements for admission welcome all those who can qualify. It is their duty to the public and to the candidates to admit those who are demonstrably qualified and to screen out those who cannot pass a test based on the necessary standards.

This is clearly indicated by the special review process which a substantial number of papers undergo after basic grading. As the AICPA booklet "Information for CPA Candidates" points out, papers which come within reasonable reach of a passing mark are singled out for special attention. This involves not only review of the grades for each separate question but also consideration of over-all performance and a decision as to the general competence of the candidates.

Occasionally a candidate's paper ends abruptly with the hastily written words "Ran out of time." This does not mean that the time limitation is unduly restrictive, but rather that the candidate has not allocated time properly. When each examination is prepared, particular attention is paid to the time required for adequate performance. Examination questions are actually tried out to establish a reasonable period for completion.

The "Note to the Candidates" at the beginning of each examination sets forth the time limitations. For each question there is an estimated minimum and maximum time for "adequate answers." It is urged that these estimates be used as a guide and that no more time than the *estimated maximum* be spent on any one question *until* all other questions have been answered.

These suggestions are so simple that they cannot be misunderstood. When a candidate cannot finish the examination within the allotted time, he may have insufficiently prepared in one or both of the following ways: He may have insufficient command of the general subject to answer promptly; or he may not be able to express his conclusions and explanations readily. The basic preparation therefore relates directly to the time element.

When a well-prepared candidate has an appreciable number of minutes left over, he can use this time to great advantage. He should use it to make certain that he has answered all questions, and has followed the general instructions in all other particulars. He can also use his extra minutes to expand some answer which might warrant it. Maximum time for a three-and-a-half-hour period is 210 minutes. Minimum estimated time for adequate answers can be as low as 140 minutes. The difference of 70 minutes represents time which a candidate may have available to review his paper in full or in part before turning it in.

FREQUENCY OF AREAS COVERED ON
(O = Objective Questions

Business Law Topics	5/61	11/61	5/62	11/62	5/63	11/63	5/64	11/64
Accountant's Legal Responsibility		X			⅓X	X	X	X
Contracts	O	X	O	X	X	X	XO	O
Commercial Paper and Banking	X		O	X	O	O		X
Agency	O		X	O	X	X	O	
Partnerships		X		O	O	X	X	O
Corporations	O	X	O	X	O	X		O
Sales	X		X	X			X	
Secured Transactions			X					½X
Federal Securities Regulation				⅓X				
Antitrust				⅔X				
Insurance		O			⅓X	O	O	X
Suretyship	O		X		⅓X			X
Bankruptcy		X			O			
Property		½O				½X		
Wills and Estates and Trusts		X		½O				
Employer-Employee Relationship								½X

USING THIS BOOK

Some comments on studying the outlines that follow will be of value. Each substantive topic of this review outline should be gone over separately and finished before another is begun. Divisions and subdivisions of an outline that are immediately clear should cause no further concern. Their immediate recognition and comprehension assure practically instantaneous recall in pertinent situations.

The time spent in each outline should be determined by the frequency with which the subject is encountered in the CPA examination questions. For example, more time should certainly be devoted to the outline for Contracts than to that for Wills and Estates and Trusts. The chart indicating the frequency of areas covered plus the length of the respective outlines and questions will furnish a useful criterion. It is desirable, naturally, to be well grounded in all fields. But it is more important to be particularly well qualified in the areas in which most questions were asked in past examinations.

An especially valuable feature of these outlines is the inclusion of related questions from CPA examinations of at least the past twenty examinations. The problem-type questions have been arranged in the order of the basic material. Thus they accomplish two purposes: (1) like the outline itself, they serve as a comprehensive review of fundamentals (2) they serve to indicate whether a student's grasp of the outline is as good as he thinks it is. In effect, he must prove it. Furthermore, the large number of objective questions and answers provide an excellent review and a unique opportunity to solidify one's knowledge.

CPA COMMERCIAL LAW EXAMINATION
X = Subjective Questions)

5/65	11/65	5/66	11/66	5/67	11/67	5/68	11/68	5/69	11/69	5/70	11/70
X X	X⅔O	XO	X	X	X O	⅓X	O	X X	X O	O X	X OX
½O X⅓O X	X X O	X X O X	X O O	O O X X ½O	X X O O ½X	O O	X X X O O X	O O X X	X O X ½O	X O O X	X X X O
X ⅓O O ½O	⅔O ⅓O X	X ⅓O ⅔O	X O X	½O XX	X ½X	⅔X O X X	X	O X	X X ½O	X X	½O ½O

Occasional reference has been made in this introduction to the booklet "Information for CPA Candidates" issued by the AICPA. Express authority has been granted to cite this valuable work here. However, the writer's references to actual content of that booklet and all other materials herein represent his own personal views and opinions only, and are not intended to reflect or to indicate anything as official or as approved by any other source.

POSTSCRIPT

There have been many significant changes in the design and format of the examination questions since the original edition of the *Shortened CPA Law Review*. Many of these changes have been indicated in the preface. However, since most readers often skip the preface, we urge you to go back and read it carefully if you have not already done so. In addition, the following changes should be noted.

In recent exams both the objective and subjective type of questions have been based exclusively upon fact situations. These require, first, a thorough understanding of the facts, followed by determining the problem involved, and finally, concluding with an application of the relevant law to the facts. This type of question is more demanding than the prior type of question, which merely asked the candidate to define a term or list the requirements of a contract or negotiable instrument. The current questions are more sophisticated and require a greater ability to analyze the facts and apply the law to them. The most recent questions following each topic are of this type and should be studied carefully. Try at least one set from each topic. You can compare your answers to the objective questions with the solutions found in the Appendix.

In all instances answer questions on the basis of the law prevailing in the majority of jurisdictions. This is the law stated in the overwhelming preponderance of textbooks, and this review book is based almost exclusively upon it. The AICPA Business Law Examination has not specifically required knowledge of the minority rule in fifteen years. In the event that a question does ask for both the majority and minority rules, it will only be those instances where the standard textbook treatment covers both. Finally, the AICPA in its *Information for CPA Candidates* states: "For questions requiring knowledge of only the majority rule, credit will be awarded for the minority rule, when given in lieu of the majority rule, if the response is clearly identified as being that of the minority rule." From a practical standpoint, it is obvious that mastery of the majority rules is the key to success in passing the law part of the examination.

PART ONE

BUSINESS LAW TOPICS FOR THE CPA EXAMINATION

TOPIC ONE

ACCOUNTANT'S LEGAL RESPONSIBILITY

CONTENTS

ACCOUNTANT'S LEGAL RESPONSIBILITY. Knowledge of the accountant's common law civil liability to clients and third parties is tested under this topic. The common law civil liability is based either upon contract or tort (negligence or fraud). Also included is *the accountant's civil and criminal liability imposed by federal statutes, such as the Federal Securities Acts of 1933 and 1934. Finally, the accountant's rights regarding his working papers and privileged communication are included.**

I. CIVIL LIABILITY TO CLIENTS

A. Imposed by common law.

1. Basis: a contractual relationship. Much of the relationship is implied rather than explicitly stated in the contract. Generally an accountant is considered an independent contractor in relation to his clients. (See Agency, p. 128, I.C.4.a)
2. Relationship to other areas of law. In general, the major legal concepts governing the accountants were drawn from contracts, negligence, fraud, agency, and partnerships. Where the accountant's legal responsibility is not defined in this topic, the general rules set forth in those topics would apply.
3. Nature of the standard imposed:
   a. Similar to that imposed upon all professional men.
   b. Must possess average degree of learning and skill of accountants in the particular area and exercise same with reasonable care.
   c. In effect, the law imposes upon the accountant the profession's generally accepted standards of competence and care.
4. Sources of guidance for the CPA in respect to his legal liability:
   a. His contractual undertaking as defined in the agreement with the client. This should be explicitly and carefully defined.
   b. The standards established by the profession, i.e., generally accepted accounting principles and auditing procedures.
   c. Court decisions defining and interpreting the accountant's contractual and tort liability.
   d. The special standards established by state and federal regulatory agencies (e.g., the S.E.C. and I.R.S.).
5. Limitation:
   a. Responsibility is limited to the usual standard unless a greater responsibility is assumed.
   b. Greater responsibility may be assumed by express provision in the contract's terms or by the wording of the audit report.
   c. To insure limitation of responsibility to the usual standards, the reports should indicate clearly the nature and extent of responsibility assumed.
6. Defalcations:
   a. Most legal actions by clients involve claims based on shortages, defalcations, or irregularities not uncovered, and in such actions the general responsibility of accountants to clients has

* Source: AICPA, *Information for CPA Candidates* (July 1970).

been most clearly defined.

b. The usual audit is intended to express professional opinion as to financial position and operating results, not primarily to uncover irregularities. Although the ordinary audit is not especially designed to disclose irregularities, their discovery frequently results as a consequence.

c. In an ordinary audit the accountant does not insure or guarantee clients against losses through irregularities.

d. In examining the statements and reporting thereon he is obligated to exercise ordinary or reasonable care (i.e., he will be liable if negligent).

e. Responsibility for failure to discover an irregularity in an ordinary audit for the examination of statements results only when the examination itself has been performed with a lack of reasonable care and the irregularity would have been discovered had the audit been made with average professional skill and related reasonable care.

7. Negligence:

a. Where the action is based on negligence, the degree of care requisite is reasonable care.

b. Contributory negligence of the client may be a defense if the client's act caused the loss and the client failed to exercise reasonable care.

8. Fraud:

a. When the action is based on fraud, the fraud may be actual or constructive (see Contracts, pp. 48–50, III.A.3.a,b.).

(1) In constructive fraud there need not be *actual* intent to deceive. Such intent may be inferred when statements meant to be relied on are made with reckless disregard or an insincere statement of opinion as to their truth.

(2) Lack of even slight care indicates a reckless disregard of truth and gross negligence. Hence, while negligence does not of itself constitute constructive fraud, it may be possible to infer fraud reasonably from evidence of gross negligence.

9. A firm of public accountants may not escape liability to clients or third persons (see below) by reason of the fact that whatever wrong was committed was not the personal act of the accountants but instead was that of their subordinates. The partners in the firm (principals) are liable for the wrongful acts of their subordinates (agents) if committed within the scope of the employment.

II. COMMON LAW CIVIL LIABILITY TO THIRD PARTIES

A. Negligence and contract:

1. Accountants may only be held liable for ordinary negligence (lack of reasonable care) by third parties when the accountant knows that the services for a client are primarily for the benefit of a third party.
2. When the services are primarily for the benefit of a third party, the third party is, in effect (even though not in actuality), a party to the contract between the accountant and client (a third party beneficiary—see Contracts, p. 54, VI.C.).
3. When services by accountants for clients are primarily for the benefit of the clients as a convenient instrumentality for use in developing their business, and only incidentally or collaterally for the use of third parties to whom the accountants' reports may be exhibited, the accountants have no liability to such third parties for ordinary negligence (lack of reasonable care) or even gross negligence (lack of slight care).

B. Fraud:

1. Accountants owe a duty to all third parties to make their reports without fraud, whether such reports are intended primarily for the benefit of third parties or primarily for the benefit of clients (see p. 14, I.A.8.).

III. LIABILITY TO THIRD PARTIES CREATED BY FEDERAL STATUTES

A. Securities Act of 1933:

1. The Act regulates public offerings of securities through the mails or in interstate commerce.
2. The Act requires the filing of a registration statement with the Securities and Exchange Commission prior to the offering of securities in which full disclosure of all material facts concerning the securities to be offered must be made. The Act is known as the "truth in securities law" and is aimed at protecting the investing public.
3. The registration statement must include financial statements certified by independent public accountants (invariably CPA s).
4. Any person acquiring securities covered by the registration statement may sue the accountant. This, of course, includes third parties (the investing public) who are not clients of the accountant.
5. The basis for the claim is an alleged false statement or omission of a material fact in the certified financial statements.
   a. Such a claim by the party sueing (the plaintiff) establishes a

prima facie case, i.e., one which will suffice unless contradicted by other evidence.
   b. Thus, the plaintiff does not have the added burden of proving that the accountants were negligent or fraudulent in certifying the financial statements.
   c. Plaintiff need not prove reliance upon the financial statement or that the loss suffered was the proximate result of the false statement or misleading omission.
   d. In effect, much of the burden of proof, typically required of a plaintiff, has been shifted to the accountant (defendant).
6. The accountant has the burden of proving he was neither negligent nor fraudulent in certifying the financial statements.
   a. He may satisfy this burden by showing that he made a reasonable investigation, had a reasonable basis for his belief, and did believe the financial statements to which he certified were true.
   b. His duty as to the truth of the statements certified is *as of the time when the registration statement becomes effective,* and not the typical time which is as of the date of the financial statements. Thus, once again, potential liability has been increased.
7. The accountant may also avoid or reduce his liability by showing that the plaintiff's loss was caused in whole or part by factors other than the false statements or omissions of material facts in the financial statements.
8. The Act contains a two-part statute of limitations, which bars actions under its provisions.
   a. First, any action must be brought within one year after discovery of the untrue statement or omission, or after such discovery should have been made by the exercise of reasonable diligence.
   b. Second, in no event can an action be brought more than three years after the security was offered in good faith to the public.

B. Securities Exchange Act of 1934

1. The Act regulates securities exchanges and the securities listed and traded thereon. In addition, post 1964, most provisions of the Act apply to companies whose securities are traded over-the-counter and have in excess of $1 million in total assets and a class of equity securities held by 500 or more persons as of the last day of the fiscal year.
2. The SEC requires each corporation subject to the Act to file an annual report (form 10-K) within 120 days after the close of the fiscal year. The 10-K report must be distinguished from the annual report to shareholders.
   a. Form 10-K is subject to specific SEC information requirements and to provisions governing the form and content of the

financial statements which must accompany the report (see *infra,* Federal Securities Regulation, p. 266).

b. With limited exceptions, the form and content of annual reports to shareholders are basically determined by the company issuing them.

3. The accountant's chief source of liability under the Act results from the required filing of certified financial statements which must accompany the annual report to the SEC.
4. The Act imposes civil liability upon any person (including the certifying accountant) who in any report makes a statement which is false or misleading in respect to any material fact.
5. Any buyer or seller of the security to which the false statement relates may sue provided he can prove that he:
   a. Bought or sold at a price affected by the false or misleading statement,
   b. Relied upon the statement, and
   c. Did not know of its falsity.
6. The accountant may avoid liability if he proves that he:
   a. Acted in good faith, and
   b. Had no knowledge that the statement was false or misleading.
7. The Securities Exchange Act has the same time limitations for bringing an action as discussed above in relation to the 1933 Act.
8. At present, there is much discussion of the possibility of liability of the accountant under Section 10b and Rule 10b-5 of the 1934 Act. Liability, in general, under this provision is covered in Federal Securities Regulation.
9. A comparison of the major features of both Acts makes it apparent that the 1933 Act is much stiffer in respect to the imposition of liability on accountants. The most obvious differences are in the burden of proof of the respective parties, the requirements necessary to establish the defense of lack of knowledge of falsity, and the time at which the statements are to be tested as to truth (the 1933 Act goes beyond the date of the financial statements to the time the registration statement becomes effective).

IV. CRIMINAL LIABILITY

A. Federal statutes.

1. The Federal Securities Acts of 1933 and 1934: Any person convicted of a willful violation of any provision of the Acts or their regulations, willful falsification of any material fact in a registration statement, or willful omission of any material fact required to be stated therein or necessary to make the statements therein not misleading, is subject to a fine of not more than $10,000, or imprisonment for not more than five years, or both.
2. Federal Internal Revenue Code (Sec. 7206, 7207): provides fines or imprisonment for any person violating its provisions. For example:

a. Willfully making a statement, return, or other document, which contains a written declaration that is made under the penalties of perjury, and which he does not believe to be true and correct as to every material matter; or

b. Willfully aiding in the preparation of any matter arising under internal revenue law which is fraudulent or false in any material matter whether or not such falsity or fraud is with the knowledge or consent of the person authorized or required to present such matter; or

c. Fraudulently executing documents required by provisions of the internal revenue law or procuring the false execution thereof; or

d. Removing or concealing goods with intent to evade any tax imposed by the internal revenue law; or

e. Willfully delivering documents that are known to him to be fraudulent or false.

B. State statutes: Most states have statutory provisions declaring criminal liability for such offenses as knowingly certifying to false or fraudulent reports, falsifying, altering, or destroying books of account, failing to make material entries and obtaining property or credit by use of false financial statements.

V. ACCOUNTANT'S WORKING PAPERS

A. Common law.

1. In the absence of express agreement that working papers of accountants are to belong to clients or to be held for them, ownership of such working papers is held to rest in the accountants.
2. Common law recognition of ownership by the accountants rests upon the *Ipswich Mills* v. *Dillon* case.

B. Statute.

1. In thirteen, or more, jurisdictions it is provided expressly by statute that, in the absence of express or written agreement to the contrary, ownership of working papers rests in the accountants.

C. Limitation of ownership.

1. Ownership of working papers by accountants is actually so restricted as to be basically custodial, with the dual purpose of permitting the accountants to retain them as evidence of the nature and extent of the services rendered and to prevent confidential information therein from being transmitted to others

(including other accountants) without the actual consent of clients. Accountants may, in general, render services to competing clients.

2. It has been held that an accountant (a sole proprietor) could not dispose of his working papers by will and that they must be destroyed unless needed to protect the estate against claims.
3. Ownership of working papers by accountants is not a valid ground for refusing to testify regarding matters covered thereby or to produce them in evidence when such testimony or production is required by legal process.

VI. PRIVILEGED COMMUNICATIONS

A. Common law: At common law no status of privileged communication exists between an accountant and his client, and, therefore, privilege is not available as a valid ground for refusing to testify as to such communications when such testimony is required by legal process.

B. Statute: In fourteen, or more, jurisdictions, the status of privileged communication has been given by statute to confidential communications between an accountant and his client.

C. Waiver of privilege: The status of privilege being established for the benefit of clients, waiver of such privilege in any instance can only be by the client.

INTRODUCTORY NOTE TO EXAMINATION QUESTIONS*

Each substantive section in this book will be followed by applicable questions from at least the 20 most recent exams of Uniform Certified Public Accountant Examinations in Commercial Law. These examinations are administered twice a year under the auspices of the American Institute of Certified Public Accountants. All questions have been included except those which are merely repetitious. The first group (subjective questions) is arranged in the order in which the material is presented in each outline; this arrangement readily enables the student to consult the outline for the answer to those questions which still prove troublesome. The second group (objective questions) serves as an excellent review of your general knowledge of the area. The answers are contained in the Appendix.

Each question in the first group is followed by a citation, the first part of which indicates the month and year in which the examination question was given. The second part of the citation refers to the appropriate page of this text in which the answer appears. Thus, the citation to the first question below is to the May 1969

* Prepared by the board of examiners of the American Institute of Certified Public Accountants and adopted by the examining boards of all states, territories, and the District of Columbia.

Uniform CPA Examination, the answer to Part (1) may be found on page 15 of this text.

ACCOUNTANT'S LEGAL RESPONSIBILITY: SUBJECTIVE QUESTIONS*

CIVIL LIABILITY

Q. Williams, a CPA, was engaged by Jackson Financial Development Company to audit the financial statements of Apex Construction Company, a small closely held corporation. Williams was told when he was engaged that Jackson Financial needed reliable financial statements which would be used to determine whether or not to purchase a substantial amount of Apex Construction's convertible debentures at the price asked by the estate of one of Apex's former directors.

Williams performed his examination in a negligent manner. As a result of his negligence he failed to discover substantial defalcations by Brown, the Apex controller. Jackson Financial purchased the debentures but would not have if the defalcations had been discovered. After discovery of the fraud Jackson Financial promptly sold them for the highest price offered in the market at a $70,000 loss.

(1) What liability does Williams have to Jackson Financial? Explain.

(2) If Apex Construction also sues Williams for negligence, what are the probable legal defenses which Williams' attorney would raise? Explain.

(3) Will the negligence of a CPA as described above prevent him from recovering on a liability insurance policy covering the practice of his profession? Explain.

5/69; p.15

Q. Give a detailed account of the nature of the certified public accountant's legal responsibility to (1) clients and (2) third parties as to skill and care in performing an engagement and submitting a report.

5/65; p.13-15

Q. The S Surety Company has written a general fidelity bond covering defalcations by employees of the Able Corporation. Upon being informed of shortages caused by the wrongful activities of an employee of Able Corporation, the S Surety Company paid the Able Corporation the full amount of its loss. The S Surety Company now seeks to hold the CPA firm that gave an opinion upon the corporation's statements liable for the shortages. The shortages were the result of clever forgeries, collusive fraud, and unrecorded transactions which would not be uncovered by an examination made in accordance with generally accepted auditing standards.

* See Introductory Note, p. 19.

(1) The S Surety Company claims that the CPA firm is, in effect, an insurer insofar as detection of defalcations is concerned. That is, the CPA firm is liable if it fails to discover a defalcation. Is this correct? Explain.

(2) What is the general legal standard governing a CPA's liability for negligence?

5/63; p. 13, 14

Q. Mio & Mio, Certified Public Accountants, were engaged for several years by Famous Carpet Company, manufacturers of woolen carpet, to conduct an annual audit. Excellent Carpet Company, a competitor of Famous, now seeks to engage the Mio firm to install a more advanced accounting system and to conduct an annual audit. The officers of Excellent approached Mio & Mio because of its outstanding reputation in the community and its acknowledged expertise in the carpet industry. May Mio & Mio accept the Excellent Carpet Company as a client? Explain.

11/69; p. 19

Q. (Continuing the facts in the question above.) Subsequently, one of the officers of Excellent offered to pay Mio & Mio a substantial bonus if they would disclose confidential financial information about Famous' operations to permit the officer to make a comparative study of the operating performance of the two carpet companies. May Mio & Mio accept this offer? Explain.

11/69; p. 18

Q. As an accommodation to its clients, the CPA firm of Ross, Smith and Lewis sometimes served as the agent to receive the balance of the sales price due a client at a real estate closing. The CPA firm's practice was to deposit the sums received in the firm's checking account and issue its own check to the client when notified to do so.

On September 14, 1969 the CPA firm received a $10,000 payment on behalf of its client, Rosewell, and deposited the money to its own account in the Security State Bank. On September 20, 1969, after an examination by the state banking examiners, the Security State Bank closed and indicated to its depositors that the bank had failed. Who must bear the loss resulting from the Security State Bank's failure? Explain.

11/69; p. 13

Q. The CPA firm of Bigelow, Barton and Brown was expanding very rapidly. Consequently it hired several junior accountants, including a man named Small. Subsequently, the partners of the firm became dissatisfied with Small's production and warned him that they would be forced to discharge him unless his output increased significantly.

At that time Small was engaged in audits of several clients. He decided that, to avoid being fired, he would reduce or omit entirely some of the standard auditing procedures listed in audit programs prepared by the partners. One of the CPA firm's clients, Newell Corporation, was in serious financial difficulty and had adjusted several of its accounts being examined by Small to appear financially sound. Small prepared fictitious working papers in his home at night to support purported completion of auditing procedures assigned to him although he in fact did not examine the adjusting entries. The CPA firm rendered an unqualified opinion on Newell's financial statements which were grossly misstated. Several creditors subsequently extended large sums of money to Newell Corporation relying upon the audited financial statements.

Would the CPA firm be liable to the creditors who extended the money in reliance on the erroneous financial statements if Newell Corporation should fail to pay them? Explain.

11/69; p. 15

Q. The Henry Manufacturing Company was hard pressed financially. Its president therefore applied to the X County Bank for a $10,000 loan. The Bank was unwilling to lend money to Henry without financial statements on which a CPA had given his opinion. Henry engaged an accounting firm to perform the audit. The X County Bank attended the final meeting wherein Henry engaged the firm. The Bank made clear to both parties at that time that the loan was contingent upon certain minimum financial tests being met (e.g., at least a 1 : 1 current ratio). Henry's president, to insure that the loan would be made, inserted several substantial bogus accounts into the accounts receivable files. The CPA firm negligently failed to detect these fraudulent accounts. On the strength of the financial statements and the auditor's unqualified opinion, the X County Bank made the loan. Henry is now insolvent and has been placed in the hands of a receiver.

(1) In a suit brought by the bank against the CPA firm, under what legal argument would the bank be most likely to prevail? Explain.

(2) What is the most likely legal argument that the attorney for the CPA firm will make in order to attempt to avoid liability to the bank? For the purpose of this question take the facts as stated as being proven and do not give any consideration to the question of whether the argument will prevail.

(3) Suppose that in the above case the CPA firm was not aware of the Bank's request for the financial statements and that it gave an unqualified opinion on the statements without performing any verification procedures on the account's receivable, which constituted a substantial part of the total assets. Would the Bank prevail? Explain.

(4) In addition to the contract with the client, what are the three principal sources of guidance for a CPA in respect to his legal liability?

11/64; p. 15

Q. Mark, a certified public accountant, was engaged by Franklin Corporation to compute the net income attributable to the sale of certain products by the Corporation for 1964. The purpose of this special engagement was to provide the basis for determination of the year-end bonuses payable to sales personnel. Mark was fully informed of the purpose of the engagement and was negligent in it, and several of the key salesmen received substantially less than they were entitled to. The Franklin Corporation is currently bankrupt and unable to pay the claims of the salesmen. However, in 1964 the Corporation was solvent and could have paid the proper amounts. Can the salesmen recover from Mark the loss they suffered as a result of his negligence? Explain.

11/67; p. 15

Q. Henry, a wealthy industrialist, bought all the outstanding stock of the Zebra Manufacturing Company from Phillips and Vogel. In deciding to purchase the stock of the Corporation and in determining the purchase price of the stock, Henry relied heavily on the company's financial statements; these had been examined by Charles, a CPA, who had rendered an unqualified opinion on them. At the time Charles did the audit, Henry had not approached Phillips and Vogel regarding the possible purchase of Zebra. Several months after the sale of stock had been consummated, a lawsuit for a substantial sum was brought against the Zebra Corporation. The basis for this liability was present, although contingent, at the time the audit was performed. The financial statements of the Corporation failed to disclose this contingent liability. This error was due to Charles' negligence in that he failed to make a reasonable investigation of the claim. A valid judgment was subsequently rendered against and paid by the Corporation. Can Henry recover from Charles the loss in value of the stock attributable to the liability? Explain.

11/66; p.15

Q. The basic facts are the same as stated above except that the financial statements in question were prepared for submission to the Securities and Exchange Commission in connection with a public offering of the Corporation's stock pursuant to the provisions of the Securities Act of 1933. James is one of the parties who bought some of the shares of stock offered to the public. Can James recover from Charles the loss in value of the stock attributable to the liability? Explain.

11/66; p.15-16

Q. Johnson, a CPA, was engaged by Frank & Co., a lending institution, to examine the financial statements of the Sare partnership. Frank & Co. was considering lending the Sare partnership a large amount of money. One of the partnership's current assets consisted of $25,000 face value negotiable bearer coupon bonds which were kept in the partnership's safe deposit box. Johnson, in performing the audit, went to the box and examined the bonds. Unfortunately the bonds were not genuine; they were clever forgeries which only an expert could detect. This fraud was not discovered until Sare defaulted on the loan and Frank & Co. attempted to sell the bonds, which had been pledged as collateral to secure the loan. Frank & Co. asserts that Johnson is liable for the loss to the extent of the value of the bonds. If the bonds had been genuine, they would have been sufficient, along with the other Sare partnership assets, to satisfy the loan. Johnson denies liability. Is Johnson liable for the loss? Explain.

11/66; p.14

Q. Williams, a CPA, was engaged by Andrews, the president of a small corporation, to examine the corporation's financial statements. Williams was pressed for time and decided to withdraw from the engagement. Without consulting Andrews, Williams asked Franklin, another CPA to whom he owed a favor, to handle the client on his own behalf. Franklin was in all respects as competent as Williams. Andrews took a personal dislike to Franklin and refused to accept him. Is Andrews liable for breach of contract as a result of refusing to accept Franklin? Explain.

11/66; pp. 13, 54

Q. The AB&C accounting firm audited the books of account of the E Corporation and gave an unqualified opinion on its financial statements. It was admitted by all parties concerned that the audit was made in good faith and was not a grossly negligent audit. However, it was at best a slovenly job, one which would be correctly categorized as a negligent audit. The net worth on the balance sheet was incorrect to the extent of $300,000. This was due to fraudulent overvaluations of the assets and understatements of the liabilities by the Corporation. As a result of these inaccuracies, the Corporation appeared to have a net worth of $250,000 whereas, in fact, there was an excess of liabilities over assets of some $50,000. The president of E Corporation used this balance sheet in persuading several creditors to lend $75,000 to the Corporation. The Corporation is now hopelessly insolvent, and the creditors seek to recover their losses from the AB&C accounting firm.

(1) Will the AB&C accounting firm be liable for the losses to the creditors which were caused by the negligent audit? Explain. Discuss the underlying rationale for the rule.

(2) If the AB&C accounting firm had been engaged by the creditors to make the audit, would your answer be different? Explain.

5/64; p.15

LIABILITY TO THIRD PARTIES CREATED BY FEDERAL STATUTES

Q. The Federal Securities Act of 1933, which regulates the public offering of securities through the mails or in interstate commerce, included some major provisions regarding accountants' legal liability. List and explain the Act's major provisions affecting accountants' legal liability.

11/67; pp. 15-16

CRIMINAL LIABILITY

Q. In addition to the civil liability imposed upon the accountant, certain federal statutes impose criminal liability on those preparing financial statements. List three well-known statutes which have so imposed liability and with which accountants are frequently concerned.

11/61; pp. 17-18

ACCOUNTANT'S WORKING PAPERS

Q. The X Corporation engaged Y, a CPA, to examine its financial statements. Nothing was expressly agreed between the parties as to the ownership of Y's working papers. In a subsequent year the client engaged another firm to examine its statements. The client demanded the return of the working papers from Y.

(1) To whom do the working papers belong? Explain the reasons why this is the rule.

(2) What restrictions, if any, are placed upon the ownership of the working papers? Explain.

11/63; pp. 18-19

Q. Keen, a certified public accountant and sole practitioner, was retained by Arthur & Son, a partnership, to audit the company books and prepare a report on the financial statements for submission to several prospective partners as part of a planned expansion of the firm. Keen's fee was fixed on a per diem basis. After a period of intensive work, Keen completed about half of the necessary field work; he then suffered a paralyzing stroke. He was forced to abandon all his work and in fact retired from the profession. The planned expansion of the firm failed to materialize because the prospective partners would act only upon the basis of the report which Keen was to have submitted and lost interest when the report was not available.

(1) Arthur & Son sues Keen for breach of his contract. Will it recover? Explain.

(2) Keen sues Arthur & Son for his fee for the work he was able to complete or, in the alternative, for the reasonable value of the services performed. Will he recover? Explain.

(3) Arthur & Son demands from Keen all of the working papers relative to the engagement, including several cancelled checks, the articles of co-partnership, and some other records of the firm. Will the firm succeed in its demand? Explain.

5/65; pp. 18-19

PRIVILEGED COMMUNICATION

Q. Peter is a certified public accountant and Frank is one of his clients. Frank was sued and Peter was called as a witness by the opposing party. After being sworn in, Peter was asked certain questions which related to confidential business matters of Frank's which came to Peter's attention in his professional accounting capacity. Frank's attorney immediately objected to the questions, claiming that the admission of such evidence would be violative of the "privileged communication" rule.

(1) Explain the meaning of the term "privileged communication."

(2) What is the policy factor which has led to the recognition of privileged communication as a valid reason for the exclusion of evidence.

(3) Indicate the most common types of relationships that give rise to privileged communication.

(4) Based upon the attorney's objection, what will the result be in the above fact situation according to the common law rule? Explain.

5/64; p.19

Q. For several years Martin engaged Watson, a CPA, to prepare the financial statements for the construction business which Martin owned and operated in his own name. Franklin is the owner of a building which Martin built on a cost-plus-fixed-fee basis. Franklin sued Martin alleging that Martin overcharged him by inflating the cost to construct his building. In preparing for trial, Franklin obtained a court order requiring Watson to turn over to Franklin all his (Watson's) working papers and correspondence relating to Martin's construction business.

At the subsequent trial, Franklin's attorney sought to introduce in evidence the working papers and correspondence subpoenaed pursuant to the court order. Martin's attorney objected claiming that the papers were inadmissible evidence.

(1) What is the legal basis for Martin's attorney's objection to the admission of the papers in evidence? Explain.

(2) Will the evidence be admitted? Explain.

(3) Who owns the working papers prepared by Watson? Explain.

5/69; p.19

ACCOUNTANT'S LEGAL RESPONSIBILITY: OBJECTIVE QUESTIONS

(1) Marshall, Clay, Henry and Company is a brokerage firm which deals in over-the-counter stocks and commodities. The brokerage firm engaged the accounting firm of Smith and Wilson to examine quarterly financial statements. Smith and Wilson performed the audit for three years (1966-1968) and the business appeared to be prosperous. Early in 1969 Baron, a trusted employee in charge of the commodities de-

partment confessed to fraud after an office investigation by Marshall, Clay, Henry and Company. As a result it was learned that Baron had stolen over one million dollars during the four-year period preceding his confession. Baron had falsified the books of the firm to avoid detection. Marshall, Clay, Henry and Company have sued the accounting firm.

(a) The accounting firm is liable for the loss for breach of contract in that the standard audit contract guarantees the discovery of defalcations.
(b) The standard of care that must be used in the audit is the care which a reasonably prudent and skillful accountant would use under like circumstances.
(c) If it can be shown that the brokerage firm failed to exercise reasonable care and thus contributed to Baron's continued defalcations, the accountants will not be liable for the losses.
(d) In the event a surety paid the brokerage firm for a portion of the defalcations under a blanket fidelity bond which covered Baron, the surety company could obtain reimbursement from the accountants if they were negligent in performing any of the audits.
(e) If the audit contract were not in writing, the accountants could plead the Statute of Frauds and avoid liability.

(2) Watts and Williams, a firm of certified public accountants, audited the accounts of Sampson Skins, Inc., a corporation that imports and deals in fine furs. Upon completion of the examination the auditors supplied Sampson Skins with 20 copies of the certified balance sheet. The firm knew in a general way that Sampson Skins wanted that number of copies of the auditor's report to furnish to banks and other potential leaders.

The balance sheet in question was in error by approximately $800,000. Instead of having a $600,000 net worth, the Corporation was insolvent. The management of Sampson Skins had "doctored" the books to avoid bankruptcy. The assets had been overstated by $500,000 of fictitious and non-existing accounts receivable and $300,000 of non-existing skins listed as inventory when in fact they had only empty boxes. The audit failed to detect these fraudulent entries. Martinson, relying on the certified balance sheet, loaned Sampson Skins $20,000. He seeks to recover his loss from Watts and Williams.

(a) If Martinson alleges and proves negligence on the part of Watts and Williams, he would be able to recover his loss.
(b) If Martinson alleges and proves constructive fraud, i.e., gross negligence on the part of Watts and Williams, he would be able to recover his loss.
(c) Martinson is not in privity of contract with Watts and Williams.
(d) Unless actual fraud on the part of Watts and Williams could be shown, Martinson could not recover.

(e) Martinson is a third party beneficiary of the contract Watts and Williams made with Sampson Skins.

(3) The Dandy Container Corporation engaged the accounting firm of Adams and Adams to examine financial statements to be used in connection with a public offering of securities. The audit was completed and an unqualified opinion was expressed on the financial statements which were submitted to the Securities and Exchange Commission along with the registration statement. Two hundred thousand shares of Dandy Container common stock were offered to the public at $11 a share. Eight months later the stock fell to $2 a share when it was disclosed that several large loans to two "paper" corporations owned by one of the directors were worthless. The loans were secured by the stock of the borrowing corporation which was owned by the director. These facts were not disclosed in the financial report. The director involved and the two corporations are insolvent.

(a) The Securities Act of 1933 applies to the above described public offering of securities in interstate commerce.

(b) The accounting firm has potential liability to any person who acquired the stock in reliance upon the registration statement.

(c) An insider who had knowledge of all the facts regarding the loans to the two "paper" corporations could nevertheless recover from the accounting firm.

(d) An investor who bought shares in Dandy Container would make a prima facie case if he alleged that the failure to explain the nature of the loans in question constituted a false statement or misleading omission in the financial statements.

(e) The accountants could avoid liability if they could show they were neither negligent nor fraudulent.

(f) Accountants' responsibility as to the fairness of the financial statements is determined as of the date of the auditor's report and not beyond.

(g) The accountants could avoid or reduce the damages asserted against them if they could establish that the drop in price was due in whole or in part to other causes.

(h) The Dandy investors would have to institute suit within one year after discovery of the alleged untrue statements or omissions.

(i) It would appear that the accountants were negligent in respect to the handling of the secured loans in question—if they discovered the facts regarding the loans to the "paper" corporations and failed to disclose them in their financial statements.

(j) The Securities and Exchange Commission would defend any action brought against the accountants in that the SEC examined and approved the registration statement.

(4) Filmore Hale, Charles Hardy and Alfred Boggs were all successful certified public accountants. They operated as sole practitioners but found it difficult to handle the increasing number of clients who

wished to retain them. Therefore, they decided to join together in a partnership to be known as Hale, Hardy and Boggs. In accordance with this understanding they drafted and signed the following partnership agreement:

> We, Filmore Hale, Charles Hardy and Alfred Boggs do hereby join together as equal partners in the Hale, Hardy and Boggs partnership for the purpose of practicing accounting. The duration of this partnership will be for a minimum of three years and in no event may any partner withdraw prior to the expiration of said period.

Two juniors were hired to help with the firm's work. One proved to be an incompetent and was negligent in auditing the accounts of several clients.

(a) The firm could avoid liability for the junior accountant's negligence if it could show he disobeyed specific instructions regarding performance of the audit.
(b) Any partner has the legal power to dissolve the partnership at any time.
(c) Any partner acting individually, without the express consent of the others, has the apparent authority to borrow money on the firm's behalf.
(d) A new partner may be admitted to the firm upon the affirmative vote of any two members of the firm.
(e) The partnership agreement had to be in writing.
(f) If the assets of the firm were insufficient to satisfy the claims of clients who were harmed by the negligence of the junior accountant, the partners would be personally liable.
(g) If the firm had an insurance policy covering malpractice and the insurance company paid the negligence claims of the clients, the insurance company would succeed to the firm's rights against the negligent junior.
(h) Profits will be shared according to which partner's client the profit is allocable to.
(i) Confidential correspondence between the firm and its clients is privileged in the Federal courts.
(j) Clients who terminate their relationship with the firm have the right to demand and receive any and all working papers relating to work the firm did for them.

5/70

TOPIC TWO | CONTRACTS

CONTENTS PAGE

*CONTRACTS. This topic is concerned with the fundamental legal question of which promises between two or more persons are to be afforded the status of contracts, and hence, are enforceable in a court of law. Subject matter includes offer, acceptance, consideration, legality, capacity to contract, unfairness in the bargaining process (e.g., fraud), the Statute of Frauds, third-party rights, performance, breach, and remedies. In addition, Article 2 (Sales) of the Uniform Commercial Code must be considered in light of the substantial changes it caused to contracts for the purchase or sale of goods.**

I. DEFINITION: FOR ANY AGREEMENT BETWEEN TWO OR MORE PARTIES TO BE ENFORCEABLE IN LAW—THAT IS, A CONTRACT—THERE MUST BE:

A. An offer (statement of intent) to be bound to do or refrain from doing something, which has been accepted

B. Sufficient consideration

C. A valid subject matter

D. Legal capacity of parties and

E. For those contracts to which the Statute of Frauds applies, its requirements must be met.

II. TYPES OF CONTRACTS

A. Express contract: an actual agreement of the parties, the terms of which are openly stated or declared at the time of making it, in distinct and explicit language, either orally or in writing.

* Source: AICPA, *Information for CPA Candidates* (July 1970).

B. Implied contract.

1. Implied in fact: one inferred by law, from the acts or conduct of the parties; the circumstances surrounding the transaction making it a reasonable or even a necessary assumption that a contract existed between them by tacit understanding.
2. Quasi contract: implied in law, not actually a contract, since it is not necessarily pursuant to the intention of a party and is possibly against his will. However, the law imposes such agreements to prevent unjust enrichment, by the equitable doctrine that no person should be allowed to enrich himself inequitably at another's expense. (E.g., when money is improperly paid there is an implied obligation to return it, and when money is improperly received there is an implied obligation to account for it.)

C. Bilateral contract: a promise given in exchange for a promise, i.e., mutual promises. (E.g., I promise you $10 if you promise to cut my hedge.)

D. Unilateral contract: a promise on one side only, the consideration for the promise being an act by the other party. (E.g., I promise to give you $10 for your act of cutting my hedge.)

E. Joint contract: a contract made by two or more promisors, who are jointly bound to fulfill its obligations, or made to two or more promisees who are jointly entitled to require performance of the same obligations.

F. Joint and several contract: a contract in which two or more persons are both equally obligated together (jointly obligated), but also individually obligated (severally obligated) in that one or more promisors or promisees has a legal right (either from the terms of the agreement or the nature of the understanding) to enforce his individual interest separately from the other parties (e.g., sue or be sued individually).

G. Entire contract: entire fulfillment of the promise by either is necessary as a condition precedent— see p. 57, VII.B.1.b.(2) (B) (i)—to the partial or full performance of the other individual (e.g., a contract to pay $100 for a painting when completed).

H. Severable contract: a contract is divisable and enforceable in portions; some performance may be given by one side so as to correspond to the consideration given by the other side (e.g., an installment contract calling for the delivery of coal, ice, and oil over a six-months' period).

I. Options (see p. 34, III.A.1.e.).

J. Unconscionable contract: one which no sensible man not under delusion, duress, or in distress would make, and such as no honest and fair man would accept. Court will find no contract under such conditions.

UCC RULE [2–302]: *If the court finds the contract for the sale of goods or a clause thereof to be unconscionable, it may either refuse to enforce it* or *enforce the remainder* or *so limit the application of the clause as to avoid any unconscionable result.*

NOTE: The Uniform Commercial Code (hereinafter UCC) has made substantial inroads in the common law of contracts, which is the basis for this chapter. Such changes are of major significance and are included throughout the contracts chapter in *italics* in order to highlight their importance and to provide a meaningful contrast. However, it should be clearly recognized that *the UCC changes in contract law apply almost exclusively to contracts for the sale of goods.* The older common law rules still apply to all other contracts, such as contracts for the sale of real property, employment contracts, insurance contracts, etc.

III. ELEMENTS NECESSARY FOR AN ENFORCEABLE AGREEMENT

A. Offer and acceptance—manifesting mutual assent to be bound.

1. Offer.

a. Offer may be either written or oral.

b. There must be clear intention to contract.

(1) If offeree (person to whom offer is made) knows or has reason to know that there is no intention on the part of the offeror to express an offer, there is no offer (e.g., offers made in jest). The test is an objective one; i.e., would a reasonable man believe that the offer was made with the requisite intent. (See p. 36, III.A.3.)

(2) Invitations to trade (such as price lists, ads, quotes, and bids) and mere proposals to negotiate are usually not found to constitute offers—the test being whether from the words and conduct of the parties a reasonable man would believe an offer had been made.

c. Offer must be definite and certain.

(1) A court cannot enforce an agreement where the things to be done are indefinite or uncertain, i.e., the court cannot determine what was agreed upon.

(2) Offers originally need not be certain if certainty can be determined at a later date. Indefinite offers will create valid contracts where they may become definite by subsequent words or agreement. (E.g., X promises to sell Y a house, to

be chosen by Y from a number of houses that X owns, and Y promises to pay a specified price for it. Since X must give up a house that Y will choose and Y must pay for it, there is a contract, although at the outset it is not clear which house will be sold.)

UCC RULE [2–204]: Even though one or more terms of a contract for the sale of goods is left open, the contract will not fail for indefiniteness if the parties intended to make a contract and there is a reasonably certain basis for giving an appropriate remedy. The UCC thus liberalizes contract law in respect to the definiteness and certainty requirement, thereby fostering the formation of a greater number of sales contracts than would be the case at common law.

d. Offers must be communicated to the offeree by the offeror or his agent.

e. Option: an irrevocable offer which is actually a contract if it is supported by an independent consideration (see p. 39, III.B.) sufficient to make the offer irrevocable. Some states, however, do not require any consideration for an irrevocable offer if it is in writing, signed by the person to be charged, and states its irrevocability.

UCC RULE [2–205]: In respect to merchants (see p.219), *an* option or firm offer *which states that it will not be withdrawn, if contained in a signed writing, binds the offeror-merchant even though there is no consideration for his promise. However, in no event can the period of irrevocability for such options exceed three months. This change applies only to option contracts for the sale or purchase of goods. E.g., X, a merchant, grants Y an option contained in a signed writing to buy widgets at $10 per 100 and indicates that such offer will remain open for five days. This option or firm offer is a contract to which the offeror-merchant is bound despite the fact that there is no consideration for his promise. However, when the offeree-merchant supplies the form on which the firm offer appears, said form must be separately signed by the offeror-merchant.*

The rules described above, i.e., the signed writing requirement and the three months' limitation, do not apply if consideration is given the option. Nor is it necessary that the grantor be a merchant. In such a case, general contract rules apply (e.g., X grants Y an oral six months' option to buy his car for $150 in exchange for $1).

2. Acceptance.

a. Acceptance may be either oral or written.

(1) Oral mutual manifestations of assent form a contract even

where a later writing embodying the agreement is contemplated. However, oral assent may, if so intended, be merely a preliminary expression which is only to become final with the adoption of a writing.

(2) In an auction "with reserve," acceptance is by fall of the hammer.

(3) In reward cases, acceptance is by doing the act requested.

b. Offer may call for an acceptance in the form of a promise (bilateral contract—see p. 32, II.C.) or an act (unilateral contract—see p. 32, II.D.).

c. Acceptance must be made with knowledge of the offer. (E.g., B, returning A's lost watch without knowledge of A's offer of $100 reward, would not be entitled to the reward.) Cross offers do not constitute a contract since the acceptance requirement is not satisfied.

d. Acceptance must conform to all terms of the offer, be unequivocal and unconditional.

(1) A reply to an offer which adds qualifications or conditions is not an acceptance but a counter-offer.

(2) Acceptance which "requests" a change or addition of terms is valid if the acceptance is not made to depend on assent to the proposed change. (E.g., A offers to sell B 50 boxes of oranges at $10 a box. B accepts but adds his wish that, if possible, delivery should be made in installments. A and B have a contract, but A is not bound to make delivery in installments.)

(3) Where a type of acceptance is specified (i.e., a promise or act), the offeree must conform to the specification; however:

(A) Where a promise is requested and the offeree, instead of promising, fully performs within the time allowed for acceptance, the offeree's tender of full performance is equivalent to a promise of performance. (E.g., A writes B that he will pay him $5 for painting his fence if he will promise within the week to do it. B does not promise, but he does paint the fence and tells A he has done the work before the week is up. There is a contract.)

(4) Where an offer describes the time or manner of acceptance, it must be complied with; however, if the offer merely *suggests* a time or manner, another method of acceptance is not precluded.

e. When an offer calls for a promise, acceptance must be communicated to the offeror; when an offer calls for an act, notification of completion of the act is not necessary unless the offeror has no means of knowing that the act has been completed.

f. Silence is not of itself an acceptance—except when:

(1) The offeree, instead of rejecting, uses services that reasonably appear to be offered only if payment will be made. (E.g., X gives tennis lessons to Y intending to charge Y. Y, although not requesting these lessons, remains silent knowing they are being given with the expectation of payment from Y. Y is bound to pay for these lessons.) Or,

(2) The offeror indicated that silence would constitute an acceptance, and the offeree intended his silence as an acceptance. Or,

(3) Previous dealings and consequent reliance create the understanding that silence is acceptance.

g. Offer can only be accepted by or for the benefit of the person to whom it is made.

UCC RULE [2–207]: *A literal and unequivocal acceptance is not required under the code. An acceptance that contains additional terms is a valid acceptance. The additional terms are treated* as proposals for additions to the contract. As *between* merchants *these additional terms become a part of the contract unless the offer precludes such an occurrence; or the new terms materially alter the offer; or the original offeror gives notification of objection to such changes within a reasonable time after he receives notice of them.*

An order or other offer to buy goods for prompt or current shipment shall be construed as inviting acceptance, either by a prompt promise to ship (thereby forming a bilateral contract) or by the prompt or current shipment of the goods (thereby forming a unilateral contract).

These are major conceptual changes from the above common law rules, supra, *p.35, 2.d; again they foster formation of the sales contract.*

3. Objective theory.

a. Validity of offer and acceptance is determined in court by an objective standard of apparent intent.

(1) Only the overt acts and words of the parties are considered in a determination of mutual assent.

(2) Subjective feeling (secret intent) is immaterial.

4. Transmission of acceptance and time when it takes effect.

a. Offeror may signify the manner in which he desires the acceptance transmitted and any time limit thereon.

b. Unless otherwise indicated, either by facts or in the offer, an acceptance may be sent by the means used by offeror, or any reasonable means offeree wishes to use.

c. If acceptance is transmitted by the means authorized by offeror, or by the same means used to transmit the offer if no means was specifically authorized, the acceptance is effective as soon as it is put out of the offeree's possession and into the possession of an independent agency for transmission. (E.g., X received via the mails an offer that did not specify the means of acceptance; therefore, a letter of acceptance forms a contract upon its being posted.) The acceptance must be correctly addressed and the fee or postage properly paid.

(1) Whether the acceptance ever reaches its destination is immaterial unless offeror provides otherwise—the theory being that the offeror has impliedly designated the independent agency as his agent for acceptance.

(2) Acceptance sent from a distance will only operate upon dispatch, provided it is sent with precautions ordinarily taken to insure safe transmission (e.g., adequate postage, proper address).

d. If acceptance is not by authorized means, it is not operative upon dispatch, but it will take effect upon receipt, if received within the time in which an authorized acceptance would have arrived. (E.g., acceptance by public messenger is valid when received, if promptly delivered by acceptor's own messenger.)

UCC RULE [*2–206*]: *Unless otherwise* unambiguously *indicated, an offer for the sale or purchase of goods shall be construed as inviting acceptance in* any *manner and by* any *medium reasonable in the circumstance. The code therefore does not require the use of the same means as the offer to make acceptance effective on dispatch as does the common law.*

5. Termination of offer.

a. Rejection by the offeree.

(1) Communication declining acceptance is rejection.

(2) Counter-offer is a rejection unless an intent of reserving original offer for further consideration is manifested. (E.g., I am interested in your offer to sell for $60, but I am willing to buy at once if you will accept $55). For the UCC rule, see p. 36.

(3) Rejection does not terminate possibility of acceptance until it is received, but it limits the power of a later acceptance to create a contract upon dispatch. (E.g., X mails Y an offer which Y rejects by mail; however, within the time allowed for acceptance and before the rejection is received by X, Y's telegram

of acceptance reaches X. A contract arises upon the receipt of the acceptance.)

(4) Where a rejection is received by the offeror before a later acceptance, the acceptance, not creating a contract upon its dispatch—see (3)—can only be considered a counteroffer, since an offeror, who received a late or otherwise defective acceptance, cannot at his election regard it as valid.

b. Lapse of time.

(1) Termination occurs upon the lapse of the time specified in the offer for acceptance.

(2) If no time is specified in the offer, termination occurs upon lapse of a reasonable time, which is a question of fact. However, where an offer is sent by mail, acceptance sent on the day of receipt of the offer is sent within a reasonable time.

(3) Time for acceptance is not extended by a delay in communication (regardless of fault of the offeror) if the offeree knew of the delay. However, if the offeree had no knowledge of the time taken by the delay, that amount of time is added to offeree's time for acceptance. (E.g., X sent Y an offer which is delayed in the mail. The markings upon the envelope make it apparent that there has been a three-day delay. If X has given Y 10 days in which to accept, Y now must accept within 7 days. However, if it was not apparent from the markings and Y had no knowledge of the delay, the delay would not affect the amount of time allowed for acceptance.)

c. Revocation by the offeror.

(1) A communication stating or implying a revocation is effective if received before the offeree's power of acceptance is exercised.

(2) Where an offer is for the sale of goods, it is revoked upon the offeree's learning of the sale of the goods by the offeror if that sale has actually been made. (E.g., X makes Y an offer to sell his car, acceptance to be in one week. Within a week Y is told by Z that X has sold his car to another; however, Y proceeds to accept. If X has sold his car, there is no contract. If Z's information was incorrect, there is a contract.) This rule applies generally to all offers (e.g., an offer to sell land).

(3) An offer publicized to a group of unknown persons is revoked by an equal publicizing of a revocation by the offeror.

(4) An offeror may revoke the remaining unaccepted offers which were part of a series of proposed contracts although some binding contracts have already been created through

acceptance. However, if the original offer was for formation of a single contract, rather than a series of contracts calling for a series of acceptances, the offeror can no longer revoke. (E.g., X offers to sell 50 pounds of coal to Y every week and does so for two months. X then revokes the offer and stops delivery. If the parties intended a new contract to be formed each time there was a delivery, the revocation of X prevents the formation of new contracts. If they originally intended the formation of a single contract to run for one year, Y's acceptance of X's original offer prevents X from effectively revoking.)

(5) Where there has been part performance in response to an offer of a unilateral contract, the majority rule is that the offeror has no power of revocation, unless full performance is not completed within the time allowed, or, if no time for performance is stated, within a reasonable time. The minority rule permits revocation but reimburses the offeree by allowing recovery for part performance in quasi contract (see p. 32, II.B.2.). (E.g., X tells Y that if Y will carry his bag to the station X will promise to pay him $5. Y carries the bag halfway and X revokes. Under the majority rule X's revocation is ineffective, and if X does not allow Y to finish this job he will be liable for $5 damages.)

UCC RULE [2–206]: The code adopts the majority view but in addition requires that notice of acceptance be given to the offeror within a reasonable time after the offeree begins performance.

(6) Option contracts (see p. 34, III.A. 1.e. above) may not be revoked until after the time given for acceptance has elapsed, or if no time is stipulated, a reasonable time.

d. Offeror's death or insanity before acceptance: Offer is terminated upon death or insanity of offeror; however, death or insanity does not affect rights under an option since a contract (the option) is already binding upon the parties.

e. Illegality or impossibility: If after making an offer but before acceptance the proposed contract becomes illegal or impossible to perform, the offer is terminated.

B. Consideration.

1. Definition: an act or forbearance, or the promise thereof, which is offered by one party to an agreement, and accepted by the other as an inducement to that other's act or promise.
2. Legal consideration: some value given or promise of same or detriment sustained or promised (forbearance of some legal right which otherwise could be exercised, e.g., giving up smoking)

which is recognized by the law as capable of supporting a contract. Examples of promises which will *not* fulfill this requirement are:

a. Promises based only on a moral rather than legal obligation (e.g., parents' love for a child).

b. Promises to fulfill a duty already in existence, i.e., a preexisting legal duty (e.g., a promise to continue one's employment under an already existing contract in exchange for a promise by the employer to pay an additional amount, or a promise not to commit a tort or crime).

c. Promises which are merely illusory and, therefore, do not give rise to any mutuality of obligation, i.e., a promise which, in effect, means no more than the promisor can perform if he wishes but which does not bind him to perform.

3. Consideration need not have a pecuniary value or a value equal to the value of the act for which it is exchanged, i.e., courts will not inquire into the adequacy of consideration, except when unequal amounts of fungible goods or money are exchanged (e.g., I promise to give you $10 for your $5).

4. Contracts without consideration.

a. Contracts under seal (specialties) derive their validity from their form alone, and not from any fact of agreement or consideration. Consideration was unnecessary at common law since there was a conclusive (unrebuttable) presumption of consideration where there was a sealed instrument; however, most states have abolished this presumption and a few have retained it only in the form of a rebuttable presumption.

The UCC has abolished the legal effect of the seal insofar as contracts for the sale of goods are concerned.

b. Moral obligation: generally not consideration, except:

(1) Void usurious agreements—see p. 58, VII.B.1.e.(5). At common law usurious agreements were void, but if the usurious elements are eliminated and the debtor subsequently promises to repay the original loan, some courts hold a moral consideration and enforce the promise.

(2) Promise to perform a previously voidable duty. A ratification or promise to perform an antecedent voidable legal duty, not previously avoided, if made after the privilege of avoidance has terminated, is binding and enforceable (e.g., ratification by infant upon reaching majority).

c. Promise to pay a debt barred by some positive rule of law if such promise is evidenced by a writing and signed by the party to be charged thereunder.

(1) Bankruptcy: A promise to pay all or part of a debt is binding if made any time after bankruptcy proceedings are begun.

(2) A new promise to pay a debt barred by the statute of limitations—see p. 63, VII.D.5.e.(2)—is virtually always enforced.

d. Waiver: Some courts hold that a new promise to fulfill a duty originally conditional upon the performance of a condition by another is binding in spite of the nonperformance of the condition by the other, if the promise was made with full knowledge of the fact that the condition would not be performed and the condition was not a substantial part of what was to have been given as consideration (e.g., X waives the requirement of a $10 deposit, originally required as a condition for his starting performance). See p. 55,VII.A.1.

e. Options or irrevocable offers (see p. 34, III.A.1.e.).

f. Written agreement to change, modify, or discharge an obligation (see p. 55, VII.A.1.b.).

g. Promissory estoppel.

(1) In some states in varying degrees a promise lacking consideration will be enforced, where:

(A) A promisor makes a definite promise which he expects will induce action or forbearance of a substantial nature on the part of the promisee, and

(B) The promise in fact induces such action or forbearance of a substantial character, and

(C) Injustice can be avoided only by enforcing the promise.

(2) Promissory estoppel is distinguished from ordinary estoppel, which occurs when there is a misrepresentation of existing facts. (E.g., A knew or should reasonably have known that he would mislead B, who was misled to his damage. The court would stop A from denying the truth of his own statement.)

UCC RULE: The code has made several major inroads into the rigid consideration requirement in respect to waivers, modifications, and options. They should be studied with great care (see pp. 61, 55, 34).

C. Valid subject matter: An agreement is unenforceable if its object is illegal.

1. Violation of positive laws.

a. Rules of common law: commission of crime or tort, i.e., a civil wrong (e.g., defrauding of others, breach of public or fiduciary duty).

b. Statutory rules: legislature in exercising police power may regulate the making of contracts (e.g., services rendered without the required license; gaming, lottery, and wagers, including prohibited buying and selling of stocks or commodities for future delivery, where the parties intend no actual delivery, but only a settlement by paying the difference between the market and contract price).

2. Agreements contrary to public policy.

   a. Contracts may be illegal and void even though the acts contemplated are not expressly prohibited by common law or statute (e.g., agreements of immoral tendency, agreements obstructing justice or affecting the freedom or security of marriage).

   b. Agreements restraining trade and competition (antitrust) and promises not to compete are against public policy and unenforceable if the restraints are unreasonable (e.g., time limitations and geographical restrictions not reasonably necessary to protect the interests of the contracting party).

   c. Agreements which relieve a party from liability resulting from his negligence toward the other party are not favored; however, most courts will enforce such agreements between private parties in relatively equal bargaining positions. Where activities of the party affect the public interest such agreements will not always be enforced (e.g., common carriers).

3. Enforcement of illegal agreements.

   a. Void agreements will not be enforced; however, a court may enforce agreements that are illegal, but not so offensive as to be found void. (E.g., X subdivides lots and sells homes but forgets to obtain a license to do so. Y, a buyer, refuses to pay for a home. The court may allow X to recover, regardless of the fact that it was illegal to sell without a license.)

   b. If the agreement is illegal only in part, the part which is legal may be enforced if it can be separated from the rest of the agreement, but not otherwise.

   c. Agreement may be void regardless of the knowledge of the parties, since in general ignorance of the law is no excuse.

4. Recovery of money.

   a. There is no action to enforce an illegal agreement, but the court may allow recovery in an action to disaffirm (repudiate) the contract, where:

(1) The party seeking recovery is less guilty, or

(2) Recovery is sought by a person the statute meant to protect (e.g., a borrower suing on usurious contract), or

(3) The transaction has not been consummated and the party repents.

b. There is no recovery in quasi contract (see p. 32, II.B.2.).

D. Legal capacity of the parties.

1. Infants.

a. Contracts are voidable only by him: An infant can disaffirm his contracts without being liable on them, unless they are contracts made for necessaries.

(1) As to personal property, he can disaffirm at any time during his minority and within a reasonable time after attaining his majority (21 years of age in most states).

(2) As to realty, he can disaffirm within a reasonable time after attaining his majority.

(3) Upon disaffirmance, he must return the property or the proceeds from the sale if he has either.

(4) Necessaries include whatever is reasonably needed for his subsistence, health, comfort, or education, considering age and his customary economic status; the infant is liable only for the reasonable value of necessaries furnished him.

(5) The privilege of disaffirmance is personal, and only if the infant dies or becomes insane can his heirs or guardian disaffirm for him.

(6) A fraudulent misrepresentation by the minor of his age will preclude his disaffirmance in many states or give rise to a counterclaim for fraud.

b. Upon attaining majority, the infant can ratify any contract which could have been disaffirmed.

(1) Ratification binds the infant. Failure to disaffirm with reasonable promptness constitutes a ratification.

(2) Ratification may be by an express new promise or implied from declarations or conduct clearly showing an intention to be bound.

(3) Contract cannot be ratified or disaffirmed in part only.

2. Married women: generally no disabilities in contracting (elimination by statute of common law disabilities).

3. Insane persons.

a. Contract is void from inception if made after adjudication of insanity.

b. Contract is voidable if made prior to adjudication of insanity.

(1) Contract is valid if there was no knowledge of the insanity by the other party who has contracted in good faith and performed up to this time so that disaffirmance would cause him loss, i.e., the insane person can only avoid liability under the contract if he can restore the consideration he has received.

(2) Quasi contracts—see p. 32, II.B.2.—are valid.

4. Drunkards: Contracts are enforceable unless the drunkard was so intoxicated at the time of contracting that he lacked capacity to make an intelligent offer or acceptance. If he lacked such capacity, the contract is voidable by the drunkard.

a. Quasi contracts (see p. 32, II.B.2.) are valid.

5. Corporations.

a. Can only contract through the authority of an agent.

b. Power to contract is limited by charter in respect to the subject matter of contracts. Agreement must reasonably accomplish some object for which the corporation was created (see Corporations, p. 180, I.C.7.c.).

6. Aliens: no contractual disability, except that contracts made by enemy aliens in time of war are void.

E. The Statute of Frauds requirement.

1. Contracts *within* the provisions of the Statute of Frauds must be in writing and signed by the party to be charged thereunder in order to be enforceable. Many contracts are not subject to the Statute of Frauds requirements (e.g., contracts for the sale of goods for less than $500). In addition, even though the contract is within the Statute of Frauds, the statute may be satisfied in a way other than a writing in the case of contracts for the sale of goods or contracts for the sale of real property (see below, E.2.).

a. A contract may be contained in a signed memo, but the memo must contain all the material terms of the agreement.

b. Several writings (e.g., letters) may be pieced together to fulfill the requirement of a memo.

c. Writing need not be delivered unless it is a deed to land.

d. Writing must contain:

(1) The subject matter.

(2) The names of the parties.

(3) The consideration.

(4) The terms of contract.

(5) The signature of party to be charged, i.e., the party seeking to avoid the contract.

e. Writing need not come into existence at time of the agreement—it need only be the evidence of an agreement.

UCC RULE [2–201]: The UCC contains a Statute of Frauds section in its treatment of sales (Article 2). It applies exclusively to the sale of goods having a value of $500 or more (see below, E.2.f.). All that is required to satisfy the UCC Statute of Frauds section is some writing sufficient to indicate that a contract for the sale of goods has been made between the parties and signed by the party against whom it is sought to be enforced or by his authorized agent. A writing is not insufficient because it omits or incorrectly states a term of the contract albeit material, but it must at least state the quantity of goods sold. This represents a major liberalization of the writing requirement in respect to the sale of goods.

The UCC requires a writing for contracts for the sale of securities (stocks, bonds, etc.) sufficient to indicate that a contract has been made for sale of a stated quantity of described securities at a defined or stated price (see below, E.2.g.).

The UCC requires a writing signed by the debtor to create an enforceable nonpossessory security interest (i.e., the creditor does not take possession of the collateral). It must contain a description of the collateral and a description of the land concerned. When the security interest covers crops or oil, gas or minerals to be extracted, or timber to be cut. In describing collateral, the word "proceeds" is sufficient without further description to cover proceeds of any character.

2. Contracts *within* the statute include contracts which:
   a. By their terms are not to be performed within one year from the making thereof. (E.g., X makes a contract for a year's duration beginning one week from the date of the agreement; the contract is unenforceable if not in writing. However, a contract made today for one year's duration with work beginning tomorrow is not within the statute.)
   b. Are for sale of real property. Part performance of a substantial nature will also satisfy the Statute of Frauds (e.g., a purchaser under an oral land contract takes possession and makes either partial payment or valuable improvements).
   c. Promise to answer for the debt, default, or miscarriage of another where such a promise is collateral rather than an original promise. (E.g., X says to Y, "If you will sell Z goods worth $30, I will guarantee Z's account." Such a promise comes under the statute; however, where X says, "Sell Z goods worth $30 and I will pay the bill," the promise is not under the statute, for it is an original promise.)

d. Are promises by an executor or administrator to pay with his own funds obligations of the estate.

e. Are in consideration of marriage, except mutual promises to marry.

f. *UCC RULE* [*2–201*]: *A contract for the sale of goods for the price of $500 or more is generally not enforceable without some writing signed by the party to be charged sufficient to indicate that the contract had been made* (*see above*). *However, the UCC provides the following additional ways of fulfilling its requirements:*
(1) *Written confirmations: A written confirmation of the contract of sale of goods between merchants will satisfy the statute as long as the confirmation binds the sender and as long as the recipient has knowledge of or reason to know its contents and does not object to the confirmation within 10 days.*
(2) *Specially manufactured goods: Where a seller has made a substantial beginning towards the manufacture of goods not suitable for sale to other than the buyer* (*e.g., custom-built golf clubs*), *the statute will be satisfied without a signed writing if the contract is valid in other respects.*
(3) *Admissions by a party: If the party against whom enforcement is sought admits in his pleading, testimony, or otherwise in court that a contract for sale was made, the contract will be enforceable without a signed writing to the extent of the quantity of goods admitted.*
(4) *Part performance: With respect to those goods for which payment has been made or which have been received or accepted, the contract will be enforceable without a signed writing, but only to the extent of those goods received or paid for.*

g. Are contracts for the sale of "securities" as defined in Article 8 (Investment Securities), which, in general, means an instrument commonly dealt in upon securities exchanges or markets or commonly recognized in any area in which it is issued or dealt in as a medium of investment (e.g., corporate stocks, corporate bonds, municipal bonds, transferable warrants, etc.).
UCC RULE [8–318] provides a contract for the sale of securities is not enforceable by way of action or defense unless
(1) there is some writing signed by the party against whom enforcement is sought or by his authorized agent or broker sufficient to indicate that a contract has been made for sale of a stated quantity of described securities at a defined or stated price; or
(2) delivery of the security has been accepted or payment has been made but the contract is enforceable under this provision

only to the extent of such delivery or payment; or
(3) within a reasonable time a writing in confirmation of the sale or purchase and sufficient against the sender under paragraph (4) has been received by the party against whom enforcement is sought and he has failed to send written objection to its contents within ten days after its receipt; or
(4) the party against whom enforcement is sought admits in his pleading, testimony, or otherwise in court that a contract was made for sale of a stated quantity of described securities at a defined or stated price.

h. Are contracts which create a nonpossessory "security interest" in the creditor (see Secured Transactions, p. 253, for the UCC definition of "security interest").

i. Are contracts for the sale of intangible personal property (choses in action) not covered by f., g., or h. above and having a value in excess of $5,000 (e.g., the sale by a party of his rights under a bilateral contract or rights to royalties having a value in excess of $5,000).

IV. REALITY OF ASSENT

A. Mutual assent being essential to every contract, agreements may be void or voidable because of:

1. Mistake: a belief not in accordance with the actual facts.

a. Mutual mistake (both parties are mistaken) may relate to:

(1) The terms of the contract, or

(2) Identity of the parties, or

(3) The existence, nature, quantity, or identity of the subject matter, or

(4) Other material facts assumed by the parties as the basis on which they entered into the transaction.

(A) Mutual mistake in regard to a material provision of the contract makes the contract *voidable* by the party whose obligations under the contract will be materially increased if the mistake is enforced, unless:

(i) The welfare of innocent third parties will be unfairly affected, or

(ii) The party seeking to avoid the transaction can obtain reformation, performance of the contract according to its original intent, or compensation from any loss he may sustain because of the mistake.

(B) Where, because of the nature of the mutual mistake, there was in effect no contract made by the parties, the mistake makes the contract *void*.

b. Mistake does not make the contract voidable where:

(1) There is a unilateral mistake (where only one party to the contract is mistaken) unless there is:

(A) Fraud (see below, IV.A.3.), or

(B) Knowledge by the other party of the existence of the misapprehension or reason to know of same.

(2) The acceptor is bound in contract, though he is actually ignorant of the terms of a written offer or of their proper interpretation. Failure to read the terms of a contract will not excuse a party from performance. The acceptor binds himself to any clause in writing that can be reasonably construed as part of the offer.

(3) One party knows of an ambiguity unknown to another, and he does nothing to clarify the ambiguity, i.e., knowing the other party may attach an alternative meaning to the contract, he binds himself in accordance with the other party's interpretation of the ambiguity.

2. Innocent misrepresentation: An innocent misstatement (i.e., one made with an honest and justifiable belief), if material, gives the other party an action for rescission which restores the parties to the position they would have had if there had been no contract at all; each party must return any benefits received.

3. Fraud: known or reckless misrepresentation of a material fact with the intention that the misrepresentation shall be acted upon by the other party, and which is acted upon by him to his injury.

a. For actual fraud to exist there must be:

(1) A false representation and not mere nondisclosure. However, nondisclosure or concealment is enough where:

(A) There are active steps taken to prevent discovery of the truth, or

(B) There is suppression of the facts by revealing only part truths, or

(C) Under the circumstances, failing to disclose defects implies that they do not exist.

(2) A misrepresentation of a past or existing material fact. Therefore, there is no fraud where:

(A) There is an expression of opinion, belief, or expectation, or

(B) There is a mere expression of intention. However, the representation that a certain intention presently exists when it does not is a false representation of existing fact.

(3) A representation known to be false. Such representation

is fraudulent if:

(A) It is actually known to be false, or

(B) It is made in reckless disregard of whether true or not, or

(C) The party represents it as his personal knowledge and his statements are relied upon.

(4) Justified reliance upon a representation which was made with an intent to be relied upon. Thus, no fraud exists where:

(A) There are only opinions of value, especially where parties are equally incapable of giving opinions (e.g., neither party is an expert), or,

(B) There are means of checking the accuracy of the opinion available, but they are not used.

(C) Representation need not be made directly to the other party if it is intended to be communicated to him and acted upon by him.

(5) Representation must deceive, induce, and cause injury (i.e., be relied upon to one's detriment or damage).

b. Constructive fraud:

(1) Is based not on a misrepresentation of fact, but on a violation of legal duty or a relationship between the parties which requires the use of exceptional good faith (e.g., contract between husband and wife, guardian and ward).

(2) Exists as a matter of law declared by the court. (E.g., the directors of a corporation buy goods and resell them at a profit to the company.)

c. Fraud may occur:

(1) In the inducement: antecedent fraud.

(A) Occurs during the negotiation which precedes the making of the contract.

(B) The contract is valid, but *voidable* at the option of defrauded party.

(2) In the execution.

(A) Exists when a person by trickery is made to sign an instrument other than the one intended, so that there is no meeting of minds.

(B) Contract is then *void*.

d. Remedies for fraud.

(1) If contract is voidable:

(A) Defrauded party may:

(i) Affirm and sue for damages for deceit, or if sued on the contract, set up the fraud in reduction of the damages, or

(ii) Bring an action at law for rescission (a return to the state at which the parties began, each returning any consideration received), thereby waiving damages for deceit, or

(iii) Sue in equity for both avoidance of the contract and equitable relief.

(B) Defrauded party cannot rescind after affirming the contract (e.g., accepting benefits, or suing on it).

(i) Delay in rescinding after discovery may amount to an affirmance or bar action on the grounds of laches (delay in enforcing claim making enforcement inequitable).

(ii) Right to rescission may be defeated where there are third persons who have acquired an interest under the contract for value, without notice of the fraud.

(C) The transaction cannot be avoided in part, i.e., it must be entirely avoided or not avoided at all.

(2) If the contract is void, defrauded party may sue for fraud (action for deceit) and recover damages.

4. Duress.

a. Duress is the actual or threatened causing of an action or inaction which, contrary to a party's free will and judgment, forces him to enter into a contract.

(1) The duress must have been against the contracting party, or his wife, husband, parent, child, or close relative under such circumstances as to deprive the contracting party of freedom to contract.

(2) The duress must have been initiated by the other party to the contract, or by one acting with his knowledge or on his behalf.

(3) The duress must have induced the party to enter into the contract.

(A) Threat of criminal prosecution, regardless of guilt or innocence, constitutes duress; however, threat of civil suit normally does not.

(B) Unlawful detention of another's goods under oppressive circumstances or their threatened destruction may constitute duress.

b. Effect of duress: Contract is voidable at option of the victim.

5. Undue influence.
   a. Brought about where unfair advantage is taken of:
      (1) The relationship of the parties (e.g., through the abuse of a close relationship or position of trust), or
      (2) Weakness of mind.
   b. Effect: renders contract voidable at option of injured party.

V. INTERPRETATION OF CONTRACT—PAROL EVIDENCE RULE

A. Agreements reduced to writing bind the parties, and they may not offer any proof of oral agreements contradicting the terms of the writing.

B. Exceptions: Parties may present oral proof:

1. Of the invalidity of the contract—the proof, rather than contradicting, goes to the entire existence of a written contract and destroys it (e.g., oral proof of fraud, or lack of consideration, mistake, illegality, or duress), or
2. Of a condition precedent— see p. 57, VII.B.1.b.(2) (B) (i)—proof that parties agreed to a condition that had to be fulfilled before agreement was effective, thereby showing no contract exists, or
3. To explain an ambiguity or omission—proof cannot contradict terms in the contract but can explain them, or
4. Of a subsequent modification—a later oral agreement must be supported by consideration and not subject to the Statute of Frauds, or
5. Of an agreement such as might naturally be made as a separate agreement by parties situated as were the parties to the written contract.

UCC RULE [2–202]: Under the UCC, written terms may be supplemented or explained by course of dealing, usage of trade, or course of performance. Thus, a specialized meaning attached to the terms by the parties will be recognized. This section also honors a statement of the writing's exclusivity, by refusing to admit additional terms when such a clause appears.

VI. ASSIGNMENT OF RIGHTS, DELEGATION OF DUTIES, AND THIRD PARTY BENEFICIARY CONTRACTS

A. Assignment of rights.

1. Under some circumstances, a person not a party to a contract may obtain the rights of one of the parties; an assignment may result from:

a. A voluntary act of the party to whom the right is owed.

(1) Contract rights may be assigned unless:

(A) The contract involves exclusively personal services, personal credit, trust, or confidence.

(B) The assignment would materially vary the duty or the risk agreed to by the obligor (person obligated to perform).

(C) Provisions in the contract prohibit assignment (look to intent of parties) or a statute forbids assignment (e.g., non-assignment of a claim against the United States).

UCC RULE [2–210]: The UCC favors assignments. The most important change in the prior law of assignments made by the UCC is to negate attempted contractual agreements prohibiting the assignment of non-executory *rights. Thus, the UCC provides, "a right to damages for breach of* the whole-contract *or a right arising out of the assignor's due performance of* his entire obligation *can be assigned despite agreement otherwise" [emphasis ours]. E.g., X, a seller, has fully performed his contractual undertaking. Despite the fact that the contract provides that the rights arising under the contract are non-assignable, X may nevertheless assign his rights to another party. The prohibition is invalid since X's rights are no longer executory.*

(2) Effect of an assignment.

(A) A debtor without notice of the assignment may assert against the assignee all defenses and counterclaims good against the assignor, including payment.

(B) Where the debtor has been given notice, the assignee takes subject to all defenses good against the assignor. With regard to counterclaims, however, the debtor may assert only those based on facts existing prior to his receipt of notice.

UCC RULE [9–318]: A debtor who has received notice may assert all defenses and all counterclaims which arise from the contract sued upon. He may also assert all other counterclaims which accrued prior to the receipt of notice. In non-consumer contracts the UCC permits the debtor to expressly waive all defenses and counterclaims as against the assignee [9–206].

(3) Validity of an assignment.

(A) An assignment may be oral or written.

(B) Assent to assignment by assignee is necessary.

(i) Presumption of assent exists, but

(ii) Assignee has the privilege of disclaimer within a

reasonable time after he acquires knowledge of assignment.

(C) As between the assignor and assignee the assignment is valid without notice to the debtor, who would be discharged if he paid the assignor without notice of the assignment.

(D) If an assignor of accounts receivable is permitted to retain control over the receivables and has the right to use the proceeds in his business, the assignment may be held void as to creditors because it could be considered a fraudulent assignment made to defeat the creditors' rights.

(E) Assignment of future rights or earnings under:

(i) An existing contract is valid.

(ii) A nonexistent contract is invalid (e.g., assignment of wages from a job to be obtained).

UCC RULE [9–204]: *All future interests are assignable under the UCC, whether based on existing or non-existing contracts. This is a highly significant liberalization of the common law rule.*

(F) An option contract is assignable.

(4) Gratuitous assignments: Assignments given without consideration are valid although subject (unlike assignments for a consideration) to revocation upon:

(A) Assignor's death, or

(B) Subsequent assignment for value by assignor, or

(C) Notice of assignor's revocation actually received either by assignee or by obligor, unless:

(i) Assignee reduced the debt to possession, e.g., by collection or obtaining judgment, or

(ii) Assignment was embodied in a writing or tangible token whose surrender is required to be made to the debtor by the original agreement (e.g., an I.O.U., savings passbook), or

(iii) Assignee received payment in good faith, or

(iv) Assignee received a new contract right against obligor by novation (see p. 56, VII.A.2.).

(5) Priority between assignees: Where an assignee wrongfully makes several assignments of the same right, one of the following rules will be used to determine the rights of the successive assignees who have given consideration for the assignment:

(A) English rule: First assignee who gave notice of the assignment to the debtor or person liable prevails.

(B) New York rule: Assignee who obtained the first assignment from the assignee prevails.

UCC RULE [9–302]: An assignee must file a financing statement to "perfect" his interest in the assigned rights. Between assignees of the same right, the first to file will prevail.

b. Operation of law: Rules of law operate to transfer rights and liabilities (e.g., a transfer of an interest in land includes an assignment of covenants running with the land).

B. Delegation of duties.

1. Performance or unconditional offer of performance by delegatee has same legal effect as performance by the party who was originally bound, and who still remains liable for any default, except the party bound cannot delegate, nor is obligee legally bound to accept performance of delegatee where:
   a. Materially different performance would result, or where contract calls for skill or is founded on personal confidence.
   b. Delegation is forbidden by:
      (1) Statute, or
      (2) Policy of equity or common law, or
      (3) Provision of contract.

C. Third party beneficiaries: those persons who are intended to receive benefits from agreements made between promisors and promisees although they are not parties to the agreement and have given no consideration.

1. A third party is permitted by a majority of states to enforce a promise if he is a:
   a. Creditor beneficiary: a third party to whom a debt is owed and which his debtor intends to discharge by contracting with another for a performance to be rendered to the third party. (E.g., X lent Y $1,000 on Y's promise to repay it to Z, a creditor of X's to whom X owes $1,000. On Y's failure to repay, Z may sue Y as a creditor beneficiary. Of course, Z retains all rights he formerly had against X.) Or,
   b. Donee beneficiary: a third party to whom the promisee intends to confer a gift by contracting with a promisor for a performance to be rendered to the third party. (E.g., X lent Y $1,000 on Y's promise to repay the sum to Z, on whom X intended to confer a gift. On Y's failure to repay, Z may sue as a donee beneficiary.) The donee beneficiary normally must be either a close relative or the public.
2. Incidental beneficiary: a third party whom the contract was not intended to benefit, but who nevertheless may derive an incidental benefit. Such a party has no enforceable rights.

3. Under the English and Massachusetts rule, the third party beneficiary doctrine is not recognized.
4. A beneficiary's rights are subject to the defenses which the promisor had against the promisee.

VII. DISCHARGE OF THE CONTRACT

A. By agreement.

1. Release, waiver, mutual rescission, or cancellation.
   a. Mutual release: an express agreement that the contract shall no longer bind either party.
      (1) Waiver is a relinquishment of a condition—see p. 57, VII. B.1.b.(2)—under a contract; release is an abandonment of a right (e.g., discharging a party from his obligation under the contract).
      (2) Mutual rescission is a complete undoing of the contract and contemplates restoration of the parties to their original position, i.e., as if the contract had never been made.
         (A) Normally, only divisible contracts may be rescinded in part where this is essential to a just result.
      (3) Cancellation signifies defacing of a written contract with intent to destroy its legal effect.
   b. Consideration is necessary to support such agreements; however, statutes in many states provide that an agreement to change, modify, or discharge an obligation shall not be invalid because of the absence of consideration, provided the agreement or release is in writing and signed by the party to be bound.

UCC RULE [*2–209*]: *An agreement modifying or rescinding a contract for the sale or purchase of goods needs no consideration to be binding. Thus, the UCC permits the parties readily to modify or rescind certain of their contractual undertakings that would fail at common law because of lack of consideration. Furthermore, this may be done* orally *unless the contract* as modified *is within the Statute of Frauds or there is a signed writing that precludes modification or rescission except in writing. However, even if a signed writing is required, the writing need not be supported by consideration to be valid. For example, X contracts to sell Y 200 widgets at $10 per 100. The price of widgets drops drastically, and X orally agrees to reduce the price to $5 per 100. The contract has been effectively modified, and Y need only pay $5 per 100 widgets unless there is a signed agreement precluding such oral modifications. The Statute of Frauds would not apply, due to the dollar amount. In any event, even if a writing were required, the modification will not fail for want of* *consideration as would be the case under the common law pre-existing legal-duty rule. See p. 40, III.B.2.b.*

2. Novation: a substituted contract.
   a. A new contract duty is expressly substituted for the old.
   b. The old contract is entirely terminated.
   c. A new contract with at least one new party is substituted for the old one.
   d. A novation discharges the contractual obligation of the old promisor; there is no standby obligation when the delegation is accomplished via novation.
   e. Novation is distinguished from a merger. In a merger the new contract is nothing more than another form of old contract merged into the new.
3. Provisions for discharge contained in the contract.
   a. Condition subsequent—see p. 57, VII.B.1.b. (2) (B) (ii). Contract contains an express or implied provision for its determination under certain circumstances and it will be discharged upon:
      (1) The nonfulfillment of a specified term, or
      (2) Occurrence of a stipulated event, or
      (3) Exercise of right of discharge provided for in the contract or exercised by right of custom which forms a part of the contract.

B. By performance.

1. Where promises have been performed (bilateral) or a promise has been performed and an act given (unilateral):
   a. Time of performance.
      (1) Where no time is specified for performance, it must be performed within a reasonable time.
         (A) What constitutes a reasonable time depends on the circumstances.
      (2) If the contract specifies a time for performance, it must be performed within that time; if not, the other party may offset, against payment, any damage caused by the delay, or if time is "of the essence," he may reject performance entirely.
         (A) Time is of the essence when:
         (i) The parties so stipulate, or
         (ii) Non-performance within the time fixed will defeat the purpose of the contract.

b. Satisfactory performance.

(1) In absence of specific provisions, performance is satisfactory if it should satisfy a reasonable man.

(2) Satisfactory performance must comply with conditions of the contract.

(A) Conditional contracts: an executory contract, the performance of which depends upon a condition.

(B) Classification of conditions:

(i) Precedent: one which is to be performed or happen before a particular duty of performance arises.

(ii) Subsequent: a future event upon the happening of which the obligation is extinguished.

(iii) Concurrent: mutually dependent events to be performed at the same time; unless otherwise provided, conditions are presumed to be concurrent.

(C) Satisfaction guaranteed: where one party guarantees satisfaction, the contract will be held to require satisfaction of a reasonable man and not personal satisfaction of the individual, unless personal taste or fancy is involved and the contract contemplated personal satisfaction.

(i) Parties may agree that performance shall be to the satisfaction of some third person and, if so, there is no liability until said person is satisfied, unless fraud or collusion can be shown.

c. Substantial performance: Under common law an express contract had to be completed to the last detail, but under doctrine of substantial performance, performance is satisfied if:

(1) There was a substantial performance of the contract, and

(2) There was a bona fide effort to comply fully, and

(3) There was no willful or deliberate departure from the terms, and

(4) The deviations were minor, and

(5) The damage sustained from the defects was deducted from the price.

d. Payment: consists of the performance of a contract by:

(1) Delivery of money, or

(2) Delivery of a negotiable instrument which is taken in absolute discharge of payee's right, or (as presumed in most jurisdictions) conditionally, in that if it is not paid when due, payee will revert to his original rights.

(3) If at or before the time of payment, debtor specified the application which is to be made of the payment, this direction must be followed (e.g., apply to principle rather than interest). Where there is no direction, some courts require payment to be applied first for interest due; others allow the creditor the choice in allocating payment to principle or interest; but if he does not exercise this choice, payment will go towards interest.

e. Interest.

(1) Interest is allowed on matured debts of specific amounts. Parties, subject to (5) below, may fix the applicable interest rate. Where no interest rate is stated but interest is to be paid, the law provides a specific rate called the legal rate of interest.

(2) Interest is not allowed on running accounts which are unliquidated until they are settled and become liquidated, unless permitted by statute or trade usage, and parties agree to it.

(3) Interest on a debt payable on demand accrues and starts from time of demand or, where there is no specific demand, at commencement of suit.

(4) Where there is an undated instrument providing for interest but not specifying the date it is to run from, interest runs from date of issue.

(5) Usury is taking a greater sum for use of money than law permits; it voids the contract. The maximum lawful rate of interest (contract rate) is a limit set by law and which the parties cannot exceed. This maximum rate is normally higher than the legal rate discussed above.

f. Tender: an offer or attempt to perform:

(1) Where there is an offer to pay something promised, refusal by promisee to accept payment does not discharge the debt which can be collected later, but prevents the running of interest.

(2) Where there is an offer to do something promised, refusal to accept by promisee discharges the promisor from the contract and allows him to sue for breach (see p. 60, VII.D.3.).

(3) Late tender may subject defaulting party to action for damages incurred.

C. By operation of law.

1. Impossibility of performance: excuses performance which:

a. Has become objectively impossible, as opposed to subjectively impossible (e.g., through personal lack of funds), which will never excuse performance. Objective impossibility is created where:

(1) Legislation makes the purpose unlawful.

(2) Subject matter, which is essential to performance, is destroyed without fault of the promisor.

(3) Personal service is required and incapacity prevents discharging these services (e.g., death, illness).

2. Impracticality of performance: Unexpected difficulty and expense encountered by the promisor generally do not excuse his duty. However, in extreme cases a few courts accept this as an excuse.

3. Frustration of purpose (doctrine not widely recognized in the United States).

   a. Where the value of the performance bargained for is destroyed by supervening events, promisor's duty is discharged. (E.g., a lease on property to be used only as a saloon is discharged when prohibition law prevents this.)

      (1) Performance may still be possible.

      (2) Theory is based on failure of consideration.

         (A) Value of performance must be totally or almost totally destroyed, and

         (B) Frustrating events must not have been anticipated at the time contract was made.

4. Alteration of a written instrument. A deed or contract in writing altered by an addition or erasure is discharged, if the alteration is made:

   a. In a material part, so that it changes the legal effect of the instrument, even if not prejudicial to the other party.

   b. By a party to the contract, or a stranger with his consent.

   c. Intentionally.

   d. Without consent of the other party.

D. By breach of contract.

1. Renunciation of contract.

   a. Anticipatory breach, i.e., renunciation before the time of performance, discharges the other party if he so chooses, and entitles him to sue at once for the breach. (Accepted in a majority of states, and under the UCC.)

   b. Renunciation of contract in course of performance discharges other party from a continuing performance and entitles him to sue at once for breach.

2. Impossibility created by one party (either before or in course of performance), making performance by the other party impossible, discharges the other party, who may sue at once for breach.

3. Violation of terms of contract.
   a. Failure of performance may discharge the obligation of the other party or merely give him a right of action for breach, depending upon whether the promises are:
      (1) Conditional upon each other. There is a discharge.
      (2) Independent of each other. Normally there is no discharge, for there is an absolute promise wholly unconditional upon performance of other party. The intention of the parties must clearly have been to have independent promises; if this is found, performance must be completed by one party, regardless of the non-performance of the other.
   b. Tortious interference with a contract, i.e., inducing a party to violate terms of the contract, makes the inducer liable in damages to the injured party.
4. Remedies for breach.
   a. Where contract is breached there is:
      (1) Right of action on contract—suit for damages. Recovery is generally designed to place party suing in same position as if the contract had been performed, allowing him recompense for his loss which directly and naturally resulted from the breach.
         (A) Damages must have been within contemplation of both parties at the time of contracting as the natural result of a breach. Unless special damages were provided for, i.e., damages arising from special circumstances beyond the normal course of events, they are not recoverable.
         (B) Liquidated damages: Parties may assess damages themselves by provision in the contract, but cannot provide for amounts which are so high as to be considered a penalty. (I.e., recovery should only attempt to place a party in the position he would be in if there had been performance as determined at the time of contracting, *not* at the time of breach.)

UCC RULE [2–718]: Under the UCC the amount of the liquidated damages need only be reasonable in the light of the anticipated or actual harm caused by the breach.

      (2) Specific performance: a suit in equity to enforce performance where no adequate remedy at law exists, i.e., where money damages will not suffice. (E.g., a court will enforce a contract to convey a unique object, as in the conveyance of land.)
      (3) *Quantum meruit:* a suit for reasonable value of services,

i.e., recovery for anything the party suing may have done on the contract. The action is based upon quasi contract, rather than arising under the terms of the original contract.

UCC RULE: For a discussion of the rights and remedies of the parties upon breach of a sales contract, see infra, *pp. 221–235.*

5. Discharge of right of action arising from breach.
   a. By agreement of the parties:

      (1) Release and covenant not to sue: a formal writing supported by consideration that recites a present relinquishment of rights therein described; effect is to immediately relieve one of the parties of some or all of his duties.

UCC RULE [1–107]: The code does not require consideration for the waiver or renunciation of any claims arising out of an alleged breach if the waiver or renunciation is in writing signed and delivered by the aggrieved party. This rule applies to all types of claims and rights under the UCC; it is not limited to contracts for the sale of goods. E.g., X breaches his security agreement on the purchase of an automobile by failing to make his installment payment on the due date. Y in a signed writing agrees to waive his right to sue for breach of contract. This waiver is valid without consideration. This is another major shift from the common law rules regarding consideration. See p. 39, III.B.2.

      (2) Accord and satisfaction: agreement between parties to a dispute to accept new arrangement in place of the *disputed one* (e.g., agreeing upon a given sum as due, in place of conflicting claims on the amount due).

         (A) Where accord is carried out it is said to be "satisfied," and there is an accord and satisfaction which is binding although there is no new consideration for this agreement.

         (B) Where an accord is executory, i.e., not yet followed by a satisfaction, any party is free to press his original claim. The minority rule states that the parties to a valid accord must be given a reasonable time in which to perform the satisfaction.

         (C) For an accord there must be:

         (i) Genuine dispute, and

         (ii) An unliquidated (undeterminable) claim—as contrasted with an account stated, which is an agreement as to an account where there is a liquidated damage claim (the sum is arrived at by way of computation, rather than by compromise).

         (D) Assent by the creditor.

(1) There is no accord unless there is an offer by the debtor for substituted performance, and acceptance thereof by the creditor.

(ii) Retention or cashing of a check offered as settlement is almost always held to operate as full satisfaction if at the time no word of dissent is sent to the debtor; if the creditor promptly informs the debtor that he will not accept this as full performance, but only apply it to the balance, a few jurisdictions will hold that no accord or satisfaction occurs, whereas most jurisdictions hold that an accord and satisfaction has occurred.

b. Discharge by arbitration:

(1) Definition: The voluntary submission of legal disputes to resolution outside the courts. It is estimated that over 70% of private legal disputes, excluding personal injury cases, are resolved in this manner.

(2) Characteristics: Relative to court proceedings, arbitration is generally speedy, informal, convenient, inexpensive, private, and conclusive.

(3) Agreements to arbitrate existing disputes are generally enforceable. Agreements in contracts to submit *potential* disputes to arbitration are also enforced by many states.

(4) Benefits: The extensive use of arbitration to resolve legal disputes is beneficial to the judicial process since it diverts a large workload from heavily burdened courts. In addition, legislatures have been stimulated to encourage, through reform of procedural statutes, a more speedy, efficient, and simplified administration of justice.

c. Discharge by judgment: Right to sue for breach is terminated upon final judgment of a court of competent jurisdiction whether in favor of or against a party.

(1) Where a party wins a suit, the cause of action merges in the judgment.

(2) Where a party loses, the judgment estops him.

d. Bankruptcy effects a statutory release from debts and liabilities which are provable and dischargeable under the Bankruptcy Act when the bankrupt has obtained a discharge from the court.

e. Lapse of time:

(1) May effect the remedy of the parties to a contract (e.g., laches-neglect or delay in enforcing a right, making it inequitable to permit the party to enforce it).

(2) Statute of limitations bars actions at law on contracts unless they are brought within prescribed periods of time. Statute does not effect a discharge, but constitutes a bar to enforcement which may be pleaded as a defense by a defending party.

(A) Statute is "tolled" (suspended) by:

(i) Disability of a plaintiff to sue (e.g., infancy, insanity), or,

(ii) Absence of a defendant from jurisdiction so as not to be subject to legal process.

(B) Full time allowed under the statute will begin to run anew when there is:

(i) Clear acknowledgment of the debt, or

(ii) Part payment on account.

(C) Statute begins to run from the date the cause of action accrues:

(i) On open book accounts from the date of entry of the last item in the account.

(ii) On a bill or note payable, from date of maturity. In case of a demand note, statute runs from the date of execution unless there are circumstances showing that the intention of the parties is that the statute shall not run until making of the demand (e.g., note payable three days after demand).

(D) A written promise to pay money due is binding if the antecedent debt was once enforceable and still would be except for the effect of the statute of limitations— see p. 41, III.B.4.c.(2). But if the promise is conditional, performance becomes due only upon the happening of the condition.

CONTRACTS: SUBJECTIVE QUESTIONS*

TYPES OF CONTRACTS

Q. You were engaged by Bridge Builders, Inc. to conduct a special study to project the net income or loss which the Corporation should expect from a contract to build a bridge and were shown the following documents:

a. A letter dated September 1, 1968 from Robert Jones, president of Bridge Builders, Inc., to Henry Adams, president of Allied Steel Company. The text of the letter read as follows:

* See Introductory Note, p. 19.

"We can use 10,000 #4 grade C 'Allied Brand' steel pipes for which we will pay the present market price.

As in the past, unless we hear from you to the contrary by return mail, we will assume you have agreed to promise to deliver. The pipe must arrive before the end of September or we will lose a $100,000 bonus payment for early completion of work."

b. A letter dated September 25, 1968 from Henry Adams to Robert Jones. The text of the letter read as follows:

"We were pleased to receive your order of September 1, for 10,000 #4 grade C 'Allied Brand' steel pipes. We have not contacted you before because until today we were sure we could deliver and intended to do so.

Unfortunately, our last supply of pipe, which had been set aside for you, was shipped to another customer by mistake. Unless we go to great expense it will be impossible for us to produce new pipe for two months. But Master Steel Company, our competitor, has an equivalent pipe which meets all of your specifications except that it does not bear our brand name. Their price will be the same as ours and we have arranged to have them ship their pipe to you to meet our obligation."

c. A telegram dated October 5, 1968 from Robert Jones to Henry Adams. The text of the telegram read as follows:

"Master never delivered. We lost our bonus. We intend to hold you responsible."

(1) Did Bridge Builders intend to create a bilateral or a unilateral contract? Explain.

(2) List the requirements for a valid contract and explain how each of these requirements was or was not met in the above.

(3) Assume a valid contract existed. Could Allied Steel Company successfully assert that its mistake or the doctrine of impossibility of performance excused its failure to perform?

(4) Assume a valid contract existed and that Master Steel made a timely delivery to Bridge Builders. Can Bridge Builders collect damages from Allied Steel Company for its failure to deliver "Allied Brand" steel pipe? Discuss the legal theory or theories which apply to your answer.

5/69; pp. 32-41, 58

OFFER AND ACCEPTANCE

Q. Dennis, a wholesale appliance dealer, had thirty-five dishwashers which he wished to sell. He telephoned William, a retailer, and offered him the entire lot at a most advantageous price. William recognized that it was a real bargain, but felt he could not handle that number alone. He, therefore, asked Dennis to give him a ten-day option on the thirty-five dishwashers. William explained that in the meantime he would be arranging financing and storage and attempting to get another retailer to agree to take some of the dishwashers. Dennis said he would consider this request and that he would contact William again. Having no other prospective buyer at the moment, Dennis decided to grant William's request. He typed out the following option: "I, Dennis, do hereby promise William that my offer to sell thirty-five (35) dishwashers (described below at the prices indicated) will be held open for ten days from this date (April 15, 1964) and will not be withdrawn prior to the expiration of such time." This statement was followed by a description of the dishwashers and the prices and was signed by Dennis. Dennis then sent this writing to William by mail and William received it the next day. On April 16 Frank, another retailer, came to Dennis' store and inquired about the dishwashers. He offered to buy them immediately. Dennis sent William a revocation of the offer, telling him that he was going to sell the dishwashers to another party. This was received by William on April 20. William disregarded the revocation and on April 22 sent Dennis a letter accepting the offer. This letter was delayed in the mail and did not reach Dennis until April 30, 1964.

(1) Is the option binding upon Dennis? Explain.

(2) Assume for the sake of answering this part of the question that the option was binding. Was there a *timely acceptance?* Explain.

(3) Assume for the sake of answering this part of the question that a contract did arise for the purchase of the thirty-five dishwashers. Would William be entitled to the remedy of specific performance? Explain.

5/64; pp. 32-39

Q. On May 1 William Harrison, a textile manufacturer, mailed to Donald Franklin a written and signed offer to sell 1,000 bolts of blue denim (with a sample enclosed) at $40 per bolt. Each bolt would contain 25 square yards. The offer stated that "it would remain open for 10 days from the above date (May 1) and that it could not be withdrawn prior to that date."

Two days later, Harrison, noting a sudden increase in the price of blue denim, changed his mind. After making great personal efforts to contact Franklin, Harrison sent Franklin a letter revoking the offer of May 1. The letter was posted on May 4 and received by Franklin on May 5.

Franklin chose to disregard the letter of May 4; instead, he happily continued to watch the price of blue denim rise. On May 9, Franklin posted a letter accepting the original offer. The letter was sent registered mail and was properly addressed and contained the correct postage. However, it was not received by Harrison until May 12, due to a delay in the mails.

Franklin has demanded delivery of the goods according to the terms of the offer of May 1, but Harrison has refused.

What are the legal problems and implications of the above facts? Discuss.

5/70; pp. 33-39

Q. In auditing the accounts of the Martin Glassware Company the following problem was revealed as a result of an examination of the "purchase orders outstanding" file. The correspondence between Martin and Fairview Glass Works (the seller) was as follows:

[Letter of April 20 from Martin to Fairview]

April 20, 1970. Gentlemen: Please advise on lowest price you can make us on our order of ten car loads of Mason green jars, complete, with caps, packed one dozen in a case, either delivered here, or f.o.b. cars your place as you prefer. State terms and cash discount.

Very truly yours,
Martin Glassware.

[To this Fairview replied]

April 23, 1970. Martin Glassware Co., Gentlemen: Replying to your favor of April 20, we quote you Mason green jars, complete, in one dozen boxes, delivered railroad depot your city: pints, $4.50, quarts, $5.00, half gallons, $6.50 per gross, for immediate acceptance, and shipment not later than May 15, 1970; sixty days acceptance, or 2% off, cash in ten days.

Yours truly,
Fairview Glass Works.

[In response to the above letter Martin replied by telegram]

April 24, 1970. Fairview Glass Works: Your letter April 23 received. Enter our order ten car loads as per your quotation. Specifications will be mailed promptly. Martin Glassware.

[The final communication was a telegram sent in response to the above telegram]

April 24, 1970. Martin Glassware: Impossible to book your order. Output all sold. Fairview Glass Works.

Martin insists that a contract was created by its telegram of the 24th of April. Fairview insists that there was no contract and it had the right to decline to fill the order at the time it sent its telegram of the 24th.

These additional facts were noted. The price of Mason green jars has increased rapidly since April 24. The term "car load" is an expression invariably used in the trade as being equivalent to 100 gross.

Indicate and discuss the legal problems and implications of the above facts.

5/70; pp. 33-39

Q. On September 13, 1962, Baker, a New York wholesale beer distributor, received a general advertisement from the Brand X Beer Company of Delaware which indicated it had certain quantities of regular and premium bock beer available in barrels which it wished to sell. On September 18th Baker sent Brand X a telegram as follows: "Relative barrels of bock beer, we order 30 barrels of regular at $8 per barrel and 25 barrels of premium at $10 per barrel. Order subject to immediate acceptance, prices net, F.O.B. your place of business wire confirmation and forward papers." Brand X received this telegram at 11:38 a.m. on September 18th and at 7:14 p.m. of the same day sent Baker a telegraphic night letter stating: "We accept your order as follows: 35 barrels of regular and 22 barrels of premium at the prices and terms indicated in your telegram of the 18th, confirm immediately." This telegram was received at Baker's office on September 19th at 8:29 a.m. At 11:16 a.m. Baker deposited a telegram in the telegraph office which was received by Brand X at 12:05 p.m., reading, "We acknowledge your acceptance our order of bock beer, as modified, forward papers draft attached First City Bank, New York. Wire immediately, our expense, when the papers will go forward." At 11:02 a.m. that day (19th) Brand X sent Baker a telegram reading as follows: "Cannot hold your offer of September 18th open any longer." This was received by Baker at 11:46 a.m. At noon Brand X sold the beer in question to another firm at $9 per barrel for regular bock beer and $11 per barrel for premium. These prices represented the prevailing prices of beer at that time. Baker sues Brand X for breach of contract.

(1) Indicate the legal effect of each communication commencing with September 13th. Discuss fully.

(2) Using the facts and the analysis you made in (1) above, determine whether a contract was made. Explain your reasoning.

11/62; pp. 35-39

Q. On March 10 Supplier sent a written offer to User to sell 3,000 tons of steel rails on certain specified terms. User received this letter on March 11 and on March 25 telegraphed to Supplier an acceptance which reached him at 3 p.m. on that day. On the same day, March 25, at 2 p.m. Supplier mailed to User a revocation of his March 10 offer which was received the following day.

(1) Is there a contract? Explain.

(2) Assume there is a contract. At what point in time was it formed? Explain.

5/65; p.38

CONSIDERATION

Q. Star, a certified public accountant, accepted an offer from Granite Corporation to become the Corporation's controller. The contract was for three years and expressly provided that it was "irrevocable by either party except for cause" during that period of time. It was in writing and signed by both parties to the contract. After a year elapsed, Star became dissatisfied with the agreed compensation which he was receiving. He had done an excellent job as controller, and several larger competing corporations were attempting to lure him away from Granite. Star, therefore, demanded a substantial raise, and the Corporation agreed in writing to pay him an additional amount at the end of the third year. Star remained with the Corporation and performed the same duties he had agreed to perform at the time he initially accepted the position as controller. At the end of the three years Star sought to collect the additional amount of money promised. The Corporation denied liability beyond the amount agreed to in the original contract. Can Star recover the additional compensation from Granite Corporation? Explain.

11/67; pp. 39-41

Q. The basic facts are the same as stated in the question above except that one of Granite's competitors, Jackson Corporation, successfully lured Star away from Granite Corporation by topping Granite's offer of additional compensation. Jackson Corporation did this with full knowledge of the terms of the original three-year contract between Star and Granite.

(1) Does Granite Corporation have any legal redress against Jackson Corporation? Explain.

(2) Granite Corporation, relying on the contract's stated irrevocability for three years, seeks the equitable relief of specific performance, i.e., an order by the court compelling Star to perform his contractual undertaking. Will Granite prevail? Explain.

11/67; p. 60

VALID SUBJECT MATTER

Q. Peters, a certified public accountant, decided to retire from practice. During a period of 25 years he had personally built up a lucrative practice in Petersburg Township. He sold all his professional assets, including the good will, to Douglas, CPA, for an agreed-upon sum. As a part of the sale Peters covenanted that he would not engage in the public practice of accounting anywhere within the United States for a period of five years. Can this agreement be enforced against Peters? Explain.

5/63; p. 42

Q. The accounting firm of Smyth, Smyth & Smith of Los Angeles, California hired Watson as a junior. Watson was required, as a condition of employment, to agree in writing that if he left the employ of the firm he would neither establish his own firm nor work for another accounting firm on the West Coast of the United States, including Alaska, for a period of ten years from the date of termination of employment.

Watson worked for several years for Smyth, Smyth & Smith. Subsequently, he left the firm's employ to return to his hometown of Eugene, Oregon where he established his own accounting firm.

Smyth, Smyth & Smith seek to specifically enforce the prohibitory provision contained in Watson's written employment contract.

Will Smyth, Smyth & Smith be able to preclude Watson from

engaging in the practice of accounting? Explain.

5/68; pp. 42, 60

LEGAL CAPACITY OF THE PARTIES

Q. Young, a minor, is studying to become a television repairman. He agrees to overhaul a television set belonging to Olds, a friend of the family, for $75 with a thirty-day parts and workmanship guaranty. Young does the work in such a negligent manner that the television set is ruined beyond repair.

(1) Olds sues Young for damages for breach of contract. Will he recover? Explain.

(2) Olds sues Young for the tort (wrong) of negligence. Will he recover? Explain.

5/65; p. 43

STATUTE OF FRAUDS

Q. You have been engaged by Stark Industries, Inc. to examine the financial statements of Murz Corporation for the six months ending June 30, 1965. The management of Stark Industries, Inc. is negotiating for the purchase of the outstanding capital stock of Murz Corporation. The purchase price will be determined, in part, by the book value of the stock. Your audit of Murz Corporation's records and books disclosed the following information:

(a) The minutes of the December 1964 meeting of the board of directors revealed approval of the employment, to begin January 1, 1965, of John Laurel as general manager. Upon further investigation, you determined that Laurel had orally accepted the Corporation's offer of this position, which provided for compensation "at the rate of $1,000 per month plus a large percentage of the net income before income taxes." You also determined that no written contract of employment was executed.

(b) Laurel had vehemently opposed the proposed merger with Stark Industries, Inc. and resigned on June 30, 1965. His letter of resignation demanded the payment of $15,000 as his percentage of the net income under his contract of employment. He computed the payment as 15% of $100,000. His estimate of the net income as $100,000 is close to the Corporation's actual net income for the period before any provision for profit-sharing and income taxes.

(c) The management and board of directors of Murz Corporation refuse to recognize any liability to Laurel. They were dissatisfied with his services and would have discharged him if he had not resigned. Furthermore, they had intended that the profit-sharing computation would be very flexible and that the percentage would not exceed 5%.

(1) (a) List four kinds of contracts to which the Statute of Frauds is applicable.

(b) What is the basic requirement for contracts to which the Statute of Frauds is applicable?

(c) What is the legal consequence if a contract to which the Statute of Frauds is applicable is not executed in compliance with it?

(d) Is the Statute of Frauds applicable to the contract between Murz Corporation and Laurel? Explain.

(2) Does Laurel have a cause of action in contract against Murz Corporation? Explain.

(3) Does Laurel have a cause of action against Murz Corporation under any other theory of law? Discuss.

(4) What professional advice or recommendation, if any, would you give to your client in connection with determining if there is a liability to Laurel?

11/65; p. 45

Q. On January 1, 1962, Brian borrowed $1,000 from Lynch and orally promised to repay the money on January 1, 1964. Brian failed to repay the loan when it became due and shortly thereafter he was adjudicated a bankrupt. Lynch filed a claim against the estate which the trustee in bankruptcy resisted on the ground that the promise to repay was not evidenced by a writing and therefore is unenforceable. Is the trustee's contention correct? Explain.

5/65; p. 45

REALITY OF ASSENT

Q. The M Corporation, a well-known radio and television manufacturer, had in its inventory several odd lots of discontinued models which it desired to clear out. M invited the owner of the D Discount Chain to come in and examine the different models and make M an offer for the entire lot. The sets were segregated from the regular inventory. Fifteen radios which were not discontinued models were inadvertently included in this segregated group. D was unaware that M did not intend to include the fifteen radios in the group. D made M an offer of $9,000, which represented a sharp reduction in price from the normal sales price, for the entire lot. Being unaware of the error, M accepted the offer. M would not have accepted had he known of the inclusion of the fifteen current models. Upon learning of the error M alleged mistake as a defense and refused to perform. D sued for for breach of contract.
Will D be able to recover? Explain.

11/63; pp. 47-48

ASSIGNMENT OF RIGHTS AND DELEGATION OF DUTIES

Q. Martinson made a contract on July 1, 1967 with Penn Oil, Coal and Coke Company for the purchase of 16,000 tons of coal at $9 per ton. The contract was in writing and signed by both parties. Under its terms delivery was to be made as follows: "4,000 tons on October

1, 1967 and 4,000 tons in each of the succeeding months."

Penn decided to terminate its coal and coke operations. Pursuant to this decision, it sold its coal and coke facilities and all related assets on September 1, 1967 to one of its competitors, Banner Coal Company. The assets sold included "all rights under existing contracts for the purchase of coal or coke by our customers."

Penn notified all its former customers of the sale of its coal and coke operations, indicating that henceforth deliveries and service would be supplied by Banner. Banner delivered the agreed upon 4,000 tons to Martinson on October 1, 1967 and Martinson accepted and paid Banner for the coal without objection. Banner then decided it was unprofitable to make further deliveries to Martinson at the contract price. Banner, therefore, notified Martinson that unless he agreed to pay $10 per ton on future deliveries, Banner would cancel the contract.

Martinson refused to pay the $10 and Banner failed to make the remaining deliveries.

(1) Discuss the legal implications and the relationship between Penn and Banner that arose as a result of the September 1, 1967 transfer of the Martinson contract.

(2) Is Banner liable to Martinson for failure to deliver the coal? Explain.

(3) Can Martinson sue Penn? Explain.

(4) Assuming that Penn performed after learning of Banner's action, will it have any rights against Banner?

5/68; pp. 54-55

THIRD PARTY BENEFICIARY CONTRACTS

Q. Terrance owns and operates a gas station and restaurant on a highway about a mile from a beautiful but undeveloped lake region. Regis, seeing the value of the lake region as a potential resort area, purchases several acres of lake front property. He then enters into a contract with Mike, a building contractor, to have him construct an elaborate hotel and ten beautiful cottages. Terrance, learning of these facts from a conversation with Regis, expands his restaurant and gas station facilities in contemplation of a substantial increase in business. Subsequently, Regis decides not to go ahead with his plans, but instead to breach the contract with Mike. He promptly notifies Mike not to commence construction and Mike complies with instructions. Terrance, learning of the change in plans, sues Regis for breach of contract. He claims that he (Terrance) is a third party beneficiary under the contract between Regis and Mike and therefore entitled to damages for the costs incurred in expanding his business and the profits he would have reaped had the contract been performed.

(1) Can Terrance recover? Explain.

Statute of Frauds is applicable?

(2) List and define the three kinds of third-party beneficiaries.

11/60; pp. 54-55

DISCHARGE OF THE CONTRACT

Q. Charles, a famous interior decorator and music lover, ordered a custom made, high fidelity, stereophonic, console radio-phonograph from the Pure Tone Phonograph Company. Charles maintained a lavish apartment which he used as a showcase to impress his wealthy clientele. In making the contract Charles insisted that the set meet with his personal approval, and the contract guaranteed personal satisfaction. Skilled craftsmen worked for months on the set and even rivals of Pure Tone considered it one of the finest products ever produced. Charles, however, was not satisfied. He didn't like the finish nor did he find the tone to be as outstanding as he wished. He, therefore, refused to accept the set unless it was refinished and substantial improvements made in the tone quality. Pure Tone, stating that the set was the best that could be made, refused to make the changes and sued Charles for breach of contract. Will Pure Tone prevail? Explain.

11/63; p. 57

Q. You are auditing the accounts of the Ajax Manufacturing Company, a manufacturer of electronic equipment for industrial uses. One of the correspondence files you examined contained a contract with Brown Ball Bearing Company, one of Ajax's best customers. The file involved a dispute between the parties about the amount due on the contract. You therefore sent a positive confirmation of the account receivable to Brown. Brown in its response stated it had paid in full.

The file indicated that Ajax had entered into an agreement with Brown to supply 100 electronic testing devices at $200 each. Delivery was to be made not later than six months after the date of execution of the contract. Prior to commencing production of the devices, one of the suppliers who manufactures a major component used by Ajax in its electronic products raised its price by $25 per component. Because Ajax was only making a 10 per cent profit per electronic testing device, management decided to attempt to renegotiate the contract with Brown.

Accordingly, the president of Ajax sent a letter to Brown proposing that they share equally the $25 cost increase. An agreement was enclosed which was labeled "Amendment of Ajax (seller)—Brown (buyer) Electronic Testing Devices Contract" and which contained a provision raising the price to $212.50 per device. This was signed by the president of Brown Ball Bearing.

All went smoothly; Ajax completed the manufacture and delivery of the electronic testing devices and sent Brown a bill for $21,250 based upon the amended contract. In reply Brown sent a letter indicating that they were not bound by the amendment and would pay $20,000. A check for that amount was enclosed with an indication above the place for the endorsement that it was tendered in complete and full satisfaction of the amount due on the Ajax-Brown contract. Ajax cashed the check and has demanded payment of the additional $1,250.

What are the legal problems and implications of the above facts and how do they affect the financial position of Ajax? Discuss.

5/70; pp. 57-58

Q. Wingate hired Stanford as his full-time assistant to review and analyze the financial aspects of Wingate's prospective real estate investments. Stanford's hiring came after working with Wingate on similar projects on a part-time basis for several years and resulted because Wingate was satisfied with Stanford's work and experience in the field. The lengthy employment agreement prepared by Wingate's attorney and signed by the parties provides that employment is to terminate after three years unless the contract is renewed. It also provides, in part: "It is distinctly understood and agreed that the services to be rendered by Stanford hereunder must meet Wingate's approval, and Wingate shall be sole judge as to the adequacy of the services. If at any time Wingate is in any way dissatisfied with any of the services, he is free to terminate the services." Stanford, who left an excellent position to accept employment with Wingate, had not read the clause in the contract set out above. He was, therefore, shocked when two months after starting his new job Wingate referred to the contract clause and requested Stanford to leave his employ. Stanford has commenced a suit for damages against Wingate, alleging breach of the contract.

(1) (a) Explain the doctrine of mutuality of obligation.
  (b) Did this doctrine exist between the parties to the contract? Explain.

(2) Was the contract clause allowing Wingate to terminate the agreement effective even though Stanford did not read it? Explain.

(3) If a contract existed and the contract clause allowing Wingate to terminate the agreement was effective, would Wingate be liable for breach of contract if a jury found:
  (a) That Wingate was not in fact dissatisfied with Stanford's services but that the real motivation for firing Stanford was Wingate's plan to retire from business and he, therefore, no longer required Stanford's help. Explain.
  (b) That Wingate was dissatisfied with some of the conclusions Stanford reached but that any reasonable man would disagree with Wingate and find Stanford's work proper and satisfactory. Explain.

5/67; pp. 40, 57

Q. Price and James, a New York accounting firm, was engaged by East Coast Builders to perform an annual audit. East Coast is a wholly owned subsidiary of Nationwide Builders, a national building company with headquarters in Los Angeles, California. The agreement signed by East Coast and Price and James for the audit was prepared by counsel for Nationwide. Except for the insertion of names, the fee, and the service to be performed, it was the standard agreement for accounting services used by Nationwide. The agreement has five pages and the clauses contained therein are written in small type. On page 4, the agreement provides: "This agreement incorporates by reference all the Rules and Regulations of Nationwide's Hiring and Procurement Department which are on file and available for inspection at Nationwide's home office in Los Angeles, California." Price and James signed the agreement and proceeded to perform the audit. A dispute regarding fees has now arisen. East Coast has informed Price and James that the Rules and Regulations incorporated into the agreement provide for the final settlement of any disputes by arbitration in Los Angeles before a panel of arbitrators selected by the American Building Association, an organization of builders.

(1) Are the parties to a contract free to incorporate an arbitration clause into their contract by reference? Explain.

(2) If Price and James never read the Rules and Regulations incorporated into the contract, is it possible that it may be bound to arbitrate? Explain.

(3) If Price and James attempts to set aside the arbitration requirement in court, discuss fully the arguments that it could assert and the opposing arguments that East Coast Builders could use for upholding its right to an arbitration.

(4) Assuming the parties arbitrate and Price and James loses the arbitration, may it successfully appeal to a court to overturn the arbitrators' findings if it can prove that the findings were not made in good faith? Explain.

5/66; p. 62

CONTRACTS: OBJECTIVE QUESTIONS

INSTRUCTIONS. Each of the following numbered phrases or clauses states a legal conclusion as it completes the related lettered material. You are to determine whether each of the legal conclusions is true or false according to the general principles of contract law. Your grade will be determined by deducting your total of incorrect answers from your total of correct answers; if you omit an answer it will not affect either total.

(1) Lucky Fastener Corporation sent a letter to Foster Box Company which was signed by Donald Voltz, Lucky's sales manager. The letter read as follows:

"We hereby offer you 100 type #14 Lucky Fasteners at $4 per fastener. This offer will be irrevocable for 10 days."

(a) The offer is a firm offer and irrevocable without consideration for the period stated.
(b) If the offer stated it was irrevocable but did not contain a stated period of irrevocability, it would be revocable from inception.
(c) If the offer were for the sale of land it would be revocable.
(d) If the offer had been made by phone it would be revocable.
(e) Acceptance must be made within the time stated and by mail.

(2) Wilkins, a purchasing agent for Rose Sales Corporation, telegraphed Major Manufacturing Corporation on May 1: "What price will you sell 1,000 standard bathroom scales, delivery by May 15?"

On May 2, Major telegraphed back: "We will sell 1,000 standard bathroom scales at $2 each for delivery at our shipping platform on the 15th of May."

On May 3 at 10:30 a.m. Wilkins telegraphed: "We accept, ship C.O.D. via Red Trucking Company."

(a) Wilkins' communication of May 1 was an offer to buy 1,000 standard bathroom scales.
(b) Major Manufacturing's communication of May 2 was too indefinite and uncertain to constitute either an offer or counteroffer.
(c) Wilkins' purported acceptance on May 3 was a variance of the terms offered but was a valid acceptance.
(d) Assuming that an acceptance did take place, it was at the time that Major Manufacturing received Wilkins' communication of May 3.
(e) Major Manufacturing need not accept the term calling for a C.O.D. shipment by Red Trucking if Major notified Wilkins of its objection within a reasonable time.

(3) Strong made a contract with Johnston Drug Corporation for the sale of Strong's Drug Store. The terms of the sale called for a payment of $8,000 to Strong, a promise by Johnston Drug to pay all outstanding firm debts listed by Strong in the contract of sale and a $1,000 gift to Strong's faithful employee, Cramford.

(a) Strong made a delegation of his duty to pay his former creditors.
(b) Cramford is an incidental beneficiary and cannot recover on the contract.
(c) Strong's creditors may sue Johnston Drug even though they have not given any consideration for Johnston's promise to pay them.
(d) Strong's creditors are donee beneficiaries.
(e) If the transaction were a novation, it would release Strong from his debts to the creditors.

(4) Abrams sent Dawson a letter offering to sell twelve acres of land

suitable for a construction site. Abrams stated that acceptance must be made within two weeks of receipt of the offer. Six days after receipt of the offer, Dawson posted a letter of acceptance. Shortly thereafter, and prior to Abrams' receipt of the letter of acceptance, Abrams telegraphed Dawson and advised that he was withdrawing the offer. The telegram arrived prior to the letter.

(a) Abrams made a firm offer to Dawson and could not withdraw it for two weeks.
(b) The Statute of Frauds applies to the above transaction regardless of the purchase price.
(c) The telegram withdrawing the offer could not be effective until it was received.
(d) The mail was the authorized means of acceptance.
(e) Dawson can hold Abrams to the contract.

(5) Evans gave Bishop the following letter of introduction to Frost, a wholesaler:

"This will introduce you to my good friend and former customer, Bishop, who desires to purchase about $5,000 worth of goods from you on open credit. If you will let him have the goods, I will make good any loss up to $5,000 if he is unable to pay.

(signed) Evans"

Bishop presented the letter to Frost on May 1 and Frost sold and delivered $4,500 worth of goods to Bishop.

(a) Evans is a surety or guarantor.
(b) It is essential that Frost have Evans' promise in a signed writing if Frost is to prevail.
(c) The extension of credit by Frost constituted an acceptance of Evans' offer to enter into a unilateral contract.
(d) Frost was obligated to communicate his acceptance of Evans' offer prior to the extension of credit.
(e) Since Evans received no consideration for his promise, Frost will be unable to enforce it.

(6) Barton, upon retiring from business, offered to sell his office equipment for $1,000. He told Francis, a prospective buyer, "The equipment is almost as good as new and a good buy at the asking price. I originally paid $3,000 for it." None of the statements were true and Barton knew he had originally paid only $1,200 for the equipment. The equipment was worth $750. Francis purchased Barton's office equipment relying on the above misrepresentations.

(a) The statement that the equipment was "almost as good as new" was a material misrepresentation of fact.
(b) Francis could sue Barton for damages based upon the tort of fraud (deceit) in that Barton knew he was lying.
(c) Even if Barton honestly believed all the above statements, Francis could still rescind the contract.
(d) In order to rescind, Francis would have to show he relied on Barton's statements.

(e) Since the statements were oral, the Statute of Frauds will apply.

11/69

(7) James Mann owns a manufacturing plant in which radios are assembled. A CPA conducting an audit determined that several radios were missing. Theft by one or more of the workers was suspected. Accordingly, under Mann's instructions, the following sign was placed in the employees' cafeteria:
"REWARD—I believe employees are stealing radios. I want all employees to watch other employees to see they do not steal. A reward of $500 will be paid for information given by any employee which leads to the apprehension of an employee who is stealing radios.
James Mann"

(a) The posting of the sign constituted an offer to enter into a unilateral contract.
(b) The posting of the sign constituted an irrevocable offer which will remain in effect for a reasonable period of time.
(c) If an employee gave information which led to the apprehension of another employee who was stealing, the employee who gave the information may not collect the reward if he was not aware of the offer at the time he reported the other employee.
(d) If an employee began to carefully observe his fellow employees to determine who was stealing, the act of observing would constitute partial acceptance of the offer of reward.
(e) The offer of reward may be effectively revoked immediately upon the removal of the sign.

(8) Albert orally ordered a $600 standard model television console for his home from Mastercraft Appliances. Mastercraft accepted the order and later sent Albert a purchase memorandum in duplicate with a request that Albert sign and return one copy. Albert did not sign or return the purchase memorandum and he refused to accept the television console. Mastercraft sued and Albert asserted the Statute of Frauds as a defense.

(a) The purchase memorandum sent by Mastercraft will be sufficient to defeat Albert's reliance on the Statute of Frauds.
(b) If Albert admits in court to making the oral contract, the contract will be enforceable.
(c) A purchase memorandum will be insufficient to satisfy the Statute of Frauds if it omits any of the terms agreed to by the parties.
(d) A writing sufficient to satisfy the Statute of Frauds would not be necessary if Albert had received and accepted the television console.
(e) Specific performance is the only remedy Mastercraft can obtain in its suit against Albert.

(9) Lester and Brookings entered into a written employment contract in January under which Lester promised to employ Brookings and Brookings promised to work for Lester as a bookkeeper for 1 year commencing on June 1 at a salary of $100 per week. In April Lester said to Brookings, "Unless business improves I am afraid I will not be able to keep my promise to employ you in June."

(a) After hearing Lester's statement Brookings may immediately accept other employment without losing his right to enforce Lester's promise on June 1.
(b) After hearing Lester's statement Brookings must be available for employment by Lester on June 1 or he will breach his contract if Lester wishes to hire him.
(c) If prior to June 1 Brookings dies, his estate will not be liable to Lester for breach of contract.
(d) If on June 1 Lester is unwilling to hire Brookings and Brookings is able to obtain a position as a stockboy for another employer at a salary of $100 per week, Brookings is under a duty to accept this employment in order to mitigate the damages resulting from his not being hired by Lester.
(e) If prior to June 1 Lester's only plant is shut down by government order Lester's obligation to hire Brookings is excused.

(10) While verifying Jarman's liabilities a CPA learned that during 1967 Jarman contracted with Pauling to purchase Pauling's business. As a part of the purchase price Jarman promised to be responsible for all of Pauling's business debt outstanding on the date that Jarman assumed control of the business.

(a) Jarman's promise to be responsible for Pauling's business debts could be enforced by Pauling's creditors.
(b) Jarman's promise to be responsible for Pauling's business debts constitutes a novation.
(c) If a misunderstanding arises as to the meaning of the term "business debts," the parol evidence rule would prevent the introduction of evidence of a subsequent oral agreement between Jarman and Pauling defining the term.
(d) Although Jarman has agreed to be responsible for Pauling's business debts, Pauling would continue to remain liable to his creditors on such debts.
(e) The contract to purchase the business would not be enforceable because the actual price to be paid for the business was uncertain at the time the contract was made.

(11) Morrison's factory badly needed painting. Atkins, a painter in need of work, wrote to Morrison stating that unless Morrison objected by return mail Atkins would proceed to paint Morrison's factory with two coats of paint for the cost of the paint plus $2,000. The parties had not previously done business together.

(a) If Morrison received Atkins' letter, tore it up and did not reply, Morrison's silence would not be an effective acceptance.
(b) If Morrison effectively accepted Atkins' offer and Atkins refused to paint the factory, Morrison may successfully sue Atkins for specific performance and force him to paint his factory.
(c) If Atkins commenced painting the factory with Morrison's approval and applied only one coat of paint, Atkins may rightfully demand payment of one half of the contract price if he needs money.
(d) If Morrison effectively accepted Atkins' offer and the factory burned down before Atkins could commence painting, Atkins is not entitled to receive the $2,000 although he remains ready to paint the factory and cannot find other work.
(e) If Atkins did not receive a reply from Morrison and proceeded to paint the factory, and Morrison (who did not know of Atkins' letter) returned from an extended vacation and was pleased to find his factory painted, Morrison would still not be responsible to Atkins in contract although he received a benefit which he needed and which cannot be returned.

(12) The following letter on company letterhead was sent to Jones, a noted artist, by John Able, the president of Able Corporation which is your audit client:

"Dear Mr. Jones:

"My company offers you the opportunity of painting my portrait next month. The painting must be completed within 30 days after you start work and I must be completely satisfied with the result. If you meet both of these conditions my company will pay you your usual fee plus an additional $1,000. On the other hand, if you are not able to meet these conditions I will expect you to pay my company $500 because you will have wasted my time.

"If you do not effectively accept this offer by mail within 10 days from the date of this letter the offer shall no longer be in effect.

"Sincerely,
John Able, President"

(a) If Jones mailed a properly stamped and addressed letter of acceptance to Able within 10 days of the date of Able's letter, an effective acceptance was made even if Jones' letter is never received.
(b) If Jones effectively accepted Able's offer, began work on the painting but then saw that he could not complete it within 30 days, Jones may rightfully withdraw his acceptance of the offer in order to avoid being liable to Able Corporation for $500.
(c) If Jones effectively accepted Able's offer but before starting

to work obtained a much better offer from another source, Jones may delegate the painting of Able to his assistant provided Jones carefully supervises the work.

(d) If Jones effectively accepts Able's offer, Able must cooperate with Jones to allow him to finish his work within the time allotted or Able will have breached the contract.

(e) If Jones effectively accepted Able's offer and completed the work and Able in good faith was not completely satisfied with the finished painting, Jones must pay Able Corporation $500 even though a group of noted art critics found that the work was a remarkably good work.

11/68

(13) In order to have an enforceable contract there must be

(a) An agreement.
(b) A legal obligation.
(c) A writing.
(d) At least two parties.
(e) Mutual assent.

(14) Anderson visited his accountant to arrange for the preparation of his tax return. A fee was not discussed, although Anderson expected to be charged. Under these circumstances

(a) An express contract to pay a reasonable fee is created.
(b) An implied contract to pay a reasonable fee is created.
(c) No contract is created.
(d) A voidable contract is created.
(e) An express bilateral contract is created whether or not mutual promises were exchanged.

(15) Anfeld said to his accountant, Crane, "I promise to pay you $100 if you will agree to prepare my tax return."

(a) Anfeld's statement constituted an offer.
(b) When Crane agrees to prepare the return an executed contract exists.
(c) When Crane agrees to prepare the return an executory contract exists.
(d) A contract cannot exist prior to Crane's commencing the work.
(e) If Crane does not expressly agree, but he prepares the return, such action may constitute the making of the contract.

(16) Peters offered in writing to sell his land to Sigaud for $10,000. Peters further promised in writing that he would hold his offer open for thirty days if Sigaud would promise to pay him an additional $100 anytime within the thirty day period, and Sigaud so promised.

(a) Sigaud has obtained a valid thirty day option to purchase Peters' land.
(b) Peters may revoke his offer to sell his land anytime prior to Sigaud's payment of $100.

(c) Sigaud may not effectively accept Peters' offer to allow Sigaud to purchase the land within thirty days at the specified price until Sigaud pays Peters $100.
(d) Peters may not rightfully sell his land to anyone other than Sigaud for thirty days, but Peters may revoke his offer to sell at anytime if he decides to keep the land for himself.
(e) If Sigaud accepts Peters' offer to sell the land within thirty days, he need not pay an additional $100.

(17) Riley embezzled funds while employed by Jones Company. Kara, internal auditor for Jones Company, later detected the embezzlement, and the Company offered a reward for information leading to Riley's arrest. Simon provided information, and as a result Riley was arrested. Simon is not entitled to receive the reward
(a) If he did not know of the offered reward when he gave the information.
(b) If he knew of the offered reward, but the offer to pay the reward was made to a limited group of individuals which did not include Simon.
(c) If he knew of the offered reward and the offer was made to him but he gave the information solely to relieve his conscience.
(d) If he knew of the offered reward and the offer was made to him but he gave the information solely to avoid his own threatened arrest.
(e) If he intended to accept the reward and the offer was made to him but he gave no indication before providing the information that he wanted to accept the offer.

(18) Jaul offered Gold terms for a contract and asked Gold to accept his offer to contract by mail.
(a) Gold's acceptance will not become effective until it is received by Jaul.
(b) Gold's properly mailed letter of acceptance will be effective as of the date it is mailed only if it reaches Jaul within a reasonable time.
(c) Gold's properly mailed letter of acceptance will be effective as of the date it was mailed even if it is lost in the mail.
(d) Gold's acceptance communicated by telegraph will not be effective until it is received by Jaul.
(e) If Gold properly mails a letter rejecting Jaul's offer and then changes his mind, Gold may not telephone Jaul before he receives the rejection letter and effectively accept the offer.

(19) Although no consideration is given, a written promise may be enforceable where
(a) The promise is to pay a past debt still existing and enforceable.
(b) The promise is to pay a past debt barred by the Statute of Limitations.

(c) The promise is to pay a past debt barred by bankruptcy.
(d) The only reason that the promise is made is the promisor's love and affection for the promisee and the promisee took no action in reliance upon the promise.
(e) The doctrine of promissory estoppel is applicable.

(20) The Statute of Frauds
(a) Does not apply to contracts created by law.
(b) Does not apply to contracts which have been fully executed.
(c) Does not apply to any contract involving less than $50 of value.
(d) When applicable, may be satisfied by an unsigned written memorandum.
(e) When applicable, may never be satisfied unless a writing evidencing the transaction has been delivered by one of the contracting parties to the other.

(21) Where a written contract has been entered into, the parol evidence rule may be applied to prevent the admissibility of proof
(a) Of an oral agreement made prior to the execution of the contract which contradicts the contract.
(b) Of a written agreement made prior to the execution of the contract which contradicts the contract.
(c) Of an oral agreement made prior to the execution of the contract which shows that no valid contract was entered into.
(d) Of an oral agreement made prior to the execution of the contract which shows that the written contract does not contain the entire understanding of the parties.
(e) Of an oral agreement made subsequent to the execution of the contract which contradicts the contract.

(22) The doctrine of impossibility of performance will excuse a promisor from performing where
(a) The subject matter of the contract is destroyed by an act of God.
(b) Illness prevents the promisor from performing a personal service contract.
(c) A change of law renders performance illegal.
(d) The promisor's financial condition makes it impossible for him to perform.
(e) A supplier of the promisor refuses to deliver goods which the promisor needs in order to be able to perform.

(23) Decker contracts in writing to sell his house to Besen and then refuses to perform.
(a) Besen may sue Decker and obtain specific performance of the contract and also a punitive money damage award.
(b) Specific performance is the only possible remedy available for Besen.
(c) Specific performance is not an available remedy if a similar house is available at a reasonable price.

(d) Specific performance may be granted on the ground that a contract for the sale of real property is unique.
(e) Only a court of law, as opposed to a court of equity, is empowered to grant the specific performance remedy.

(24) Canale owes Murzin $100 and Murzin owes Stark the same amount. It is agreed among all three parties that Canale will pay Stark instead of Murzin, and that Murzin will terminate his legal relations with both and will be discharged.
(a) The agreement is unenforceable because of lack of consideration.
(b) The agreement constitutes an executed accord and satisfaction.
(c) The agreement constitutes a novation.
(d) The agreement constitutes merely an assignment of Murzin's rights against Canale to Stark.
(e) Canale's becoming bankrupt prior to paying Stark would have no effect upon the agreement.

11/67

(25) The following promises are sufficiently definite to create a contract:
(a) A promises B to sell to B, and B promises A to buy from A, all goods of a certain character and price which B shall need in his business during the ensuing year.
(b) A promises B to sell to him, and B promises A to buy from A, goods "at cost plus a nice profit."
(c) A and B promise that specified performances shall be mutually rendered by them "in about nine months' time."
(d) A promises B to employ him for a stated compensation, and B promises A to serve as long as B is able to do the work or as long as business is carried on.
(e) A promises B to do a specified job, and B promises A to pay a specified amount therefor if performance is satisfactory to B.

(26) In an auction
(a) The auctioneer invites offers.
(b) The auctioneer invites acceptances.
(c) That is announced to be without reserve, the auctioneer cannot withdraw the item to be auctioned under any circumstances.
(d) That is announced to be without reserve, a bidder cannot withdraw his bid once it has been made.
(e) Any bidder can withdraw his bid before a sale is completed.

(27) If an offer of a reward is made for information leading to the capture of a criminal, the reward may be collected by
(a) A, a policeman who knew of the reward and arrested the criminal in the line of duty.

(b) B, a citizen who knew of the reward and gave information leading to the arrest of the criminal but did not participate in the arrest.
(c) C, a citizen who captured the criminal without knowledge of the reward.
(d) D and E jointly, if they knew of the reward and their information and acts, taken together, caused the capture of the criminal.
(e) The criminal who surrendered to a policeman.

(28) If all communications are properly addressed and stamped and sent through the mails and the offeror has not specified the means of acceptance, a contract exists where
(a) An acceptance is sent and lost.
(b) The offeree sends a rejection and then an acceptance, and then the offeror receives the rejection, and then the acceptance.
(c) The offeree sends an acceptance and then a rejection, and the offeror receives the rejection, and then the acceptance.
(d) The offeree sends a rejection and then an acceptance, and the offeror receives the acceptance, and then the rejection.
(e) The offeree sends an acceptance and then a rejection, and the acceptance is lost and the offeror receives the rejection.

(29) The doctrine of consideration
(a) Has been totally abolished in several jurisdictions.
(b) Has been abolished in all jurisdictions recognizing the doctrine of promissory estoppel.
(c) Has been eliminated, in part, by statute in several jurisdictions.
(d) Is a common law doctrine.
(e) May consist of an act, a forbearance, or a return promise.

(30) Under the Statute of Frauds, a writing will be required to evidence
(a) An offer to sell land.
(b) An acceptance of an offer to sell land.
(c) An agreement made in consideration of marriage.
(d) A promise by an executor to use estate funds to pay a decedent's debts.
(e) A promise made to a debtor to be responsible for his debt.

(31) The parol evidence rule
(a) Applies only to an integrated contract.
(b) Affects the admissibility as evidence of subsequent oral statements which contradict an earlier written contract.
(c) Affects the admissibility as evidence of oral statements, made at the time the contract was signed, which explain the terms of a writing.
(d) Affects the admissibility as evidence of an oral statement,

made prior to the date of the contract, which conditioned the existence of the contract.

(e) Affects the admissibility as evidence of a writing which contradicts the terms of a subsequent integrated contract.

(32) If an agreement is illegal and both parties were aware of the fact when they entered into the agreement,

(a) Neither party may sue the other for damages for breach of contract.

(b) Either party may sue the other for return of any consideration tendered.

(c) Either party may sue the other for the benefit he bestowed on him.

(d) Either party may sue the other for the value of his services.

(e) The contract is void as to both parties.

(33) A third party beneficiary contract

(a) Requires that three persons enter into a contract together.

(b) Is enforceable by a donee beneficiary.

(c) Is enforceable by a creditor beneficiary.

(d) Is enforceable by an incidental beneficiary.

(e) Is enforceable by the promisee.

(34) The doctrine of substantial performance

(a) Has most frequently been applied in cases of building contracts.

(b) If applied, will require payment of the full contract price.

(c) May be applied even though there has been an express waiver of any defect.

(d) May be applied if the obligor intentionally departed from the contract in a minor detail.

(e) May be applied even though the obligor unintentionally departed from the contract in a minor detail if the cost of replacement would be grossly and unfairly out of proportion to the good to be accomplished by complete performance.

(35) An anticipatory breach of contract

(a) May involve the breach of an express term of a contract.

(b) May involve the breach of an implied term of a contract.

(c) Does not give the innocent party a right to elect to wait until the time for performance to sue for breach of contract.

(d) Of an employment contract always allows the prospective employee to collect full damages even if at the time of suit he has a better job at higher pay.

(e) Occurs if there is a present inability to perform, even if there is a willingness and capability to perform at the future time called for by the contract.

(36) In assessing contract damages, a court will usually grant a plaintiff

(a) Compensatory damages.
(b) Foreseeable damages.
(c) Punitive damages.
(d) Damages stipulated in a liquidated damage clause.
(e) Specific performance whenever plaintiff prefers such recovery to a money judgment.

5/66

TOPIC THREE

COMMERCIAL PAPER

AICPA DESCRIPTION OF THE TOPIC

*COMMERCIAL PAPER. The major provisions of Article 3 (Commercial Paper) and Article 4 (Banking) of the Uniform Commercial Code come under this topic which is traditionally referred to as Negotiable Instruments. It includes the types of negotiable instruments, the concept and importance of negotiability, the requisites for negotiability, negotiation, holding in due course, defenses, and the rights of the parties to the instrument.**

I. TYPES †

A. Introduction: The law of negotiable instruments has undergone its most recent codification in Article 3 of the Uniform Commercial Code. This topic is based exclusively on the Code. The outline reorganizes the provisions of UCC Article 3 and Article 4, Part 4 (in the section on checks) and paraphrases their contents to provide a logical presentation and to facilitate the student's comprehension.

B. Draft (formerly termed a bill of exchange): a written order addressed by one person‡ called the drawer, to another called the drawee, directing the drawee to pay a sum certain in money to the order of another, called the payee, or to bearer of the bill.

1. Domestic draft: one which on its face is both drawn and payable within the United States.

* Source: AICPA, *Information for CPA Candidates* (July 1970).

† Commercial paper is an aggregate term for four types of negotiable instruments (draft, check, certificate of deposit, and note). Investment securities, documents of title, and money are negotiable instruments not included in the term "commercial paper." As this chapter outlines the law of commercial paper, these three additional types of negotiable instruments will not be treated here.

‡ "Person" as applied to parties to negotiable instruments is not restricted to legal entities. (E.g., an unincorporated association may be the payee of a negotiable instrument.) A party need only be identified with reasonable certainty by the instrument.

2. Foreign draft: one which on its face is either drawn or payable outside the United States.
3. Sight draft: draft payable upon delivery and presentment to the drawer.
4. Documentary sight draft: sight draft accompanied by a shipping document, e.g., a bill of lading.
5. Time draft: payable at some future, determinable time, usually accepted by the drawee.
6. Trade acceptance: draft drawn by seller of goods on the buyer and accepted by the buyer.
7. Money order: instrument with name of its purchaser and the payee on its face, and drawn on a bank or a post office.
8. Banker's acceptance: draft drawn on and accepted by a bank.

C. Check: a draft drawn on a bank and payable on demand.

1. Bank draft: a check drawn by one bank against funds deposited to its account in another bank.
2. Cashier's check: a check drawn by a bank on itself payable to its customer's order.

D. Certificate of deposit: an acknowledgment by a bank of receipt of money with an engagement to repay it.

E. Note: a written promise other than a certificate of deposit by a person called the maker to pay a sum certain in money to the order of another called the payee or to the bearer of the note.

II. THE CONCEPT OF NEGOTIABILITY

A. Importance of the concept.

1. The concept of negotiability is the leading principle of the law of negotiable commercial paper. This paper is used to supplement the money supply, and in order to foster its ready acceptance in commerce it is given many distinct benefits not afforded to ordinary contract rights (see below). The key to this area of law is the ability or legal power of a transferor, under certain circumstances, to transfer better rights than he has.
2. In order to obtain the distinct benefits of negotiability, the party holding the instrument must attain the status of a *holder in due course.* At the outset it will be helpful briefly to summarize in logical sequence the steps which must be followed to obtain these benefits:

a. The instrument must be *negotiable* (see III).

b. The person asserting the rights must be a *holder,* i.e., he must take via *negotiation* (see IV).

c. The holder must satisfy the requirements for *holding in due course* (see V.A.).

d. The defense asserted must be a "*personal defense*" as contrasted with a "*real defense*" (see V.B.).

3. It may be helpful to think of these four steps as rungs in a ladder —you must satisfy each one of them to reach the top. Study them with great care in the succeeding parts of the text.

B. Characteristics: differences between negotiable instruments and ordinary contracts.

1. Negotiable instruments may pass freely from hand to hand. (This is not true of ordinary contract rights which, in some cases, cannot be transferred at all.)

2. Negotiable instruments are transferred by indorsement and delivery or sometimes by delivery alone. Contract rights in some cases may be assigned orally.

3. In all but a very few cases the rights of the assignee of a contract right are the same as those of his assignor. In the case of negotiable instruments, a holder in due course (see p. 96, V.) acquires greater rights because he takes free of most defenses. (I.e., the major advantage of a negotiable instrument is that it circulates, unburdened by claims of ownership or personal defenses of the maker, drawer, or subsequent transferees.)

4. Every negotiable instrument is deemed *prima facie* to have been issued for a consideration.

a. The words "value received" need not be in the instrument, as the presumption of consideration exists without them.

b. The necessary consideration for the issue of a negotiable instrument is any consideration that would support a simple contract.

c. In the hands of a holder in due course, consideration is conclusively presumed.

III. REQUISITES OF NEGOTIABILITY

A. Instrument must be in writing and signed by the maker or drawer.

1. If instrument is signed by an authorized agent, the agent must disclose his principal's name and his own representative capacity, or he will be personally liable upon the instrument.

2. The signer may use his own name, an assumed name, a symbol, or a rubber stamp, so long as what he uses is intended by him as a signature.

B. Must contain an unconditional promise or order to pay a sum certain in money.

1. Promise: an engagement to pay which is more than an acknowledgment of an obligation (e.g., an "I.O.U." is a mere acknowledgment, hence non-negotiable).
2. Order: a direction to pay which is more than an authorization or request addressed to one or more persons (drawees) identifiable with reasonable certainty.
3. Promise or order must be unconditional.
   a. A promise or order is not rendered conditional although the instrument:
      (1) States its consideration, or
      (2) Refers to the transaction out of which it arose or any other separate agreement, or
      (3) States that it is secured by a mortgage or other security device, or
      (4) Indicates a particular account, fund, or source from which payment may be drawn, or
      (5) If issued by a government or a governmental agency, states that it is to be paid only out of a particular fund or source, or
      (6) Is payable only out of the entire assets of a partnership, unincorporated association, estate, or trust.
   b. A promise or order is not unconditional if the instrument:
      (1) States that it is "subject to" or "governed by" another agreement, or
      (2) States that it is to be paid only out of a particular fund or source except as mentioned in III.B.3.a.(5) and (6).
4. Sum certain: the sum payable is certain although it is to be paid:
   a. With stated interest, including different rates of interest before and after default, or
   b. By stated installments, or
   c. With a stated discount or addition for early or late payment, or
   d. With exchange added or deducted, whether at fixed or current rate, or
   e. With costs of collection or attorney's fees or both upon default.
5. Money: defined as a medium of exchange authorized or adopted by a domestic or foreign government as part of its currency.

a. If the sum payable is stated in a foreign currency it may be paid in that number of dollars which said sum would purchase on the day of payment unless the instrument specifies the foreign currency as the medium of payment.

6. Instrument which contains an order or promise to do any act in addition to the payment of money is non-negotiable; however, the negotiable character of an instrument is not affected by a provision which:

   a. States that collateral has been given and authorizes its sale upon default, or

   b. Requires maintenance or protection of collateral or giving of additional collateral, or

   c. Authorizes a confession of judgment upon default, or

   d. Waives the benefit of any law intended for the advantage of the obligor, or

   e. States that by indorsing or cashing a draft the payee acknowledges full satisfaction of drawer's obligation.

C. Instrument must be payable on demand or at a definite time.

1. Instrument is payable on demand if:

   a. It so states, or

   b. It is payable at sight or on presentation, or

   c. No time for payment is stated, or

   d. It is issued when payment is overdue.

2. Instrument is payable at definite time which by its terms is payable:

   a. On or before a stated date or at a fixed period after a stated date, or

   b. At a fixed period after sight, or

   c. At a definite time subject to any acceleration. An acceleration clause is a term allowing the payee or his successor to demand full payment immediately. Such acceleration is allowed only if provided for in the instrument, or

   d. At a definite time subject to extension either at the option of the holder or of the maker or acceptor, or automatically upon the occurrence of a specified act or event.

3. Instrument which is payable *only* upon the occurrence of an act or event uncertain as to time of occurrence (e.g., a promise to pay C $500 upon B's death) is not payable at a definite time and therefore not negotiable.

D. Instrument must be payable to order or to bearer.

1. Instrument is payable to order when it is payable to the order or "assigns" of any person which it specifies with reasonable certainty or to him or his order.
   a. Instrument may be payable to the order of:
      (1) Maker or drawer, or
      (2) Drawee, or
      (3) Payee other than maker, drawer, or drawee, or
      (4) Two or more payees together or in the alternative. (If payable to payees in the alternative, it is payable to any one of them, and any one of them with possession of the instrument may negotiate, discharge, or enforce it. If payable to payees jointly, it is payable to all of them and may be negotiated, discharged, or enforced only by all of them), or
      (5) An estate, trust, or fund (in such case it is payable to the order of the representative of the estate, trust, or fund), or
      (6) An officer or an officer by his title alone, or
      (7) A partnership or unincorporated association.
   b. Instrument is payable to bearer if it states it is payable to:
      (1) Bearer or the order of bearer, or
      (2) A specified person or bearer, or
      (3) "Cash" or to the order of "cash," or any other indication in which a specific payee is not designated.
   c. Instrument may be payable to one or more persons jointly or in the alternative but not in succession.

E. Amplification and rules of construction.

1. An instrument may be non-negotiable but nevertheless enforceable as a contract.
2. An instrument may still be negotiable even though it is antedated or postdated (providing this was not done for fraudulent or illegal purposes).
   a. The person who receives such an instrument acquires title thereto as of the date of delivery.
   b. An instrument need not be dated at all in order to be negotiable.
3. An instrument is not rendered non-negotiable because place for payment is not specified.
4. An instrument expressly payable at a bank or other special place is referred to as a "domiciled" instrument.

5. An instrument which is signed but is incomplete in some necessary respect (e.g., failure to state amount payable) cannot be enforced until it is completed.
   a. It may be completed by any one given the authority to do so, and when it is completed in accordance with authority given, it is effective as completed.
   b. An unauthorized completion of such instrument is a material alteration (see p. 99, V.B.2.e.).
   c. The party who asserts that completion was unauthorized has the burden of proving that fact.
6. Ambiguities: rules of construction.
   a. Written words control over sums denoted by figures unless words are ambiguous or uncertain.
   b. Instrument not dated is considered dated as of the time of issue.
   c. Written provisions prevail over printed provisions.
   d. Interest runs from the date of the instrument if there is no specification to the contrary, and, if there is no date, it runs from the date of issue.
   e. Where a signature is so placed that it is not clear in what capacity a person signed, he is deemed an indorser.
   f. Where an instrument containing the words "I promise to pay" is signed by two persons, those persons are deemed jointly and severally liable.
   g. Where there is doubt whether the instrument is a draft or a note, the holder may treat it as either at his election.
   h. The drawer and drawee of a draft may be the same; if so, the holder may treat it as a note.

IV. ISSUE AND NEGOTIATION

A. Issue: the first delivery (voluntary transfer of possession) of an instrument to a holder (normally to the person to whom the instrument is payable, i.e., the payee).

B. Negotiation: Subsequent transfer of the instrument in such a way that the transferee is a "holder."

1. Bearer paper is negotiated *by delivery alone.* (However, the holder may be required to indorse or may indorse if he wishes.)
2. Order paper is negotiated *by an indorsement* by the person to whose order the instrument is payable, *and delivery.*
   a. Indorsement: signing one's name, with or without other words, on the instrument.

(1) May be typewritten or rubber stamped if intended as an indorsement.

(2) May be by an agent on behalf of the holder.

(3) Indorsements are also made for purposes other than the transfer of the instrument. (E.g., X, not a party to the instrument, writes his name on the back of Y's note as an accommodation indorser—see p. 105, VI.F.1. and 2.—so that Y may obtain a loan.)

C. Types of indorsement.

1. Blank: transferor's signature alone. Converts order paper to bearer paper.
2. Special: made to a specified person called an indorsee (e.g., "Pay X," signed Y). Bearer paper so indorsed becomes order paper. Further negotiation requires the indorsee's signature.
3. Restrictive.
   a. Conditional. (E.g., "Pay X if but only if . . . ," signed Y.)
   b. Indorsements containing the words "For deposit," "For collection," "Pay any bank or banker," or like terms. These indorsements and conditional indorsements require the immediate (first) transferee and all subsequent transferees (with the exception of intermediary and payor banks* in the instrument collection process which may disregard the restrictions) to comply with the restrictions in paying value for the instrument. To the extent that said transferees do so, they are holders and are not prevented from being holders in due course if they fulfill the other requirements for that status (see p. 96, V.A.).
   c. Indorsement purporting to prohibit further transfer (e.g., "Pay X only," signed Y). Neither such an indorsement nor any other restrictive indorsement prevents further transfer or negotiation.
   d. Indorsee payable only for the use or benefit of another (e.g., "Pay X in trust for Z," signed Y). "Trust" indorsement requires only the immediate transferee to comply with the restriction. Any subsequent tranferee may disregard the restriction, and his holder in due course status (see p. 96, V.A.) is not affected thereby unless he knows that the first transferee did not comply with the restriction.
4. Qualified (e.g., "Without recourse," signed Y): Transferor disclaims liability on the instrument, to pay upon dishonor (see p. 105, VI.E.2.). Does not prevent transferee from being a holder in due course.

* A "payor bank" is a bank at which an instrument is payable as drawn or as accepted. A drawee bank is a payor bank.

D. Amplification and explanation.

1. Above types of indorsement can be used in combination so long as the combination is not by definition inconsistent (e.g., "Pay X Bank, for deposit" is both special and restrictive).
2. Transfer for value of order paper without an indorsement operates as an assignment, and title to the instrument vests in the transferee. Such a transferee has the right to require the transferor to indorse the paper subsequent to the transfer. However, the transferee becomes a holder as of the date of the indorsement. It is at this later time that he must meet the requirements for holding in due course. (E.g., X takes a negotiable instrument payable to Y's order by mere delivery. He will not become a holder until he obtains Y's indorsement. If at any time prior to his obtaining Y's indorsement he learns of a defense to the instrument, he will not qualify as a holder in due course.)
3. A payee or indorsee whose name is incorrectly spelled on the instrument should so indorse the instrument. The transferee may require his proper signature in addition.
4. Negotiation in the following ways is effective to transfer the instrument but is subject to rescission except as against a subsequent holder in due course.
    a. Where transferor is an infant, a corporation exceeding its powers, or any other person without capacity, or
    b. Where obtained by fraud, duress, or mistake of any kind, or
    c. Where part of an illegal transaction, or
    d. Where made in breach of duty.
5. Only the entire amount of the instrument can be negotiated; i.e., an attempted transfer of part of the face value of a negotiable instrument will be treated as a partial assignment, not a negotiation.

V. HOLDER IN DUE COURSE

A. Requisites.

1. The person must be a holder (i.e., the payee or a transferee who takes via negotiation) of a negotiable instrument.
2. Holder must take the instrument for value. A holder gives value in the following ways:
    a. By performing the agreed consideration. Any consideration sufficient to support a simple contract may be value, but only to the extent that it has been performed. When part of the agreed consideration is executory (unperformed), at the time of notice of an infirmity or defect in an instrument, the holder will qualify as a holder in due course only to the extent that he

has performed. (E.g., X brought notes from Y aggregating $1,000. X paid $250 and promised to pay $500 at a later date. Before X had paid any additional money, he learned that Y had obtained the notes from the maker by duress. X may recover only the $250 from the maker.)

b. By acquiring a security interest in or a lien on the instrument otherwise than by legal process (e.g., X in order to borrow money from the bank pledges bearer negotiable instruments with the bank. The bank will have given value to the extent of the loan).

c. By taking the instrument in payment of or as security for an antecedent claim (e.g., debt, contract right) against any person. As in the case above where the instrument is taken as security for a loan, the holder qualifies as a holder in due course only to the extent of his interest therein.

d. By giving his own negotiable instrument in exchange (despite the fact that in the case of a check, for example, the party could stop payment after learning of a defense).

e. In the case of a bank, by the depositor withdrawing the value of the instrument from his account. (E.g., X deposits a $500 check in B Bank. B Bank credits X's account with that amount. Later X withdraws the $500 from his account.) In determining when a depositor has withdrawn the amount of the item in question, the FIFO (first-in-first-out) rule prevails.

f. Even though a negotiable instrument sells at a substantial discount, the value requirement is nevertheless fulfilled and the holder will qualify as a holder in due course for the face value (full amount of the instrument) provided he took it in good faith. (E.g., X, in good faith, pays $75 for a $100 promissory note.)

3. Holder must take the instrument in good faith (honestly) and without notice that it is overdue or has been dishonored or that any person has a defense against or claim to it. This requirement as interpreted and applied is almost exclusively a subjective test (i.e., did *the particular person* asserting holder in due course status take in good faith or have knowledge). The test is not whether he was negligent or whether a reasonable man (an objective test) would have known.

   a. Holder has notice of a claim or defense when he knows or has reason to know of it.

   b. The instrument itself puts the holder on notice of a defense if it is so incomplete as to suggest forgery or alteration or is otherwise so irregular as to call into question its validity, terms, or ownership.

c. A domestic check is presumed to be overdue after 30 days following its issue. Other demand instruments are overdue after a reasonable time has elapsed.

d. Knowledge that an incomplete instrument has been completed does not put the holder on notice of a defense unless the holder knows or has reason to know of any improper completion.

e. Notice that one or more but less than all of the prior parties have been discharged does not put the holder on notice of a defense as far as the remaining parties to the instrument are concerned. However, those discharges of which the holder *does* have notice will be effective against him although he may be a holder in due course as to the other parties.

B. Rights of a holder in due course.

1. Any holder of a negotiable instrument has the right to transfer or negotiate it, to discharge it or enforce payment in his own name, and to strike out any indorsements not necessary to his title.

2. A *holder in due course,* in addition, takes the instrument free from all claims to it by any person and free from all defenses of any party with whom he has not dealt except the following:

   a. Infancy. To the extent that the law of the jurisdiction makes this a defense to a simple contract, it is effective against a holder in due course (see Contracts, p. 43, III.D.1.).

   b. *Void* instruments. To varying extents in different jurisdictions the following may render the instrument void:

      (1) Incapacity other than infancy (see Contracts, p. 43, III.D.).

      (2) Duress in the execution.

      (3) Illegality of the transaction.

   c. Fraud as to the nature and essential terms of the instrument—fraud in the execution; see Contracts, p. 48, IV.A.3.c.(2). For example, X is asked to sign a "receipt" for the delivery of goods. The "receipt" is in fact a negotiable instrument.

   d. Unauthorized signatures.

      (1) Negligence inviting forgery or otherwise unauthorized signing prevents a party from (he is estopped from) raising the defense.

      (2) Two types of forgery of instruments are not included in this defense and do not run against a holder in due course:

         (A) Indorsement in the name of a named payee by a person who induced issuance of the instrument by posing as the payee, e.g., an imposter poses as X, a prominent person, obtains a check payable to X's order, and indorses the check by signing X's name on the back, and

(B) Indorsement in the name of a fictitious payee by *a person* who made or induced another to make the instrument payable to such a fictitious payee. (E.g., a payroll clerk draws a check payable to a fictitious payee, has it signed by the company treasurer, and later indorses the fictitious payee's name himself.)

e. Material alteration.

(1) Negligence inviting alteration prevents a party from raising this defense (estoppel).

(2) The following alterations are material:

(A) Date.

(B) Sum payable.

(C) Time or place of payment.

(D) Medium of payment.

(E) Number or relationship of parties.

(F) Adding a place of payment where none is specified.

(G) Anything that alters the contract of the party to the instrument in any respect.

(3) If the instrument is materially altered, the maker or drawer and/or prior indorser remains liable on the instrument to a holder in due course, according to its original tenor. A wrongful or unauthorized filling in or completion is treated as a material alteration. However, if the wrongful filling in or completion is done without knowledge of its invalidity on the part of the holder in due course, he takes free of this defense.

f. Discharge in insolvency proceedings, i.e., bankruptcy.

3. The defenses listed above are termed "real" defenses. All defenses other than those listed above are termed "personal" defenses and are not available against the holder in due course. (E.g., simple contract defenses, fraud in the inducement—see Contracts, p. 48, IV.A.3.c.(1)—payment, lack of delivery.)

4. One can acquire rights of holder in due course without being one, by taking title through a holder in due course. (E.g., X, a holder in due course of a note originally procured through fraud, gives it to Y, who knows of the fraud. Y, although not a holder in due course, acquires X's rights as a holder in due course and can collect the proceeds if he did not take part in the fraud.) The exception to this rule is that a holder of an instrument who does not qualify as a holder in due course cannot better his rights by

transferring the instrument to a holder in due course and then reacquiring it.

VI. CONTRACTUAL LIABILITY OF THE PARTIES

A. Conditions precedent to holding certain parties liable.

1. Introduction: Drawers of drafts and checks and indorsers of drafts, checks, and notes do not assume primary liability for payment of the instrument. Instead, it is contemplated that a person other than those persons will pay. In the case of drafts and checks, the drawee is the party who should make payment and, in the case of notes, the maker should pay. Thus drawers and indorsers are said to be *secondarily liable*. This means that, unless excused or waived, the party seeking payment from drawers and indorsers must fulfill certain conditions precedent (presentment, notice of dishonor, and, in certain cases, protest) in order to charge these people with liability on the instrument. The importance of this distinction is that failure to comply with these conditions precedent completely discharges indorsers from secondary liability and discharges the drawer at least to the extent he has been injured by failure to fulfill the conditions precedent. Each of these conditions is discussed in detail below.

2. Presentment for acceptance: The drawer's act of drawing a draft does not make the drawee liable on the instrument. Oddly enough, no one has primary liability on a draft at the time of its issue. Drafts payable at a stated date may be required to be presented, or may be voluntarily presented, for acceptance. If the drawee then promises to pay the draft when due, he is said to have accepted or "honored" the draft and thereby becomes *primarily liable*. Presentment for acceptance applies only to time drafts.

   a. Presentment for acceptance is only required to hold the drawer and indorsers when:

      (1) Draft so provides, or

      (2) Draft is payable elsewhere than at drawee's residence or place of business, or

      (3) Date of payment depends on such presentment (e.g., draft payable 30 days after presentment or sight).

   b. The failure to make valid presentment for acceptance, *where required* discharges indorsers entirely and discharges drawers to the extent of the injury (i.e., to the extent that the drawer has been harmed by the failure to meet the requirement—see p. 104, VI.C.2.).

c. Otherwise, time drafts may be voluntarily presented for acceptance or may simply be presented for payment on the due date, without prior presentment for acceptance.

d. Acceptance is made only by the drawee's writing his signature, with or without other words, on the draft.

e. General acceptance: drawee accepts draft exactly as presented.

f. Acceptance varying draft (e.g., acceptance varying time or amount of payment or designating exclusive place for payment.)

(1) Holder may refuse such acceptance and treat draft as dishonored.

(2) Assent by the holder to such acceptance discharges any drawer or indorser who does not also affirmatively assent.

g. If drawee refuses to accept the draft or fails to accept it before the close of the next business day following presentment, the draft is dishonored.

h. Time of presentment: Where necessary presentment must be made on or before date payable. For drafts payable after sight, presentment must be made within reasonable time after issue or date of draft, whichever is later.

i. Excuse of delay in presentment for acceptance (see p. 103, VI.A.6.).

j. How presentment may be made (see p. 102, VI.A.3.g.).

3. Presentment for payment.

a. Relates to any commercial paper.

b. Made to maker of note, drawee or acceptor of draft, drawee of a check, or other payor.

c. If the party to pay refuses to pay or fails to do so before the close of business on the day of presentment, the instrument is dishonored.

d. Due presentment for payment necessary to fully hold maker of bank-domiciled note (see p. 104, VI.C.2.), acceptor of bank-domiciled draft, any drawer, or any indorser.

(1) Failure to make a valid presentment for payment completely discharges all indorsers, and

(2) Discharges others mentioned immediately above to the extent they have been injured (see p. 104, VI.C.2.).

e. Time of presentment.

(1) Demand note must be presented within a reasonable time after issue.

(2) Demand draft (excluding checks), to hold a drawer or indorser, must be presented within a reasonable time after the party sought to be held becomes liable on it.

(3) Check must be presented 30 days after date or issue, whichever is later, to hold the drawer, and seven days after a person's indorsement to hold said indorser.

(4) Where an instrument is accelerated (p. 92, III.C.2.c.), presentment must be made within a reasonable time after the acceleration.

(5) Instrument which states date on which it is payable must be presented on that date. If said date is not a full business day, presentment must be made on the next full business day.

f. Excuse of delay in presentment for payment (see p. 103, VI,A.6.).

g. How presentment for payment or acceptance may be made:

(1) By mail, with receipt of the mail effecting presentment, or

(2) Through a clearing house (a group of banks or other payors which meets so that each member may present instruments to the other members for payment and acceptance), or

(3) At the place of payment or acceptance specified in the instrument. If there be none, then at the place of business or residence of the party to pay or accept.

(4) May be made to any one of multiple makers, acceptors, drawees, or other payors, or to any person who has the authority to make or refuse the payment or acceptance.

(5) Drafts accepted or notes made payable at a bank in the United States must be presented at such bank.

(6) The person to whom presentment is made may require exhibition of the instrument, identification of person making presentment and evidence of his authority to do so, and a signed receipt on the instrument upon payment full or partial, with surrender of the instrument upon full payment.

h. Instrument payable at a bank (bank-domiciled) is treated in some jurisdictions as equivalent to a draft drawn on the bank designated. In other jurisdictions such an instrument is deemed merely to designate a place of payment, giving no order or authority to the bank to pay it.

4. Notice of dishonor.

a. Dishonor is non-acceptance of a time draft or non-payment of a draft or note. However, return of an instrument because of lack of a proper indorsement is not a dishonor.

b. Due notice of dishonor is necessary to fully hold maker of bank-domiciled note, acceptor of bank-domiciled draft, any drawer, or any indorser. Indorsers are completely discharged; the others mentioned above are discharged to the extent they were harmed by failure to meet the notice requirement.

c. May be given orally or in writing.

d. Must identify the instrument and state that it has been dishonored.

e. Return of the instrument bearing a stamp, ticket, or other writing to the effect that it has been dishonored, or notice of debit of the account is sufficient notice of dishonor.

f. Time of notice of dishonor.

(1) By banks: by midnight of the next banking day.

(2) By other parties: by midnight of the third business day after knowledge of dishonor.

g. Excuse of delay in giving notice (see below, VI.A.6.).

h. Any party who may be compelled to pay the instrument may notify any party who may be liable on it. (I.e., the person notified need not be liable to the person giving notice for said notice to be effective.)

i. Notice operates for the benefit of all parties who have rights on the instrument against the party notified.

j. Notice to joint parties who are not partners must be given to each individually, unless one has authority to receive such notice for the others.

k. Notice to a party dead or incompetent may be sent to his last known address or given to his personal representative.

5. Protest: formal attestation of dishonor.

a. Not necessary except on drafts drawn or payable outside the United States ("foreign" drafts).

b. Must be made and sealed by United States consular officer, or notary public, or other person authorized to make protest by the law of the jurisdiction where dishonor occurs.

c. Any necessary protest is due at the time notice of dishonor is due.

d. Failure to comply with the protest requirement completely discharges all indorsers and drawers (see p. 104, VI.C.2.).

6. Excuse of delay in presentment, notice of dishonor, or protest.

a. Excused when the party is without notice that it is due (e.g., when note accelerated without his knowledge), or

b. When caused by circumstances beyond his control; when cause of delay ceases to operate he must act with reasonable diligence.

7. Presentment or notice of dishonor or protest not required:
   a. As to party who dishonored the instrument, and
   b. As to any party who waives it before or after it is due, and
   c. When the maker, acceptor, or drawee of any instrument except a documentary draft is dead or in insolvency proceedings instituted after issue of the instrument.

B. Contract liability (liability on instrument) of maker of non-bank-domiciled note and acceptor of non-bank-domiciled draft. Note that here, as elsewhere, the UCC stresses the importance of the distinction between non-bank-domiciled and bank-domiciled instruments (see below, C).

1. Each engages to pay it according to its terms at the time of making or acceptance respectively, or as later completed when completed as authorized.
2. Each admits the existence of the payee and then his capacity to indorse.
3. Acceptor of draft is liable to holder in due course even though draft bears a forged drawer's signature.
4. None of the conditions of presentment, notice of dishonor, and protest is necessary to hold these parties, as they are primarily liable.

C. Contract liability of maker of bank-domiciled ("payable at a bank") note and acceptor of bank-domiciled draft.

1. Each engages to pay as stated in VI.B.1. above, *provided that* due presentment of the respective instrument for payment at the bank designated (domiciliary bank) is made and that any necessary notice of dishonor or protest is given.
2. Delay in fulfilling or failure to fulfill presentment or notice of dishonor conditions discharges such maker or such acceptor (or any drawer) only when he is deprived of funds maintained with the drawee or other payor bank to cover the instrument because such bank becomes insolvent during the delay. In addition, such party must assign in writing his rights against the bank in respect of such funds. Failure to meet the protest condition, where required, completely discharges the above parties.
3. Each admits the existence of the payee and his then capacity to indorse.

D. Contract liability of any drawer.

1. Engages that upon dishonor of the draft and notice of dishonor or protest, if necessary, he will pay the amount of the draft to the holder or to any indorser who assumes responsibility on it.
2. Effect of delay in fulfilling or failure to fulfill these conditions (see p. 104, VI.C.2.).
3. Admits the existence of the payee and his then capacity to indorse.
4. Drawer may disclaim his liability by drawing without recourse.

E. Contract liability of indorsers.

1. Every indorser *other than a qualified indorser* engages that upon dishonor and any necessary notice of dishonor or protest he will pay the instrument according to its terms at the time of his indorsement to the holder or to any subsequent indorser who assumes responsibility on it.
2. A qualified indorser disclaims this liabilty by writing a disclaimer (e.g., "without recourse") on the instrument.
3. Delay in fulfilling or failure to fulfill the conditions precedent (i.e., presentment, notice of dishonor, or protest) *completely* discharges any indorser.
4. Indorsers are liable to one another in the order of indorsement unless they agree otherwise.

F. Liability of accommodation party.

1. Accommodation party is in effect a surety in that he signs the instrument and thus assumes possible liability on it in order to accommodate another party to it. This is done to facilitate a loan or transfer the instrument. As between the accommodation party and the party accommodated, the latter should perform and bears the ultimate liability. E.g., X wishes to borrow $1,000 from Y and offers to give his promissory note for the loan. Y is unwilling to loan the money unless X obtains another party (a surety) against whom Y can seek recovery if X defaults. Z, in order to accommodate his friend X signs the negotiable promissory note either as a co-maker or indorser. As such, Z is an accommodation party.
2. Accommodation party is liable in the capacity in which he signs (e.g., maker, acceptor, indorser, etc.), even though the taker knows of the accommodation as long as the instrument has been taken for value before it is due.
3. Accommodation party is not liable to the party accommodated and can proceed against the party accommodated if he has to pay the instrument.

VII. WARRANTY LIABILITY OF THE PARTIES

A. Introduction: In addition to the contractual liability discussed in VI above, certain implied warranties attach to the sale of commercial paper.

B. Warranties to persons accepting or paying.

1. A person other than a holder in due course making presentment for acceptance or payment and any prior transferor of the instrument warrants to the person accepting or paying that:
   a. He has good title (i.e., all indorsements are genuine and authorized) or is an authorized representative of a person with good title, and
   b. He has no knowledge that the signature of the maker or drawer is unauthorized, and
   c. The instrument has not been materially altered.
2. A holder in due course making presentment:
   a. Warrants that he has good title.
   b. Does not make warranty 1.b. if he is acting in good faith to a maker or drawer with respect to their respective signatures, or to an acceptor to whom he is making presentment for payment.
   c. Does not make warranty 1.c. to a maker or drawer, to an acceptor with respect to an alteration made prior to acceptance if the holder in due course took the draft after acceptance, or to an acceptor with respect to an alteration made after acceptance.

C. Warranties to transferees and subsequent holders.

1. Any person who transfers by indorsement and for consideration warrants to his transferee and to any subsequent holder that:
   a. He has good title or is an authorized representative of a person with good title, and
   b. All signatures are genuine or authorized, and
   c. The instrument has not been materially altered, and
   d. No defense of any party is good against him, and
   e. To his knowledge no insolvency proceedings have been instituted with respect to the maker or acceptor or the drawer of an unaccepted instrument.
2. An indorser who transfers "without recourse" (qualified indorser) makes the same warranties listed in 3.a–e., with the exception

that with respect to 3.d. he warrants only that to his knowledge no defense of any party is good against him.

3. A person who transfers for consideration but without indorsement (e.g., transfer of a bearer instrument) makes the same warranties listed in 3.a–e., but he makes them only to his immediate transferee and not to subsequent holders.
4. The official draft of the UCC eliminates warranty liability for the accommodation party who does not receive consideration, but some adopting states (e.g., New York) have added a provision making him liable on warranties a., b., c., and e. of C.1. *supra*, p. 106.

VIII. CHECKS

A. Draft, drawn on a bank, payable on demand. Note that we have already considered many of the rules applicable to the parties to a check in prior parts of the text, i.e., the contractual liability of the parties and especially in the warranty liability of the parties. When a check is received in payment of a debt, the underlying obligation for which the check is given is not extinguished, except in rare instances; i.e., the check is not taken in absolute payment.

B. Relationship of bank and depositor.

1. Ordinary deposit or checking account: A debtor and creditor relationship exists, and the bank has title to the deposits.
   a. A check does not operate as an assignment in the absence of special facts.
   b. Bank may set off debts owed it by its depositor.
2. Special deposit for a specific purpose: a bailee and bailor relationship exists, and depositor has title to the deposits.

C. Right to compel payment.

1. Payee has no right to compel payment as against drawee bank, even though depositor has funds on deposit.
2. Payee can compel payment by drawer, if drawee bank refuses to pay and the proper procedural steps (see p. 105, VI.D.) have been taken in respect to dishonor.
3. Payee can compel payment by drawee bank after certification of check (see p. 108, VIII.D.).
4. Only the drawer has a right of action against the bank for a wrongful dishonor (e.g., slander of credit).
   a. When dishonor occurs through mistake, liability is limited to actual damages proved.

b. A bank is under no obligation to pay a check more than six months old, other than a certified check; hence, dishonor is not wrongful. However, it may pay such a check without being liable to its customer.

D. Certification: bank's recognition of a depositor's check and acceptance of it as a valid appropriation of the amount specified. The bank warrants that sufficient funds are on deposit and have been set aside.

1. Major advantage: Drawee bank becomes liable to the holder on the instrument.
2. Holder procures certification.
   a. Bank becomes primarily liable.
   b. Drawer and indorsers are discharged.
3. Drawer procuring certification.
   a. Bank is primarily liable.
   b. Drawer remains secondarily liable.
4. Bank's refusal to certify is not dishonor; only refusal to pay is dishonor.
5. Certification of overdraft.
   a. Holder may collect full amount of check from drawee.
   b. Drawer is liable to drawee for the difference.
   c. If certification of the overdraft was knowingly made by bank official, he is liable to bank.

E. Drawer's right to stop payment.

1. Stop-payment order must reach bank in time for bank to avoid certifying the check or making final payment on it.
2. Oral stop-payment order lapses after 14 days but may be confirmed in writing within that period. Written order is effective for six months unless renewed in writing.
3. Bank is liable to drawer if it pays after effective stop-payment order.
   a. This liability may be varied by agreement; however, no agreement can disclaim or limit a bank's liability for damages caused by its own lack of good faith or its negligence.
4. The drawer has the burden of proving that the failure to obey his stop-payment order caused the loss.
5. If drawer stops payment, he is liable to the holder of the check unless he has a valid, assertable defense.

F. Drawer's responsibility with respect to unauthorized signatures or alterations.

1. If drawer's negligence has substantially contributed to the unauthorized signatures or alterations, he bears the loss resulting from a good faith payment by the bank.
2. Drawer who knowingly or unknowingly makes a check payable to an imposter or to a fictitious payee bears the loss.
3. Drawer who receives a bank statement with paid checks enclosed may not recover from the bank any amount paid on a forged or altered check if he is negligent in informing the bank promptly after receipt of the paid check and the bank can prove it has been harmed by said failure to give prompt notice. In addition, a negligent failure to notify the bank of the forgery or alteration within 14 days causes the drawer to bear the loss on additional checks, forged or altered by the same wrongdoer, thereafter paid in good faith by the bank.
4. If the drawer can prove that the bank was also negligent in paying a forged or altered check, then his negligence in notification of the bank does not preclude his recovery against the bank.
5. Regardless of negligence on the part of the drawer or the bank, a drawer who fails to report his unauthorized signature or any alteration within one year after receiving his bank statement or fails to report any unauthorized indorsement within three years bears the loss on the forged or altered check.
6. Where bank bears loss resulting from payment of a forged or altered check it may look to the warranties of the party making presentment and prior transferors of the check for recovery. As to whether the bank will prevail, see p. 106, VII.A. and B. In addition, the forger is liable to the bank independently of these warranties.

COMMERCIAL PAPER: SUBJECTIVE QUESTIONS*

TYPES

Q. Arthur purchased securities from William, giving William his check payable to William's order and drawn on Produce Bank in payment. At William's insistence, the check was endorsed by Arthur's friend, Gregory, before it was delivered. William then endorsed the check to the order of Robert, "without recourse," and it was accepted by Robert in payment of a debt owed him by William. Robert endorsed the check in blank and delivered it to his son, Charles, as a birthday

* See Introductory Note, p. 19.

gift. Arthur has discovered that the securities sold him by William are worthless and has directed Produce Bank to stop payment.

(1) Identify the status of all parties to the check described above at each step in its negotiation, explaining such identifications.

(2) When Produce Bank refuses to pay Charles on the check and Charles sues Arthur, may Arthur assert the defense of failure of consideration against Charles? Explain.

(3) Assuming Charles knew Gregory signed the check as an accommodation to William and received no value for his accommodation, may Charles nevertheless recover from Gregory on the Bank's failure to honor the check? Explain.

(4) Assume Arthur has no defense on the check and is insolvent, that Charles took the check from Robert for value and that the Bank refused to pay the check for lack of funds in Arthur's account. Discuss the rights and liabilities of Charles, Robert, William and Gregory.

5/70; pp. 98, 105

REQUISITES OF NEGOTIABILITY

Q. Baker offered to lend Able $20,000 at 5% interest per annum if Able agreed to pledge 100 shares of his stock in XYZ Corporation to secure the loan. At the closing of the loan, Able found that he only owned 75 shares of XYZ Corporation stock and could not pledge the agreed number of shares until the next day, when he would be able to purchase an additional 25 shares of stock. As a courtesy to Able, and in order to allow the closing to proceed, Charlie, who was present at the closing, suggested that he (Charlie) sign the note for the amount to be loaned as a co-maker with Able. An "understanding" was reached that as soon as Able purchased additional shares of stock and pledged them the note which Charlie signed would be destroyed and a new note, executed solely by Able, would replace it. Upon reaching agreement on the above arrangement, Able delivered 75 shares of XYZ Corporation to Baker, and Able and Charlie executed as co-makers and delivered to Baker a negotiable promissory demand note for $20,000, with interest at 5%, payable to Baker's order. The note contained no mention of the parties' "understanding." Able, Baker, and Charlie also signed a separate agreement referring to the note and outlining the "understanding" the parties had come to with regard to the substitution of a new note, executed solely by Able, upon delivery of an additional 25 shares of XYZ stock to Baker as security. The agreement stated that Baker was not to transfer the first note. Baker then delivered to Charlie his check in the amount of $20,000. Immediately after the closing, Baker went to the local bank and discounted the note. At the bank's request, Baker endorsed the note by signing his name on the back. The next day Able purchased 25 shares of XYZ stock, heard of the transfer of the note to the bank, and tendered the shares to the bank. Able showed the separate agreement and asked to be allowed to substitute his note, executed solely by himself, in place of the note the bank held. The bank refused to allow the substitution. Shortly thereafter, Baker disappeared. His check has proved to be worthless.

(1) List the requisites needed for an instrument to be negotiable.

(2) (a) What is Charlie's relationship to Able? Explain.
  (b) What is Baker's relationship to the bank? Explain.

(3) Is the bank a holder in due course of the note? Explain.

(4) Did the bank have a right to refuse to allow Able to substitute a new note? Explain.

(5) (a) What right, if any, does the bank have against Charlie? Explain.
  (b) If Charlie has to pay, what right does he have against Able? Explain.

5/66; pp. 90-93

NEGOTIATION

Q. Y holds a negotiable instrument made out to his order which he transfers to X for value. Y forgot to indorse his name on the back and X did not notice the omission.

(1) What is the effect of the transfer? Explain.

(2) When, if ever, will X become a holder in due course?

5/61; p. 94

HOLDER IN DUE COURSE

Q. Able obtained a check, drawn on City Bank, for $1,500 from Baker by a fraudulent scheme involving the sale of bogus oil stock. He immediately negotiated it to Carl by a blank indorsement. Carl met the requirements for holding in due course. Carl then deposited it in the National Bank after indorsing it as follows: "Without recourse to me, Carl." The balance in his account after depositing this and other checks was $6,000. The next day he deposited some additional checks totaling $7,000 and he drew one check for $10,000 which he gave to his broker in payment of some bonds he had purchased. This check for $10,000 was paid by the National Bank. Upon discovering the fraud, Baker notified the City Bank to stop payment on the check. City Bank stopped payment as requested and returned the check to National Bank. National Bank then demanded payment from Baker. Baker refused. He claimed that the National Bank was not a holder in due course because it took the check with a "without recourse" indorsement and, therefore, should have been on notice of some defect; i.e., he claims that the check was not taken in good faith. He also claimed that National had not given value since the bank had $3,000 of Carl's money on deposit, an amount which was sufficient to cover the check.

(1) Can the National Bank qualify as a holder in due course despite the "without recourse" indorsement? Explain.

(2) Had the National Bank given value? Explain.

(3) If it be assumed that the National Bank itself cannot qualify as a holder in due course, what alternative course of action is available to it against Baker on the check?

11/62; p. 97

Q. Albert executed a contract with Blake for the construction by Blake for Albert of a factory building. At the closing of the contract, in accordance with the terms of the agreement, Albert presented Blake his signed promissory non-interest-bearing demand note in the amount of $14,000, payable to bearer, as a down payment required by the contract. On the lower left corner of the note, Albert wrote, "This payment arises out of a construction contract." Two weeks later Blake took the note to Charlie, a long-time creditor, and asked him to accept the note in partial payment of a past due debt owed by Blake. Charlie read the legend on the lower left corner of the note and asked Blake if he had breached his contract with Albert. Blake said he had not and Charlie accepted this answer and took the note, although he mistrusted Blake and he knew Albert well and could have easily checked with him as to the truthfulness of Blake's statement. Shortly after receiving the note, Charlie presented it for payment to Albert, who refused to pay since, in breach of their contract, Blake had failed to begin work on Albert's job.

(1) Was the instrument negotiable? Explain.
(2) Was Charlie a "holder" of the instrument? Explain.
(3) Was Charlie a "holder in due course" of the instrument? Explain.
(4) If Charlie brings suit against Albert on the instrument, what decision would be rendered? Explain.

11/66; pp. 97-98

Q. Jarrett Corporation is a manufacturer of folding boxes which it sells to bakeries. Cooks Bakery was indebted to Jarrett in the amount of $500 and Cooks' manager suggested to Jarrett's bookkeeper that Cooks be allowed to satisfy the obligation by negotiating to Jarrett a certified check in the amount of $500 which Cooks had received from a customer.

The bookkeeper examined the check and found that it was drawn four days before on The National Bank by Richard Smith and was payable to the order of Donald Jones. Cooks' manager explained that J & H Caterers received the check from Jones in payment for a catered party and that J & H Caterers had refused to take the check from Jones unless it was first certified. Jones obtained the certification from The National Bank, which stamped the words "certified payable as originally drawn" on the face of the check. The check was then indorsed by Jones to J & H Caterers, who in turn properly indorsed the check to Cooks. With knowledge of the facts Jarrett's bookkeeper agreed to accept the check. The check was properly indorsed by Cooks and delivered to Jarrett's bookkeeper.

Jarrett's bookkeeper then cashed the check at The National Bank. Later the bank called and demanded the return of $400, explaining that the check had been originally issued for $100, that the check had been stamped "certified as originally drawn," and that it had been raised by Jones to $500 prior to certification. The bank agreed with Jarrett's bookkeeper that no one but an expert would have realized that the check had been raised.

(1) Is Jarrett Corporation a holder in due course? Explain, including a description of the requirements for a holder in due course in your answer.

(2) What was the amount and the nature of Smith's liability, if any, on the check after it was certified by The National Bank at the request of Jones? Explain.

(3) For the purpose of examining the financial statements of Jarrett Corporation, should a CPA consider that the check is worth $500 or worth only $100? (Is it necessary that Jarrett record a liability of $400 to The National Bank?) Explain.

11/68; pp. 99, 106

DEFENSES

Q. David, who bore a remarkable physical resemblance to Frank, one of the town's most prominent citizens, presented himself one day at the Friendly Finance Company, represented himself as Frank, and requested a loan of $500. The manager mistakenly, but honestly, believed that David was Frank and accordingly, being anxious to please so prominent a citizen, required no collateral and promptly delivered to David a $500 check payable to the order of Frank. David took the check and signed Frank's name to it on the back and negotiated it to Harold who took in the ordinary course of business (in good faith and for value). Upon learning the real facts, Friendly Finance Company stopped payment of the check. Harold now seeks recovery against the Friendly Finance Company.

(1) Can Harold collect on the negotiable instrument against the Friendly Finance Company? Explain.

(2) What right of action does Friendly Finance Company have against David? Explain.

5/61; pp. 98-99

Q. Charles owed the XYZ brokerage firm several thousand dollars on some recent investments he had made. He decided to make a trip to the financial district to see some of his clients and to pay the amount he owed to the brokers. Before leaving his office, he drew a check payable to cash and signed it. However, he left the amount blank because he was not sure of the exact figure. He placed the check in his attaché case. Charles, while riding downtown to the broker's office in a bus, placed the attaché case under his seat in order to read the morning paper. When he got off the bus, he absentmindedly forgot the attaché case. Another passenger found the check, filled it in for fifteen hundred dollars ($1,500), and negotiated it to Ernest. Ernest took the instrument in good faith and without notice of any defect therein in payment of the finder's prior indebtedness to him. Charles immediately notified his bank in writing to stop payment on the check. When Ernest's bank presented the instrument for payment through the normal banking channels, payment was refused. Ernest now sues Charles for the face value of the check.

(1) Will Ernest prevail? Explain.

(2) If Charles' bank, after receiving notice to stop payment, inadvertently paid the check in the above situation, could Charles recover the amount so paid? Explain.

11/64; p. 106

Q. Franklin, a depositor of the Milltown Bank, orally ordered the cashier of the bank to stop payment on a check which he had issued. The check was issued in payment for goods which were not received. Franklin learned that the seller was a notorious confidence man. The cashier in turn notified the tellers that an oral stop order had been given. Ten days later one of the tellers, who was not paying much attention to his business, paid the seller's wife, who had been sent to the bank to cash the check for the seller. Franklin, while examining his cancelled checks at the end of the month, discovered the error and promptly notified the cashier. The cashier apologized but pointed out that the original application, which Franklin signed at the time that the checking account was opened, contained a clause disclaiming any and all liability on the bank's part for erroneously paying an item in disregard of a customer's outstanding stop order. The cashier further indicated that the stop order was not in writing and, therefore, was invalid in any event.

(1) Was the oral stop order valid? Discuss.

(2) Can the bank rely upon the disclaimer clause to avoid liability? Discuss.

(3) Suppose the bank limited its liability on improper payment of checks to $10 per item despite the presence of an outstanding stop order. Would the bank be liable for any amount in excess of $10? Discuss.

11/67; p. 108

Q. Newton, a holder in due course, presented a check to the Marshall Bank, the drawee bank named on the face of the instrument. The bank examined the signature of the drawer very carefully, but the signature was such an exact forgery of the drawer's signature that only a handwriting expert could have detected a difference. The bank therefore paid the check.

(1) Assume that the check was promptly returned to the drawer-depositor but that he did not discover the forgery until thirteen months after the check was returned to him. Can he compel the bank to credit his account for the loss?

(2) Assume that the bank discovered the forgery before returning the check to the drawer-depositor and credited his account. Can the bank in turn collect the amount paid to Newton? Discuss.

(3) How would your answers to (1) and (2) above be modified if the forged signature was that of the payee or an indorser rather than the signature of the drawer? Discuss.

11/67; p. 109

Q. On January 29 Edwards, a wholesale grocer, made a large deposit in cash to his account at Cattlemen's Bank. In error, Edwards' deposit was posted to the account of Edmunds, another depositor. On the following day, Nevins, a local produce jobber, deposited a check to his account at Watermill Bank drawn on Cattlemen's Bank to Nevins' order by Edwards. When the check was presented for payment, Cattlemen's Bank refused to honor it and stamped it "Insufficient Funds." The check was promptly returned to Nevins by Watermill Bank. If Edwards' deposit on January 29 had been properly posted, his bank account balance would have been substantially greater than the amount of his check to Nevins.

(1) Have the above described events exposed the Cattlemen's Bank to any liability to Edwards? Explain.

(2) Assume that Edwards' check had been given to Nevins in payment for a carload of produce which Edwards had arranged to resell at a large profit, that the Bank was aware of this, that on dishonor of the check Nevins stopped the goods in transit, and that Edwards as a result lost his profit on the resale of the goods. May Edwards recover such lost profits from the Bank? Explain.

(3) Does the Cattlemen's Bank have any liability to Nevins? Explain.

11/69; p. 107

Q. On Thursday, May 15, Fox, the payee on a check drawn by Owens on Riverside Bank, endorsed the check to the order of Granger who, on the same date, endorsed the check to the order of Hines, a mutual friend of Granger and Owens. On Friday, May 16, Hines presented the check for payment at the Bank and payment was refused because of insufficient funds in Owens' account. Not wishing to embarrass Owens, Hines telephoned and advised Owens of the Bank's refusal to pay and the reason therefor. Owens promised to make a deposit to his bank account on the following Monday and told Hines to again present the check at the Bank on that day and it would be paid. Hines agreed but unexpectedly had to go out of town on business and could not again present the check for payment until the following Thursday, May 22. When Hines again presented the check at the Bank, payment was again refused for the same reason. Hines thereupon promptly and properly notified Granger, Fox and Owens of the dishonor of the check. It was later determined that Owens was insolvent, Granger and Hines were holders in due course, all endorsements were unqualified, and there were no defenses on the check.

(1) Does Hines have a cause of action against Granger and Fox? Explain.

(2) Assuming Hines may recover from Granger and Fox and recovers from Fox only, may Fox recover from Granger? Explain.

(3) Assume Hines promptly notified Granger and Fox of dishonor of the check the first time (Friday, May 16) Hines presented the check to the Bank and that Fox's endorsement to Granger was "without recourse." What rights, if any, would Hines have against Granger and Fox? Explain.

(4) Assume Fox had forged Owens' signature to the check, that the check was paid when Hines presented it at the Bank, that Owens promptly notified the Bank of the forgery when his cancelled checks were returned to him by the Bank, and that the Bank thereupon recredited Owens' account with the amount of the check. Could the Bank recover the amount from Hines or Granger? Explain.

11/69; pp. 105-106

COMMERCIAL PAPER: OBJECTIVE QUESTIONS

Each of the following numbered phrases or clauses states a legal conclusion as it completes the related lettered material. You are to determine whether each of the legal conclusions is true or false according to the provisions of Article 3 (Commercial Paper) and Article 4 (Bank Deposits and Collections) of the Uniform Commercial Code. Your grade will be determined from your total net score obtained by deducting your total of incorrect answers from your total of correct answers; an omitted answer will not be considered an incorrect answer.

(1) James Clemens purchased an automobile from Charles Dunlop. As consideration Clemens executed and delivered the following instrument to Dunlop:

New York, N.Y., May 2, 1969

For value received, I promise to pay to the order of Charles Dunlop, ONE THOUSAND DOLLARS ($1,000) payable at my principal place of business on May 1, 1970. If at any time the holder of this instrument shall deem himself insecure, he may declare the instrument due and payable immediately.

James Clemens

(a) The instrument is a trade draft.
(b) The instrument is a bearer instrument.
(c) The language "For value received" is unnecessary to satisfy the requirements of negotiability.
(d) The acceleration clause destroys negotiability.
(e) Clemens has negotiated the instrument to Dunlop.

(2) Henry Fenimore had a negotiable draft in his possession. The draft was originally payable to the order of Walter Barnes. The back of the instrument contained the following indorsements:

(1) *Arthur Thomas*
(2) *Walter Barnes*
(3) Pay to the order of Frank Small, *Donald Keith*
(4) Pay to Henry Fenimore, without recourse, *Frank Small*
(5) For deposit, *Henry Fenimore*

(a) If Thomas signed as an accommodation indorser, he did not make any warranties to Fenimore.
(b) The instrument was bearer paper when it contained only the signatures of Thomas and Barnes.
(c) Small has no warranty liability on the instrument since he signed "without recourse."
(d) The last indorsement is a restrictive indorsement.
(e) The last indorsement prohibits any further negotiation.

(3) Harper fraudulently misrepresented the value of oil stock he knew to be worthless and received a negotiable check for $9,000 from Goodwin in exchange for the worthless stock. Harper promptly cashed the check at the Acme Finance Company, paying off a loan of $1,000 and receiving the balance in cash. Harper's indorsement was "without recourse."

(a) The fraudulent misrepresentation constitutes a real defense.
(b) Acme Finance only gave value to the extent that it paid Harper cash.
(c) Acme Finance cannot qualify as a holder in due course because of Harper's indorsement "without recourse."
(d) Even if Acme Finance is a holder in due course a timely stop order will eliminate Goodwin's liability on the check.
(e) If the drawee bank arbitrarily refused to cash the check Acme

Finance could sue the bank and recover any loss resulting from the bank's arbitrary action.

(4) The following handwritten instrument was negotiated by Elmer Dodd for value to Jane Maples:

Toronto, Canada, May 5, 1969

Sixty days after date pay to the order of Elmer Dodd, one hundred and fifty dollars ($150), payable at New National Bank, U.N. Plaza, New York, N.Y. Value received and charge the trade account of Olympia Sales Corporation, New York, New York.

W. Stark

(a) The instrument is a negotiable foreign time draft.
(b) In the event of dishonor a formal protest is required to hold secondarily liable parties.
(c) A timely presentment for payment can be made at any time within a week following the expiration of 60 days from the date of issue (May 5, 1969).
(d) Olympia Sales has primary liability on the instrument.
(e) In the event Olympia Sales is insolvent and cannot pay, W. Stark will be liable to Jane Maples if she has complied with the proper procedural steps and sues him.

(5) Hills issued a check to the order of Lewis on April 3, 1969. It was postdated May 6, 1969. Lewis negotiated the check to Gordon. On May 6 Gordon had the check certified by the drawee, Wilson National Bank.

(a) At the time of issue the instrument was not negotiable because it was postdated.
(b) At the time of issue Hills was primarily liable on the instrument.
(c) A refusal to certify the check at Gordon's request would have constituted a dishonor by the bank.
(d) Upon certification the bank became primarily liable on the instrument.
(e) Upon certification Hills and all indorsers were discharged from liability.

(6) Barnaby's Department Store drew a refund check to the order of Flynn for $100 on Merchant Bank. The check was stolen from Flynn's mail box. The thief forged Flynn's signature and raised the amount to $400. James, a subsequent holder in due course, presented the check for payment and the bank paid him $400, charging Barnaby's account. Barnaby's promptly discovered the alteration and forgery and immediately notified the bank.

(a) Barnaby's has a right to have Merchant Bank credit its account for $400.
(b) Flynn will not be able to collect the $100 from anyone except the thief.
(c) James is entitled to keep the $400 if the bank seeks to collect it from him.

(d) If the bank had dishonored the check James could recover from any prior endorser.
(e) The forged indorsement and the raised amount constitute real defenses.

5/69

(7) An instrument reads as follows:

	No. 452
Pay	April 1, 1968
to the	
Order of Richard Smith	$100.00
One Hundred and no/100	Dollars
Fireman's Bank	
Chicago, Illinois	Roberta Jones

(a) This instrument is a bill of exchange.
(b) Roberta Jones is the drawee.
(c) Fireman's Bank is the drawer.
(d) Richard Smith is the payee.
(e) This instrument is a draft.

(8) An instrument reads as follows:

$250.00	Chicago, Illinois	April 1, 1968
Thirty days	after date I promise to pay to the	
order of Cash		
Two hundred and fifty		Dollars
at New York City		
Value received with interest at the rate of six per cent per annum. This instrument arises out of a separate agreement.		
No. 20	Due May 1, 1968	Robert Smith

(a) This instrument is a draft.
(b) This instrument is order paper.
(c) This is not a negotiable instrument.
(d) Robert Smith is the maker.
(e) This instrument may be negotiated without an indorsement.

(9) Andrews owed Martin, his accountant, a fee for services rendered. Andrews drew a check on his bank payable to "Cash" and signed it. He left the amount blank because he was not sure of the exact amount owed. On his way to Martin's office Andrews lost the check. Oliver found the check, filled it in for $500 and handed it to Ernest to satisfy a $500 debt which Oliver owed to Ernest. Ernest accepted the check in good faith as payment for the debt. Meanwhile, Andrews stopped payment on the check.

(a) If Andrews' bank is told the circumstances under which Ernest accepted the check when he presents it for payment, the bank would be acting improperly if it obeyed the stop payment order.

(b) Martin must now look to Oliver rather than Andrews for payment of the fee due from Andrews.

(c) If Ernest sues Andrews on the instrument, Andrews will have a real defense.

(d) If Ernest sues Andrews on the instrument, Ernest may be able to prove he is a holder in due course.

(e) If Andrews orally requested his bank to stop payment on the check the request would not be binding on the bank.

(10) Roberts was a holder in due course of a properly drawn check payable to "Bearer." He indorsed the check as follows:

"Pay to the order of Wilson Hall without recourse.
Peter Roberts"

Roberts then transferred the instrument to Hall who in turn negotiated it to Miles, who is now a holder in due course.

(a) Roberts' indorsement is both a qualified indorsement and a special indorsement.

(b) Hall must have been a holder in due course.

(c) By his indorsement Roberts made warranties to Miles.

(d) By his indorsement Roberts made warranties to Hall but these warranties are not the same as the warranties which would be made by an indorser who indorses an instrument in blank.

(e) Roberts' indorsement of the instrument and his transfer of it to Hall represents a negotiation.

(11) Justin was a holder in due course of a properly drawn check payable to "Bearer." He indorsed the check as follows:

"Pay to Edward Evans or order.
John Justin"

Justin then transferred the check to Evans. Evans in turn negotiated the check to Diamond who proceeded to have the bank on which the check was drawn certify the check.

(a) Until the bank certified the check the drawer of the check was primarily liable for its payment.

(b) Diamond is a holder of the check.

(c) Evans did not have to indorse the check in order to negotiate it to Diamond.

(d) The bank on which the check was drawn was not obligated to certify the check unless it had specifically agreed to do so.

(e) When the bank on which the check was drawn certified the check at Diamond's request both the drawer and all the indorsers were discharged.

(12) Casey held a negotiable instrument payable to his order. He transferred the instrument to Dale for value. At the time of transfer Casey failed to indorse his name on the back of the instrument and Dale accepted the instrument as given to him.

(a) If Dale realized that Casey did not indorse the instrument when he accepted it, Dale waived his right to receive Casey's indorsement.
(b) Casey may not deny Dale the right to his indorsement but Casey has the right to qualify the indorsement.
(c) If Casey is a holder in due course of the instrument Dale will be entitled to assert Casey's rights from the time the instrument was transferred to him if Dale has acted in good faith and without notice of any defects.
(d) The instrument cannot be negotiated to Dale without Casey's indorsement.
(e) Even if Dale receives Casey's indorsement Dale cannot be a holder in due course of the instrument.

5/68

(13) In respect to drafts
(a) The drawer and payee may be the same person.
(b) The drawee is primarily liable at the time of issue.
(c) The drawer is secondarily liable at the time of issue.
(d) A draft must be payable on demand in order to be negotiable.
(e) The check is the most common type of draft.

(14) The trade acceptance
(a) Must be signed by the drawer and drawee in order to be negotiable.
(b) Is normally used in conjunction with a title document, and the trade acceptance is forwarded through banking channels for acceptance or payment by the buyer.
(c) Imposes no liability upon the buyer prior to acceptance.
(d) May be either a sight or time draft.
(e) Must be accepted by the acceptor's signing before a notary, and the acceptor's acknowledgment must be taken.

(15) The certificate of deposit
(a) Is an acknowledgment by a bank of receipt of money with a promise to repay.
(b) Is typically payable on demand.
(c) Is payable to order by use of the words "payable upon return of this instrument properly indorsed."
(d) Is the same as a cashier's check.
(e) May contain the printed signature of the appropriate bank official in lieu of his actual signature.

(16) An instrument is a bearer instrument if it is payable
(a) To the order of an imposter.
(b) To the order of bearer.
(c) To cash.
(d) To the order of a named person and indorsed in blank.
(e) To bearer initially and the last indorsement is a special indorsement.

(17) A promise or order, otherwise unconditional, is not made conditional by the fact that the instrument
- (a) Contains a provision indicating the instrument is subject to a certain contractual agreement.
- (b) Is limited to payment out of a particular fund and is issued by a governmental agency.
- (c) Is limited to payment out of the entire assets of a partnership.
- (d) States that it is secured by a mortgage.
- (e) States that the instrument matures "as per" the transaction out of which it arose.

(18) The sum payable is certain even though it is to be paid
- (a) With the cost of collection upon default.
- (b) With attorney's fees upon default.
- (c) With a stated addition to the face amount if paid after maturity.
- (d) By stated installments with interest.
- (e) With the current rate of exchange added to the face amount.

(19) An instrument is payable at a definite time if by its terms it is payable
- (a) At the end of a period of time after a stated date.
- (b) Upon the happening of an event which is uncertain as to the time of occurrence.
- (c) At a definite time subject to an option in the hands of the holder to extend the time.
- (d) One year after the date of death of the maker.
- (e) At a definite time but subject to acceleration.

(20) A person (other than the payee) in possession of an instrument is a *holder* (as distinguished from a mere possessor, transferee, or assignee) if he acquired ownership by
- (a) An indorsement which purports to transfer less than the full face amount of the instrument.
- (b) Mere delivery of a bearer instrument.
- (c) Delivery for value of an order instrument which is not indorsed.
- (d) Finding a bearer instrument in the street.
- (e) Delivery of an order instrument along with a separate detached indorsement in blank by the transferee.

(21) An indorsement is restrictive if it
- (a) Is conditional.
- (b) States that it prohibits further negotiation.
- (c) Indicates it is "without recourse" to the indorser.
- (d) Includes the words "pay any bank or banker."
- (e) Includes the words "for deposit to my account."

(22) A restrictive indorsement
- (a) Limits the indorser's liability in respect to warranties given to the transferee.
- (b) Prevents further negotiation of the instrument.

(c) Prevents all subsequent parties from becoming holders in due course of the instrument.
(d) Does not put intermediary banks on notice or otherwise affect their rights as a result of the restrictive indorsement.
(e) Imposes upon the indorser's depository bank the obligation to pay or apply any value given it consistent with the indorsement.

(23) An unindorsed order instrument was duly delivered to Milton. He will be considered
(a) A holder of the instrument if at the time he received it he took it in good faith.
(b) A mere transferee.
(c) To have obtained all the rights of his prior transferor if he took it in good faith.
(d) A holder in due course, irrespective of good faith, upon obtaining the prior party's signature.
(e) A holder, if he subsequently obtains the proper indorsement of his transferor.

(24) A holder in due course takes the instrument free from
(a) All claims of ownership to it by any person.
(b) The defense of infancy even if local law makes it a defense to a simple contract.
(c) Discharge in bankruptcy.
(d) Fraud in the execution.
(e) The illegality of the underlying transaction such as would render the obligation a nullity.

5/67

TOPIC FOUR | AGENCY

CONTENTS PAGE

FORMS OF BUSINESS ORGANIZATIONS. Three major areas of business law are covered by this topic. One is the area of agency with the main focus upon the subject of imposition of liability in contract and tort by the agent upon his principal. This area of law may be tested in situations relating to proprietorships, partnerships, *or corporations. Another major area is partnership law which encompasses the characteristics of the partnership and limited partnership; the rights, duties, and liabilities of the partnership and the partners among themselves and to third parties; and the rights of the various parties upon dissolution. The third major area is corporate law with emphasis on traditional state law regulation of the corporation as contrasted with federal regulation of the corporation. Included in the subject matter are corporate characteristics; incorporation; corporate rights, powers, and liabilities; corporate financing; directors' and officers' duties and liabilities; and stockholder rights.*[*]

I. CHARACTERISTICS

A. Definition: the relationship which results from the manifestation of consent by one person, called principal, to another, called agent, that the other (agent) shall act on the principal's behalf and subject to his control, and the consent of the agent so to act.

1. It is a fiduciary relationship.
2. It is *always* consensual.

B. Capacity of the parties:

1. To be a principal, i.e., to appoint an agent:
   a. Infant: In a majority of states an infant may appoint an agent. Appointment of agent, where not for purposes of obtaining necessaries, is voidable at infant's option, without his being subject to a suit for breach of contract.
   b. Married women: by statute under no disability because of marital status.
   c. Insane persons: contract of agency voidable if made before adjudication of insanity, void if made after such adjudication.
   d. Corporations: act exclusively through their agents.
   e. Partnerships: act through the partners who are its agents; can appoint agents in addition to the partners.
   f. Unincorporated associations: not competent to appoint agents since they are not recognized as legal units, i.e., have no power to do business under a firm name. Individual members, acting jointly, may be held as principals, if they appoint agents.
   g. Joint principals: Two or more parties may act through one agent if they so agree.

[*] Source: AICPA, *Information for CPA Candidates* (July 1970).

2. To act as an agent:
   a. General capacity needed. Any person, including an infant, who possesses sufficient physical and mental capacity to exercise authority delegated to him may be an agent.

      (1) For infants the test is one of mental capacity, not that of age. Imbeciles and lunatics are ineligible.

      (2) One incompetent to make a specific type of contract may nevertheless make it as an agent, because agent's contracts are those of his principal and not his own.

      (3) Power conferred on joint agents is presumed to be joint; thus, unless otherwise authorized, they can act for principal only by acting together.

C. Classification of agents.

1. Scope of authority:
   a. General agent has broad authority to represent his principal.
   b. Special agent has authority limited to a specific task or series of routine tasks.
2. Manner of appointment:
   a. Express agency: created by written contract or oral appointment.

      (1) One common type of appointment is made by a power of attorney, an instrument authorizing another to act as one's agent.

         (A) Whatever a principal cannot do, he may not delegate to be done by an agent through a power of attorney. (E.g., a minor cannot delegate conveyance of real estate or confession of judgment against himself, since he may repudiate a conveyance of real estate and he has no capacity to confess judgment against himself.)

         (B) Attorney in fact: an agent whose authority to do a type of transaction is conferred by a written instrument, such as a power of attorney.

      (2) Statute of frauds (see Contracts, p. 44, III.E.): If agent's duties involve the making of a contract governed by this statute, some states require agency to be in writing (e.g., agency for the sale of real property).
   b. Implied agency: one created by acts or deduced from circumstances evidencing an intention to create the relationship. (E.g., an agent with possession of an authority to sell personal property would have implied authority to do whatever is reasonably necessary to carry out agency, including power to

make usual representations and warranties and receive payment, but not including unusual powers such as the power to mortgage, exchange, or pledge goods or give credit or sell at an auction.)

3. Special types of agents.
   a. Attorneys at law: qualified by admission to the bar to represent other persons in matters of a legal nature.
   b. Auctioneer: authorized and licensed by the state to conduct a public sale of property; agent for the seller until fall of the gavel, and then agent for both parties.
   c. Factor or commission merchant: a commercial agent employed by principal to sell or dispose of goods.

      (1) Factor is entrusted with possession of goods; however, title remains in principal, the factor being merely a bailee for the purpose of the agency.

      (2) Compensation is called factorage or commission.

      (3) Having possession of principal's goods, he is the ostensible owner of them; thus, he can sell them in his own name, and collect the proceeds subject to his duty to account to his principal.

      (4) Factor can convey better title than he has to the goods. (I.e., a third party who buys goods in good faith and for value, from factor who has exceeded his authority, gets title as against principal.)

      (5) Factor has duty to give principal full accounting.

      (6) Factor has a general lien on goods for expenses incurred in his capacity of factor for the principal and for any unpaid amounts due him from the principal (e.g., advances made by factor to principal).

   d. Exclusive agency: agreement by owner that during the life of the contract he will not sell the property to a purchaser procured by another agent. Agreement does not preclude owner himself from selling to a purchaser he procures.
   e. Exclusive sale: agent given exclusive rights to act for principal in sale of his property during the duration of the agency, with no right of sale remaining with owner.
   f. *Del credere* agent: a sales agent who has assumed, generally for a higher commission, an obligation to pay his principal what the purchaser fails to pay (i.e., he guarantees the accounts of his customers).

      (1) If debt is not paid when due, action will at once lie against *del credere* agent.

(2) Although his guaranty is a promise to answer for the debt of another (see Contracts, p. 45, III.E.2.c.), it is considered as having been given primarily for his own benefit and, therefore, not within the statute of frauds.

g. Real estate broker: authorized to negotiate for purchase or sale of real property.

(1) Must usually be licensed to qualify as agent and earn commissions.

(2) Entitled to commissions only when there is an express or implied contract with principal.

(3) Hiring usually subject to automatic termination in case of a prior sale.

(4) Broker not entitled to commission unless buyer he produces is ready, willing, and able to meet seller's terms.

h. Agency coupled with an interest or obligation: the only agency relationship that courts generally enforce specifically in that the agent has a property interest in the thing to be disposed of or managed under the power created by the agency. It is referred to as an "irrevocable agency" relationship. (E.g., X owes Y $100 and Z owes X $500; X makes Y his agent for collection from Z with instructions to pay himself out of the proceeds and remit the surplus to X.)

i. Gratuitous agent: one who assumes the role of an agent without expectation of compensation. He is not bound to perform even though he promises to do so; but once he does begin performance he must perform in a nonnegligent manner.

4. Agent distinguished from:

a. Independent contractor: work not subject to control and supervision of one who employs him.

b. Trustee: acts in his own name; has legal, but not equitable title to property, and retains authority until purpose of trust is fulfilled; he can be removed only for cause.

c. Servant: a low-level type of agent, used to distinguish supervised employees (e.g., manual workers, factory hands, chauffeurs, drivers) from those whose task involves primarily the creation of new legal relationships between the principal and third parties (e.g., salesmen, executives of corporations). *Respondeat Superior* applied to and arose out of this type of agency.

(1) An agent has broader authority and responsibility than a servant or employee, and is usually empowered to bind his principal by contract, whereas a servant or employee is not.

d. Subagent: derives authority not from the principal, but from an agent, who is expressly or impliedly authorized to appoint subagents.

(1) Intent to allow agent the power to delegate may be gathered from:

(A) Expressions of the principal.

(B) Character of the business.

(C) Usages or prior conduct of the parties.

(D) Necessity of meeting an emergency.

(E) Character of acts committed to subagent, being ministerial only.

5. Agency distinguished from:

a. Sale: the buyer is not usually the seller's agent.

b. Assignment: is irrevocable; agent's authority can be withdrawn at will if not coupled with an interest.

c. Lease: is an interest in land; tenant is not the agent of the landlord.

II. CREATION OF AGENCY RELATIONSHIP

A. Agency by appointment: See p. 126, I.C.2.

B. Agency by ratification: approval of an unauthorized act done by an agent, or acts done by one who was not an agent.

1. Principal may ratify an act which is not unlawful. Hence a tort may be ratified and subject the person so ratifying to liability; a crime, however, may not be ratified.
2. Principal must be competent to have appointed agent in order to be able to ratify act done by agent (see p. 125, I.B.1.).
3. Act must be purported to have been done in name and on behalf of the person ratifying.
4. Principal must have full knowledge of the facts.
5. Ratification must cover the entire act; principal cannot ratify in part and reject in part; it is retroactive, but not retractable.
6. Ratification may be express (written or oral) or by implication, as by accepting the benefits of an act with full knowledge of facts. Even silence may amount to ratification.
7. A person seeking to ratify an act must have been in existence at the time when the act was done. (E.g., a corporation cannot ratify acts of promoters done on its behalf prior to incorporation. However, it can adopt them and become liable—see Corporations, p. 182, II.A.3.).

8. Ratification requires the same formalities as authorization.

C. Agency by estoppel: created by operation of law; prevents party from denying the existence of an agency where a third person relies on circumstances that would reasonably lead to the conclusion that one exists. (E.g., X permits Z to pose as his agent and Y acts on the belief that there was an agency and relies thereon to his detriment in dealing with Z.)

D. Apparent or ostensible agency: based upon principal's manifestations to third party; differs from estoppel in that reliance (change of position) is not necessary.

E. Agency by necessity: implied in law where a situation exists or an emergency arises which makes it necessary to presume an agency as a matter of public policy. (E.g., a wife is an agent of necessity of her husband when he fails to provide her with necessaries and she obtains them; or an agency is implied in emergencies to contract for medical, hospital, or first aid expenses.)

III. MUTUAL RIGHTS AND DUTIES

A. Duties of principal to agent.

1. To compensate agent:
   a. Amount ordinarily a matter of contract; or, if there is no agreement, the reasonable value of services will be inferred.
   b. Drawing account: deemed to be agent's salary unless specifically provided that it is a loan.
2. To reimburse agent: Agent is entitled to expenses expressly or implicitly authorized and incurred during course of agency.
3. To indemnify agent against loss and liability for acts performed at principal's direction when said acts are not manifestly illegal or known to be wrong.
4. Agent's lien: attaches to principal's money or property in agent's hands in connection with which agent made advances, incurred expenses, or sustained losses.

B. Duties of agent to principal:

1. Utmost loyalty and good faith: agency is a fiduciary relationship.
   a. Agent cannot represent two principals with conflicting interests unless they consent.
   b. Dealing for agent's own interest absolutely prohibited.
   c. Agent must not engage in business competing with principal's unless with principal's knowledge and consent.

d. Violation of the above duty deprives agent of his **right to** compensation, reimbursement, indemnification or to agent's lien, and subjects him to liability for resulting loss and dismissal.

2. Obedience.

   a. When duties are routine in nature, agent must adhere to instructions in all cases in which they can be obeyed by the exercise of reasonable and diligent care.

   b. When duties involve use of discretion, agent must act competently and carefully, and is liable for failure to use reasonable care.

3. To use necessary skill, care, and diligence to perform task properly; however, agent is not an insurer (i.e., will not be liable without fault) of services he renders unless he guarantees the result by express contract.

4. Not to make a delegation or substitution: Agency relationship normally involves trust and confidence and therefore cannot be delegated without consent—see p. 129, I.C.4.d. (1).

5. Duty to account: duty to render unto principal that which is, or in good faith should be, the principal's.

   a. All profits and advantages gained by the agent in the execution of the agency belong to the principal, regardless of whether the profit results from strict performance or from violation of the agent's duty.

6. Not to commingle funds. If agent commingles funds and they are somehow lost (e.g., a bank fails), agent will be liable.

7. Right of employee (agent) to use the fruits of his employment: employee is entitled to his own invention even though made on his employer's time and with use of his employer's equipment.

   a. Called the "shop rights doctrine."

   b. This license (i.e., right to use the invention) is irrevocable, non-assignable, and non-exclusive.

IV. AGENCY AND THIRD PARTIES

A. Principal's liability on contracts.

1. Disclosed principal is liable on contract made by his agent when contract was:

   a. Authorized (either expressly or implicitly).

      (1) Where agent has no authority, express or implied, third party deals with him at his peril. (E.g., a third party paying

an agent who has no authority to collect funds remains liable to principal for purchase price.)

b. Unauthorized initially but subsequently ratified.

c. Made under circumstances where principal is deemed to have clothed his agent with certain apparent authority. An act performed by an agent within the usual scope of authority is binding upon the principal, for his agent has apparent authority even though the particular act has been forbidden. An innocent third party will be protected if the act done by the agent is the usual practice, and the principal has not taken steps to make the third person aware of his agent's disability to contract in this area. (E.g., where an agent is properly appointed to sell personal property he has implied authority to make usual warranties of title and to collect the purchase price when he delivers the goods.)

2. Undisclosed principal: where third party has no notice that the agent is acting for a principal.

   a. Principal is liable on a contract which agent was authorized to make unless:

      (1) Contract is fully performed by agent.

      (2) Contract is a negotiable instrument.

      (3) Contract specifically excluded an undisclosed principal as a party thereto.

      (4) Contract is under seal, in some states.

      (5) Third party, later ascertaining the existence of the undisclosed principal, has elected to hold agent exclusively.

   b. Principal is liable on contract which general agent was not authorized to make, but which was usual or necessary to a transaction which agent was authorized to conduct.

   c. Principal has benefit of election theory. Third party, upon ascertaining the existence of an undisclosed principal, may elect to hold either the agent or the undisclosed principal.

      (1) This election is irrevocable in some jurisdictions:

         (A) If, after disclosure of agency, the third party proceeds to judgment against agent with knowledge of principal's identity, only agent is liable, but,

         (B) If he proceeds to judgment against principal, principal is liable and agent is not.

      (2) In a few jurisdictions a third party may proceed to judgment against both principal and agent, but may obtain only one satisfaction.

B. Principal's liability for servant-agent's torts.

1. Principal is liable for agent's torts if they are within the scope of his employment and committed during the course of his duties. This rule is known as *Respondeat Superior*. As to agents who are not servants, the principal is liable for such agents' torts if committed within the scope of the agent's authority.
   a. Rule applies even though servant-agent violated principal's instructions in committing the tort.
   b. Some states presume that the driver of an auto (other than the owner) is the agent for the owner and thus impose liability on the owner for torts of the driver.

C. Principal's liability for agent's crimes: Principal is not liable for agent's crimes unless he planned, directed, ordered, or acquiesced in their commission.

D. Notice to agent will constitute notice to principal unless:

1. Disclosure to the principal would be adverse to the agent's personal interest.
2. Notice was given prior to commencement of the agency relationship, except where agent remembers the notice while he is acting for principal and is under no duty to a prior principal to keep it secret.

E. Agent's liability to third parties: Although generally not liable, an agent becomes liable to third parties when he:

1. Acts for nonexistent or incompetent principal, i.e., one under contractual disability (e.g., an infant in connection with a luxury, or an insane person), and he:
   a. Knows of the principal's lack of capacity,
   b. Knows that third party is ignorant of principal's disability or nonexistence, or
   c. Represents to third parties that principal is competent or in existence.
2. Acts for undisclosed principal and third party elects to hold him liable.
3. Signs a negotiable instrument in his own name. (Only agent is liable, not principal; agent should always sign negotiable paper: "P, Principal, by A, Agent.")
4. Contracts in his own name.
5. Misrepresents his scope of authority to third party, who is thereby misled and who is unable to hold principal liable.

6. Wrongfully receives money on behalf of principal and has not delivered it to principal (agent is also responsible to principal).
7. Personally guarantees certain acts of his principal.
8. Commits a tort, even if it is in the course of discharging his duties. (If tort was committed within course of employment, principal will also be liable to third party.)

V. TERMINATION OF AGENCY

A. Termination by act of parties:

1. Agreement may provide for termination after the expiration of a definite period of time or upon the happening of a stipulated event.
2. Parties may terminate relationship despite the agreement calling for a greater duration.
   a. Principal may revoke agency.
      (1) If he does so wrongfully he is liable to agent for damages (e.g., if he revokes a valid contract for an irrevocable agency of fixed duration).
      (2) Principal may rightfully revoke when agent violates his duties to principal.
      (3) Where agency is coupled with an interest or obligation (see p. 128, I.C.3.h.), principal neither has right nor any power to revoke.
   b. Agent may renounce or abandon agency (same right as principal), but if he does so wrongfully, he is liable to principal for damages for breach of the agreement unless:
      (1) Principal violates agency agreement, or
      (2) Agency is gratuitous, or
      (3) Agency is terminable at the will of either party.

B. Termination by operation of law: results when there is:

1. Illegality of subject matter. Relationship is therefore void.
2. Impossibility (e.g., destruction or loss of subject matter).
3. Death or disability of parties.
4. Bankruptcy or insolvency of principal. But bankruptcy of agent will not terminate the agency unless it is a matter of consequence to the principal and affects the agency relationship.

C. Notice of termination.

1. Notice of revocation by principal or renunciation by agent must be such as is specified in contract, or if no specification, reasonable notice must be given.

a. Notice by letter takes effect when received and read.
b. Where authority has been given to perform several different acts, principal may terminate authority as to some without impairing agent's authority as to others. However, where performance of one act is dependent on performance of another, termination of authority to perform one will terminate authority to perform the other.

2. Third parties must receive personal notice, or they may act as though agency continued, and thus hold principal for acts of former agent, if they had prior dealings with the agent (see p. 130, II.C.).
3. As to third parties who have had no prior dealings with agent, constructive notice by publication in a local paper will be sufficient.

AGENCY: SUBJECTIVE QUESTIONS *

CHARACTERISTICS

Q. John Barry, a world famous golfer, represents Golf Cart Company, Inc., as a sales agent to promote sales of the Company's product, a golf cart. The Company sells a new type of golf cart, which it has named the "Barry Golf Cart," and it has commenced an extensive marketing campaign. As a part of this campaign the Company sends letters advertising the cart to presidents of golf clubs. In its letter the Company represents that the new cart "can be driven a full 18 holes of golf under any conditions" and that "the cart will not require any major repair for two years." Also in the letter, which is signed by John Barry as vice president in charge of sales promotion, there is a statement by John Barry that he "personally tested the cart and was delighted with its performance." Jones, a president of a golf club, bought a golf cart after reading the letter and corresponding with the Company to determine the model which best suited his needs. He now finds that the cart is totally unsatisfactory since it continually breaks down when it is driven on the golf course. He has informed Barry that he intends to bring a suit for damages against both the Company and Barry in his individual capacity. However, he further states that if he could be sure that Golf Cart Company, Inc. is solvent he would not sue Barry individually but would sue only the Company. To determine the Company's financial status, he asks Barry to secretly allow him access to the Company's financial records. Barry suspects that Jones may have other motives for wishing to secretly view the Company's records.

(1) Explain the legal relationship which exists between Barry and Golf Cart Company, Inc.

* See Introductory Note, p. 19.

(2) What should Barry do with regard to arranging for Jones to secretly examine the Company's financial records to avoid a suit against himself individually?
(3) What legal theory would support a suit brought by Jones against Golf Cart Company, Inc.? Describe the necessary elements to be proved to justify a recovery.
(4) In the event that Barry is sued individually by Jones, what defense(s) is (are) available to him? Explain.

11/67; pp.125, 130

CAPACITY OF PARTIES

Q. Peter, a minor, engaged his brother-in-law, Allen, as his agent for the purchase of a used sports car from Tom. Allen knew that Peter was a minor, and that Tom did not know this, but made the purchase to accommodate Peter. He acted without compensation and with a written authorization to make the purchase. At the time of the sale Allen exhibited the authorization to the seller and signed the contract in such a way as to clearly indicate he was acting in an agency capacity. Peter, after driving the car for several days, decided he could obtain a better deal elsewhere. He disaffirmed the contract, stopped all payments, and returned the car to Tom. Tom seeks to hold Peter or Allen to the contract. May he do so? Explain.

5/62; pp. 125, 133

CLASSIFICATION OF AGENTS

Q. On January 1, 1963, Baker loaned Able $1,000. Able owned a painting for which the X Museum had offered $2,000. On January 20, 1963, Able gave Baker a writing by which Baker is given the authority, in case of nonpayment of the loan by March 31, 1963, to sell the painting to the X Museum for $2,000 and to retain out of the proceeds the amount of the loan. He was to pay the surplus to Able. On April 1, 1963, Able informed Baker that at that time he could not repay the loan and that the authority to sell the painting was revoked. On the same day Able informed the curator of the X Museum that the painting was not for sale. An April 4, 1963, Baker showed the written authorization to the curator and they executed a sale of the painting for $2,000.

(1) Does Able have any remedy against Baker for selling the painting? Explain.

(2) Does Able have any remedy against the Museum for buying the painting? Explain.

5/63; p. 126

CREATION OF AGENCY RELATIONSHIP

Q. Brian purchased an electric typewriter from Robert under a written contract by which Robert reserved the title until the purchase price was fully paid and reserved the right to repossess the typewriter if Brian failed to make any of the required ten payments. Arthur, an employee of Robert, was instructed to repossess the machine on the ground that Brian had defaulted in making the third payment. Arthur took possession of the typewriter and delivered it to Robert. It was then discovered that Brian was not in default.

(1) May Brian recover damages from Arthur? Explain.

(2) May Brian recover damages from Robert? Explain.

(3) Assuming that Brian recovers damages from Arthur, does Arthur have the right of indemnification from Robert? Explain.

11/63; pp. 130, 134-135

Q. A CPA examining the financial statements of Excellent Storm Window Company seeks to determine the collectibility of a $300 past due account receivable from Evans. He is given the following information:

Martin, a general home contractor, was authorized by Excellent to solicit orders for storm windows. Evans told Martin that he wanted storm windows and Martin showed him Excellent's brochure and contract form for ordering storm windows. The contract form contained prices and specifications and indicated that Excellent was the seller. The contract order form contained several provisions and clearly specified that "storm windows are sold as is without any warranty, express or implied, unless a warranty is requested from Excellent's home office and received in writing from an authorized agent."

Evans reviewed the form and asked Martin to install windows costing $300 after Martin said, "As an experienced general contractor I personally warrant that these storm windows will do the job." Martin completed the form properly and Evans executed the form. Within a short time Martin personally delivered and installed the storm windows.

After the windows were installed, Evans, following Martin's instructions, gave Martin a check, payable to his order, for $300. Martin cashed the check and disappeared without fulfilling his obligation to remit payment to Excellent. Under Martin's contract with Excellent, he had no authority to collect payment and Excellent maintains therefore that Evans is still responsible for payment. Evans, on the other hand, has informed the Company that he is not responsible for payment and that he intends to hold Excellent liable because the windows are not adequate for his needs although the storm windows Martin installed do meet the specifications indicated on the contract form.

(1) Identify the legal relationship between Martin and Excellent Storm Window Company.

(2) May Evans validly disclaim liability to Excellent on the basis that he has already made payment to Martin? Explain.

(3) Assume that Evans has correctly determined that the storm windows he received are not adequate for his needs. Does Evans have a cause of action against Excellent which should be reflected in Excellent's financial statements?

(4) If Evans agrees to purchase a new set of storm windows from Excellent, can he demand that he be allowed to return the storm windows he received and obtain full credit toward the purchase of the new windows?

11/68; pp. 131-132

AGENCY AND THIRD PARTIES

Q. (1) What is the general rule concerning the rights and liabilities of an undisclosed principal and a third person who has entered into a transaction with the agent of the undisclosed principal?

(2) State four defenses that are exclusively available to an undisclosed principal in a suit against him by the third person.

11/65; p.132

Q. Acme Manufacturing Company wished to acquire a site for a warehouse. Knowing that if it negotiated directly for the purchase of the property the price would be substantially increased, it employed Anson, an agent, to secure lots without disclosing that he was acting for Acme. Anson's authority was evidenced by a writing signed by the proper officers of Acme Company. Anson entered into a contract in his own name to purchase Thomas' lot, giving Thomas a negotiable note for $1,000, signed by Anson, as first payment. Believing that Stuart would succeed better with Davis for the purchase of Davis' property, Anson employed Stuart for that purpose, giving him written authorization. Stuart signed a contract in his own name to buy a lot owned by Davis. Davis' lot was not within the area of the proposed site and therefore not within the actual authority given by Acme to Anson. Unaware that the lot was not a part of the site, Acme wrote both Anson and Stuart approving their individual purchases. Acme's identity as principal became known to Thomas and Davis.

(1) Is the Acme Company liable to Thomas on the note? Explain.

(2) Is the Acme Company liable to Davis on the contract to buy Davis' lot? Explain.

(3) Could Davis hold Stuart personally liable on their contract? Explain.

11/63; pp.129, 132

TERMINATION OF AGENCY

Q. Amos was a traveling salesman employed by the Paper Box Corporation. His express authority included the solicitation of orders and the collection of accounts. After Amos had worked for the Corporation for five years, he was discharged; the fact that he was discharged was published by the Corporation in a newspaper of general circulation. Immediately thereafter, Amos called upon Richard, an old customer, and collected an account from him. The publication by the Corporation had not come to Richard's attention. He also called upon Charles, a new prospect who knew of Amos' express authority but who had never dealt with the Corporation. Amos secured a substantial order from Charles, collected the price of the order, sent the order to the Corporation, and disappeared. The Corporation delivered the goods to Charles in accordance with the order.

(1) Will the Corporation recover if it sues Richard for his account? Explain.

(2) Will the Corporation recover if it sues Charles for the agreed price of the goods? Explain.

11/65; p.135

AGENCY: OBJECTIVE QUESTIONS

Each of the following numbered phrases or clauses states a legal conclusion as it completes the related lettered material. You are to determine whether each of the legal conclusions is true or false according to the general principles of agency law. Your grade will be determined from your total net score obtained by deducting your total of incorrect answers from your total of correct answers; an omitted answer will not be considered an incorrect answer.

(1) The Gordon Company, a manufacturer of cosmetics, employed Wood as its agent to promote its products. Under the terms of the contract signed, the agency is to last one year and is renewable at the Company's option. The contract provides that Wood is to be paid a 1 per cent commission on gross sales of the Company. In addition, the Company is to provide $100,000 to Wood to be used over the year to advertise the Company's products. Wood made no promise to work a specific amount of time during the year for the Company. Wood started to place advertising for the Company and to arrange promotional events. Three months after entering into the contract the Company marketed a new type of cosmetic. Marketing studies conducted by an independent firm engaged by the Company indicate that the new product will sell so well without any promotion that gross sales of the Company should more than triple, but that the product will not sell any better if it is promoted. The Company has notified Wood his contract is being terminated early.

(a) Wood has no rights under the contract because all contracts of agency are terminable at will.

(b) Wood has no rights under the contract because he has not given any consideration in return for the Company's promise to employ him.

(c) The Company is not free to terminate the contract on the grounds that the marketing of the new product is an unexpected development which substantially changes the relationship of the parties.

(d) The contract must remain in force, but Wood will not be entitled to commissions on the sale of the new product.

(e) Wood may recover damages in a suit against the independent firm that studied the market for the new product for interfering with his contract with the Company.

(2) Charles Jackson borrowed $20,000 from the Morgan Loan Company. He executed a note and a real property mortgage on his land and factory to secure payment of the loan. Subsequently, Jackson defaulted on the loan and authorized the Morgan Loan Company in writing to sell the factory on his behalf and retain an amount sufficient to satisfy the debt.

(a) Unless the Morgan Loan Company filed the mortgage on the property it will be unable to enforce against Jackson.
(b) The mortgage did not include the inventory stored in the factory.
(c) Jackson can terminate the agency relationship with Morgan at any time prior to the consummation of the sale of the land and factory.
(d) The death of Jackson would terminate the agency relationship but would not affect Morgan's rights on the mortgage.
(e) Morgan has an agency coupled with an interest.

(3) Philip Star was a car salesman employed by the Modern Motor Company. The Company instructed Star not to sell an antique car belonging to the Company which was kept on the Company's premises. When Roger Bloom came to purchase a car and expressed an interest in the antique car, Star informed Bloom that the car belonged to him personally and that he would sell it for $500 although it was worth $2,000. Bloom agreed and paid Star $500 cash and received a bill of sale. Star then disappeared.

(a) Bloom is entitled to the antique car since he dealt with an authorized agent of Modern Motor Company.
(b) When Bloom entered the Modern Motor Company showroom, he could properly assume that any car salesman was authorized to sell any new car on the premises.
(c) When Bloom paid Star $500 cash for the antique car, Bloom could not properly assume that Star had apparent authority as an agent to sell the car.
(d) Modern Motor Company must pay Bloom $500 because the Company was negligent in failing to place a sign on the antique car which stated "This car is not for sale."
(e) Modern Motor Company must pay Bloom $500 because as a principal it is responsible for the wrongful acts of its agent done in the course of his employment.

(4) John James, a local jobber, purported to act as the agent for Fairway Department Store when he in fact had no authority to bind Fairway. James made a contract in Fairway's name with Frank Williams to purchase 100 desk lamps at $4.75 each. James did this with the expectation of receiving a commission from Fairway because he believed the 100 lamps were a bargain at $475.

(a) James would be personally liable on the contract if Fairway refuses to purchase the lamps.

(b) Williams would not be liable to anyone if he repudiated the contract prior to any action by Fairway.

(c) If Fairway learned of the transaction and affirmed the contract prior to any action by Williams, Fairway may enforce the contract against Williams.

(d) If the contract were consummated and Fairway made a large profit on the lamps, Fairway must pay James a commission.

(e) Since James committed a fraud at the initial stage of the contract, it was void at the inception.

(5) Majestic Merchandise Mart employed Paul to deliver merchandise purchased by its customers and provided Paul with a light truck to make deliveries. Paul was told not to drive over 35 miles per hour, which was 5 miles less than the speed limit. Paul, while making his deliveries, drove at 40 miles per hour and hit and injured Elaine. Paul was also injured.

(a) Paul would be entitled to workman's compensation even if he were shown to have been negligent.

(b) If Paul were negligent, Majestic may be held liable for Paul's actions only if Majestic were negligent in its hiring of Paul.

(c) Majestic could not be held liable even if Paul were negligent since he disobeyed company instructions.

(d) If Elaine sued and recovered from Paul, she could not recover from Majestic also.

(e) If Paul were held liable to Elaine, he could obtain indemnification from Majestic since he was acting as an agent for and on behalf of his principal when the accident occurred.

(6) Michael Evans was employed as the purchasing agent for Restaurant Corporation. He purchased goods on credit for the Corporation in his own name from the Martin Food Supply Company. Martin Food Supply did not know that Evans was acting as an agent when he purchased the goods. The goods were used by the Corporation. When Martin Food Supply attempted to collect the cost of the goods from Evans, Evans informed Martin that he (Evans) was an employee and had purchased the goods for Restaurant Corporation's account. Later, Owens, who was the sole stockholder of Restaurant Corporation, sold all of his shares of stock to Diamond.

(a) Prior to the sale of the Restaurant Corporation shares to Diamond, the Corporation was responsible to Martin Food Supply for the goods Evans bought as purchasing agent.

(b) As sole stockholder of the Corporation, Owens would be personally responsible to satisfy the claim of Martin Food Supply if Restaurant Corporation were liable and did not have sufficient assets to meet the obligation.

(c) Evans' liability for the cost of the goods purchased did not end after the fact that he was an agent became known.

(d) Owens was not an undisclosed principal of either Restaurant Corporation or Evans and therefore had no liability to Martin.

(e) After the purchase of the Restaurant Corporation shares by Diamond, a defense which would preclude liability on the part of the Corporation would be that Diamond was unaware of the debt owed to Martin Food Supply when he purchased the shares of stock.

11/69

(7) Wallace, a traveling salesman for Excellent Appliances, sold Jackson a washer-dryer for $600. The bill of sale specified that Wallace was authorized to collect 10 per cent of the purchase price as a down payment and that the appliance would be delivered within one week. Three days after Jackson received the washer-dryer, Wallace, without authority from Excellent Appliances, collected the $540 balance. Wallace has absconded with the entire $600.

(a) The Statute of Frauds could be relied upon by Jackson to defeat Excellent Appliances' claim for payment.
(b) The appointment of Wallace as the sales agent for Excellent need not be in writing.
(c) Excellent will recover the $540 balance from Jackson because Wallace had no apparent authority to collect.
(d) The collection of the 10 per cent down payment was expressly authorized and therefore bars Excellent from recovering this amount from Jackson.
(e) To the extent that either party suffered a loss, recovery may be sought in an action against Wallace.

(8) Franklin was employed by the Gordon Department Store as a driver of one of its delivery trucks. Franklin was carefully chosen and was exceptionally well qualified. He was assigned a designated route and made his deliveries during the regular working hours of the store. Upon completion of his deliveries he was required to return the truck to the store's garage. One day while making his usual deliveries he negligently drove the truck through a red light and collided with Bunt's car. Both Bunt and Franklin were injured and their vehicles were damaged. The collision was solely Franklin's fault.

(a) Franklin was an employee agent (servant).
(b) Franklin cannot be held personally liable since he was carrying out Gordon's business.
(c) The fact that Franklin was carefully chosen and exceptionally well qualified will prevent Bunt's recovering from Gordon.
(d) If Franklin has to pay Bunt for the damages he caused, he is entitled to a reimbursement from Gordon.
(e) Franklin's negligence will not bar his recovery of workman's compensation.

(9) Baxter owns several cigar stores. He employed Arthur to open a new store in Arthur's home town. He told Arthur to use his own (Arthur's) name on the store front and make all purchases and sales without disclosing that Baxter owned the business. In this way Baxter hoped to

obtain the benefits of local ownership and trade on Arthur's popularity in the community. Arthur agreed and made many sales and purchases in his own name.

(a) Baxter is an undisclosed principal.
(b) Baxter cannot be held liable to third parties on contracts they made with Arthur in his own name in that they did not rely on Baxter's credit.
(c) Third parties who learn of Baxter's ownership of the business may disaffirm the executory contracts they made with Arthur.
(d) Such an arrangement between Arthur and Baxter is against public policy and therefore illegal.
(e) Upon Arthur's default after Baxter's identity is revealed, a third party who dealt with Arthur and elects to sue Arthur would be precluded from suing Baxter for breach of contract.

(10) Vaughn appointed Hawks, his real estate agent, to sell all of his extensive holdings in the state except Blackacre which Hawks expressly promised Vaughn he would not sell. At a press conference to announce Hawks' appointment Vaughn stated that he was selling out his real estate holdings in the state and anyone interested in purchasing any of his land should contact Hawks who had "complete authority." Nothing was indicated regarding the agreed limitation on the sale of Blackacre. Hawks mistakenly sold Blackacre to Williams who was unaware of the limitation.

(a) The relationship between Hawks and Vaughn was an agency coupled with an interest.
(b) Hawks had implied authority to sell Blackacre.
(c) Williams can enforce the contract of sale of Blackacre made by Hawks on Vaughn's behalf.
(d) The mistake in question was a mutual mistake in fact thereby allowing rescission.
(e) Specific performance is the only remedy that would be available to Williams if he were to win his case against Vaughn.

(11) Dawson hired Fee as his sales manager at $2,000 per month. A written contract signed on December 15, 1968 specified that the contract was "absolute and irrevocable" for one calendar year beginning on January 1, 1969. Prior to commencement of the employment Dawson notified Fee that he no longer wished to perform and that he was cancelling the contract.

(a) The Statute of Frauds requires the above described contract to be in a signed writing.
(b) Fee may seek and obtain specific performance of the contract.
(c) The contract created an agency coupled with an interest.
(d) At the time Dawson cancelled the contract Fee was released from any further obligation to perform.
(e) Fee may immediately sue Dawson for damages for breach of contract based upon anticipatory repudiation.

(12) Filmore, a manufacturer, hired Gladstone as a traveling salesman to sell goods manufactured by Filmore. Gladstone also sold a line of

products manufactured by his uncle. He did not disclose this to Filmore. The relationship was unsatisfactory and Filmore finally fired Gladstone after learning of Gladstone's sales of his uncle's goods. Gladstone, enraged at Filmore for firing him, continued to make contracts on Filmore's behalf with both new and old customers which were almost uniformly disadvantageous to Filmore. Filmore upon learning this gave written notice of Gladstone's discharge to all parties with whom Gladstone had dealt.

(a) Gladstone breached his fiduciary duty to Filmore and was rightfully fired.
(b) Filmore can bring an action against Gladstone to have him account for the secret profits he made selling his uncle's goods.
(c) Prior to notification Gladstone retained some continued authority to bind Filmore despite termination of the agency relationship.
(d) The new customers who contracted with Gladstone for the first time cannot enforce the contracts against Filmore even though they were unaware that Filmore had terminated the agency.
(e) If Filmore had promptly published a notification of termination of Gladstone's employment in the local newspapers and in the trade publications he would not be liable for Gladstone's wrongdoing.

5/69

(13) The doctrine that a master is liable for the negligent acts of his servant
(a) Is founded in the law of torts.
(b) Is founded in the law of contracts.
(c) Applies only if the master expressly commanded his servant to do wrong.
(d) Applies only if the master commanded his servant to do wrong, either expressly or impliedly.
(e) Applies only if the servant was acting in the scope of his employment and in the execution of his service.

(14) A written power of attorney given by A to B
(a) Is invalid unless accepted by B.
(b) Expressly authorizes B to act as A's agent.
(c) Expressly authorizes B to act as A's servant.
(d) Impliedly creates a principal-agent relationship.
(e) Vests B with apparent authority to act for A beyond the terms of the power of attorney.

(15) An independent contractor
(a) Can never become an agent.
(b) Is a particular type of agent.
(c) Usually promises a definite result.
(d) Acts in a fiduciary capacity.
(e) Enters into contracts in his principal's name.

(16) A person is an agent when he is acting in the capacity of

(a) A partner.
(b) The president of a corporation.
(c) An executor.
(d) An auctioneer hired to conduct a public sale.
(e) A lien holder.

(17) If a principal intends to grant to his agent the power to enter into a contract for him and he manifests this intent only to the third party who is to contract with the agent and not to the agent,

(a) The agent thereby gains "apparent" authority.
(b) The agent thereby gains "real" authority.
(c) The principal would not be bound to the contract so long as the agent entered it without knowing he had authority to do so.
(d) If the agent later learns of his authority, accepts it, and enters into the contract, he thereby acts as a factor.
(e) If the agent later learns of his authority, accepts it, and enters into the contract, the third party could hold the principal to the contract by invoking the doctrine of agency by estoppel.

(18) If an agent makes a contract within the scope of his authority for an undisclosed principal,

(a) The agent does not have "real" authority.
(b) The agent does not have "apparent" authority.
(c) The principal is ordinarily bound by the contract when his identity is disclosed.
(d) The party contracting with the agent may elect to hold either the agent or the principal when the principal's identity is disclosed.
(e) The agent is liable on the contract only until the identity of the principal is disclosed.

(19) An agent acting on behalf of a known principal may not be held liable on a contract entered into with a third party on behalf of the principal, even if

(a) The agent misrepresents his scope of authority.
(b) The agent signs a negotiable instrument in his own name without indicating his agency.
(c) The agent commits a tort in the course of discharging his duties.
(d) The third party deals only with the agent and never speaks to the principal.
(e) The third party mistakenly believes the principal is a wealthy man.

(20) If an agent enters into an unauthorized contract with a third party on behalf of his principal,

(a) The principal on learning of the act may affirm and ratify the contract although at the time the act was done the principal did not have capacity to authorize the act.
(b) The principal on learning of the act may affirm and ratify the contract by remaining silent and receiving the benefits derived from the contract.

(c) The principal on learning of the act may affirm and ratify the contract by suing the third party on it.
(d) The third person learning that the agent was unauthorized is entitled to withdraw from the contract only so long as the principal has not yet affirmed it.
(e) The principal may not affirm the contract unless the third party agrees to allow him to do so.

(21) A, a chief clerk for B, is asked by B to assume the management of his retail store while B is away on a world tour for six months. If B cannot be reached for advice, A is justified in
(a) Borrowing money in B's name for the purpose of expanding the store.
(b) Discharging an incompetent employee.
(c) Purchasing new inventory in the regular course of trade.
(d) Selling the business on receiving an excellent offer.
(e) Conducting the traditional semiannual sale.

(22) Circumstances which may be looked to in order to determine the intent of the principal to allow an agent to delegate his authority to a subagent include
(a) The prior conduct of the parties.
(b) The character of the act to be delegated.
(c) The skill of the subagent.
(d) The availability of the agent to do the job when it is to be done.
(e) Trade practice in the industry.

(23) P places an ad in the newspaper to sell his car for $1,000. A, his servant, believes the car is worth $1,500 and tells T to buy the car. A has breached his duty of loyalty to P if
(a) A allowed P to sell the car to T without informing P that T was his friend.
(b) A does not inform P that he believes the car is worth $1,500.
(c) A accepts a payment from T for giving him the information about the car.
(d) A agreed to repurchase the car from T for $1,200.
(e) A misrepresented the condition of the car to P in order to induce P to sell it for a lower price.

(24) A and B are adjoining land owners. A agrees to allow B six months in which to attempt to sell their properties as a joint parcel and obtain a price of at least $5,000 for A's land. B agrees to attempt to effect a sale for A on these terms.
(a) B has become A's agent for the purpose of selling his land.
(b) A and B are partners.
(c) A and B are joint venturers.
(d) B has a power coupled with an interest.
(e) A may terminate his agreement with B at any time by giving notice to B.

11/66

(25) A lender is given, as security, authority to collect rents due to the borrower and to apply those rents to the payment of the debt owed him.

(a) This is an agency coupled with an interest.
(b) This agency can be terminated by act of the principal.
(c) This agency is not revoked by death of the agent.
(d) This agency will be terminated by a supervening illegality.
(e) This agency will be revoked by insanity of the principal.

(26) An agent is ordered by his principal to repossess certain property from a third party. The agent does so unaware that the repossession is illegal.

(a) The principal is liable to the third party.
(b) The agent is liable to the third party.
(c) The agent can get indemnity from his principal only if he is required to answer to the third person.
(d) The third person can look only to the agent for compensation for an injury caused by the agent's wrongful act.
(e) The principal can get indemnity from the agent if the principal is required to answer to the third person.

(27) A principal gives his agent an exclusive agency to sell specified personal property and collect the proceeds.

(a) The creation of this agency need not be evidenced by a writing unless required by statutes.
(b) The principal has the right to appoint other agents to accomplish the sale.
(c) The agent may hold back from the proceeds enough money to insure reimbursement for expenses necessarily incurred in making the sale.
(d) The principal can compete with the agent in seeking a buyer.
(e) The creation of such an agency imposes upon the agent the liability of an insurer of the services he renders.

(28) If a ratification is to be effective,

(a) The ratification must be in writing.
(b) The third person must not have withdrawn from the transaction prior to ratification.
(c) The principal must ratify the entire transaction.
(d) The act must have been done on behalf of the person who ratifies it.
(e) The principal must be competent to ratify at the time the unauthorized act was performed.

(29) Notification of termination of an agent's authority

(a) Will be effective only if it comes from the principal.
(b) Will be effective as to all parties if published in a newspaper of wide circulation.
(c) Need not be given when the termination of authority is due to the principal's death.
(d) Need not be given when the termination of authority is due to the agent's breach of duty.

(e) Must be given to third persons who have been dealing with the agent.

(30) A real estate broker
(a) Is a special agent.
(b) Has a lien on the seller's property for his commission.
(c) Is not entitled to his commission unless the buyer he produces is ready, willing, and able to meet the seller's terms.
(d) Is not entitled to his commission in the absence of an express or implied contract of hiring.
(e) Must have a brokerage license in force throughout the entire period during which services are rendered.

5/65

TOPIC FIVE

PARTNERSHIPS

CONTENTS

PARTNERSHIPS. The AICPA description of partnerships is contained in the discussion of the forms of business organization at the beginning of Agency (see p.125): "Another major area [of business law] is partnership law which encompasses the characteristics of *the partnership and the partners among themselves and to third parties; and the rights of the third parties upon dissolution."**

I. CHARACTERISTICS

A. Definition: The Uniform Partnership Act (a uniform statute adopted by the majority of states) defines partnership as "an association of two or more persons to carry on as co-owners a business for profit."

B. Distinctive features of a general partnership:

1. Voluntary association of persons as individuals; not considered a separate entity for most purposes.
2. Organized by simple agreement without governmental sanction; must be for a legal purpose and licensed if this is required (see Contracts, p.41, III.C.1).
3. Fiduciary relationship among the partners.
4. Co-ownership: Each partner has a proprietary interest in the subject matter of the partnership (tenancy in partnership).
5. Association must be one for profit.
6. Mutual agency of partners: Each partner is agent for the others and for the partnership in respect to all transactions "within the scope of the partnership business."
7. Mutual and unlimited joint and several liability for partners' acts; each partner is financially responsible for all partnership acts.

C. Distinguished from:

1. Corporations, as to:
   a. Initial expense. (Corporations' initial charges and fees are greater.)
   b. Liabilities for debts of the business. (Stockholders of corporations have limited liability.)
   c. Liability of owners of the business for the acts of one another. (Corporations normally have no liability for the acts of individual stockholders.)
   d. Continuity of existence and effect of death, bankruptcy, or sale of one's interest in business. (Corporation, being a separate legal entity, is not affected by the death, bankruptcy, or sale of stockholder's interest.)
   e. Necessity of obtaining permission to do business from governmental agencies. (Corporation cannot come into existence without state approval; normally approval is readily granted.)

* Source: AICPA, *Information for CPA Candidates* (July 1970).

f. Right to practice a profession. (Corporation is prohibited from practicing most professions.)

g. Advantages of partnership:

(1) Less formality necessary for partnership action; normally greater equality and control of business by partners.

(2) Possibly a lighter tax burden.

(3) Relatively free from public supervision.

(4) Freedom to unite professional skills in fields forbidden to corporations (e.g., to practice law).

(5) Theoretically greater borrowing power in that partners are personally liable for firm debts.

2. Joint ventures: partnership for a particular transaction or series of transactions.

a. Co-ownership only for a given limited purpose.

b. Somewhat less power to bind associates.

c. Otherwise legal rules similar to partnership.

3. Joint stock associations: rarely used as a form of business organization today; possesses some partnership and some corporate characteristics.

a. Issues stock against capital; shares are transferable.

b. Does not come into existence through state sanction as does a corporation.

c. Enjoys corporate advantage of continuous succession.

d. Liability is unlimited as in a partnership; however, creditors must first proceed against the association.

e. Affairs managed through directors and officers.

f. Association must sue in the name of members, or president or treasurer, not in its registered name.

4. Business trusts.

a. Trust device used to carry on a business; title to property transferred to trustees.

b. Duration of a trust may be limited.

c. Limited liability—only if trustees are completely free of beneficiaries' control.

D. Capacity to become a partner.

1. Generally, any person who is competent to make a contract.

a. Infants:

(1) May become partners.

(2) Have right to disaffim; however, may not withdraw investment after debts are incurred unless remaining assets are sufficient to pay such debts.

(3) Only liable up to amount of capital contribution.

b. Corporations:

(1) Lack capacity in absence of specific authority conferred by state corporation laws.

(2) May become partners by estoppel.

c. Partnerships: may become partners if all partners agree.

d. Married women: may become partners; some states prohibit them from becoming partners with their husbands.

E. Classification of partnerships.

1. General: created for usual partnership purposes.

a. Trading: engaged in trade and commerce and which buys and sells goods as a part of its ordinary course of business.

b. Non-trading: formed for professional or quasi-professional purposes; renders service rather than trade.

(1) Third parties are entitled to assume that members of trading partnerships have wider authority than members of non-trading firms.

2. Limited partnership: See p. 160, IV.

F. Classification of partners.

1. General (active):

a. Share in the management of the business.

b. Liability is unlimited.

c. Must give notice to firm's customers and creditors upon withdrawal in order to avoid future liability.

2. Limited (special):

a. Liability limited by statute.

b. Must not share in any way in management of the firm's business.

3. Secret (undisclosed):

a. May be active in conduct of business.

b. Connection with firm not disclosed.

c. If active, liability similar to that of undisclosed principal (see Agency, p. 132, IV.A.2.).

d. Unlimited liability if active in firm business.

4. Silent:

a. Have no voice in management of business, but generally known as partners.

b. Liability same as that of general partners.

5. Dormant: undisclosed principal has a right to management par-

ticipation although infrequently used; liability same as general partners, if connection with the firm is discovered.

6. Nominal (ostensible):
   a. Appear to be partners (e.g., allow their names to be used) although they are not partners.
   b. May be liable as partners regardless of whether they have an actual interest in business.
   c. Sometimes known as partners by estoppel (equitable doctrine to prevent injustice to one who has relied upon a misrepresentation by not allowing the misrepresentor to deny the truth of the assertion he has expressly or impliedly made).

G. Creation of a partnership.

1. Contract may be:
   a. Express: oral or written. Writing is needed only when statute of frauds is applicable (see Contracts, p. 44, III.E.).
   b. Implied from the acts of the parties involved (e.g., sharing profits and losses and joint management).

      (1) Under the Uniform Partnership Act receipt of a share of the profits of a business by a person raises a presumption he is a partner. However, if payments are for services rendered, interest on loans, payment of debts, as annuity to a widow of a deceased partner, as rent to a landlord, and so on, the presumption of a partnership no longer holds.

      (2) Receipt of gross returns does not in itself establish a partnership.

      (3) To be protected against liability an employee should request the following provisions in his contract for employment:

         (A) He has been hired as an employee and is not a partner.

         (B) Profits are received as salary or bonus, not as profits.

         (C) Employee is not required to contribute to capital or losses.

         (D) Employee's name is not to appear on firm stationery.

         (E) Employee is to receive a minimum guaranteed salary in any event.

         (F) Employee is in no way to be held out as a partner.

2. Articles of co-partnership: some important provisions:
   a. Firm name and names and addresses of partners.
   b. Date when partnership becomes effective.
   c. Nature, purpose, and scope of partnership activity.
   d. Location of place of business and field of operations.
   e. Admission of new partners, in absence of which consent of

all partners is necessary.

f. Duration of partnership.

g. Payment of interest on invested capital.

h. Computation and sharing of profits and losses—if not stated, shared equally.

i. Salaries to be paid.

j. Powers and duties of partners and limitations, if any.

k. Dissolution and right to continue business upon withdrawal of any partner.

l. Distribution of surplus upon dissolution.

m. Disposition of firm name and good will.

n. Liquidating partners.

o. Provision for arbitration, in absence of which consent of all partners is necessary to submit a matter to arbitration.

II. RIGHTS, DUTIES, AND LIABILITIES OF PARTNERSHIP AND PARTNERS

A. Partnership property rights.

1. Firm name:

a. May consist of actual names of partners.

b. May consist of fictitious or assumed names; however, statutes will usually require filing of certificate which discloses the true names of the partners.

c. May not be such as to mislead the public. Statutes provide:

(1) That no person may conduct business in the name of a partner not associated with the firm, except where an established business continues in existence and the name of a former partner is retained.

(2) That when the designation "and Company," "and Co.," or similar designation is used, it must represent an actual partner, except where a pre-existing firm or corporation discontinuing business consents to the use of its name.

d. In most states partners must sue or be sued in their individual names.

(1) Common law so provides, and a partnership is not a legal entity for this purpose.

(2) Statutes in some states permit partnership to sue or be sued in the firm name or in the name of a specified officer.

e. Firm can hold property in the firm name and is considered a legal entity for this particular purpose. This is the Uniform Partnership Act rule, which is contrary to the common law.

2. Good will: reputation for honesty, efficiency, and fairness which a firm builds up in the eyes of the business world.
3. Capital contributions.
   a. Aggregate of individual contributions in money or property contributed by partners to the partnership.
   b. Distinguished from partnership property in regard to:
      (1) Amount, in that capital is an agreed amount whereas property continually varies in amount.
      (2) Undivided profits; capital does not necessarily include them, while property does.
      (3) Distribution upon dissolution. Capital is repayable in proportion to amounts contributed; property is not necessarily so distributed.
4. Partnership property includes:
   a. All property originally brought into the partnership or subsequently acquired on account of the partnership.
   b. Property acquired with partnership funds unless a contrary intent appears.
   c. Undivided profits.

B. Relation, rights, and duties of partners to one another.

1. Unless the partnership agreement provides otherwise the following rules apply:
   a. Profits and losses are shared equally.
   b. Partners are indemnified for payments made, or personal liability reasonably assumed, in behalf of the partnership.
   c. A partner who makes an advance beyond his agreed contribution is entitled to interest from the date of the advance; on his capital contribution, however, he is only entitled to interest from the date when repayment thereof should have been made.
   d. Partners have equal rights in management and conduct of partnership business.
   e. No partner is entitled to salary for acting in partnership affairs.
2. A partner is accountable as a fiduciary to the partnership and must exercise good faith and loyalty to the firm interests.
3. Partners must exercise reasonable skill and enterprise in conducting firm business.
4. Right to be informed: Whether he has an active part or not, partner has a right to be informed particularly as to firm's operations.
5. Right to an accounting: A partner is entitled to a formal account-

ing as to partnership affairs whenever circumstances render an accounting just and reasonable. A demand for an accounting is usually, but not necessarily, joined with a demand for a dissolution. However, one cannot have a dissolution without an accounting, because dissolution is followed by distribution, which requires an accounting.

6. A partner has a right of access to firm's books and records, which, in absence of a contrary agreement, are kept at principal place of business.
7. A partner has the right to return of capital upon dissolution after partnership property has been applied to partnership debts.
8. Property rights of a partner: rights in specific partnership property:
   a. Co-owner of specific property (tenancy in partnership):
      (1) Right to possess and use property for partnership purposes.

      (2) Right to participate in management not assignable without consent of all partners. However, partner's right to share in profits and receive a share upon dissolution of partnership is assignable.

      (3) Partner's right to specific partnership property is not subject to attachment or execution.

      (4) Remaining partners have survivorship rights in a deceased partner's interest in specific partnership property. However, remaining partners must account to the deceased partner's estate for his partnership interest.

      (A) Partner's right in specific partnership property is not subject to allowances to spouse, heirs, or next of kin.

      (B) Partner's interest in partnership realty is personal property. Partner's share upon distribution is personal property and in case of death will pass by rules of descent of personal property.

C. Liability to third parties dealing with the partnership.

1. Mutual agency of partners:
   a. Each partner is an agent of the partnership and for every other partner, and while acting within actual or apparent scope of partnership business he binds the other parties. (E.g., a partner who receives payment, although misapplying funds, binds partnership to payment.) Agreements among partners limiting their powers are not binding on third parties unless they have knowledge of them.

      (1) Any partner in a trading partnership may purchase a customary amount of goods on credit and bind the partnership

regardless of his actual authority.

(2) Agents or employees hired by a partner may assume that partner was authorized to hire them.

(3) Partnership is liable to an innocent party from whom a partner borrowed money in behalf of the firm.

b. Acts of a partner which are not apparently for the carrying on of the partnership business in a usual way do not bind the partnership unless authorized by the other partners.

(1) No partner has power to bind the firm on accommodation paper or contracts of suretyship or guaranty unless expressly authorized, or in furtherance of firm business.

(2) No partner has power to make a gift of partnership property.

(3) A conveyance made by one partner of real property held in the firm name may be rescinded by the firm unless it has been subsequently resold to a bona fide purchaser for value. However, where there is a conveyance of firm property which has only the name of the conveyor on record (with no indication of rights of partnership), title passes to an innocent purchaser for value.

c. Liability of partnership begins when it is actually formed, although articles of partnership are not executed until later.

d. Majority of partners can control ordinary decisions of business, but fundamental changes (e.g., change from retail to wholesale selling) require unanimous consent. Also, the following acts require unanimous consent unless there is an abandonment of the firm business:

(1) Assigning partnership property in trust for creditors.

(2) Confessing a judgment.

(3) Submitting a claim to arbitration.

(4) Disposing of good will of the business.

(5) Doing any act making it impossible to carry on ordinary business of partnership (e.g., selling out entire stock).

2. Tort liability of partners: General partners are liable for torts committed during the course of the partnership; limited partners are not.

3. Criminal liability of partners: Partners are not liable for crimes committed by other partners unless they themselves participated, planned, aided, or acquiesced in their commission.

4. A deceased partner's estate is liable for firm debts incurred while he was a partner.

5. An incoming partner, under the Uniform Partnership Act, is

liable for existing firm obligations only to the extent of his capital contribution. At common law he would not be liable even to this extent.

a. He may, however, become personally liable by assumption or novation.

6. A retiring partner is liable to creditors for existing debts of the partnership, but not for those incurred after retirement, so long as creditors had notice of the retirement before extending the credit.
7. No person can become a member of a partnership without the consent of all the partners unless the partnership agreement provides otherwise.

III. DISSOLUTION OF THE PARTNERSHIP

A. Definition: The Uniform Partnership Act defines dissolution as "the change in relation of the partners caused by any partner ceasing to be associated in the carrying on, as distinguished from the winding up, of the business." On dissolution, the partnership is not terminated, but continues until the winding up of partnership affairs is completed.

B. Voluntary dissolution: brought about by agreement of partners, either in original agreement or by subsequent agreement.

1. Where partnership provided for a definite term which has expired, partners may continue in partnership for an indicated term by agreement, or, if the parties continue without agreement, it is a partnership at will.

C. Dissolution by operation of law (involuntary) occurs:

1. Upon death of a partner, unless partnership agreement specifically provides to the contrary (executor can then require winding up of partnership and payment to estate).
2. Upon bankruptcy of a partner or of the partnership.
3. When partnership enterprise becomes illegal or participation by a partner becomes illegal.
4. When, upon the outbreak of war, partners are citizens of enemy countries.
5. Upon the withdrawal and retirement by a partner either in accordance with the term fixed or before the time fixed by agreement; however, if withdrawal is before time fixed the partner is liable for breach of contract.

   a. Assignment of interest in a partnership by one partner will not dissolve the partnership, since the assignee does not displace the liability of the assigning partner.
   b. When a new partner is admitted into an existing partnership,

business may be continued without liquidation of the affairs of the previous partnership but the former partnership is dissolved.

6. Upon application by a partner, a judicial decree of dissolution must be granted when:
   a. A partner is shown to be of unsound mind, or
   b. A partner is shown to be permanently incapacitated so that he cannot conduct his duties, or
   c. There is misconduct sufficiently serious so as to affect prejudicially the success of the business, or
   d. The business is a failure (i.e., conducted at a heavy loss so that further activities would be futile), or
   e. There is any situation which would make it equitable to do so (e.g., lack of harmony).

D. Unless otherwise provided in agreement, no partner can be expelled; however, a similar result may be achieved by dissolving the partnership and forming a new one excluding the undesirable partner.

E. Effect of dissolution:

1. Partners have no authority to conduct new business.
2. Partners are trustees for the purpose of winding up affairs of the firm and should proceed to:
   a. Discharge the firm debts, and
   b. Distribute remaining assets, or
   c. Court may appoint a receiver when partners disagree as to proper distribution.
3. Disposition of the firm name on dissolution.
   a. If there is no provision, any partner may use it, so long as public is not misled (see p. 154, II.A.1.c.).
   b. Right to use the firm name may be sold as a business asset.
   c. Retiring partner may give or sell the right to continue to use his name in the firm name.
   d. Court may order sale of assets upon death of a partner, and the firm name must then be accounted for.

F. Order of distribution of firm assets of a general partnership: Order is different for limited partnership (see p. 161, IV.E.).

1. Firm (i.e., partnership) assets (in order of priority):
   a. To firm creditors other than partners.
   b. To partners for liabilities other than for capital and profits.

c. To partners for liabilities arising from capital contributions made by them.

d. To partners for liabilities arising from undistributed profits of the firm.

2. Where there are insufficient firm assets, partners are personally liable for firm debts.

a. Each partner must contribute toward the losses (including capital losses) according to his share in profits.

(1) Profits and surplus in absence of agreement will be distributed in equal portions after all liabilities, including those to partners, are satisfied.

b. Marshaling of assets (equitable doctrine):

(1) Firm assets must first be made available for payment of firm debts; surplus, if any, goes toward payment of individual partner's debts to the extent of his partnership interest.

(2) Personal assets of a partner are applied to his personal debts; surplus, if any, goes toward payment of firm debts.

IV. LIMITED PARTNERSHIP

A. Definition: a partnership formed pursuant to a statute (not recognized at common law) and consisting of one or more general partners, jointly and severally liable as ordinary partners, and by whom the business is conducted, and one or more special or limited partners who contribute capital to the common fund, *but who do not manage the firm business,* and who are not liable for debts of the partnership beyond the amount they contributed.

B. The Uniform Limited Partnership Act, adopted in a majority of states, requires that:

1. A certificate signed and sworn to by all parties must be filed, recorded, and published, and must contain:

a. The name of the firm and the address of its principal place of business.

b. The general nature of the partnership business and duration of the partnership.

c. The names and residences of the general and limited partners.

d. Capital contributions of each limited partner.

e. The method for determining changes of personnel and continuance of business in the event of death or retirement of general partners.

2. There must be at least one general partner.

3. Contributions of limited partners can be in cash or property but cannot consist of services.
4. Firm name cannot contain name of limited partner unless it is the same as that of a general partner.
5. In absence of statutory restriction, the limited partnership may carry on any business which a partnership without limited partners may carry on.

C. Rights of limited partner: in general, the same rights (except in management) as a general partner; he has the right:

1. To receive profits and compensation as provided in the agreement.
2. To have books kept at principal place of business, to inspect the books and formal accounts, and to make copies of them.
3. To demand a formal accounting whenever the circumstances warrant.
4. To obtain return of capital contribution upon withdrawal, subject to creditors' rights.
5. To have a dissolution and winding up by a decree of a court of competent jurisdiction.

D. Restrictions on limited partner (determined by statute):

1. Limited partner will be held liable as a general partner:
   a. Where he takes an active part in the business.
   b. Where he interferes in management.
   c. In most states, for failure to comply with, or violation of, the requirements of the statute.
   d. In some states, as a result of the withdrawal of any part of the sum contributed by a special partner, either as dividends, profits, or otherwise, at any time during the continuance of partnership. In most states, such withdrawal merely renders special partner liable to restore the sums withdrawn with interest.

E. Order of distribution of assets after dissolution as provided for by the Uniform Limited Partnership Act:

1. To creditors in order of priority as provided by law.
2. To limited partners in respect to their share of undistributed profits and other compensation by way of income on their contributions.
3. To limited partners in respect to their capital contributions.
4. To general partners other than for capital and profits.

5. To general partners in respect to profits of the firm.
6. To general partners in respect to capital contributions.

F. The utility of a limited partnership:

1. It secures the advantages of corporate liability for investors in business organizations that cannot conveniently incorporate.
2. Certain tax advantages: treated the same as a general partnership for tax purposes; i.e., not recognized as a separate tax entity.

PARTNERSHIPS: SUBJECTIVE QUESTIONS*

CHARACTERISTICS

Q. Arthur and his brother John, residents of X state, formed a partnership for manufacturing and selling alcoholic beverages. Federal and X state licenses to run the business were obtained under John's name without stating that Arthur had any interest in the firm. Both the federal and X state statutes required that the holder of such licenses disclose the names of all persons interested in the firm and imposed criminal penalties for failing to do so. After the firm had been in operation for several years, Arthur sued John for an accounting of his profits in the partnership. Will Arthur recover against John? Explain.

11/63; pp. 155-156

PARTNER'S RIGHTS AND DUTIES

Q. Peter, a member of the Peter and Paul partnership, invested various sums of money in the partnership. On January 15, 1950, he initially invested $15,000 in the partnership as a contribution to capital. On January 15, 1957, he made an additional $10,000 contribution to capital. There was an agreement that this $10,000 would be returned to him in five years. On January 15, 1963, he loaned the partnership $5,000. Animosity having developed among the partners, Peter on January 15, 1964, demanded that he be paid interest on the entire $30,000 which is still retained by the partnership. Will Peter be entitled to interest on all or any part of the $30,000 in question? Explain.

5/64; p.155

LIABILITY TO THIRD PARTIES

Q. S, a member of the AB&S partnership, encountered personal financial difficulties as a result of an unexpected fall in stock prices. His bank called him on the phone and indicated that he would have to repay

* See Introductory Note, p. 19.

a part of his loan or pledge more collateral. The AB&S partnership is a trading partnership which deals in woolens. It had in its safe $10,000 worth of stocks which were purchased as an investment during the off-season. The face of the certificates indicated that the AB&S partnership was the owner. S, feeling that the market would quickly rebound, took the stocks from the safe, signed the partnership name in blank in the appropriate place, and signed his name beneath the partnership name as partner. He then turned the stock over to the bank as collateral. The stock market took another severe drop and the bank sold all the collateral. The bank realized exactly the amount that was due on the loan. The other members of the AB&S partnership, upon learning of S's activities, demanded that the bank replace the partnership's securities.

(1) Distinguish between a trading and non-trading partnership.
(2) Why is the distinction important in partnership law? Explain.
(3) As between the AB&S partnership and the bank, who will prevail? Explain.

5/64; pp. 152, 157

Q. Johnson was a general partner in a machine tool merchandising partnership. Johnson applied for a personal loan at Empire Loan Company. The intended purpose of the loan, as disclosed by Johnson to Empire, was to purchase a new automobile for his wife. Empire refused to lend Johnson the money unless an accommodation indorsement by his firm was obtained. Johnson signed his name on the face of the note and then signed the firm name on the back. All this was done in the presence of the Empire agent.

Johnson is now bankrupt and Empire seeks to collect from the partnership or alternatively to obtain Johnson's interest in the partnership.

(1) Can Empire hold the partnership liable on the note? Explain.
(2) Can Empire obtain Johnson's interest in the partnership? Explain.
(3) What effect does Johnson's bankruptcy have upon the partnership?

11/68; p. 157

DISSOLUTION OF THE PARTNERSHIP

Q. A, B, and C formed the ABC Company, a partnership, with A contributing $12,000 of capital, B contributing $8,000, and C contributing $6,000. In their partnership agreement, A, B, and C provided that the partnership was to exist for twenty years, but the partners made no provision as to the proportions in which profits and losses were to be shared. During the course of operating the partnership, A made a loan of $1,000 to the partnership which has not been repaid, and the partnership also owes outside creditors additional amounts which exceed the value of partnership assets by $3,000.

(1) Under the Uniform Partnership Act, in absence of a specific

agreement between the parties, how is the compensation and profit for each partner determined during the course of operating the partnership?

(2) Under the Uniform Partnership Act

(a) If A wishes to terminate the partnership but B and C do not, does A have the right to withdraw from the partnership? Explain.

(b) If A, B, and C agree to terminate the partnership, how will losses be divided?

(3) Discuss

(a) The rule of marshalling of assets.

(b) The distinction between the "dissolution" of the partnership and the "winding up" of partnership affairs.

(4) If D becomes a partner in ABC Company and replaces A, what is D's liability with respect to obligations arising before his admission to the partnership?

5/66; pp. 158-160

Q. Bradley and Smith are the only partners in an insolvent partnership. The firm has assets of $10,000 and liabilities of $100,000. The creditors are Donaldson ($50,000), Charles ($40,000), and Williams ($10,000). The three creditors rank equally in order of priority. Bradley does not have any personal assets or liabilities. Smith has personal assets of $80,000 but he owes the Security Bank $50,000. Smith has no other personal debts.

How much are Donaldson, Charles, Williams and Security Bank each entitled to receive? Explain.

11/68; pp. 159-160

Q. Upon examining the books of account of a partnership you ascertain the following facts:

(1) The partnership was created six months ago and consists of three partners, Monroe, Adams and Madison, who share profits equally. The partnership agreement is silent on the sharing of losses.

(2) Monroe loaned the partnership $10,000 and made a capital contribution of $20,000; Adams made a $10,000 capital contribution; Madison made no capital contribution.

(3) The partnership now has assets of $80,000 and owes outside creditors $55,000.

(4) The partners have decided to dissolve the firm.

Monroe requests that you explain how the distribution should be made to the partnership's creditors and its partners. He is particularly concerned about his own rights on dissolution.

Prepare the explanation requested above. Give the reasons for the conclusions you reach.

11/68; pp. 159-160

LIMITED PARTNERSHIPS

Q. Tom, Jerry, Neil, and Jay decided to form a limited partnership for the purpose of operating a farm. They selected the limited partnership as the form of business entity most suitable for their purpose. Jerry was to serve as the general partner and contribute $5,000 in capital. Tom, Neil, and Jay were to contribute $10,000 each and were to be limited partners. All the above mentioned capital contributions were made and the necessary limited partnership papers were duly filled out and properly filed in the appropriate state office designated for such purpose. The partnership agreement and the papers filed clearly indicated that Jerry was the sole general partner. The others were to be treated as limited partners and liable only to the extent of their capital contributions. Jerry managed the partnership during the first two years. However, during the third year Tom and Neil overruled Jerry as to the type of crops to be planted, exercised the power to draw checks on the firm account and finally replaced Jerry with a new and more receptive general partner. Jay did not join his fellow partners in these activities. However, his name was used, with his knowledge and consent, on the partnership stationery as part of the firm name. Some of the creditors knew that Jay was only a limited partner.

(1) Are Tom and Neil personally liable for any of the partnership debts? If so, to what extent? Explain.

(2) Is Jay personally liable on any of the partnership debts? If so, to what extent? Explain.

11/61; p. 161

Q. What is the order of priority of payment of limited partnership obligations in settling accounts upon dissolution?

11/61; pp. 161-162

Q. One year ago Orand and Scanon formed a partnership to sell insurance. Their agreement stated that the partnership would remain in existence for five years unless it was mutually agreed that the partnership should be dissolved. Under the terms of the agreement (1) the partners were specifically denied the right to unilaterally dissolve the partnership and (2) a partner who should unilaterally attempt to dissolve the partnership would be prohibited from ever again selling insurance in the United States.

Last month Scanon accepted the appointment as head of the local Redevelopment Commission for one year. This is a full-time paid position and Scanon no longer sells insurance. Nonetheless, he told Orand they were still partners and that he intends to return to the partnership full time when his term of office expires.

Orand now wishes to dissolve the partnership. Scanon maintains that the terms of the partnership agreement specifically prohibit

Orand from unilaterally ending the partnership and that if Orand attempts to dissolve the partnership he will invoke the provisions of the agreement to prohibit Orand from selling insurance.

(1) Does the agreement not to dissolve the partnership prevent Orand from unilaterally dissolving the partnership? Discuss.

(2) What procedures, if any, are available to ensure a fair dissolution and winding up of the partnership? Discuss.

(3) Discuss the effectiveness of the contract clause barring a partner who dissolves the partnership from ever again selling insurance in the United States.

5/69; pp. 158-159

Q. Marshall, Watson and Gilbert are equal partners in a partnership. Watson suffered a severe stroke and decided to retire from the partnership. He offered to sell his interest in the partnership to Malloy who would become a member of the firm in Watson's stead. Marshall and Gilbert were both willing to accept Malloy as an equal partner. It was further agreed by the parties that the firm would continue to carry on its business in the usual manner without a winding up of its affairs. Watson's name was deleted from the firm name and Malloy's name was substituted in its place.

Malloy paid Watson $20,000 for his partnership interest, contributed $5,000 in capital and expressly assumed Watson's one-third share ($10,000) of existing partnership liabilities. The creditors of the partnership were duly given notice of the change in the composition of the partnership and of Malloy's assuming Watson's share of partnership liabilities.

(1) Did Watson effectively eliminate his liability to partnership creditors existing at the time he sold his interest if the partnership should become bankrupt? Explain.

(2) Is Malloy liable for more than his capital in the partnership to the firm creditors who were in existence prior to his becoming a partner? Explain.

(3) Has a dissolution of the firm occurred? Explain.

5/69; p. 159

PARTNERSHIPS: OBJECTIVE QUESTIONS

Each of the following numbered phrases or clauses states a legal conclusion relating to each lettered material. You are to determine whether **each** of the legal conclusions is true or false according to the Uniform Partnership and Limited Partnership Act. Your grade will be determined from your total net score obtained by deducting your total of incorrect answers from your total of correct answers; an omitted answer will not be considered an incorrect answer.

(1) Vaughn is a limited partner in the Maxwell, Wallace and Grand Limited Partnership, a real estate syndication. He purchased his interest

for $5,000 when the partnership was created. Subsequently he loaned the Partnership $8,000 for five years at 6 per cent interest. The Partnership has prospered and Vogel has offered to buy Vaughn's limited partnership interest for $6,500. The general partners are opposed to the sale because they dislike Vogel.

(a) A limited partnership is formed by compliance with state statutory requirements; it is not recognized at common law.
(b) As a limited partner Vaughn would only have personal liability after the Partnership assets and the assets of the general partners have been used to satisfy creditors.
(c) Active participation in the management of the Partnership would impose personal liability as a general partner on Vaughn.
(d) Vaughn could only sell his limited partnership interest with the consent of the general partners.
(e) Assuming a valid sale of Vaughn's entire limited partnership interest to Vogel, Vogel would automatically become a substituted limited partner.
(f) Since Vaughn is both a creditor and a partner of the Partnership, his loan would rank behind outside creditors upon dissolution.
(g) The death of Vaughn would cause a dissolution of the limited partnership.
(h) Vogel would have the right to be admitted as a general partner upon purchase of Vaughn's limited partnership interest.
(i) Vaughn's limited partnership interest is real property since the Partnership is a real estate venture.
(j) Vaughn would have the same rights as a general partner to inspect the Partnership books.

(2) Franklin, an accountant, has been retained by the creditors of the Wade Limited Partnership to prepare a balance sheet. There are three general partners, two of whom are hopelessly insolvent and one general partner, Sampson, who has $10,000 in assets and $8,000 in debts. There are twenty-five limited partners, all of whom are solvent. The Partnership has $8,000 in assets and $40,000 of liabilities. Each limited partner contributed $2,000 for his limited partnership interest with the exception of Wilson who agreed to contribute $2,000 but who only contributed $1,000.

(a) The Partnership creditors would be able to obtain $2,000 from Sampson.
(b) The limited partners would receive nothing in return for their capital contribution.
(c) The partnership creditors could obtain $1,000 from Wilson.
(d) If Wilson had permitted his surname to be used in the partnership name, i.e., Wade & Wilson, he would be liable to any partnership creditor who extended credit to the partnership without actual knowledge of the fact that he was not a general partner.
(e) The Partnership creditors could validly assert claims against the

property owned by the wives of the two insolvent general partners.

(3) The Viking Partnership consisted of seven equal partners. Wells, one of the partners, purchased six shares of the Azuma Dairy Farm Corporation stock. He used partnership funds to purchase the stock. Subsequently another share was purchased and each partner's capital account was debited for an amount equal to one-seventh of the total purchase price. Furthermore, Wells had indicated that each partner owned one share.

(a) There is a presumption that the stock is Partnership property in that Partnership funds were used.
(b) If the property is partnership property, an individual partner has no right to one of the shares.
(c) In the event of insolvency, the various firm and personal creditors would be interested in the question of the ownership of the property.
(d) Partnerships are precluded from investing in corporate stock.
(e) The stock in question would be held to belong to the individual partners and not the Partnership.

(4) Adams, Webster and Coke were partners in the construction business. Coke decided to retire and found Black who agreed to purchase his interest. Black was willing to pay Coke $20,000 and promise to assume Coke's share of all firm obligations.

(a) Unless the partners agree to admit Black as a partner, he could not become a member of the firm.
(b) The retirement of Coke would cause a dissolution of the firm.
(c) The firm creditors are third party beneficiaries of Black's promise to Coke.
(d) Coke would be released from all liability for firm debts if his interest were purchased by Black and Black promised to pay Coke's share of firm debts.
(e) If the other partners refused to accept Black as a partner, Coke could retire, thereby causing a dissolution and winding up.

(5) Carson, Crocket and Kitt were partners in the importing business. They needed additional capital to expand and located an investor named White who agreed to purchase a one quarter interest in the Partnership by contributing $50,000 in capital to the Partnership. At the time he became a partner there were several large creditors who had previously loaned money to the Partnership. The Partnership subsequently failed and the creditors are attempting to assert personal liability against White.

(a) White is personally liable on all firm debts contracted subsequent to his entry into the firm.
(b) Creditors of the first partnership automatically become creditors of the new partnership continuing the business.
(c) Creditors of the old firm which existed prior to White's entry cannot assert rights against his capital contribution.

(d) White has no personal liability for firm debts existing prior to his entry into the firm.
(e) If White agreed to pay the individual creditors at the time he entered the partnership, a novation would have occurred.

5/70

(6) Edward and Arnold, two brothers, inherited their deceased father's factory under the provisions of his will. The will provided that the brothers were to own the factory jointly and run it as partners. Edward and Arnold decided, however, that they did not wish to be partners. Instead, it was agreed between them that Edward, the older brother, would employ Arnold and pay him a portion of the profits from the business as a salary. Later Edward and Arnold decided that a partnership would be better and they orally agreed to be partners. A lawyer later drew a formal partnership agreement for the brothers. After executing the partnership agreement and leaving the lawyer's office Edward and Arnold orally agreed to change the terms of the agreement.

(a) Edward and Arnold became partners when their father's will took effect at his death.
(b) Edward and Arnold became obligated at the time their father executed his will to become partners upon his death.
(c) The arrangement for Edward to employ Arnold did not constitute a partnership.
(d) A partnership was created prior to the execution of the written partnership agreement by the oral agreement between Edward and Arnold.
(e) The written partnership agreement could not be orally modified.

(7) Five individuals gathered one evening to discuss the formation of an investment club to provide for joint stock investments. The suggestion was made that the investment club be formed as a partnership and this suggestion was unanimously adopted. Then other ideas were discussed.

It would be possible to have a partnership even if it was also decided that

(a) The investment club is to be a nonprofit organization donating all of its income to charity.
(b) The investment club is to be a profit-making organization and the gains on the sale of stocks are to be divided unequally among only three members with all dividends received going to the other two members.
(c) Only four of the individuals will make capital contributions.
(d) The investment club is not to employ any personnel on a salary basis.
(e) The investment club is not to be held out as a partnership to the public.

(8) The partners in a partnership composed of seven members have

differing views on several partnership issues. If the partnership agreement makes no provision for the number of partners required to decide particular issues, the necessary authority would exist

(a) To require the discharge of a clerk accused of stealing if only two partners are in favor.
(b) To cause the dissolution of the partnership if only three partners are in favor.
(c) To require the change of the partnership business from a wholesale to a retail operation if only four partners are in favor.
(d) To require the submission of a partnership claim to arbitration if only five partners are in favor.
(e) To submit to a confession of judgment on behalf of the partnership if only six partners are in favor.

(9) Alvin, Barry and Charles are in business together as partners. Alvin is the active manager of the business. Barry and Charles are wealthy and do not work in the business. Although the partnership is a financial success, Alvin has personal losses and an involuntary bankruptcy petition was filed against him by his individual creditors. Daniel offered to purchase Alvin's interest and to enter the partnership either as a working partner or as a nonworking partner.

(a) Alvin's individual creditors may not force the partnership into bankruptcy to gain access to Alvin's interest in the partnership.
(b) After being adjudicated a bankrupt, Alvin retains full power to deal with third persons and to bind the partnership so long as he acts in good faith.
(c) After Alvin is adjudicated a bankrupt, Barry and Charles may not continue to operate as a partnership without a dissolution even if a satisfactory agreement is reached to pay the value of Alvin's interest to the trustee in bankruptcy.
(d) Daniel may not enter the partnership as a nonworking partner because the partnership must have at least one member working in the business in a managerial capacity.
(e) If Daniel purchases Alvin's interest and enters the partnership as an active partner, Daniel will not be personally liable for partnership debts incurred while Alvin was a member of the partnership.

(10) Frank, Gerald and James are partners in an insurance brokerage firm. Their partnership agreement states that "profits earned by them are to be shared equally." Frank's father is a well-known insurance broker and Frank, without his father's knowledge, often represents to clients that his father is associated with the firm. Gerald, to make extra money, sells real estate on weekends over the objection of his fellow partners who feel that this part-time activity damages the image of the partnership. They informed Gerald that if he continues to sell real estate his profits from real estate sales must be turned over to the partnership. James was named as an executor in a will and is now administering the estate.

(a) Frank's father may be found to be a partner by estoppel.

(b) Gerald is violating his duty to the partnership by selling real estate.
(c) If Gerald continues to sell real estate he need not share his profits from real estate sales with his partners.
(d) James must share any income earned as executor with his partners.
(e) Each partner is free to render insurance brokerage services to nonpartnership clients after normal working hours and need not inform his partners of this or bring these clients to the partnership so long as he does not handle these matters during the normal working day or use partnership supplies.

(11) Jane, Carol, Edith and Alice formed a partnership. Capital contributions were: Jane, $13,000; Carol, $10,000; Edith, $5,000; and Alice made no capital contribution. There was no provision for sharing profits or losses in the partnership agreement. The partnership owes Jane $6,000 for a loan which has not been repaid. The assets of the partnership are worth $20,000 and the partnership owes $26,000 to trade creditors. The partners decide to terminate the partnership and Edith agrees to take charge of the liquidation. Upon liquidation
(a) Each partner must contribute an additional $1,500.
(b) Jane may demand interest on the loan she made to the partnership in the absence of any provision in the partnership agreement.
(c) Carol will not be required by the partners to make an additional contribution to the partnership to cover losses.
(d) The partners can agree that Edith will receive additional compensation for her work in liquidating the partnership.
(e) Unpaid creditors may not sue the individual partners while the partnership continues to remain in existence.

5/68

You are the CPA retained by Smith, Charles, and Black, who are in business together.

(12) Smith, Charles, and Black share profits and consider themselves partners. However, they are not actually members of a partnership until
(a) A certificate of doing business as a partnership is signed and filed.
(b) They agree to the duration of the partnership.
(c) A partnership office is formally opened in the state.
(d) A partnership agreement is signed.
(e) An income tax return is filed for the partnership.

(13) If Smith, Charles, and Black are partners
(a) Each is the agent of the other.
(b) Each is the agent of the partnership.
(c) Each is personally liable on contracts made for the partnership which are within the scope of the partnership business.

(d) Each partner has implied authority to confess a judgment where a sum of money is due and owing by the partnership without consulting the other partners.
(e) Each partner has implied authority to execute a general assignment for the benefit of creditors, where it is warranted, without consulting the other partners.

(14) If the partners have made no agreement to the contrary
(a) A majority vote of the partners may control decisions connected with the ordinary partnership business.
(b) All partners have equal rights in the management and conduct of the business regardless of the amount of experience or talent each may have.
(c) No partner is entitled to receive interest on monies lent by him to the partnership.
(d) Each partner must contribute to losses according to his share of profits.
(e) Profits will be divided in proportion to the amount of each partner's capital investment in the partnership.

(15) The accounting records of the partnership
(a) Should be kept at the principal place of business of the partnership unless otherwise agreed.
(b) Are open to inspection by any former partner at any time as an absolute right.
(c) Belong to the partner keeping the records.
(d) Are admissible in evidence against the interests of the partnership.
(e) Are closed to a former partner after his withdrawal from the partnership under all circumstances.

(16) If a new partner is to be admitted to the firm
(a) All present partners must agree that he is to be admitted.
(b) The old partnership is dissolved.
(c) The old partnership must be wound up and liquidated.
(d) The new partner is not liable in any manner for any pre-existing obligations of the partnership.
(e) The new partner is liable for pre-existing obligations of the partnership to the same extent as the other partners.

(17) The requisite capacity to join the partnership is possessed by
(a) Another partnership.
(b) A minor.
(c) A trustee.
(d) An estate.
(e) An insolvent person.

(18) If a partnership agreement provides that the partnership is to remain in force for a definite term
(a) The partnership cannot be dissolved before the expiration of that term.
(b) The partnership may only be dissolved by the unanimous consent of all of the partners.

(c) The death of any partner dissolves the partnership.
(d) Any partner has the power to dissolve the partnership at any time.
(e) Repudiation of the partnership by a partner before the end of the stipulated term may subject the partner to an action for breach of contract.

(19) If the partners decided to incorporate
(a) The partners would immediately upon dissolution of the partnership and incorporation have limited liability for all outstanding debts.
(b) The parties may be personally liable after incorporation to creditors who continue to deal with them without knowledge of their incorporation.
(c) A creditor may be held to have notice of the dissolution of a partnership from surrounding circumstances even if not told directly.
(d) Notice to all creditors of dissolution is generally deemed sufficient if given by publication.
(e) Sufficiency of a published notice to creditors will vary depending on whether a creditor has dealt with the partnership in the past.

(20) Upon the death of a partner
(a) The partnership is dissolved even if its term has not expired.
(b) The deceased partner's representative has a legal interest in the assets of the partnership.
(c) The deceased partner's representative has an equitable interest in the distribution of any surplus funds remaining after payment of firm debts.
(d) The deceased partner's representative does not have the right to demand an accounting.
(e) The rights and duties of the deceased's partner's personal representative may be governed by a partnership agreement.

(21) Upon the death of a partner
(a) His estate is liable so long as the deceased partner's name is continued to be used in the firm name.
(b) The right to use the deceased partner's name is part of the goodwill of the firm.
(c) The firm name passes to the surviving partners if they purchase and continue the business.
(d) Provision cannot be made in a partnership agreement for sale of the name upon the death of the partner.
(e) A court is powerless to enjoin the misuse of a deceased partner's name.

(22) In settling accounts between partners and creditors upon dissolution, among the items to be paid prior to satisfying the general creditors are
(a) Debts of creditors entitled to a preference.

(b) Debts owing to partners on account of loans made to the partnership.
(c) Amounts owing to partners in respect of capital investments.
(d) Debts of secured creditors which remain after exhausting any available security.
(e) Back salaries due to partners.

(23) The partnership is to be liquidated. Smith has contributed $6,000 to capital; Charles $3,000 to capital; and Black has made no contribution to capital but has merely contributed his services. Liabilities of the partnership exceed assets by $9,000. The following contributions must be made by the partners from their personal assets if there is no prior agreement on sharing losses:
(a) Smith need not make a contribution.
(b) Smith must contribute $3,000.
(c) Charles must contribute $3,000.
(d) Black must contribute $6,000.
(e) Black must contribute $3,000.

5/67

(24) A partnership can be created by
(a) Mutual consent.
(b) Estoppel.
(c) State statute.
(d) Congressional legislation.
(e) Operation of law.

(25) A competent person can, under ordinary circumstances, enter into a partnership relation with
(a) Another competent individual.
(b) A corporation.
(c) An existing partnership.
(d) A trust estate.
(e) An unincorporated association.

(26) A creditor of a trading partnership would be justified in assuming that Elmer, who sells for the firm, is a partner if the creditor knows that
(a) Elmer receives 10% of the net profits from all business which he brings into the firm.
(b) Elmer receives an annual bonus of 10% of the annual net profits of the firm.
(c) Elmer's sole compensation is 10% of the annual net profits of the firm.
(d) Elmer receives 10% of the gross receipts from all business which he brings into the firm.
(e) Elmer receives a stated percentage of the profits and bears an equal percentage of the losses of the firm.

(27) In the absence of an actual partnership, Carl could hold John liable as Frank's partner for an act done by Frank if

(a) John told Carl that he and Frank were partners.
(b) Frank told Carl that he and John were partners.
(c) Frank told Carl, in John's presence, that he and John were partners and John did not deny it.
(d) David told Carl that Frank and John were partners.
(e) David told Carl, in Frank's presence, that Frank and John were partners and Frank did not deny it.

(28) A limited partnership
(a) Can only be formed pursuant to statute.
(b) Must have at least one general partner.
(c) Gives to a limited partner complete immunity from liability for firm debts.
(d) Does not limit in any way the liability of a general partner for firm debts.
(e) Limits the liability of a limited partner to his contribution to the firm capital.

(29) Under ordinary circumstances property
(a) Originally invested into the partnership is partnership property.
(b) Acquired with partnership funds is partnership property.
(c) Belonging to the partnership can be taken and used by a partner for his individual purposes.
(d) Belonging to the partnership is considered to be owned by the partners as tenants in common.
(e) Consisting entirely of real estate may be acquired in the partnership name.

(30) Arm, Bran, and Coe are partners in a firm engaged in the manufacture and sale of electrical appliances. Arm signed a thirty-day negotiable note with the firm's depository bank in the partnership name. The action was contrary to an agreement among the partners. The bank could recover on the note from the firm if
(a) The note was given in payment for a shipment of toasters purchased by the firm.
(b) The partnership had paid such notes in the past.
(c) The partnership was a CPA firm instead of a manufacturing firm.
(d) The proceeds of the note were deposited in a special account held in the firm name.
(e) The partnership had previously notified the bank that notes given in the partnership name must bear the signature of at least two partners.

(31) If the partnership agreement contains no applicable provision, partners
(a) Have a right to an equal voice in the management of the business.
(b) Can deny to an individual partner all participation in the management of the business.
(c) Can resort to the courts for a settlement of a dispute arising

as to ordinary matters connected with the partnership business.

(d) May grant authority to one partner to manage the business.

(e) Must give unanimous consent to the making of a fundamental change in the conduct of the business.

(32) Edgar, Frank, and George are partners in a CPA firm. The partnership will be bound by George's act if George, without the consent of Edgar and Frank, should

(a) Hire an attorney to defend a malpractice suit against the firm.

(b) Purchase land with firm monies and in the firm name.

(c) Submit a partnership claim to arbitration.

(d) Enter into an agreement to combine their partnership with another partnership engaged in the practice of public accounting.

(e) Lease a suite of offices to be used by the firm.

(33) Able and Ben are partners in a trading firm. There are no articles of partnership and no oral agreement regarding their rights and duties as between them.

(a) Each partner owes a duty to disclose to the other all information material to the business.

(b) If Able sells his interest in the partnership to Ben, each owes a duty to disclose facts appearing on the books or records of the partnership.

(c) Ben will be entitled to wages provided that he spends more time than Able in carrying on the business.

(d) Either partner can engage in outside business activities which do not interfere with the performance of his partnership duties.

(e) Able is entitled to interest on any loans he makes to the firm.

(34) Martin, Lewis, and Davis are partners in a CPA firm. The firm and the other partners will be liable if

(a) Martin negligently causes an automobile accident while on his way to perform an audit.

(b) Lewis, in the transaction of firm business, fraudulently induces a third person to enter into an agreement.

(c) Davis, while on vacation, negligently causes a motor boat accident.

(d) Martin intentionally sets fire to Lewis' home.

(e) Davis misappropriates money of a third person held by the firm.

(35) The dissolution of a partnership

(a) Is tantamount to its termination.

(b) Will automatically occur upon the assignment by a partner of his interest in the firm.

(c) Will automatically occur upon the death of a partner.

(d) Will effectively discharge a partner's liability in respect to firm debts.

(e) Will subject the individual property of a deceased partner for all firm obligations incurred while he was a partner, subject to the prior payment of his separate debts.

TOPIC SIX | CORPORATIONS

CONTENTS | PAGE

CORPORATIONS. The AICPA description of corporations is contained in the discussion of forms of business organizations at the beginning of Agency (see p.124): "The third major area [of business law] is corporate law with emphasis on traditional state law regulation of the corporation as contrasted with federal regulation of the corporation. Included in the subject matter are corporate characteristics; incorporation; corporate rights, powers, and liabilities; corporate financing; directors' and officers' duties and liabilities; and stockholder rights." *

* Source: AICPA, *Information for CPA Candidates* (July 1970).

I. CHARACTERISTICS

A. Definition: an artificial person or legal entity created by or under the authority of an act of the legislature to accomplish some purpose which is authorized by the charter or governing statute.

B. Governing law.

1. State statutes regulate activities (e.g., formation, powers, liabilities, management) of corporations they charter.
2. State statutes conform to a general pattern but vary from state to state as to particulars.
3. Uniform statutes dealing with corporations:
   a. UCC Article 8 (Investment Securities).
   b. Uniform Business Corporation Act (adopted only in a few states).

C. Attributes.

1. Creation and regulation by the state.
2. Existence as a legal entity.
   a. Corporation exists separate and distinct from its stockholders, directors, officers, and employees.
      (1) Corporate property belongs to the corporation, not to the stockholders.
      (2) Corporate liabilities are liabilities of the corporation, not of its stockholders (limited liability for stockholders).
   b. Separate legal entity normally respected even if one stockholder owns all the shares.
   c. Where, however, legal entity is used to perpetrate a fraud or merely as the "agent" or "instrumentality" of its parent corporation, the courts may disregard it (i.e., "pierce the corporate veil").
3. Continuity of existence.
   a. Existence continues, regardless of death or incapacity of any of its directors, officers, or employees, and regardless of transfer of stock by shareholders.
   b. Existence may continue forever if the charter so provides.
4. Operates through its board of directors, officers, and other human agents.
5. Purposes for which corporation may be formed: generally for any lawful purpose, but cannot practice professions such as law, medicine, and so on.

6. Advantages of corporate form of business:
   a. Limited liability (see p. 195, VII.).
      (1) Stockholder is generally not liable for corporate debts.
      (2) Stockholder is not personally liable for acts of a corporation's directors, officers, or employees.
   b. Flexibility of financing: can issue common and preferred stocks and bonds in varying amounts to suit its needs and to conform to its investors' demands.
   c. Continuity of existence despite death of directors, stockholders, or officers.
   d. Transferability of shareholders' interests (may be sold, traded, given away, etc.).
   e. Relative attractiveness to investors; due to above advantages the corporation is generally favored by investors.
   f. Concentration of business strength through right to act as legal entity.
7. Disadvantages of corporate form of business:
   a. Expense: fees for incorporating.
   b. Taxation:
      (1) State franchise tax, stock issuance, and transfer taxes.
      (2) Federal and state income tax burden may be heavier for corporations than for individuals in the lower tax brackets.
   c. Scope of authority: limited by express powers contained in charter.
      (1) When a corporation is acting beyond its powers it is said to be acting *ultra vires*.
      (2) This problem has been diminished by the current practice of drafting the corporate charter so broadly as to permit the corporation to do anything within reason.
   d. Right to do business in other states is subject to limitations imposed on foreign corporations by individual states (see p. 199, IX.).
   e. Greater governmental supervision.
   f. Denied right to practice most professions.
8. Comparison with other associations (partnerships, joint ventures, joint stock associations, business trust, and limited partnership): see Partnerships, p. 150, I.C.

D. Classification.

1. Public corporation: corporation created as an agency of the state for governmental purposes.

a. Municipal corporation: includes any county, town, school district, village, city, or other territorial division of the state established by law with powers of local government.

b. Public-benefit corporation: any corporation organized to construct or operate a public improvement in which the profits inure to the benefit of the government (e.g., a state-operated bridge); stock of which is typically owned entirely or largely by the government.

2. Quasi-public corporation (public utility): engaged in rendering service of such general public importance as to justify privilege of eminent domain and amenability to public regulation under public power.

3. Private: organized for non-governmental purposes.

   a. Stock corporation: one having shares of stock and authorized by law to distribute dividends to holders.

   b. Nonstock corporation (membership corporation): includes every other private corporation (e.g., athletic clubs, co-op apartments).

   c. Many states provide for the formation of charitable, educational, social, and other non-profit corporations.

4. Domestic: A corporation doing business in the state wherein it was incorporated is a domestic corporation in that state.

5. Foreign: A corporation doing business in any states other than that in which it was incorporated is a foreign corporation in all such states (see p. 199, IX.).

6. Closed corporation: one whose stock is closely held by a limited number of persons. Normally restrictions are placed upon the transfer of stock in closely held corporations in order to prevent outsiders from becoming shareholders.

II. PROMOTION, INCORPORATION, AND ORGANIZATION

A. Promotion.

1. Relates to plans and steps which precede and determine the formation, purpose, and structure of a corporation and the way its shares and interests are to be issued and distributed.

2. Promoter.

   a. Definition: the person who takes the preliminary steps to organize a corporation, such as issuing its prospectus, procuring stock subscriptions, and securing a charter.

   b. Responsibility for profits: The promoter is in a highly fiduciary relationship to the corporation and is not permitted to make secret profits at the expense of the corporation or its subscribers.

3. Corporate liability for promoter's contracts.
   a. Promoter is not the agent for the corporation since one cannot be the agent for a nonexistent principal.
   b. Corporation not bound unless and until it approves and thereby adopts the agreement upon coming into corporate existence.
   c. Without corporation's approval, promoter alone is bound, unless contrary intent was clearly understood.
   d. Adoption of contract, if it occurs, should be reflected in corporate minutes. However, adoption may also be inferred from corporate conduct (i.e., acceptance of the benefits).
4. Corporation's liability for promoter's services: no liability for pre-incorporation services unless the board of directors approves payment after the corporation comes into existence.

B. Incorporation.

1. Relates to the legal steps by which a corporation is brought into existence.
2. Source of authority:
   a. Sovereign power to grant corporate charters vested in states.
   b. Federal government can grant charters only as an incident to the conduct of its own business (e.g., Federal Bank, T.V.A.).
   c. Charters are granted subject to the right of the state at any time to repeal, alter, or amend.
   d. *De jure* corporation: one duly and properly formed under the law.
   e. *De facto* corporation: see p. 183, II.D.
   f. Corporation by estoppel: an equitable doctrine to prevent injustice wherein a party has acted to his detriment in reliance on corporate existence; therefore, a corporation will be deemed to exist for the purpose of a specific transaction, even where the elements of a *de facto* corporation are missing.
3. Qualifications of incorporators:
   a. Vary from state to state. Incorporators must look to state law in order to insure fulfillment of any particular state's requirements.
   b. Most states require one or more natural persons of 21 years or over and who are United States citizens.
4. Contents of certificate of incorporation:
   a. Proposed name (must not have the same name as, or bear too

close a resemblance to, the name of another corporation incorporated within the state, and must indicate its corporate status).

b. Purpose, objects, and powers (current practice is to draft these as broadly as possible).

c. Capital structure (including amount, types, par or no-par, etc.).

d. Location of principal office.

e. Duration.

f. Directors.

g. Subscribers to stock.

h. Designation of agent for service of process (usually secretary of state where incorporated, in addition to any other agent).

C. Organization.

1. First meeting of incorporators.
   a. "Dummies" (persons used for convenience in incorporating and who have no real interest in the corporation), if they are used in incorporating, assign their stock subscriptions to the true stockholders in interest.
   b. Issuance of stock which was authorized.
   c. Bank designated as depository.
2. Bylaws.
   a. Govern conduct of corporation and are binding upon the directors and officers.
   b. Generally, are adopted by the incorporators or directors at the first meeting, subject to any bylaws stockholders may adopt; bylaws can be altered by the board if the charter so provides.
3. First meeting of directors.
   a. Usually follows immediately after first meeting of incorporators.
   b. Directors select officers. (Corporation is now ready to do business.)
   c. Bylaws adopted.

D. *De facto* corporations.

1. A *de facto* corporation is deemed to exist, although not properly formed under the law, when:
   a. There is a *valid* law in existence under which such a corporation can be formed. (E.g., a corporation which was formed under an unconstitutional statute would not have the status of

a *de facto* corporation after the statute was declared unconstitutional.)

b. There has been a bona fide attempt to organize.

c. Some minor error or omission was made in the process of incorporation.

d. There has been an exercise or use of the corporate powers.

2. The shareholders of a *de facto* corporation have limited liability.
3. If the above requirements are not fulfilled, the general rule is that the parties concerned will be treated as partners, and they will be liable for the "corporation's" debts as general partners.
4. The status of a *de facto* corporation in general is that of a valid and existing legal entity which may not be attacked collaterally by any party but which may be attacked directly by the state (i.e., an action brought by the state to specifically question the right of the association to be a corporation).

III. CAPITAL STOCK

A. Capital: that portion of the value of property actually received by corporation for stock it issues, based upon the par value or the arbitrarily stated value of no-par stock.

B. Shares of capital stock:

1. Represent the interest the holder has in the corporation; give the holder no right to particular corporate property.
2. Issued in the form of stock certificates (shares).
3. Stockholder has a pre-emptive right to subscribe to all newly authorized issues of stock in order to maintain his equity or proportionate share of stock in the corporation; however, it is possible to negate this right by a provision in the corporate charter.
4. "Blue sky" laws: a popular name for state acts which provide for the regulation and supervision of the sale of stock and which aim at the protection of the investing public (e.g., protect the investor from investing in fraudulent corporations).
5. Types of stock:
   a. Par value stock: stock given a fixed arbitrary value, such as $1.00 per share, which is allocated to the capital account; excess of purchase price over par value is allocated to capital surplus.
   b. No-par stock: stock that has no fixed par value given to it; state statutes require that part of the price received for no-par stock be allocated to capital stock account.

c. Authorized stock: maximum amount of stock that a corporation is authorized by its charter to issue.

d. Issued stock: part of authorized stock for which certificates are made out and delivered.

e. Outstanding stock: issued stock in the hands of stockholders.

f. Unissued stock: stock which is authorized but as yet not issued.

g. Treasury stock: stock which is authorized, issued, but not outstanding.

(1) Issued stock returned to or required by the corporation.

(2) A corporation can only purchase its own stock out of surplus as permitted by state law to be used for this purpose (e.g., earned surplus, capital, or paid-in surplus); sale or purchase by a corporation of its own stock usually does not result in a taxable gain or deductible loss.

(3) Corporation cannot vote its treasury stock.

(4) Corporation may resell treasury stock without regard to par value or pre-emptive rights.

(5) Does not participate in dividends or distributions.

C. Classes of stock:

1. Common: Stockholder has the right to vote on the basis of one vote per share, unless common stock is designated non-voting, but has no right to dividends unless directors, in their discretion, declare them.

2. Preferred: Stockholder is given some kind of preference over another class of stock. Dividends are still discretionary.

   a. Normally preferences relate to a fixed dividend rate and distribution of assets upon dissolution.

   b. Cumulative preferred: If the amount of a fixed dividend is not paid, the obligation to pay it continues and accumulates; common cannot receive dividends until all accumulations have been paid.

   c. Non-cumulative preferred: If a dividend is not declared in any given year, the obligation to pay it ceases even though it is earned (provided there is a valid business reason for retention of the earnings).

   d. Participating preferred: participates in earnings over and above the amount necessary to pay dividends on the preferred; the remainder may be distributed to both preferred and common, usually on a percentage basis.

e. Voting rights:

(1) Preferred has the same voting rights as common unless the certificate of incorporation provides otherwise.

(2) Normally the certificate of incorporation provides that preferred has no voting rights unless there is default in payment of preferred dividends.

3. Redeemable (callable): subject to redemption (recall by the corporation) at a fixed price, which is usually above the issue price paid to the corporation by the stockholder.
4. Convertible: Preferred stockholders are given an option to convert into common stock.

D. Stock subscriptions.

1. Definition: contract to take and pay for a certain number of shares of capital stock of a corporation already organized or to be organized.
2. Legal effect:
   a. Ordinarily is an offer to buy stock and may be withdrawn prior to acceptance by the corporation.
   b. Not binding on the subscriber until accepted by the corporation (i.e., the corporation is in existence and the subscription is approved).

   (1) May be made binding by use of such devices as "irrevocable" power of attorney, escrow deposits, underwriting agreements, etc.

   (2) Some states by statute make subscriptions irrevocable for a stated time.

   c. Upon acceptance, subscriber becomes liable, not merely on his subscription, but as a stockholder.

E. Contract to purchase stock:

1. Executory agreement to subscribe to stock in the future; it is not a subscription.
2. Purchaser becomes liable as a stockholder only when certificate is tendered and price is paid.
3. If party fails to perform, he is liable for breach of contract.

F. Consideration for which stock may be issued:

1. Original par value stock: at least for its full par value in cash, property, or services.
   a. Outstanding capital stock is said to be *watered* if:

(1) Cash given for it was less than its par value, or
(2) Property or services were given for it whose true worth was less than the stock's par value.

b. For liability of original purchases of watered stock see p. 195, VII. B. 1.

2. Original no-par value stock: for such consideration as represents fair market value of the shares.

G. Corporate bonds.

1. Definition: a certificate or evidence of debt, with a stated interest payable at some fixed time or intervals and principal payable at face value at maturity.
2. Owners of bonds are creditors of the corporation.

IV. DIRECTORS

A. Principal duties and powers of directors:

1. Establish and guide policies of the corporation.
2. Select officers of the corporation.
   a. Furnish authority for officers' major acts.
   b. Supervise officers' conduct generally.
3. Determine whether to declare dividends.
4. Act when meeting as a board (i.e., usually must act as a unit), with the requisite number of directors present so as to constitute a quorum. A director acting in his individual capacity as a director has no power to bind the corporation.
5. Have implied power to do what is required for full discharge of their duties.
6. Directors are guided and limited by the charter, bylaws, and governing statutes.
7. One who continuously exercises the powers and duties of a director and who holds or purports to hold office under some colorable claim of an election, appointment, or a holding over in office is a *de facto* director.

B. Delegation of duties by directors:

1. May not vote by proxy in relation to discretionary powers but may delegate ministerial (routine) duties to others.
2. Executive committee: a device which, unless prohibited, permits a part of the entire board to act in designated matters. Full board delegates some of its powers to an executive committee.

C. Meetings of directors.

1. May be held outside state of incorporation. (Majority of states so permit.)
2. Parliamentary usage generally governs.
3. Must meet as a unit and conform to the procedures required by law and as set forth in the charter and bylaws. (E.g., there must be a quorum of the board present, which usually means a majority.)

D. Compensation of directors.

1. Not ordinarily entitled to compensation unless there is some provision for it in the charter or bylaws (bylaws invariably call for such compensation).
2. Entitled to compensation if services are rendered in a capacity other than that of director (e.g., if X, a director, renders services as a lawyer).
3. A retroactive voting of compensation for directors is voidable.

E. Tenure of office.

1. Director's term cannot be abridged, except for cause, without the director's consent; however, bylaws may provide that directors can be removed at any time and without cause by a vote of the other directors or shareholders.
2. Statutes generally limit tenure so as to require periodic re-election.
3. Directors whose terms have expired hold over until their successors are chosen, or until they resign or are removed.
4. It is against public policy to contrive to perpetuate directors in office by agreement or by dispensing with elections; however, it is not illegal for stockholders to unite upon a common policy for the election of certain directors (e.g., a voting trust).
5. Even though a statute or the corporate charter or a bylaw provides that tenure shall continue until a qualified successor is duly elected or appointed, a director may, nevertheless, resign at any time.
6. Personal bankruptcy of a director does not disqualify him from holding office.

F. Liability of directors.

1. Transactions with the corporation:
   a. Directors are said to be under a "fiduciary" duty to the corporation, and they will be liable for any breach of this duty.

b. Directors may deal with the corporation only if they do so openly and in good faith, i.e., permitting an "independent" majority to decide, free from the interested parties' influence. (E.g., X, a director of the Y corporation, votes for the adoption of a contract which will benefit him personally. If X's vote was necessary to constitute a majority, the contract is voidable at the option of the Y corporation.)

c. If a profit is derived at corporation's expense, party profiting must account to the corporation for such profit.

2. Liability of directors in other common situations:

a. For negligence:

(1) Not responsible for mistakes of judgment unless decisions are so patently wrong as to indicate negligence or lack of reasonable intelligence.
(2) Test is whether a director acted as a reasonably prudent and intelligent man would act in his own affairs.

(3) Directors may be negligent in failing to detect and prevent wrongs by co-directors.

b. Directors of a nonexistent or defectively formed corporation (i.e., one which is neither *de jure* nor *de facto*), are personally liable when acting for such a body.

c. For preferential transfers: Directors responsible are liable.

d. For loans to stockholders: Many state statutes expressly forbid such transactions and make the director personally liable for loans made by the corporation to its stockholders.

e. In connection with the acquisition of treasury stock, directors are personally liable if stock is acquired out of any corporate funds other than surplus as the state corporation law specifies.

f. For declaring dividends which impair the capital of the corporations, directors are personally liable.

g. For *ultra vires* acts of the corporation, directors are personally liable unless they have indicated their dissent to such acts.

3. For additional liability of directors, see Federal Securities Regulations.

V. OFFICERS

A. Distinguished from directors:

1. Officers are individual agents of the corporation.

2. Each officer may bind the corporation by his individual acts within the actual or apparent scope of his authority, whereas an individual director, by virtue of his office alone, cannot legally bind the corporation.

B. Selection and tenure:

1. Selected by directors for a definite term fixed in the bylaws, statute, or charter; some states permit shareholder to elect officers if so provided in certificate.
2. If no term is so fixed, officers are removable at the pleasure of the directors.

C. President:

1. Presides at shareholders' and directors' meetings.
2. Signs certificates of stock and major commitments on behalf of the corporation.
3. Usually must be a director.

D. Compensation: fixed by resolution of the board of directors; if none is so fixed, the law will imply that officer, who is not a director, is to be paid a reasonable remuneration for his services.

E. Officers' liability to the corporation is governed by the general rules of agency (see Agency, p.130, III.B.).

VI. RIGHTS OF STOCKHOLDERS

A. Stockholder: one recognized as the true owner of stock.

1. At law: one who holds the stock directly.
2. In equity: one for whose benefit stock is held by another.
3. Methods of acquiring stock:
   a. By original issue.
   b. By purchase of treasury stock.
   c. By stock transfer from an existing stockholder.

B. Stockholder's rights commence:

1. When one becomes the true owner of the stock either at law or in equity.
   a. In the case of a present subscription, when said subscription has been accepted by the corporation.
   b. In the case of a contract to purchase, upon payment of the purchase price and delivery of the certificate.
2. As between old and new stockholder: as soon as new stockholder buys the stock.
3. As between corporation and new stockholder:
   a. Latter not recognized as a stockholder until transfer is registered on corporate books.

b. Stockholder may institute suit to compel corporation to make the transfer on the corporate books.

C. **Rights and privileges of a stockholder:**

1. Right to a stock certificate.
2. Right to transfer stock.
   a. By delivering certificate duly indorsed.
   b. By delivering certificate accompanied by a separate assignment.
   c. In a. and b. above, a transfer on the books of the corporation is not required to validly transfer legal title; however, a bona fide payment of dividends by the corporation to the holder of record will be good as against the real owner.
   d. Limitations upon right to transfer stock may be imposed by charter, bylaw, or special contract.

      (1) Restrictions must be reasonable.

      (2) Restrictions may be placed upon holders of unpaid stock, or a stockholder may not be allowed to sell his stock to a third party without first giving the corporation or the other stockholders the option of buying it.

      (3) The Uniform Commercial Code requires that any restriction or transfer be conspicuously noted on the certificate if such restrictions are to bind an innocent third party.

      (4) A statement on the stock certificate to the effect that the stock is "transferable only on the books of the corporation" does not prevent transfer as between old and new stockholders in a. or b. above, even though the transfer has not been made on the corporate books.
3. Right to vote.
   a. Governed by the charter.

      (1) If the charter is silent on the rights of the different classes of stock, both preferred and common have equal voting rights.

      (2) Usual provision is that only common may vote.

      (3) If dividends remain unpaid for specified period on the preferred stock, preferred stockholders may be given the right to vote and participate in control of the corporation or to take over control.

      (4) Normally one vote is allowed for each director for each share of stock held.

      (5) Cumulative voting may be required by statute or be provided for in the charter.

(A) Each stockholder may multiply the number of shares he owns by number of directors to be elected, and the total may be cast for a single director or a number of directors. (E.g., X has 100 shares of stock and five directors are to be elected. X has a total of 500 votes, all of which may be cast for one or split among several of the candidates.)

(B) By the use of cumulative voting the minority is given an opportunity to place one or more of its members on the board of directors.

b. Governed by the bylaw provisions: Bylaws may require that certain corporate acts be authorized or approved by the stockholders or they will be invalid.

c. Governed by statute:

(1) If a charter or bylaw provision conflicts with a statutory provision regarding the stockholder's right to vote, the former is invalid.

(2) Since the requirements vary from state to state, the corporate law of the particular state must be consulted.

(3) Some corporate acts require approval of a majority (e.g., increasing or reducing capital stock; changing corporate headquarters).

(4) Other corporate acts require a two-thirds vote or approval (e.g., merging or consolidating with another corporation; dissolving the corporation; selling all or substantially all of the corporate assets).

d. Minority stockholders must abide by a decision of majority but may seek to restrain the majority from exercising control when the proposed action is:

(1) To the detriment of the corporation, or

(2) *Ultra vires,* or

(3) In violation of the charter, bylaws, or statute, or

(4) Illegal or fraudulent (as to suits brought by stockholders—see p. 195, VI.C.9.).

4. Right to have and participate in stockholders' meetings:

a. Regular: annual meeting as fixed in the bylaws.

b. Special: additional meetings called to handle matters requiring special attention.

c. Minutes: records of meetings which must be kept in the minutes book.

d. Quorum: the number of votes necessary to validate a meeting, normally a majority of the entire body.

e. Proxy: power of attorney given by a stockholder authorizing a designated person to cast the stockholder's ballot; proxies may not be redelegated without express permission.

f. Voting trust: agreement by which stockholders surrender their voting power and place it irrevocably in the hands of others to vote as they see fit; approved by public policy, but statutes considerably limit their operations particularly as to duration (e.g., ten years).

5. Right to dividends.

a. Payment of dividends (except liquidating dividends) must not impair capital as defined in corporation statutes (i.e., may be paid only out of surplus).

b. Except where dividends are somehow guaranteed, a stockholder has no inherent right to a dividend until one is declared.

c. When stockholders may compel the declaration of a dividend:

(1) Normally determination of whether to declare a dividend is within the exclusive discretion of the board of directors.

(2) However, when there is a surplus together with adequate cash, stockholders may be able to compel declaration of dividends if directors are withholding the dividends dishonestly, or out of spite, or for their own private purposes, or for some other reason which is a *clear abuse of discretion.*

d. Dividends normally will be made payable to the stockholders of record on a given date.

e. Corporation may refuse to recognize a stockholder of record if his stock is not fully paid for.

f. Dividends illegally declared and paid may be recovered by the corporation, a stockholder in the name of the corporation, judgment creditors of the corporation, or by a trustee in bankruptcy.

g. Dividends become a *debt* of the corporation as soon as declared, provided they are properly declared and public notice is given; dividends are irrevocable and cannot be recalled except when:

(1) The declaration is illegal, *ultra vires,* in fraud of creditors, or

(2) It is revoked at the same meeting in which it was declared, or

(3) It is payable in the future and the declaration has not been made public or communicated to the stockholders, or

(4) A stock dividend is declared and the stock has not been issued.

h. Dividends may be either:

(1) Secured: A dividend is a secured debt only if a specific fund has been set aside for payment, or

(2) Unsecured: If no fund is set aside out of which payment is to be made after the declaration of a dividend, the stockholder is only a general creditor.

6. Right to inspect the books, records, and stocklists.

a. Most jurisdictions have enacted statutes specifically defining which books, records, and stocklists must be kept for the purpose of permitting inspections by shareholders; it is both necessary (e.g., for tax purposes) and desirable that the following books be maintained at the corporation's principal place of business:

(1) Minute books of the directors' meetings.

(2) Stock certificate book (may be kept with the transfer agent).

(3) Stock ledgers.

(4) General books of account.

(5) Other records and files containing accurate records of corporate affairs. (Under the "business entry" rule, all the above books and records are admissible in evidence if kept by the corporation in the regular course of business although, ordinarily, evidence not given under oath is not permitted.)

b. A stockholder has a common law right to inspect the books of account, records, stocklists, etc., for any legitimate purpose. The right may not be denied unless the corporation can show that the stockholder's motive in seeking to inspect the books is for an unwarranted purpose (e.g., to obtain a stocklist for its commercial value), for a purpose hostile to corporation (e.g., to aid a competitor), or to gratify idle curiosity.

c. If the corporate officers wrongfully refuse to allow an inspection, the stockholder may obtain an injunction from the court ordering the corporation to open its books to the shareholder; some states also provide for fines against those parties who wrongfully deny the right of inspection.

d. A stockholder may bring an attorney and an accountant to aid him in the inspection, and transcripts may be made.

7. Right to financial statements.

a. Not generally prescribed by state statute — but see Federal Securities Regulation, p. 278.

b. Corporate practice varies widely.

c. In some states, stockholders owning a given percentage of stock are entitled by law to financial statements.

8. Pre-emptive right.
   a. Right to subscribe to new stock (newly authorized) in proportion to stockholder's existing holdings, before such stock is offered to the public.
   b. Right does not generally attach to treasury stock sold to the public.
   c. Preferred stockholders generally do not have pre-emptive rights.
   d. State statutes permit the corporation to negate the pre-emptive right by so providing in the corporate charter.
   e. In the event of a reduction of capital stock outstanding, the shareholders would have their proportionate number of shares reduced on a pro rata basis.
9. Right to sue.
   a. A shareholder in his own right may be able to obtain injunctive relief in the nature of an order prohibiting a transaction which is fraudulent, *ultra vires,* or detrimental to the continued existence of the corporation.
   b. A derivative action may be brought by a shareholder in the name of and for the benefit of the corporation against directors, officers, and others to recover damages. Any recovery goes to the corporation or is held by the stockholder in trust for the corporation's benefit.
   c. Before a shareholder may sue derivatively he must make a demand on the directors or officers to sue unless such demand would be useless, and thus excuse him from this requirement.
10. Rights on dissolution: A stockholder is entitled to a pro rata distribution of net assets after payment of debts. Preferred stock, however, may be given a preferential right on distribution.
11. Right to an appraisal and purchase of stock by the corporation: This right is available to dissenting stockholders when a fundamental corporate change is undertaken, such as a merger or consolidation.

VII. STOCKHOLDER'S LIMITED LIABILITY

A. Stockholders have no general liability for the corporation's debts; the extent of loss is, thus, normally limited to capital investment.

B. Stockholder may become specially liable to creditors over and above original capital investment:

1. Where stock is sold on original issue for less than its par value, the original purchaser may be liable for the difference between the issue price and par value.
   a. Subsequent purchaser will not be so liable provided he had no notice that stock was issued for less than par value.

2. For the unpaid balance on no-par value stock.
3. For dividends paid which impair capital.
4. For unpaid wages:
   a. Some statutes specifically provide that stockholders will be liable to employees, in excess of their capital contributions, for unpaid wages. The statutes have been construed to preclude high-salaried officers from coverage.

VIII. CORPORATE RIGHTS, POWERS, AND LIABILITIES

A. Corporate rights as a legal entity:

1. To buy, own, hold, and sell property.
2. To make contracts through its human agents in the corporate name.
3. To sue and be sued in its own name.
4. To have exclusive use of its corporate name in the jurisdiction.
5. To have a corporate seal.

B. Scope of corporate powers:

1. Those expressly conferred by its charter, and
2. Those which may be reasonably implied therefrom in order to carry out the corporate objects and purposes.
   a. Acts within its express or implied powers are *intra vires*.
   b. Acts outside its express or implied powers are *ultra vires* (see p. 198, VIII.D.2.).
3. General powers which every corporation is deemed to possess:
   a. Power to have succession or continued existence for the period stated in its charter; this may be perpetual.
   b. Power to take, hold, sell, and convey real and personal property for corporate purposes.
   c. Power to make bylaws not inconsistent with law:
      (1) For management of the business.
      (2) For transfer of stock.
      (3) For regulation of its affairs.
   d. Power to appoint such officers and agents as are necessary and to fix their compensation.

C. Law limits corporation in respect to the following rights, powers, and functions:

1. Right to become a partner: A majority of states deny the corporation the right to enter into a partnership; however, some states

permit this by statute and all states recognize that a corporation may be estopped to deny it.

2. Right to buy its own stock: Even without express authorization in the charter, a corporation may acquire and hold its own stock provided:
   a. Transaction is fair and made in good faith.
   b. Transaction is not fraudulent.
   c. Rights of creditors and stockholders will not be prejudiced by the purchase.
   d. Purchase is made out of existing, earned, and/or capital surplus as state law provides.
   e. Purchase will not cause the corporation to become insolvent.
   f. Corporation is not in the process of dissolution.
3. Right to buy stock in other corporations:
   a. Generally, corporation cannot buy stock in another corporation unless such power has been *expressly* granted to it in its charter or is necessarily implied from its existence.
   b. Statutes in some states authorize such purchases provided:
      (1) Power is *expressly* conferred by charter, or
      (2) Corporation whose stock is acquired is engaged in business similar to that of acquiring corporation so that acquisition is reasonably incidental and necessary to express objects and purpose of latter.
4. Power to lend money:
   a. Ordinarily corporation has no such power unless authorized to do so by charter, pursuant to statute.
   b. Corporation may lend money if it is necessary to do so as an incidental part of its normal functions and powers.
5. Power to guarantee obligations: ordinarily no such power unless:
   a. Guaranty and surety bonds are issued by a company engaged in such business.
   b. If the corporation owns negotiable paper it may indorse it.
   c. The corporation is the parent corporation (i.e., owns over 50% of another corporation); then the parent may guarantee an obligation of the subsidiary.
6. Power to indorse for accommodation: Corporation cannot indorse negotiable paper for another's accommodation, and one who accepts a negotiable instrument with such an indorsement cannot hold the corporation.
7. No right to practice most professions (e.g., law, medicine, accounting).

D. Corporate liability.

1. Contracts:
   a. A corporation is liable for contracts made by its agents within the scope of their express authority. Apparent authority of officers to make binding contracts is strictly construed so that those dealing with officers of corporations should make sure of their authority.
   b. Corporation is not liable on contracts made in its behalf prior to incorporation, unless such contracts are expressly or implicitly adopted (see p. 182, II.A.3.).
   c. Corporation not liable on illegal contracts.
2. *Ultra vires* acts:
   a. Where neither corporation nor third party has performed, neither party can enforce an *ultra vires* contract against the other.
   b. Where both parties have performed, neither party may sue to rescind an *ultra vires* contract.
   c. Where an *ultra vires* contract has been executed on one side but not on the other, the majority of state courts hold that party receiving full performance is estopped from raising the defense of *ultra vires*.
   d. Where there has been part performance on both sides, the law generally enforces the contract only to the extent that it has been performed.
   e. Either the state, via the attorney general, or a stockholder has the requisite standing in court to object to an *ultra vires* act; a competitor could not so object.
3. Unauthorized acts of officers:
   a. Corporation is liable for such acts, provided they are customarily delegated to such officers.
   b. Restrictions on authority:

      (1) If contained in bylaws, third parties not bound unless they have actual knowledge of those bylaws.

      (2) Third parties are chargeable with knowledge of legal restrictions and any restrictions in the certificate of incorporation.
4. Torts:
   a. Corporation is liable for all torts committed by its officers, agents, or employees during course and within the scope of their corporate duties.

b. It is no defense that the acts or transactions in connection with which such torts occurred were *ultra vires*.

5. Crimes:

a. Corporations are capable of committing some crimes (e.g., violating labor or antitrust statute), but generally corporations cannot commit crimes applicable only to human beings (e.g., bigamy, homicide).

b. Punishment typically is in the form of fines or forfeiture of charter, since the corporation, a fictitious being, cannot be imprisoned.

IX. FOREIGN CORPORATIONS

A. License requirements in order to qualify to "do business" in a state other than that of incorporation:

1. Depend on the laws of the particular state where the corporation is doing business.
2. Usual procedure requires filing a certificate in the state, with information about the corporation, and payment of a registration fee.

B. What constitutes "doing business":

1. To constitute "doing business" there must be a more or less permanent and continuous business.
2. Isolated transactions normally do not constitute "doing business."

C. Penalties and deprivations for "doing business" without a license:

1. Foreign corporation may be fined.
2. Foreign corporation may be deprived of right to sue in such state.
3. Personal liabilities and penalties are imposed by some states upon stockholders, directors, and officers.

X. MERGERS AND CONSOLIDATIONS

A. Merger: the union of two or more corporations by the transfer of one or more corporations to another (the possessor corporation) which continues in existence, the other or others being dissolved and merged therein.

1. All the property, rights, privileges, and franchises of the merged corporation shall vest in and be enjoyed by the possessor corporation but subject to all the liabilities of the merged corporation and the rights of its creditors.

2. Stockholder approval must be obtained; usually at least two-thirds of the stockholders must agree to the merger (or consolidation) with dissenting stockholders having a right to an appraisal (see p. 200, X.B.3.).

B. Consolidation: a unifying of two or more corporations into a *single new* corporation; takes place when two or more corporations are extinguished, and by the same process a new one is formed, taking over the assets and assuming the liabilities of those passing out of existence.

1. The new corporation succeeds to all the rights, franchises, and privileges of each of the consolidating corporations, and upon consummation of the consolidation, all property of each consolidating corporation automatically vests in the new corporation.
2. The rights of creditors of the consolidating corporations are in no way impaired by the consolidation, and the new corporation succeeds to all debts and liabilities existing against the consolidating corporations.
3. Dissenting stockholder's right of appraisal: Any stockholder not in favor of the consolidation or merger may, at any time prior to the vote on the plan of consolidation or merger, object to it; claim the right of an appraisal of the fair market value of his stock; and obtain payment for his stock.
   a. Mergers and consolidations are strictly governed by state statute as to the formalities to be complied with; local state law must be consulted. Moreover, mergers and consolidations must always be considered in the light of existing antitrust and tax laws.

XI. REORGANIZATION

A. Definition: rearrangement of interests of creditors and security-holders, often through the formation of a new corporation organized to take over the assets and liabilities and to conduct the business of the old one.

B. Purpose: to adjust the capital and debt structure of the corporation at a minimum sacrifice to the stockholders, bondholders, and unsecured creditors, so as to permit the corporation to carry on the business instead of going into bankruptcy, thereby avoiding losses entailed by a forced liquidation.

C. May be brought about in the following ways:

1. Voluntarily, by agreement of all parties.
2. By forced or judicial sale upon foreclosure.
3. By decree without sale.
4. By proceedings under the National Bankruptcy Act (see Bankruptcy, p. 360, I.C.5.).

XII. DISSOLUTION

A. Definition: the termination of corporation's existence by surrender, forfeiture, cancellation, or other extinguishment of its charter so that not only are the corporation's affairs wound up and its assets distributed among creditors and stockholders, but corporation ceases to exist as a legal entity.

B. Dissolution does not result from:

1. Sale of corporation's entire assets, or
2. Appointment of a receiver, or
3. Assignment for benefit of creditors.

C. Voluntary dissolution: brought about by corporation itself.

1. Expiration of duration for corporate existence as specified in the charter.
2. Merger or consolidation (see p. 199, X.).
3. Filing of certificate to bring about surrender of the charter, without a judicial proceeding, may be done by:
   a. Incorporators prior to commencement of business or issuance of shares, or
   b. Written consent of all outstanding stockholders, or
   c. Resolution at a stockholders' meeting upon a minimum required vote of approval.
4. Judicial proceedings on petition of stockholders: Petition must show that a dissolution is desirable in the interests of the corporation (e.g., when corporation is hopelessly deadlocked).
5. Unless a receiver is appointed by the court, the directors at the time of dissolution act as trustees for the creditors and stockholders to wind up the corporate affairs.

D. Involuntary dissolution:

1. May be brought about by the state, acting through the attorney general, upon one of the following grounds:
   a. Non-user. (E.g., corporation fails to organize, commence business, or undertake its duties within a given period or ceases to function over a long period.)
   b. Fraud, or fraudulent concealment, in procuring a charter.
   c. Corporation has failed to pay taxes for a specified period of time.
   d. Any other serious grounds which would tend to substantially injure the public.
2. May be brought by creditor or stockholder:

a. Must submit to the attorney general a verified statement of the facts warranting the commencement of dissolution proceedings, e.g., corporation:

(1) Has remained insolvent, or

(2) Neglected or refused to pay and discharge its notes or other evidences of debt, or

(3) Suspended its ordinary and lawful business.

b. If the attorney general fails to commence an action within a certain time after submission of the verified statement, the stockholders or creditors may apply to a court of competent jurisdiction for leave to proceed by themselves.

CORPORATIONS: SUBJECTIVE QUESTIONS*

PROMOTION, INCORPORATION, AND ORGANIZATION

Q. The XYZ Corporation was to be formed by Peter, a promoter. In order to operate the Corporation after incorporation, it was necessary for Peter to obtain stock subscriptions, lease certain facilities, and, of course, carry out the mechanics of incorporating. Peter accomplished all these things in short order including the execution of two separate leases in the corporate name, one covering office space and the other factory space, without revealing to the lessor that the Corporation had not yet been organized. The Corporation subsequently came into existence, directors were duly elected, and the board met and took the following actions:

(a) Accepted all the subscriptions that Peter had obtained.

(b) Declined to accept the lease of office space that Peter had executed in the corporate name.

(c) Voted to move, and subsequently did move all the Corporation's machinery into the factory that Peter had leased. However, at no time did they vote to accept this lease.

(d) Issued $50 par value stock to all subscribers; some of the subscribers paid $25 per share for the stock which was marked fully paid. These shares were subsequently sold at $30 per share to other people who were unaware of the original price paid for the stock.

(1) According to the prevailing rule, what is the legal status of a pre-incorporation stock subscription? When does it become binding upon the subscriber? Explain.

(2) Can the Corporation validly decline the lease of office space that Peter made in its name? Explain.

* See Introductory Note, p. 19.

(3) Does Peter have any liability on any of the leases he made? Explain.

(4) Has the Corporation accepted the contract Peter made to lease factory space? Explain.

(5) If it be assumed that the Corporation had formally accepted all the above leases, is Peter free from liability? Explain.

(6) What rights do creditors of the Corporation have against shareholders who took the newly issued stock for less than par? Explain.

(7) Do the creditors have any rights against the subsequent purchasers of the stock that was issued for less than par? Explain.

11/62; pp.182-183, 195

CAPITAL STOCK

Bullock Corporation notified its bondholders that it is unable to pay interest due on its 6 per cent bonds because the Corporation is insolvent after only two years of existence. The bondholders engaged Augustus, a CPA, to audit the Corporation's financial statements. During his examination Augustus learned the following:

(a) Several substantial subscriptions for stock of the Corporation were withdrawn by the subscribers prior to the Corporation's coming into existence.
(b) Two large shareholders paid less than par value for the shares they received at the time the stock was originally issued to them by the Corporation. The bondholders did not know of this when they purchased the bonds from the Corporation.
(c) A dividend was paid to common shareholders partially out of the legal capital of the Corporation in the first year of operation.
(d) One of the directors purchased a profitable patent right from an inventor who contacted the director to offer the patent right to the Corporation. The director told him "to forget about it, that the Corporation would not be interested, but that he would take it himself."
(e) A certified copy of the corporate charter was not filed in the county in which the Corporation's principal place of business was located as required by state law and one of the three incorporators was a nonresident alien at the time of incorporation which was prohibited by state law.

Discuss the legal implications, if any, of each of the above facts to the bondholders.

5/69; pp. 187-189

Q. The Cover Manufacturing Corporation was formed on January 1, 1964, for the purpose of manufacturing and selling umbrellas. You are engaged in the examination of its financial statements as of December 31, 1964. Your examination of the account Stock Subscriptions Receivable disclosed that it included amounts applicable to some subscriptions made before and some made after the Corporation was formed. You examined correspondence received from both types of subscribers in which it was requested that subscriptions be cancelled. No action has been taken to cancel or to collect these subscriptions. Discuss the balance sheet presentation of the subscriptions that the subscribers have requested be cancelled; include a discussion of the legal status of the subscriptions.

5/65; p. 186

DIRECTORS AND OFFICERS

Q. The Cover Manufacturing Corporation was formed on January 1, 1964, for the purpose of manufacturing and selling umbrellas. You are engaged in the examination of its financial statements as of December 31, 1964. Discuss the legal status of each of the following expenses and name all of the documents or records that you might examine for authorization of each:

(1) Directors' compensation.
(2) Officers' salaries.
(3) Promoters' organization expenses.

5/65; pp. 187-189

RIGHTS OF STOCKHOLDERS

Q. A dissident group of noncumulative 6% preferred shareholders learned that during certain recent years in which they were shareholders (some still own the shares), and in which the Endo Corporation failed to pay the 6% preferred dividend despite adequate earnings, the Corporation's directors were quietly buying in the preferred stock at 80% of the $100 par value at which the shares were originally issued and sold. The dissident preferred shareholders seek to have the directors declare a dividend to cover all prior and current years' dividends. Will they prevail? Discuss.

5/67; p. 193

Q. A well organized minority group of common shareholders have asserted that the Endo Corporation's directors and officers have been guilty of mismanagement and negligence and have allowed the corporate assets to be shamefully wasted. They demand to see the books and records of the Endo Corporation in order to obtain all the relevant facts. Furthermore they demand to be permitted to make copies of the lists of shareholders. They also demand that they be permitted to bring in their attorney and their accountant.

(1) What is the standard of care which a director or officer should exercise in respect to managing corporate affairs? Discuss.
(2) Do the shareholders have the right (1) to examine the books, (2) make copies of the lists of stockholders, and (3) bring along their attorney and their accountant? Discuss.
(3) Suppose the Corporation refuses to permit any inspection of the books, records, or lists. What recourse do the shareholders have? Discuss.

5/67; p. 194

Q. During 1966 the Endo Corporation sold a block of newly authorized shares of common stock via a private placement. An examination of the charter and the stock certificates reveals that nothing is expressly provided for regarding the existing shareholders' pre-emptive right. What problem, if any, does this set of facts generate for the Corporation? Discuss.

5/67; p. 195

Q. Doe, who has sharply criticized the management of other corporations, purchased 1,000 shares of Endo Corporation stock. The transfer agent, upon the instructions of the officers of the Corporation, refused to transfer the shares on the books of the Corporation or issue a stock certificate to the purchaser. What are the legal implications created by these facts? Discuss.

5/67; p. 191

CORPORATE RIGHTS, POWERS, AND LIABILITIES

Q. During your examination of the records of Cover Manufacturing Corporation you discovered that the president of the Corporation, who is also the principal stockholder, had committed the Corporation to a partnership agreement with Harry Gore. The partnership, formed for the purpose of importing and selling umbrellas, began operations on April 1, 1964. Discuss the legal significance of your discovery.

5/65; p. 196

FOREIGN CORPORATIONS

Q. You have been engaged to examine the financial statements of Endo Corporation for the year ended December 31, 1966. The Corporation is closely held, although there are distinct minority groups of preferred and common shareholders. Its stock is not listed on any stock exchange. Your audit of the Corporation's books and records reveals the following situations. The Endo Corporation was duly incorporated in the State of Y in 1960. During all years prior to the current year its operations and activities were all intrastate, taking place in State Y. In

1966, however, a sales office was established in State Z and two resident salesmen authorized to contact prospective customers in that state, to solicit orders, and to make sales. The Corporation has taken no action in respect to the Secretary of State of Z or the administrative agency which administers the State of Z's corporation laws. What is the danger that this set of facts raises in respect to the Endo Corporation? Discuss. Indicate the possible penalties or liabilities that may be asserted in light of the facts.

5/67; p.199

CORPORATIONS: OBJECTIVE QUESTIONS

Each of the following numbered statements states a legal conclusion. You are to determine whether each legal conclusion is true or false according to the general principles of corporation law. Your grade will be determined from your total net score obtained by deducting your total of incorrect answers from your total of correct answers; an omitted answer will not be considered an incorrect answer.

(1) Adams, Miller and James are the stockholders of Uco Corporation. The Corporation was authorized to issue 400 shares of $100 par value common stock and 100 shares of $10 par value preferred stock. Adams, Miller and James each own 100 shares of common stock which they subscribed for upon incorporation. Adams paid the Corporation $50 per share for his common stock pursuant to an offer he made which was accepted by the board of directors; Miller contributed real property to the Corporation in exchange for his stock which the board valued at $10,000; James' stock was issued by the board in consideration of his pre-incorporation services as promoter of the Corporation. Miller purchased all of the preferred stock for $1,000.

(a) Adams' common stock is validly issued, fully paid stock.
(b) Assuming the board acted in good faith, Miller's common stock is validly issued, fully paid stock.
(c) James' common stock was issued for an invalid consideration.
(d) The directors might be personally liable to the Corporation's creditors with respect to the issuance of Adams' common stock.
(e) If the Corporation should be liquidated, Miller would be entitled to receive the first $1,000 of unencumbered assets before any distribution would be made to Adams or James.

(2) Peterson and Collins decided to incorporate their retail store, which they operated as a partnership. They executed and filed all the appropriate papers required by applicable state law, issued stock to themselves and commenced operations in the corporate form. Through inadvertence, the certificate of incorporation they filed was not properly acknowledged as required by law.

(a) Since the incorporation was not validly accomplished pursuant

to law, Peterson and Collins would be personally liable to the Corporation's creditors.
(b) Peterson and Collins formed a *de jure* corporation.
(c) If the Corporation institutes suit on a note payable to it, the maker may raise improper incorporation as a defense.
(d) The Corporation may be dissolved on a suit brought by the state on the ground that it was invalidly incorporated.
(e) If the Corporation sues the state for a refund of taxes, the state may raise improper incorporation as a defense.

(3) Dodson, an accountant, performed services in connection with the organization of Beta Corporation for which he was issued shares of Beta's common stock as compensation. Three years later Dodson decided to sell his Beta stock and took an ad in a nationally distributed newspaper offering to sell the stock to the highest bidder. Dodson had performed no services for Beta other than those described above and his Beta stock represented less than 1 per cent of Beta's issued and outstanding common stock.
(a) Dodson violated the Securities Act of 1933.
(b) If Dodson sells his Beta stock to members of the public using instrumentalities of interstate commerce, he would violate the Securities Act of 1933.
(c) The answer to the preceding two questions would be different if Dodson's stock represented more than 50 per cent of Beta's issued and outstanding common stock.
(d) In the circumstances described in the preceding question, Dodson would be considered the "issuer" of the Beta stock he owned for purposes of the Securities Act of 1933.
(e) If Dodson had acquired his Beta stock under the facts in item 43 intending to resell it to the public in interstate commerce, he would be deemed an "underwriter" of the stock by the Securities Act of 1933.

(4) Bancroft and Davis are directors and substantial shareholders of Gotham Corporation, a large publicly held corporation whose securities are listed on a national securities exchange. Making use of information known only to Gotham's management, Bancroft made a large profit trading in Gotham stock. Five months ago Davis purchased additional Gotham stock on the market, which he now proposes to sell at a profit.
(a) Bancroft may have incurred liability to members of the public dealing with him in his transactions with Gotham stock.
(b) Davis, who had no knowledge of the inside information, may be liable to Gotham for any profit realized by him on the sale of his additional Gotham shares within six months from the date of purchase.
(c) The answer to the preceding two questions would be different if Gotham's stock were not listed on a national exchange but were traded "over-the-counter."

(d) If Davis should sell the remaining shares of his Gotham stock in a regular exchange transaction without first registering such stock under the Securities Exchange Act of 1933, he might violate the Act.

(e) The answer to the preceding question would be different if Davis should sell his stock to Jones, a stock broker, who bought for his own account for investment.

(5) Five of the seven directors of Baker Corporation, constituting a quorum of the directors at a meeting of the board, voted three to two to take the following actions:

(1) acquire the assets of Yalu Corporation (worth $10,000) for 200 shares of Baker's common stock (par value $100 per share) held in Baker's treasury;

(2) purchase real property owned by Everett, one of the directors who attended the meeting and voted in favor of the action; and

(3) declare a dividend on Baker's preferred stock in an amount in excess of retained earnings and capital surplus.

(a) The board's action for the acquisition of Yalu Corporation was proper.

(b) The answer to the preceding question would be the same if the Baker stock issued for the Yalu acquisition were previously authorized but unissued stock.

(c) The transactions between Baker and Everett are void.

(d) The Baker directors who voted for the dividend may be personally liable to Baker's creditors.

(e) The Baker directors who voted against the dividend and who had their dissent recorded in the minutes of the meeting may also be liable to Baker's creditors since the board acts as a board and not as individuals.

(6) The boards of directors of Inco Corporation and Still Corporation voted to merge the two corporations under a plan of merger in which Inco stockholders would exchange their Inco stock for Still stock and Still would be the surviving corporation.

(a) The merger of Inco into Still must be approved by the stockholders of both corporations.

(b) The answer to the preceding question would be the same if Inco and Still consolidate rather than merge.

(c) If, rather than merging, Still were to purchase all of the assets of Inco, approval of the purchase by the stockholders of Still would not be required.

(d) Following the merger of Inco into Still, the creditors of Inco may look to Still for payment of their claims.

(e) A stockholder of Inco who votes against the merger must nevertheless accept Still stock in exchange for his Inco stock if the required percentage of Inco stock votes in favor of the merger.

5/70

(7) Frank, Mark and John joined together to promote the formation of Eagle Corporation to construct houses. The promoters contracted with Frank's brother-in-law, George, that the Corporation would purchase a tract of land owned by George for $100,000 to be paid six months after the Corporation was formed. The contract specifically provided that Frank, Mark and John would not incur any liability as promoters. After executing the contract the promoters completed incorporation through the purchase of stock at par for cash by the promoters and several of their friends and relatives. Mark and his three sons were elected as directors and hired as officers. The Corporation then had the land surveyed, had building plans drawn, and tendered $100,000 to George for the land.

(a) Prior to the incorporation the promoters had no fiduciary duties.
(b) Upon incorporation the promoters could satisfy any obligation to make a full disclosure of their activities to the Corporation by making such a disclosure to the board of directors.
(c) The agreement made by the promoters with George did not constitute an enforceable contract at the time it was executed.
(d) The Corporation could be regarded as a third party beneficiary of the contract between the promoters and George.
(e) The actions of the officers of the Corporation would constitute an adoption of the contract between George and the promoters which would bind both George and the Corporation to the contract.

(8) You have been the auditor of Cybul Corporation for the three years it has been in existence. Upon incorporation 1,000 shares of $50 par value common stock authorized by the articles of incorporation were sold for cash to the public. The Corporation was very profitable and the board of directors, which has as its members all of the officers of the Corporation, to reward management for outstanding work, has increased the salary of each officer by $5,000. The Corporation plans to expand its production facilities and issue more stock to obtain additional capital. To date the Corporation has paid no dividends.

(a) The directors breached their duty to the shareholders by not declaring a dividend.
(b) The directors must obtain shareholder approval to amend the certificate of incorporation prior to issuing additional shares of stock.
(c) The directors may not effectively agree to raise the officers' salaries.
(d) The directors may legally agree to allow themselves to have the first opportunity to subscribe to the additional shares of stock to be issued.
(e) The general investing public must be offered a reasonable opportunity to purchase shares of the new stock to be issued when present shareholders are given an opportunity to purchase such shares.

(9) David and Sidney each own 50 per cent of the capital stock of Diamond Corporation. They are unrelated and have no other business relationship. They entered into a shareholders' agreement which provided that upon the death of either, the survivor would purchase the others' stock in the Corporation at book value with the book value to be determined annually by a CPA. The book value of each party's stock interest as determined by a CPA on the date of the execution of the agreement was $20,000. David and Sidney plan to purchase life insurance on each other so that funds will be available to meet their obligations under the agreement.

(a) The shareholders' agreement cannot remain valid for more than ten years unless it is renewed.
(b) The shareholders' agreement may remain in effect even if David and Sidney fail to have a CPA annually review the book value of their stock interests.
(c) If the premium to be paid by Sidney on the insurance policy he takes out on David's life is higher than the premium David must pay, Sidney is entitled to reimbursement for the additional cost from the Corporation.
(d) If David should die the insurance proceeds Sidney collects would constitute a dividend.
(e) If David and Sidney both sell their stock they could not take out additional insurance on each other's lives.

(10) Your client, Plywood Corporation, a manufacturer, has consistently operated at a loss since its incorporation three years ago. Plywood is now insolvent and owes twenty creditors a total of more than $50,000. Stanley is a stockholder of Plywood and Walter owns bonds issued by Plywood which are now due. Most bondholders will not demand payment until conditions improve. Stanley demands that Plywood purchase his stock at his cost and Walter demands payment for his bonds. Each threatens to force Plywood into bankruptcy if his demand is not met. Stanley also owns stock in Hardwood Corporation, a very successful enterprise, and Hardwood has offered to purchase its own stock from Stanley at a price in excess of the market price of the stock.

(a) Plywood may not repurchase Stanley's stock because it has a deficit balance in its legal capital.
(b) Walter cannot alone file a petition for the involuntary bankruptcy of Plywood if Plywood refuses to retire Walter's bonds.
(c) If Plywood repurchases Walter's bonds and immediately files a voluntary petition in bankruptcy, the trustee in bankruptcy may be able to claim that Walter received a preference.
(d) Hardwood's stock would be "watered stock" if Hardwood should repurchase its own stock from Stanley for more than the market price.
(e) Hardwood would commit an *ultra vires* act by repurchasing its own stock from Stanley.

(11) Alan is chairman of the board of directors of Shipping Corporation, one of your clients. The by-laws of the Corporation provide for a seven-man board of directors, one of whom has just died. The by-laws have no provision for filling a vacancy and Alan would like to appoint his brother. Alan has also learned that two ships, the Nina and the Pinta, are available for purchase. Alan would like to purchase the Nina himself and attempt to sell it for profit and he thinks the Corporation should purchase the Pinta.

Alan attempted to telephone the other directors and inform them of what he learned and what he would like to do. He contacted two directors who agreed by telephone to all of his plans. A third director could not be reached. The fourth director agreed to Alan's plans on behalf of himself and the fifth director, who had given his proxy to the fourth director. The substance of the telephone calls was not reduced to writing.

(a) Alan did not hold a valid director's meeting.
(b) Alan, as chairman of the board of directors, does not have implied power to fill a vacancy on the board of directors.
(c) Alan was free to purchase the Nina without disclosing his plans.
(d) The director who could not be contacted will be strictly accountable for any wrong done by his fellow directors even though he was unaware of what was happening.
(e) Directors have power to vote by proxy to the same extent as shareholders.

(12) Evan and Norman each own 50 per cent of the capital stock of Eian Corporation. They arranged a conference with their lawyer and their accountant to agree on the terms of a stockholders' agreement. If agreed upon by both stockholders the following provisions could be properly adopted as a part of the stockholders' agreement.

(a) The stockholders' agreement is to terminate if the Corporation's stock should be sold to the investing public.
(b) The Corporation can be dissolved without court approval if the stockholders disagree.
(c) A stockholder wishing to sell all or part of his stock in the Corporation must first offer the stock to the other stockholder at a price to be determined by an independent appraisal.
(d) The sale of stock is to be restricted.
(e) The activities in which the Corporation may engage under the terms of its charter are to be increased.

11/68

(13) If twenty persons are in business as partners and wish to form a corporation to carry on the business, the corporation must be incorporated in a state in which

(a) The corporation plans to carry on the major portion of its activities.
(b) At least one of the incorporators intends to reside during the time that the corporation is to remain in existence.

(c) The majority of the incorporators reside at the time of incorporation.
(d) The partnership was established.
(e) The partnership carries on the major portion of its activities.

(14) A shareholders' agreement may
(a) Provide for a mandatory purchase of shares from a shareholder's estate upon his death.
(b) Restrict the sale of securities to outside parties until present shareholders are given the opportunity to purchase the shares.
(c) Bind shareholders to vote to dissolve the corporation in the event of a deadlock.
(d) Bind shoreholders to seek arbitration in the event certain disputes arise.
(e) Bind non-assenting shareholders to its terms if a majority of shareholders sign the shareholders' agreement.

(15) In order for a corporation to obtain *de facto* status, there must be
(a) A special statute passed by the legislature allowing for such status.
(b) A statute under which the corporation might have been validly incorporated.
(c) Some exercise of corporate privileges.
(d) A good faith attempt to comply with the incorporation law.
(e) The correction of any defect prior to the payment of any debt.

(16) Rolling Corporation transferred part of its assets to a new corporation in exchange for the latter's stock and then immediately distributed such stock to Rolling Corporation's shareholders without requiring them to surrender any of their Rolling Corporation stock. Such a transaction
(a) Is illegal.
(b) Constitutes a stock split.
(c) Constitutes a spin off.
(d) Increases the par value of Rolling Corporation's stock.
(e) Constitutes an *ultra vires* act even though authorized by Rolling Corporation's charter.

(17) Lillian Corporation and Feld Corporation join to form a new corporation, Lillianfeld, Inc. Such a transaction
(a) Is referred to as a merger.
(b) Is referred to as a consolidation.
(c) Is referred to as an acquisition.
(d) May not occur without the consent of all of the shareholders of each corporation.
(e) May provide some shareholders with the right to an appraisal remedy.

(18) "Blue sky" laws
(a) Refer to outdated statutes regulating the incorporation of corporations.

(b) Need not be complied with if the stock of a corporation is publicly traded on an exchange.
(c) Refer to state statutes regulating the issuance and sale of securities.
(d) Are administered by the Securities and Exchange Commission.
(e) Refer to federal statutes regulating corporations.

(19) Directors of a corporation generally have the power to
(a) Appoint their successors.
(b) Replace officers.
(c) Declare dividends.
(d) Set salaries for executives.
(e) Require shareholders to sell stock.

(20) Where a corporation is insolvent and a dividend has been declared
(a) A shareholder may obtain a court injunction to prevent the payment of the dividend.
(b) A creditor may obtain a court injunction to prevent the payment of the dividend.
(c) The dividend may be required to be returned to the corporation if paid.
(d) The payment of such a dividend would constitute a fraud against the creditors.
(e) The declaration of such a dividend by the board of directors in good faith reliance on an improper balance sheet would not necessarily constitute a breach of trust.

(21) A cash dividend
(a) Becomes a debt of the corporation once it is validly declared.
(b) May be sued for by a shareholder if it is not paid once it is validly declared.
(c) Must be declared when more than adequate earnings exist.
(d) May be ordered by a court even if there is no evidence that withholding its declaration is an abuse of discretion.
(e) Is payable only from funds legally available for such purpose.

(22) Cumulative voting
(a) Applies only to the election of directors.
(b) Assures each voter that at least one of his candidates will be elected.
(c) Is always in effect for preferred shares.
(d) Is not as effective when the number of persons to be elected is decreased.
(e) May be made mandatory by statute.

(23) The "pre-emptive rights" doctrine
(a) Allows preferred shareholders to assume control of the corporation if dividends are not paid.
(b) Protects a shareholder's interest in the corporation in the event of the issue of additional shares.
(c) Allows the directors to replace officers of the corporation at will.

(d) Requires directors to turn over all corporate opportunities to the corporation.
(e) Insures the payment of a dividend to the shareholder of record on the record date.

(24) Treasury stock
(a) Is authorized stock.
(b) Is issued stock.
(c) Is outstanding stock.
(d) May be voted.
(e) May participate in dividends.

11/67

(25) If the existence of a corporation is challenged, a corporation would be found to exist
(a) If it is a *de jure* corporation.
(b) Even though all of the corporation's stock is owned by one individual.
(c) Even though the corporation is engaging in acts which are beyond the scope of the activities authorized by its charter.
(d) Even though A, B, and C, doing business as partners, decided to consider themselves bound as a corporation and do business using a corporate name.
(e) Even though the term of corporate existence specified in the charter has long expired, but the corporation continues to carry on its activities using the corporate name.

(26) If a corporation has been organized by promoters
(a) It cannot be a closed corporation.
(b) The promoters were the agents of the corporation prior to its formation.
(c) The corporation can sue on a contract made by a promoter which it has adopted.
(d) Before the corporation was formed, the rules of joint venture governed the promoters' relationships among themselves.
(e) And if creditors are defrauded by promoters, the creditors' sole recourse would be against the corporation.

(27) If a corporation does a substantial amount of business in a state in which it is not incorporated,
(a) It must incorporate in that state in order to enjoy the benefit of its laws.
(b) It may be required to qualify in that state in order to do intrastate business within that state.
(c) It may always incorporate under a federal incorporation law and thereby be permitted to do business in any number of states.
(d) It may be sued in that state for acts which are carried out in that state.

(e) It cannot be taxed by that state.

(28) Directors of a corporation
(a) Are elected by the officers of the corporation.
(b) May declare a stock dividend.
(c) Are agents of the shareholders.
(d) May fix executive compensation.
(e) May exercise their powers individually.

(29) Officers of a corporation
(a) Are elected by the shareholders.
(b) May be removed by the board of directors.
(c) Have no implied authority arising out of their offices.
(d) May be liable on contracts they enter into if they do not indicate that they are contracting as agents for a corporation.
(e) May not also be directors of the corporation.

(30) If an officer of a corporation does outstanding work for the corporation, he may be rewarded for his special services by receiving
(a) A stock bonus.
(b) Deferred compensation.
(c) The right to purchase property which the corporation ultimately wishes to acquire.
(d) The right to purchase corporate assets at a nominal price.
(e) The right to an unlimited expense account.

(31) A shareholder's proxy
(a) May be solicited by persons who are not officers of the corporation.
(b) May be irrevocable in some cases.
(c) Is always revocable.
(d) May not be sold.
(e) May be given for a forthcoming election by a shareholder who has sold his stock "ex-voting" rights.

(32) The shareholders of a closed corporation may agree among themselves
(a) Completely to prohibit the sale of corporate stock.
(b) To prohibit the sale of corporate stock prior to the stock's being offered to the original shareholders at a specified price.
(c) To fix a price for the purchase of a deceased shareholder's stock by the corporation.
(d) To place their shares in a voting trust.
(e) To have the corporation carry life insurance on the life of each shareholder.

(33) The right to cumulative voting
(a) Applies only to the election of directors.
(b) Is diluted by increasing the number of vacancies to be filled.
(c) Might be eliminated by amendment if it merely exists pursuant to a provision of the bylaws and is not required by statute.

(d) Helps insure majority control.
(e) Is mandatory in some jurisdictions.

(34) A derivative suit
(a) Can be brought by directors or officers of the corporation.
(b) Can be brought by shareholders of the corporation.
(c) Is sometimes referred to as a "representative" or "class" suit.
(d) Can be brought to compel the corporation to allow a shareholder to inspect corporate books and records.
(e) If successful, does not generally result in a direct recovery to the person bringing suit.

(35) A shareholder's common law right of inspection
(a) Permits inspection of corporate books for any purpose.
(b) Permits inspection of corporate books at any place or time.
(c) Would permit inspection of the corporation's physical plant.
(d) May permit inspection of the minutes of directors' meetings.
(e) Would permit the shareholder to have the assistance of his accountant in carrying on an inspection.

(36) Dissolution of a corporation
(a) Is not synonymous with the liquidation of a corporation.
(b) Must be under court supervision.
(c) Once begun, cannot be prevented even if found to be oppressive to a particular group.
(d) Automatically terminates the corporation's existence for all purposes.
(e) Terminates the corporation's right to sue.

5/66

(37) An owner of common stock of a corporation
(a) May insist upon an annual declaration of dividends.
(b) May join with other stockholders to form a voting trust.
(c) Must personally vote his stock at a stockholders' meeting.
(d) Becomes a creditor of the corporation when a cash dividend is duly declared.
(e) Has an absolute right to inspect the books of the corporation in order to ascertain its financial condition.

(38) The directors of a corporation
(a) Although elected by the stockholders become the representatives of the corporation itself.
(b) May vote by proxy at a board meeting.
(c) Are fiduciaries entrusted with the management of the corporation.
(d) Will be personally liable if they authorize the sale of treasury stock at less than par value.
(e) May exercise the voting rights of treasury stock at a stockholders' meeting.

(39) In the absence of express authorization or special circumstances, a corporation cannot

(a) Accept or endorse bills of exchange in the usual course of its business.
(b) Consolidate or merge with another corporation.
(c) Purchase, hold, or convey real property in the corporate name.
(d) Subscribe to the stock of another corporation engaged in a business completely different from its own.
(e) Become an accommodation endorser on a negotiable promissory note.

(40) The dissolution of a corporation

(a) Will automatically occur upon termination of the period fixed in the charter.
(b) Will occur upon consolidation with another corporation.
(c) May be effected by surrender of the charter to the state by the incorporators prior to the start of business or the issuance of shares.
(d) May be brought about by the state on the ground that the corporation continuously failed to file reports or pay taxes.
(e) May be brought about by the proper state official at the instance of a stockholder because the corporation has suspended its ordinary and lawful business.

5/65

TOPIC SEVEN | SALES

CONTENTS PAGE

*SALES. This topic is largely concerned with Article 2 (Sales) of the Uniform Commercial Code which includes warranty protection of the buyer, privity of warranty, allocation of risk of loss, and the buyer's and seller's rights, duties, and remedies. In addition, problems arising as a result of a bulk purchase, covered by Article 6 (Bulk Sales) of the Uniform Commercial Code, are included.**

* Source: AICPA, *Information to CPA Candidates* (July 1970).

I. CHARACTERISTICS

A. Introductory note: This section is based exclusively on the rules contained in Articles 2 (Sales) and 6 (Bulk Sales) of the UCC. At present, the UCC has been adopted in nearly every state in the United States. Its bold departures from prior law reflect the stress and upheaval of the great changes in our whole system of marketing and sales.

B. Definitions.

1. Sale: consists of the passing of title from the seller to the buyer for a price.
2. Contract for sale: includes both a present sale of goods and an agreement to sell goods at a future time.
3. Present sale: a sale which is accomplished by the making of the contract.
4. Goods.
   a. All things (including specially manufactured goods) which are movable at the time of identification to the contract for sale other than:
      (1) The money in which the price is to be paid.
      (2) Investment securities.
      (3) Things in action (intangible personal property such as accounts receivable).
   b. Includes the unborn young of animals and growing crops and other identified things attached to realty.
   c. Fungible with respect to goods means goods of which any unit is, by nature or usage of trade, the equivalent of any other like unit.
5. Merchant: a person who deals in goods of the kind involved or who otherwise by his occupation holds himself out as having knowledge or skill peculiar to the practices or goods involved in the transaction.

C. Other commercial transactions distinguished from sales.

1. Gift: a present transfer of title and possession without consideration.
2. Bailment:
   a. Definition: a delivery of personal property, by one person to another, for a particular purpose, upon condition that the property be subsequently returned, kept until reclaimed, or disposed of pursuant to agreement.
      (1) Bailor: delivers the property, has title but not possession.
      (2) Bailee: accepts it, has possession but not title.
      (3) Both have an insurable interest in the property.

b. Elements.
   (1) Personal property.
      a. No bailment of real property.
      b. Valid chattel: No rights can arise from illegal goods. (E.g., bailor cannot reclaim liquor stored in warehouse while prohibition is in force.)
   (2) Transfer of possession and control either by actual delivery of the property itself, or constructive delivery (e.g., where a key to the place where the goods are stored is delivered to the bailee or he is given documents of title representing the actual goods).
   (3) Bailments are normally contractual (express contract), but they may also be constructive (implied contract, e.g., a finder of lost goods).
   (4) Acceptance of possession: Acceptance is normally pursuant to a contract or agreement by the parties; however, acceptance may be implied as in the case of a finder of lost goods.
   (5) Title remains in the transferor (bailor). Appointment of a receiver over bailee's property would not affect bailor's title.
   (6) In a mutual benefit bailment the bailee has the duty of exercising reasonable care of the bailed property. He is not an insurer; i.e., he will not be liable unless negligent or otherwise at fault.

3. Consignment: a special type of bailment or an agency for sale.
   a. Transfer of possession, but not title for shipment or sale.
   b. Consignee normally the agent of consignor.

D. General contractual considerations: The area of sales is built upon the basic rules of contract law as set forth in Article 2 of the UCC. Many of the major contractual provisions relating to sales are covered extensively in the chapter on contracts (e.g., offer and acceptance, consideration, modification, Statute of Frauds, etc.; see *supra*, pp. 44–47) and will not be treated again here.

E. Elements of a sale.

1. Parties must have capacity to contract (see Contracts, p. 43, III.D.).

2. Price.
   a. The parties if they so intend can conclude a contract for sale even though the price is not settled. In such a case the price is a reasonable price at the time for delivery if:
      (1) Nothing is said as to price, or

(2) The price is left to be agreed upon by the parties and they fail to agree, or

(3) The price is to be fixed in terms of some agreed market or other standard as set or recorded by a third person or agency and it is not so set or recorded.

b. A price to be fixed by the seller or by the buyer means a price for him to fix honestly and according to commercially reasonable standards.

3. Subject matter: goods which have:

a. Validity (see Contracts, p. 41, III.C.).

b. Actual existence and identity.

(1) Goods must be both existing and identified to the contract before any interest in them can pass.

(2) Goods which are not both existing and identified are "future goods." A purported present sale of future goods or of any interest therein operates as a contract to sell, not a sale.

c. Where goods whose continued existence is presupposed by the agreement are destroyed without fault by either party before the risk of loss has passed to the buyer:

(1) If the loss is total the contract is avoided.

(2) If the loss is partial the buyer may avoid the contract or take the surviving goods with a price adjustment.

F. Merchants and the UCC.

1. Special rules apply to transactions among merchants (see, e.g., p. 225, II.C.3.c.). In general, the UCC fosters the creation of legal rights more easily when the agreement is solely between merchants rather than between a consumer and a merchant, since the concern for protecting the inexperienced and untutored consumer is not present.

2. Article 2 sets special standards for merchants in many specific areas. These include: firm offer by a merchant; conflicting offers and acceptances; modification of existing contracts; warranty of merchantable quality; duty to follow instructions; retention of possession; power of sale of goods entrusted to merchants; and risk of loss and goods rejected by a merchant buyer.

II. RIGHTS AND OBLIGATIONS OF THE PARTIES TO THE SALES CONTRACT

A. Unimportance of title: Under prior law, many critical legal consequences were determined by location of title to the goods. Under the UCC, however, specific provisions govern the legal consequences of various situations irrespective of title. These include provisions regarding risk of loss (see below), the seller's right of action for the price, insurable interest, and other situations.

B. Risk of loss.

1. In the event of a breach:

a. In general, the UCC quite properly places the risk of loss on the party who has breached the contract. It also takes into account the fact that the goods sold are normally insured.

b. Where a tender or delivery of goods so fails to conform to the contract as to give a right of rejection, the risk of their loss remains on the seller until cure (see *infra*, p. 233, III.C.4.) or acceptance.

c. Where the buyer rightfully revokes acceptance he may, to the extent of any deficiency in his effective insurance coverage, treat the risk of loss as having rested on the seller from the beginning.

d. Where the buyer as to conforming goods already identified to the contract for sale repudiates or is otherwise in breach before risk of their loss has passed to him, the seller may, to the extent of any deficiency in his effective insurance coverage, treat the risk of loss as resting on the buyer for a commercially reasonable time.

2. In the absence of breach:

a. Where the contract requires or authorizes the seller to ship the goods by carrier:

(1) If it does not require him to deliver them at a particular destination, the risk of loss passes to the buyer when the goods are duly delivered to the carrier.

(2) If it does require him to deliver them at a particular destination and the goods are there duly tendered while in the possession of the carrier, the risk of loss passes to the buyer when the goods are so tendered as to enable the buyer to take delivery.

(3) The UCC presumes that the seller is not obligated to deliver at a named destination and bear the concurrent risk of loss until arrival, unless he has specifically agreed to make delivery or the commercial understanding of the terms used by the parties contemplates such delivery.

(4) The UCC has made certain widely used shipping terms an integral part of its rules regarding when delivery is required, thereby determining who has the risk of loss. For example,

where the term is F.O.B. place of shipment, the seller must bear the expense and risk of putting the goods in the hands of the carrier at that place (e.g., at the freight terminal in seller's area). The buyer thus has the risk of loss once the goods are in the carrier's hands for shipment.

b. Where the goods are held by a bailee to be delivered without being moved, the risk of loss passes to the buyer:

(1) On his receipt of a negotiable document of title covering the goods, or

(2) On acknowledgment by the bailee of the buyer's right to possession of the goods, or

(3) After his receipt of a non-negotiable document of title or other written direction to deliver.

c. In any case not within the above subsections a. or b. the risk of loss passes to the buyer on his receipt of the goods if the seller is a merchant; otherwise the risk passes to the buyer on tender of delivery.

d. The application of the above subsections (a., b., and c.) are subject to the following limitations:

(1) The contrary agreement of the parties. The UCC rules apply only where the parties have not allocated risk of loss in their contract. Clearly, the parties to the sale should expressly cover this point in their contract.

(2) In "sales on approval" the risk of loss does not pass to the buyer until acceptance, and in "sale or return" transactions the risk of loss is on the buyer until the goods are returned.

(3) As previously indicated, where there has been a breach of contract, the rules contained in B.1. above apply.

3. As a matter of policy, Article 2 has made an attempt to correlate possession and risk of loss in some situations. Thus, where the goods are not to be shipped, the risk of loss passes to the buyer on his receipt of the goods if the seller is a merchant; otherwise the risk passes to the buyer on tender of delivery.

C. Warranties.

1. Introduction: The UCC's treatment of warranties represents a significant shift toward greater consumer protection. Article 2 has made express warranties of certain warranties that were implied under prior law, and the UCC defines the ambiguous term "merchantability." Also, in the area of disclaimers the code's provisions are aimed at greater consumer protection. The UCC does, however, take an equivocal position on the question of privity (see *infra*, p. 226, II.C.6. a.), leaving it to local law to decide.

2. Express warranties.

   a. Express warranties by the seller are created as follows:

      (1) Any affirmation of fact or promise made by the seller to the buyer which relates to the goods and becomes part of the basis of the bargain creates an express warranty that the goods shall conform to the affirmation or promise.

      (2) Any description of the goods which is made part of the basis of the bargain creates an express warranty that the goods shall conform to the description.

      (3) Any sample or model which is made part of the basis of the bargain creates an express warranty that the whole of the goods shall conform to the sample or model.

   b. It is not necessary to the creation of an express warranty that the seller use formal words such as "warrant" or "guarantee" or that he have a specific intention to make a warranty. However, an affirmation merely of the value of the goods or a statement purporting to be merely the seller's opinion or commendation of the goods does not create a warranty. The borderline between "affirmations of fact" or "promises" and expressions of "value" or "opinion" remains imprecise.

   c. No warranty is created when the seller is merely "puffing" his goods; that is, where the promise or affirmation is a value judgment or opinion of the goods (e.g., the clothes will "wear like iron"). However, the code's tightening of the rules of disclaimer (see below) should make the "puffing" salesman more guarded in his statements and thus add to consumer protection.

   d. UCC 2–209 has eliminated the contract requirement of consideration for agreements modifying a sales contract. (See Contracts, p. 55, VII. A.1.b.) Elimination of this requirement has validated most postcontractual promises made by the seller and has significantly expanded the consumer's express warranty protection.

3. Warranty of title and against infringement.

   a. There is in a contract for sale a warranty by seller that:

      (1) The title conveyed shall be good and its transfer rightful.

      (2) The goods shall be delivered free from any security interest or other lien or encumbrance of which the buyer at the time of contracting has no knowledge.

   b. A warranty under subsection a. will be excluded or modified only by specific language or by circumstances which give the buyer reason to know that the person selling does not claim title in himself or that he is purporting to sell only such right or title as he or a third person may have. (E.g., "I do not claim to have clear title to the goods in question and any defects in title must be assumed by you, the buyer.")

c. Unless otherwise agreed, a seller who is a merchant regularly dealing in goods of the kind sold warrants that the goods shall be delivered free of the rightful claim of any third person by way of patent or trademark infringement or the like, but a buyer who furnished specifications (e.g., plans or drawings for manufacture) to the seller must hold the seller harmless against any such third-party claim which arises out of compliance with the specifications.

d. Although it is not mentioned specifically in the UCC provision, the official comment to that provision states that the disturbance of the buyer's quiet possession of the goods is one way of establishing a breach of the title warranty.

e. For any breach of the warranty of title, the buyer must seasonably (i.e., within a reasonable time) notify seller.

f. The UCC is silent on whether this warranty is express or implied.

4. Implied warranties of quality.

a. Merchantability.

(1) Unless excluded or modified, a warranty that the goods shall be merchantable is implied in a contract for their sale if the seller is a merchant with respect to goods of that kind. The serving for value of food or drink to be consumed either on the premises or elsewhere is a sale.

(2) Goods to be merchantable must be at least such as:

(A) Pass without objection in the trade under the contract description, and

(B) In the case of fungible goods (i.e., movable goods such as grain which may be estimated according to weight, measure, and number) are of fair average quality within the description, and

(C) Are fit for the ordinary purposes for which such goods are used, and

(D) Run, within the variations permitted by the agreement, of even kind, quality, and quantity within each unit and among all units involved, and

(E) Are adequately contained, packaged, and labeled as the agreement may require, and

(F) Conform to the promises or affirmations of fact made on the container or label if any.

(3) Unless excluded or modified, other implied warranties may arise from course of dealing or usage of trade.

b. Creation of the warranty of fitness for a particular purpose.

(1) Seller must have actual or constructive knowledge of the particular purpose for which the buyer needs the goods (e.g., knowledge that shoes would be used for mountain climbing).

(2) Seller must furnish or select the goods.

(3) Buyer must rely on the seller's skill or judgment. Insistence by the buyer on a particular brand (e.g., Bab-O) would ordinarily indicate that the buyer is not relying on the seller's skill and judgment: hence, no warranty. However, the mere fact that the article purchased has a particular trade name is not sufficient to indicate non-reliance if the article has been recommended by the seller as adequate for the buyer's purpose ("Bab-O will take tobacco stains off your woodwork").

5. Cumulation and conflict of express or implied warranties.

a. Warranties, whether express or implied, shall be construed as consistent with each other and as cumulative, but if such construction is unreasonable the intention of the parties shall determine which warranty is dominant. In ascertaining that intention the following rules apply:

(1) Exact or technical specifications displace an inconsistent sample or model or general language of description.

(2) A sample from an existing bulk displaces inconsistent general language of description.

(3) Express warranties displace inconsistent implied warranties other than an implied warranty of fitness for a particular purpose.

b. The rules set forth above are not absolute but are mere guides which may be changed by evidence showing that the parties had some other intention.

6. Limitations on warranty protection.

a. Requirement of privity.

(1) Early common law restricted the scope of warranty protection to the party or parties directly contracting with the seller. (E.g., if a woman buys defective food for her family from a grocery, only she has an action of warranty against the grocer, even if other members of the family were injured by it. Furthermore, there would be no warranty action available against the manufacturer or intermediate distributor of the food because there is no privity between either of them and our housewife, the ultimate consumer.)

(2) The UCC extends the warranty protection to the buyer's

family, household, and guests if it is reasonable to expect that they would use, consume, or be affected by the goods. A seller may not exclude or limit the operation of this warranty.

(3) Many states are breaking down the privity requirement between manufacturers and distributors and the ultimate consumer. Recent landmark cases in several former citadels of privity indicate a clear trend away from this antiquated rule. This is particularly so in the case of food and drugs. The UCC takes a neutral position on this point.

b. Exclusion or modification of warranties (disclaimers).

(1) The UCC seeks to protect a buyer from unexpected and unbargained for language of disclaimer by:

(A) Denying effect to such language when inconsistent with language of express warranty.

(B) Permitting the exclusion of implied warranties only by conspicuous language or other circumstances which protect the buyer from surprise.

(2) To disclaim the warranty of merchantability, the seller must normally use the word "merchantable" in the disclaimer (e.g., "no warranty exists as to merchantability"); and if the disclaimer is written, it must be a conspicuous writing.

(3) To exclude the implied warranty of fitness for a particular purpose, the disclaimer must be in writing and conspicuous.

(4) All warranties of quality may be excluded by:

(A) Language such as "with all faults" or "as is" or other similar language which in common understanding clearly calls the buyer's attention to the exclusion of warranties and makes plain there is no implied warranty.

(B) An unrestricted examination of the goods by the buyer or a refusal to examine will negate all implied warranty protection as to defects which an examination ought in the circumstances to have revealed to him.

(C) A course of dealing or usage of trade (e.g., where an end of season sale of remaining stock to a person dealing in such property is deemed to be final and without warranty protection).

(5) As with the seller's and buyer's remedies (see p. 228, III.A.), the parties are free to bargain for their own warranties and remedies for breach of warranty. For the buyer's remedies for improper delivery, including breach of warranty, see p. 232, III.C.2.

c. The parol evidence rule: Where the contract is in writing and protected by the parol evidence rule (see Contracts, p. 51), the buyer will not be able to rely upon evidence of earlier conflicting oral express warranties relating to the goods. However, the implied warranties of merchantability and fitness are not affected except by use of a written express disclaimer which would be sufficient to preclude them (see p.227, II.C. 6.b.).

7. Statute of limitations: The UCC contains a four-year statute of limitations for the sale of goods. The parties may reduce the period to one year, but they may not lengthen it.
8. Time of breach of warranty.
   a. Breach occurs when tender of delivery is made.
   b. When the warranty explicitly extends to future goods, the cause of action accrues when the breach is or should have been discovered.

III. REMEDIES

A. Introduction: Many of the remedies discussed in this part of the text have been considered as they relate to contracts in general (see Contracts,pp. 60-63). However, the UCC has made many significant additions to, and modifications and refinements of, the traditional remedies available to parties to contracts for the sale of goods. In general, the UCC gives the parties wide discretion to determine their own remedies by specifying them in their contract. Unless construction of the contractual language precludes such an interpretation, the remedies specified are to be deemed additions to those which the UCC provides (see below). This discretion to determine the remedies is subject to the following limitations in connection with:

1. Liquidated damages: Although specifically permitted, the liquidation is enforceable only at an amount which is reasonable in light of the anticipated or actual harm caused by the breach, the difficulties of proof of loss and the inconvenience or non-feasibility of otherwise obtaining an adequate remedy. Excessive liquidated damages are void as a penalty.
2. Unconscionable modifications and limitations: In general, unconscionable clauses are invalid. Specifically, limitations of consequential damages [see *infra,* p.234, III.C.4.c.(2)] for injury to the person in the case of consumer goods is *prima facie* unconscionable, but limitation where the loss is commercial is not.

B. Seller's remedies.

1. Upon buyer's insolvency:
   a. Where the seller discovers the buyer to be insolvent he may refuse delivery except for cash, including payment for all goods

previously delivered under the contract, and stop delivery in transit as discussed in 3. below.

b. Where the seller discovers that the buyer has received goods on credit while insolvent, he may reclaim the goods upon demand made within 10 days after receipt, but if a written misrepresentation of solvency has been made to the seller within three months before delivery, this 10-day limitation does not apply.

(1) Reclamation is subject to the rights of buyers in the ordinary course of business and other good faith purchasers.

(2) Successful reclamation of goods excludes all other remedies in respect to them.

2. Before buyer's receipt or acceptance of goods: Where the buyer *wrongfully* rejects or revokes acceptance of goods or fails to make a payment due on or before delivery or repudiates either wholly or in part, then with respect to any goods directly affected (and if the breach is of the whole or entire contract then also in respect of the whole undelivered balance), the *aggrieved seller* may:

   a. Withhold delivery of such goods.
   b. Stop delivery in transit (see below).
   c. Identify goods to the contract (see below).
   d. Complete unfinished goods (see below).
   e. Resell and recover damages (see below).
   f. Recover damages for non-acceptance (see below).
   g. Recover the price in proper cases (see below).
   h. Cancel.

3. Stoppage in transit: The seller may stop delivery of goods in the possession of a carrier or other bailee (e.g., a warehouseman) irrespective of the size of shipment when he discovers the buyer to be insolvent. He may also stop delivery of carload, truckload, planeload, or larger shipments of express or freight when the buyer repudiates or fails to make a payment due before delivery. Stoppage can be made at any time until:

   a. Receipt of the goods by the buyer.
   b. Acknowledgment to the buyer by any bailee of the goods, except a carrier, that the bailee holds the goods for the buyer.
   c. Such an acknowledgment by a carrier by reshipping the goods for the buyer or such acknowledgment being made to the buyer where the goods are being held by the carrier in the capacity of a warehouseman.
   d. Transfer to the buyer of any negotiable document of title

(e.g., a negotiable bill of lading or negotiable warehouse receipt).

4. Identification of the goods to the contract: An aggrieved seller (as described in 2. above) may:
   a. Identify to the contract conforming goods in his possession or control where not already identified to the contract at the time he learned of the breach.
   b. Treat goods which have demonstrably been intended for the particular contract, even though unfinished, as the subject of resale.
5. Complete unfinished goods: Where the goods are unfinished, an aggrieved seller (as described in 2. above) may *in the exercise of reasonable commercial judgment* for the purpose of avoiding loss and of effective realization (e.g., by resale) either finish the goods and identify them to the contract or cease manufacture and resell for scrap or salvage value or proceed in any other reasonable manner.
6. Resale.
   a. An aggrieved seller (see 2. above) may sell the goods concerned or the undelivered balance thereof.
   b. Where the seller elects to resell and the resale is made in good faith and in a commercially reasonable manner, the seller:
      (1) Is not accountable for any profit made on any resale.
      (2) May recover the difference between the resale price (this in effect determines the fair market value for the purpose of computing recovery) and the contract price together with any incidental damages but less expenses saved in consequence of buyer's breach (e.g., shipping charges saved by not having to deliver to the breaching buyer).
   c. The resale may be at public (subject to certain requirements) or private (if private, seller must give buyer reasonable notice of intention to resell) and said resale must be reasonably identified as referring to the broken contract.
   d. Good faith purchasers at resale take free of any rights of the original buyer even though the seller fails to comply with the stated requirements (e.g., seller fails to give notice to original buyer of intent to resell).
7. Damages for non-acceptance or repudiation.
   a. If the aggrieved seller does not elect to proceed under the resale provisions, as discussed above, he is entitled to an amount equal to the standard measure of damages for breach of contract. That is, the difference between the market price at the time and place for tender and the unpaid contract price, plus incidental damages but less expenses saved.

b. If the measure of damages provided above is inadequate to put the seller in as good a position as performance would have done, then the measure of damages is the profit (including reasonable overhead) which the seller would have made from full performance by the buyer, plus incidental damages, less due allowance for costs, and due credit for payments or proceeds of resale. E.g., if a dealer with a large supply of refrigerators finds a buyer who at first agrees to purchase one refrigerator for the standard price of $200 and then breaks his agreement, the buyer's breach injures the seller even if the seller is able to resell the refrigerator at the identical price. This is so since the seller made only one sale rather than two. This rule allows the seller to seek his lost profit as the measure of damages. This rule will also be resorted to in situations where there is no fair market value upon which to base damages.

8. Action for the price.
   a. When the buyer fails to pay the price as it becomes due, the seller may recover the price, plus any incidental damages, in three limited cases:
      (1) The buyer has accepted the goods.
      (2) The goods have been lost or destroyed after the loss has passed to the buyer.
      (3) The seller is unable, after a reasonable effort, to effect a resale of the goods he has retained.
   b. Goods which have been identified to the contract and are still in the seller's control must be held for the buyer unless resale becomes possible.
   c. A seller who is not entitled to recover the price is nevertheless entitled to damages.
9. Incidental damages: include any commercially reasonable charges, expenses, or commissions incurred in stopping delivery, in transportation, care, and custody of goods after the buyer's breach, in connection with return or resale of the goods or otherwise resulting from the breach.
10. Cure. Where the buyer rejects a non-conforming tender:
    a. If the time for performance has not expired, the seller may "cure" or correct the deficiency by seasonably notifying the buyer of his intention and may then within the contract time make a conforming delivery.
    b. If the seller had reasonable grounds to believe the goods would be acceptable with or without money allowance the seller may if he seasonably notifies the buyer have a further reasonable time to substitute a conforming tender.

(1) The purpose of this provision is to prevent "surprise rejections" which were frequently used under prior law in situations where the buyer was seeking to avoid his contractual obligations.

(2) "Reasonable grounds" can lie in prior course of dealing, course of performance, or usage of trade, as well as in the particular circumstances surrounding the making of the contract.

C. Buyer's remedies.

1. In general:

a. Where the seller fails to make delivery or repudiates or the buyer rightfully rejects or justifiably revokes acceptance then with respect to any goods involved, and with respect to the whole if the breach goes to the whole contract, the buyer may cancel and, whether or not he has done so, may in addition to recovering so much of the price as has been paid:

(1) "Cover" and obtain damages (see *infra*, p. 234, III.C.4.b.) for the goods affected, whether or not they have been identified to the contract, or

(2) Recover damages for non-delivery.

b. Where the seller fails to deliver or repudiates, the buyer may also:

(1) Recover goods identified to the contract and paid for where seller becomes insolvent (see p. 235, III.C.6.).

(2) In a proper case, obtain specific performance or replevy the goods (see *infra*, p 234, III.C.5.).

c. On rightful rejection or justifiable revocation of acceptance, a buyer has a security interest in the goods in his possession or control for any payments made on their price and any expenses reasonably incurred in their inspection, receipt, transportation, care, and custody and may hold such goods and resell them in like manner as an aggrieved seller. However, if a profit results, it must be turned over to the seller.

2. Improper delivery (e.g., breach of warranty): if the goods or the tender of delivery fails in any respect to conform to the contract (e.g., as when fruit delivered under a contract is undersized), the buyer may:

a. Reject all of the goods. If the buyer elects to reject, he must:

(1) Do so within a reasonable time.

(2) Seasonably notify the seller of his election (said election does not preclude recovery of damages).

(3) Take reasonable care of the goods until the seller retrieves them.

(4) Not exercise ownership of them (e.g., he may not resell them for his own account; see Contracts).

(5) Particularize reasonably discoverable defects. If the buyer fails to particularize (e.g., neglects to state that the fruit was undersized), he may not later use this fact to justify his rejection of the goods. The seller may have a right to cure the defects (see *infra,* p.231, III.C.4.). (see 8)

b. If he has at first accepted defective goods, the buyer may later revoke his acceptance:

(1) If the defects were hidden (e.g., if there were worms inside the fruit) or if the seller had assured him that the defects would be cured (see below, III.B.10.) and they were not, and

(2) If he notifies the seller of the breach within a reasonable time after discovery.

(3) If he returns the goods and cancels the contract. This alternative would not preclude the buyer's right to damages for breach of contract.

c. Accept any commercial unit or units, and reject the rest and recover damages.

d. Accept all of the goods. Acceptance does not preclude the buyer from recovering damages so long as he has notified the seller of the breach. Again, the old election-of-remedies rule has been clearly overturned.

3. Disposition of rejected goods.

a. A merchant buyer must follow any reasonable instructions that the seller gives him for the disposition of the goods. If the goods are perishable or of a type that will immediately decline in value, the merchant buyer who has received no instructions must make a reasonable effort to sell the goods (i.e., he must not allow a rejected shipment of peaches to rot if there is a ready market for them).

b. A non-merchant buyer who receives no instruction from the seller may:

(1) Store the goods.

(2) Send the goods back to the seller.

(3) Resell the goods for the seller. If the goods are resold, the seller must reimburse the buyer for any expenses incurred in the sale.

4. Buyer's damages.

a. Measure of damages: the difference between the contract price and the market price of comparable goods *at the time the buyer learns of the breach* plus any incidental and consequential damages.

(1) Where the market price in the buyer's area is difficult to determine:

(A) Figures in trade journals, official publications, newspapers, and periodicals of general circulation may be used as evidence.

(B) The buyer may use the price prevailing within any reasonable time before or after the time described or at any other place which in commercial judgment or under usage of trade would serve as a reasonable substitute.

(2) Where the buyer has accepted the goods but has notified the seller of the breach, his damages are measured by the loss resulting in the ordinary course of events from the seller's breach as determined in any reasonable manner.

b. Cover.

(1) Permits a buyer to procure substitute goods in the open market when the seller has repudiated or failed to deliver. His primary damages become the difference between the actual cost of replacement and the contract price.

(2) The buyer is under no duty to "cover" or take the least expensive course of action, so long as his choice of conduct is reasonable and in good faith.

(3) If the buyer chooses not to cover, he may receive damages for non-delivery (see above 4.a.).

c. Incidental and consequential damages.

(1) Incidental damages are expenses reasonably incurred as a result of the delay or breach, including:

(A) Inspection, receipt, transportation, and care and custody of goods rightfully rejected.

(B) Any commercially reasonable charges, expenses, or commissions in connection with effecting cover.

(2) Consequential damages include:

(A) Any damage resulting from the seller's breach which the seller at the time of the contracting had reason to know, and

(B) Which could not reasonably be prevented by cover or otherwise, and

(C) Injury to person or property proximately resulting from any breach of warranty.

5. Specific performance, replevin, and recoupment.

a. To obtain specific performance:

(1) The goods must be unique (e.g., a famous painting), or

(2) Other proper circumstances must exist (e.g., inability to cover).

b. Generally, replevin (i.e., recovering possession of the goods) is given only where cover is not reasonably available.

c. Upon notification of breach to the seller, the buyer is permitted to deduct from the price still due (recoup) all or any part of the damages resulting from the seller's breach.

6. Buyer's rights on seller's insolvency. Goods whether delivered or undelivered may be recovered by the buyer if:

a. The buyer has paid all or a part of the purchase price and keeps open an offer to pay the rest.

b. The buyer has a special property interest in the goods. To create such an interest, the goods must be identified in the contract (i.e., the buyer must prove that the particular goods are the ones he contracted to buy).

c. The seller becomes insolvent within 10 days after receipt of the first installment on the price of the goods.

D. Anticipatory repudiation by either party.

1. Occurs when one party demonstrates a clear intention, with respect to a performance obligation not yet due, not to perform or acts in a way which renders performance impossible.

2. When the repudiation will substantially impair the value of the contract to the aggrieved party, that party (seller or buyer) may:

a. For a commercially reasonable time await performance by the repudiating party, or

b. Resort to any remedy for breach (see above pp. 228, 232), even though he has notified the repudiating party that he would await the latter's performance and has urged retraction, and

c. In either case suspend his own performance or proceed in accordance with provisions on the seller's right to identify goods to the contract, notwithstanding breach, or complete unfinished goods (see *supra*, p.230, III .B.5.).

E. Right to assurances: When reasonable grounds for insecurity arise with respect to the performance of either party, the other may demand in writing adequate assurance of due performance. The aggrieved party may also:

1. Suspend his own performance pending the outcome of the demand.

2. Treat the contract as broken if his reasonable grounds for insecurity are not cleared up within a reasonable time.

IV. BULK SALES: UCC ARTICLE 6

A. Article 6 applies to all those whose principal business is the sale of merchandise from stock, including those who manufacture what they sell (e.g., a toy manufacturer who produces toys in one part of his shop and sells them in another).

B. The purpose of Article 6 is to deal with two common forms of commercial fraud:

1. Where merchant, owing debts, sells out his stock in trade to a friend for less than it is worth, pays his creditors less than he owes them, and hopes to come back into the business through the back door some time in the future.
2. Where the merchant, owing debts, sells out his stock in trade to anyone for any price, pockets the proceeds, and disappears, leaving his creditors unpaid.

C. Rules.

1. A bulk transfer is valid if the seller and buyer make a schedule of the property and the buyer obtains a list of the creditors and gives them adequate notice of the intended sale.
2. There is an optional provision which, if adopted by state legislatures, would require the buyer to apply the consideration for the sale to the debts of the seller. Otherwise, he has no such duty.
3. Failure by the bulk buyer to comply with the above requirements invalidates the sale, and he must either return the goods purchased or satisfy the claims of the bulk seller's creditors.
4. Where the bulk sale is by auction, the auctioneer is required to follow the procedures required of the buyer at a regular bulk sale.
5. A subsequent *bona fide* purchaser (i.e., one taking for value, in good faith, and without notice of fraud) from a bulk buyer, in the situation where the bulk buyer has not met the above requirements, is nevertheless protected against the creditors.

V. WRONGFUL SALES TO THIRD PARTIES

A. Power to transfer title to good-faith purchaser of goods.

1. A purchaser of goods acquires all title which his transferor had or had power to transfer except that a purchaser of a limited interest acquires rights only to the extent of the interest purchased. A person with voidable title has power to transfer a good title to a good faith purchaser for value. When goods have been delivered under a transaction of purchase the purchaser has such power even though:

a. the transferor was deceived as to the identity of the purchaser, or
b. the delivery was in exchange for a check which is later dishonored, or
c. it was agreed that the transaction was to be a "cash sale", or
d. the delivery was procured through fraud punishable as larcenous under the criminal law.

B. Entrusting.

1. Any entrusting of possession of goods to a merchant who deals in goods of that kind gives him power to transfer all rights of the entruster to a buyer in ordinary course of business.
2. "Entrusting" includes any delivery and any acquiescence in retention of possession regardless of any condition expressed between the parties to the delivery or acquiescence and regardless of whether the procurement of the entrusting or the possessor's disposition of the goods have been such as to be larcenous under the criminal law.
3. The rights of other purchasers of goods and of lien creditors are governed by the Articles on Secured Transactions (Article 9), Bulk Transfers (Article 6), and Documents of Title (Article 7).

SALES: SUBJECTIVE QUESTIONS*

CHARACTERISTICS

Q. Korn, a fur coat manufacturer, wished to promote a new style of coat and approached Carter's Department Stores, Inc. with the following proposal: If Carter would allow Korn to sell the coats on a "special promotion" in Carter's store for two days, Korn would split all profits with Carter on a 50-50 basis and give Carter exclusive rights to sell the coats in the area thereafter if Carter so desired. The "special promotion" sale was to be conducted by Korn's personnel, Carter was to furnish Korn with counter space in the store and space in the fur storage vault of the store for keeping the coats during non-business hours. Carter agreed to this proposition. After the close of business on the first day of the promotion, the fur storage vault having been secured in the usual manner, Carter's was burglarized and Korn's coats were stolen from the vault. Korn asserts that Carter must make good his loss.

(1) Describe the relationship between Carter and Korn.
(2) On the facts given, was Carter liable to Korn? Explain.
(3) Assuming Carter is liable to and pays Korn and has a "floater" theft insurance policy on merchandise in the store, may the insurer

* See Introductory Note, p. 19.

defend against Carter's claim on the policy on the ground that Carter had no insurable interest in the coats? Explain.

5/70; pp. 219-220

Certain terms appear frequently in legal matters. Define each of the following:

(1) Fungible goods.
(2) Bulk transfers.
(3) Sale.
(4) Bailment.

11/65; p. 219

RISK OF LOSS

Q. A college bookstore ordered 100 copies of a standard accounting text from the publisher. The contract is ambiguous as to whether a "sale on approval" or a "sale or return" was intended. Two days after receipt of the books they were inadvertently damaged when a water pipe burst and flooded the storeroom. Which type of sale will the publisher argue was intended by the parties? Why? Explain.

5/62; p. 222

Q. Tom ordered 1,000 pairs of cordovan shoes from the Bunion Shoe Company. The terms were F.O.B. X Railroad at seller's railroad siding. The Bunion Shoe Company packed and delivered the 1,000 pairs of shoes to the X Railroad. During the transportation of the shoes to Tom, torrential rains caused widespread flooding and water seeped into the boxcar carrying the shoes. As a result, the shoes were discolored and damaged in other respects. The buyer refuses to accept the goods and claims that the risk of loss remained with the seller. Is he correct? Explain.

5/61; p. 222

Q. Acme Store had 100 boxes of special-design shirts, packed six shirts to a box, which it offered to sell to Bell for $10 per box. Bell accepted the offer, asked the Store to bill him at month's end, and said that he would send for the shirts the following day. Upon receiving Bell's acceptance, the Store tied together the boxes into five bundles, tagged each bundle with Bell's name, and placed the lot in the "pick-up" room. During that night the building accidentally, and without negligence on the part of the Store, caught fire and two of the bundles were wholly destroyed. What are the rights of the parties according to the Uniform Commercial Code? Explain.

5/65; p. 223

Q. Alpha Store had entered into a contract with Curtis for the installation of six heavy-duty sewing machines at the Store. Following the description of the sewing machines, together with the price of each article, the written contract provided: "*This outfit (six sewing machines as described) is subject to ten days' free trial and is to be installed within a week after the signing of the agreement.*" The machines were duly installed and six days thereafter were destroyed in an accidental fire which swept through the Store. Curtis contends that the Store is liable for the purchase price of the sewing machines. The Store denies liability. Is the Store liable according to the Uniform Commercial Code? Explain.

5/65; p. 223

EXPRESS WARRANTIES

Q. X Company, a manufacturer of clothing, received a brochure from Y Company extolling the virtues and describing in detail the specifications and results of laboratory tests regarding the strength, flexibility, resistance to strain, workability, and other attributes of various types of its plastic materials. Relying upon data contained in the brochure, X ordered a large quantity of one certain type of plastic material which was made into raincoats. To X's dismay, the material was wholly unsatisfactory for this purpose, as it had a definite tendency to tear under ordinary use. X seeks to recover damages from Y for breach of warranty. Does X have a valid claim against Y?

5/60; p. 224

IMPLIED WARRANTIES

Q. The Sudsy Soap Company received an order from the Williams Wholesale Distributing Corporation for one thousand boxes (12 to a box) of Sudsy's best cake soap. The shipment arrived and was accepted by the Williams Corporation. Shortly thereafter Williams discovered that the boxes were somewhat the worse for wear, because they had received rough treatment in handling. Upon opening a random sample of some 50 boxes it was found that the individual packages of each cake were discolored and that many cakes of soap were cracked in half. Williams tried to sell the soap to its customers and delayed paying Sudsy's bill. After six months had elapsed and Williams saw that there would be a considerable loss in connection with the sale of the soap it notified Sudsy that it would only take the soap at a greatly reduced price and that if Sudsy wouldn't accept this it rescinded the whole transaction. Williams also indicated that under no circumstances would it pay the face value of the bill. Sudsy demands payment in full.

(1) Is the soap of merchantable quality? Explain what is meant by

this term and list the criteria that would be used by the court in determining whether the goods in question are merchantable.

(2) Will Sudsy be able to collect the full amount of the price for the soap? Explain.

(3) List three remedies that would be available for breach of warranty.

11/62; pp. 225, 232

Q. S offers to sell B an automobile. B insists on an inspection before purchasing and S readily agrees to this. B spends several hours examining the automobile.

(1) Explain the impact of a buyer's *inspection* of the automobile upon his express and implied warranty protection.

5/64; p. 227

Q. Jerry wishes to purchase twenty radios for his appliance store. He went to the Hi-tone Radio Company, and they proceeded to show him some samples. Jerry considered one of the samples an excellent buy at the price. The sample shown had some obvious imperfections in the finish and, in addition, would only play on alternating current whereas most radios could play on either alternating or direct current. There was a sticker on the back of the radio indicating that it should not be used with direct current without a converter. Jerry examined the radio, listened to its tone, range, and volume, and decided he couldn't pass up the opportunity at that price. The rural area in which Jerry's store was located used direct current. When Jerry received the radios they all had imperfect finishes and were in all other ways exactly like the sample he inspected. When he plugged one in the socket, it blew several tubes.

(1) Which warranties (other than those expressly stated and the implied title warranties) arise in sales transactions? List them.

(2) Which of the implied warranties, if any, has been breached here? Explain.

5/61; p. 226

Q. Ozgood purchased a used automobile from Superior Auto Sales Corporation. Unfortunately the car was defective. In order to put the car in adequate running condition Ozgood had to replace the clutch and have a complete overhaul of the motor. The car was only one year old and appeared to be in good condition at the time of purchase. The salesman orally assured Ozgood that the car was an excellent buy and in "good shape." Ozgood offered to have the car examined by his mechanic, but the salesman assured him this would not be necessary. Ozgood demanded that Superior Auto Sales Corporation repair the auto, but they refused. He, therefore, took it to several authorized dealers and, after several bids on the repair job, selected the low bid. This amounted to $625. He now seeks to recover that amount based upon breach of warranty. Superior Auto Sales relies upon the following disclaimer clause: "All warranties express and implied are hereby disclaimed." This appeared on the back of the form along with a large number of standardized provisions which were all in very small type.

(1) What warranties are created as a result of the above fact situation?

(2) Will the disclaimer clause effectively preclude Ozgood from recovery of the $625? Discuss.

5/67; p. 227

Q. Fan Motor Company purchased a motor from the Excello Motor Manufacturing Company. The contract contained several written express warranties followed by a written description of the motor purchased and a disclaimer clause. It stated in the description that the motor had a kilowatt capacity of 650. This kilowatt capacity was very important to Fan Motor. It turned out that the motor had a kilowatt capacity of less than 600, which rendered the motor worthless for Fan Motor's use. Fan Motor seeks to rescind the transaction. Excello refuses, stating that the motor meets all the requirements contained in the express warranties, which is true. Excello admits that the motor did not meet the 650 kilowatt capacity but asserts that this was merely a part of the description and not an express warranty. Furthermore, the disclaimer clause admittedly effectively precludes any reliance upon implied warranty protection. As between Fan Motor and Excello, who will prevail? Explain.

5/67; pp. 226-227

Q. Martha purchased a can of Pure Best Quality Company's beef stew from the corner grocer. This was served to her maid at the luncheon meal. One hour later the maid developed an acute case of ptomaine poisoning. The maid is seeking to recover damages against the corner grocer, who asserts that he has no liability to her in that she was not the purchaser of the contaminated stew. Can the maid sue and recover from the corner grocer? Discuss.

5/67; pp. 226-227

SELLER'S REMEDIES

Q. Franks contracted to sell to Acme Construction Corporation 1,000 cases of first-quality blue roofing shingles which were to be exactly ¼ of an inch thick. The contract required that delivery be made by November 1, 1969. Franks made delivery on October 15, 1969 and was notified on October 20, 1969 that 100 cases contained shingles which were less than ¼ of an inch thick and 50 additional cases contained shingles which were off-color. These cases had inadvertently been included in the shipment as the result of a new employee's selecting some cases from an area which contained seconds.

Franks immediately notified Acme that he would ship 150 replacement cases. The cases were delivered on October 30, 1969, but Acme refused to accept them. Acme insisted that the contract had been breached and that Acme was no longer obligated to perform. Acme also indicated all cases would be returned to Franks. Assuming Acme returns all the cases of shingles, would it have any liability as a result of its action? Explain.

11/69; pp. 231-232

BUYER'S REMEDIES

Q. Typewriter Supply Company contracted to sell to Harper Corporation 75 Wonder model typewriters. The terms were $600 per typewriter, delivery and payment to be made one month from the date of the execution of the contract. Two weeks after the contract was executed Typewriter Supply notified Harper Corporation that the obligation would not be fulfilled because prior commitments had entirely depleted the supply of Wonder typewriters. Harper immediately purchased 75 Wonder typewriters elsewhere at the prevailing market price of $625 per typewriter.

Prior to the expiration of the one month delivery date contained in the original contract between Typewriter Supply and Harper, Star Typewriter Manufacturing introduced a revolutionary new model. This depressed the market price for Wonder typewriters to $550, which was the prevailing market price at the scheduled delivery date to Harper.

(1) What was the legal effect of Typewriter Supply's notification that delivery of the Wonder typewriters would not be made? Explain.
(2) What rights and remedies were available to Harper as a result of receipt of the notification that Typewriter Supply would not perform? Explain.
(3) What, if any, is the amount of damages to which Harper is entitled? Explain.

11/69; pp. 233-235

BULK SALES

Q. Several large creditors of the now defunct Valvo Plumbing Corporation have written letters to Sanitary Plumbing Corporation demanding the purchase price or the return of large quantities of plumbing supplies the creditors sold to Valvo on account. Sanitary Plumbing had purchased all of Valvo's assets, which consisted almost exclusively of its stock in trade (plumbing supplies), office equipment and fixtures. The purchase was privately negotiated and notice was not given by Sanitary to Valvo's creditors. The owners of Valvo have disappeared without paying their trade creditors. What liability, if any does Sanitary Plumbing have as a result of the above facts? Explain.

11/69; p. 236

SALES: OBJECTIVE QUESTIONS

Each of the following numbered phrases or clauses states a legal conclusion as it completes the related lettered material. You are to determine whether each of the legal conclusions is true or false according to the provisions of Article 2 (Sales) of the Uniform Commercial Code and general principles of law. Your grade will be determined from your total net score obtained by deducting your total of incorrect answers from your total of correct answers; an omitted answer will not be considered an incorrect answer.

(1) Franklin purchased a new Wizard automobile from Superior Auto Sales, Inc., the local Wizard dealer. The contract of sale was silent on the question of warranty protection except for the following clause:

"The actual buyer of this automobile is the only person entitled to any warranty protection arising from the sale by Superior Auto Sales, Inc. of this Wizard automobile."

Franklin was aware of this provision at the time he purchased the automobile.

Several days later the automobile collided with an oncoming truck. Franklin, his wife and their maid were injured. The collision also caused extensive damage to the automobile. It was conclusively determined that the collision was caused by a faulty part in the Wizard's steering mechanism.

(a) If Franklin returned the automobile to Superior Auto Sales, Inc. and received his money back, his action would constitute an election to rescind and would preclude recovery of damages.

(b) Mrs. Franklin will be precluded from recovering from Superior Auto as a result of the clause limiting warranty protection to the actual buyer.

(c) Even if the contract did not contain the clause limiting warranty protection, the maid would be precluded from suing Superior Auto because of lack of privity.

(d) The Uniform Commercial Code expressly permits a purchaser of a product purchased from a local sales representative to sue the manufacturer of the product.

(e) Since Superior Auto's contract of sale did not contain any express warranty protection, recovery can only be obtained if negligence is proven.

(2) Martin purchased an earth-mover from the Strong Equipment

Company. The written contract contained a detailed description of the capabilities of the equipment under varying conditions. In addition the contract conspicuously stated: "There are no warranties which extend beyond the description contained herein."

(a) Martin received an express warranty by description.
(b) The parol evidence rule would be asserted against Martin if he attempted to rely upon an oral express warranty made prior to the execution of the contract and which added to the description of the earth-mover's capabilities.
(c) An implied warranty of fitness was effectively excluded by the above disclaimer.
(d) An implied warranty of merchantability was excluded by the above disclaimer.
(e) If the contract of sale had contained language clearly indicating that the earth-mover was sold "as is," Martin would lose all implied warranty protection.

(3) Parker ordered 50 cartons of soap flakes from Riddle Wholesale Company. Each carton contained 12 packages of soap flakes. The terms were: Eight dollars per carton, 2/10, net/30, F.O.B. buyer's delivery platform, delivery by June 1.

During transit approximately one half the packages were damaged as a result of being crushed by other merchandise being carried by the local motor carrier. The delivery was made on May 28.

(a) Riddle had the risk of loss during transit.
(b) If Parker elects to accept the undamaged part of the shipment, he will be deemed to have accepted the entire shipment.
(c) To validly reject the goods, Parker must give timely notice of rejection to Riddle within a reasonable time after delivery.
(d) If Riddle were notified of the rejection on May 28, Riddle could cure the defect by promptly notifying Parker of its intention to do so and making a second delivery to Parker of conforming goods by June 1.
(e) The Statute of Frauds is inapplicable to the transaction in the facts given in "C."

(4) Johnston, a retail appliance dealer, agreed to buy 25 color television sets from Reliable T.V. Manufacturing Company. The sets were promptly delivered and according to the terms of the contract Johnston was granted the right to return any or all of the sets within one month from the date of delivery. The contract was otherwise silent on the type of sale contemplated and the question of risk of loss.

Two weeks after receipt of the sets Johnston's storage area was flooded, severely damaging 20 of the sets shipped by Reliable T.V. The flooding was not due to any negligence on Johnston's part. Johnston seeks to return the 20 damaged sets.

(a) Johnston would prevail if he could persuade the court that the transaction was a "sale or return."

(b) According to the facts given, the transaction should be categorized as a "sale on approval."

(c) If Reliable T.V. retained a non-possessory security interest in the T.V. sets, the risk of loss to the extent of such security interest will be placed upon Reliable T.V.

(d) Unless Johnston had title to the T.V. sets he would not have a valid insurable interest in them.

(e) If Johnston elected to return the 5 sets which were not damaged, the return would be at the buyer's expense.

(5) Andrews wished to purchase a second-hand calculator. He saw the model he wanted on sale at the Addito Calculator Company showroom. The salesman indicated that the price did not include delivery and that Andrews would have to take it with him or have it picked up within two days because storage space was scarce at Addito. Andrews agreed to these terms, signed the contract and said he would pick up the calculator the next day.

The Addito salesman marked the calculator "sold," placed Andrews' name on it and moved it to the storeroom. That night thieves broke into the storeroom and removed all items, including the calculator in question. This was in no way caused by the negligence of Addito. Andrews refuses to pay unless he receives the calculator. Addito claims the sale had been consummated, that title had passed, and Andrews therefore must pay the agreed price.

(a) Title is irrelevant in determining who bears the risk of loss in the above transaction.

(b) Because Addito is a merchant, risk of loss does not pass to Andrews until he receives the calculator.

(c) Andrews would have to pay for the calculator if the contract had expressly provided that Andrews would bear the risk of loss from the time the contract was signed.

(d) If Andrews had agreed to pick up the calculator the afternoon of the sale and failed to do so, the risk of loss would rest with Andrews to the extent that the calculator was not effectively covered by Addito's insurance.

(e) If the contract had contained the delivery term, F.O.B., place of delivery, Addito would be unable to collect the purchase price.

(6) Smart, a used car dealer, showed a 1967 automobile to Giles. Smart told Giles, "In my opinion the car is a dandy buy for the money, a real honey, and a car you would be happy owning." Smart honestly believed these statements.

Giles liked the looks of the car but insisted on a trial run and personal inspection. Giles knew very little about automobiles. He drove the car at varying speeds and examined the usual things an unsophisticated buyer would ordinarily inspect. He could find nothing wrong with the car and bought it. The car had an almost invisible hairline crack in the engine block at the time of sale.

The contract of sale contained a disclaimer clause which stated: "The buyer expressly waives all warranty protection afforded him in connection with the purchase of this automobile." This clause was in fine print in the middle of the seventh page of the contract. Giles was not aware of it at the time of the purchase.

(a) Smart's sales talk constituted an express warranty.
(b) The fact that Smart honestly believed the statements he made in connection with the sale was irrelevant insofar as Giles' warranty protection is concerned.
(c) The disclaimer described above is invalid.
(d) Giles will be precluded from recovering for breach of warranty as a result of his test drive and inspection.
(e) If Giles cannot recover for breach of warranty, he can recover damages based upon fraud.

11/68

(7) The privity of warranty requirement
(a) Where applicable, precludes suits for breach of warranty by buyers who have no direct contractual relationship with the manufacturer of the product purchased.
(b) Has been expressly abolished.
(c) Is gradually being narrowed by judicial decision and legislative action.
(d) Does not apply to suits brought against the seller by the family, household, or guests of the purchaser.
(e) Precludes suits for negligence by buyers who have no direct contractual relationship with the manufacturer of the product manufactured.

(8) A merchant seller
(a) Is deemed to give the buyer certain implied warranties of title.
(b) Warrants that the title conveyed shall be good and its transfer rightful.
(c) Warrants that the goods shall be delivered free of any security interest or other lien or encumbrance whether known or unknown to the buyer at the time of contracting.
(d) Cannot disclaim the title warranties.
(e) Warrants, as to kinds of goods that he regularly deals in, that the goods shall be delivered free of any third party's rightful claim of patent or trade mark infringement.

(9) An express warranty
(a) Created by an affirmation of fact or promise by the seller must be in writing to be valid.
(b) Can only be created if the seller uses the words warrant or guarantee.
(c) Can only be created where the seller has manifested an intention to make a warranty.
(d) Can be created by a description of the goods which is made a part of the basis of the bargain.

(e) Is created by the seller's affirmation of the value of his goods.

(10) The warranty of merchantability
(a) Cannot be disclaimed or modified.
(b) Does not apply to the serving for value of food or drink to be consumed on the seller's premises.
(c) Is implied in a contract of sale of goods if the seller is a merchant with respect to goods of that kind.
(d) Requires that fungible goods be better than average quality within the description.
(e) Implies that the goods are fit for all purposes for which such goods are used.

(11) The warranty of fitness for a particular purpose
(a) Cannot be created unless the buyer expressly makes known any particular purpose for which the goods are required.
(b) Does not apply to goods which are purchased under a patent or trade name.
(c) Is not applicable if the buyer relies on his own skill or judgment to select suitable goods.
(d) Will be effectively disclaimed if the seller indicates the goods are sold "as is."
(e) Will not be effectively disclaimed by language such as "all implied warranties are hereby disclaimed."

(12) A sells B 1,000 yards of carpeting at $1 a yard using a sample piece of the carpet to induce B to buy.
(a) In that this is a sale by sample, the Statute of Frauds will not apply.
(b) B has obtained an implied warranty that the whole of the goods will conform to the sample.
(c) B cannot assert an implied warranty of merchantability.
(d) B, having examined the sample as fully as he desired, cannot rely upon implied warranty protection with regard to defects which he ought under the circumstances to have discovered.
(e) Whatever warranties B has received, whether expressed or implied, shall be construed as consistent with each other and cumulative.

(13) On January 1, S, a dealer, wrote to B: "I hereby offer to sell you the following goods (describing them) for $600. This offer will remain open for six months."
(a) This offer may be withdrawn at any time before acceptance unless there is consideration for the assurance to keep the offer open.
(b) This offer is irrevocable for the time stated.
(c) This offer is irrevocable for only three months.
(d) This offer cannot be accepted during the fourth month even though it has not been withdrawn.
(e) This offer would be irrevocable for its entire duration if it were supported by consideration.

(14) The Sales Article Statute of Frauds requirements

(a) Apply to contracts for the sale of goods for the price of $300 or more.
(b) Do not apply to the sale of choses in action.
(c) May bind a merchant who receives and ignores a signed written confirmation by a fellow merchant of the sale of goods.
(d) Provide that a written memorandum of sale will be insufficient if it fails to indicate the agreed quantity of goods sold.
(e) Provide that a written memorandum of sale will be insufficient if it fails to indicate the price agreed upon.

(15) In a "sale or return" transaction
(a) Risk of loss passes to the buyer at the time the buyer manifests his final acceptance of the goods.
(b) The option to return must be exercised within ten days from receipt of the goods if no time is stated.
(c) The return is at the buyer's risk and expense unless otherwise agreed.
(d) The goods are subject to the claims of the buyer's creditors while in the buyer's possession.
(e) The buyer may return the goods even if they are wholly as warranted.

(16) Risk of loss, in the absence of breach of contract,
(a) Passes to the buyer at the time the contract of sale is made in respect to specific goods in a deliverable state.
(b) Can be agreed upon by the parties to the contract.
(c) Passes to the buyer when the seller delivers the goods to the carrier for the required delivery to a particular destination.
(d) Depends upon when title to the goods passes to the buyer.
(e) Remains with the seller whether or not he is required to make delivery at a particular destination so long as he retains a security interest in the goods.

(17) Where conforming goods are shipped pursuant to a shipping term, risk of loss
(a) Passes to the buyer upon delivery to the carrier if the term is F.O.B. the place of shipment.
(b) Remains with the seller until the goods are loaded on the carrier where the term is F.O.B. railroad car, seller's place of business.
(c) Passes to the buyer at the same time whether the terms are C.I.F. or C. & F.
(d) Will be determined by a shipping term in the contract unless it is used in connection with the stated price and destination.
(e) Cannot otherwise be allocated by the parties.

(18) The seller may recover the price if
(a) The goods are accepted by the buyer.
(b) The goods have been lost or destroyed and risk of loss has passed to the buyer.

(c) The goods are in transit and title has irrevocably passed to the buyer.
(d) The seller is unable, after reasonable effort, to resell the goods identified to the contract at a reasonable price.
(e) The buyer has wrongfully rejected the goods.

11/66

(19) Unless a contrary intention appears, a buyer purchasing equipment is protected by a warranty that
(a) The price charged for the equipment is a reasonable one.
(b) The seller's title to the equipment conveyed is good.
(c) The seller of the equipment is financially solvent.
(d) The seller of the equipment will remain in business for a reasonable length of time to be able to service the goods sold.
(e) The equipment shall be delivered free from any security interest which the buyer at the time of contract has no knowledge of.

(20) Express warranties are created
(a) By a seller's stating his opinion as to the value of goods.
(b) By a seller's stating his opinion as to the length of time the goods will provide trouble-free service.
(c) By a seller's displaying a sample or model and stating that all of the goods shall conform to it.
(d) By a seller's describing the goods and stating that all of the goods shall conform to the description.
(e) By a seller's making an affirmation which is excluded from being part of the basis of the bargain.

(21) Fassler sells Karasyk a washing machine to be delivered within 30 days after the sale. When a machine was delivered within five days after the sale, it was found that a mistake was made and the wrong model was delivered. In such a case
(a) Karasyk must accept delivery of the nonconforming machine and sue Fassler for damages.
(b) Karasyk may reject delivery and refuse to take immediate delivery of the correct machine.
(c) Fassler may within the 30 days allowed for delivery notify Karasyk of his intention to supply the correct machine and may then make a proper delivery within the 30 days allowed.
(d) Fassler may within the 30 days allowed for delivery notify Karasyk of his intention to supply the correct machine and then make a proper delivery within a reasonable time after the 30 days have elapsed.
(e) Since he has breached the sales contract, Fassler may not deliver the correct machine to Karasyk without first obtaining his consent.

(22) The warranty of merchantability

(a) Is an implied warranty only if the seller of goods is a merchant with respect to the goods sold.
(b) Is an implied warranty in any sale.
(c) Does not extend to the serving for value of food or drink in a restaurant as this is a service and not a sale.
(d) Means that goods must always be above average quality.
(e) Extends to the adequacy of the container in which the goods are packaged.

(23) The warranty of fitness for a particular purpose
(a) Is never an implied warranty.
(b) Cannot exist if goods are purchased by trade name.
(c) Cannot exist if the buyer has not relied on the seller's skill or judgment to select suitable goods.
(d) If applicable, cannot be excluded by disclaimer.
(e) If applicable, may be excluded by a course of dealing between the parties.

(24) A seller's warranty
(a) Extends to any person who comes in contact with the goods sold.
(b) Extends only to the buyer.
(c) May extend to persons other than the buyer only if the warranty is an express warranty.
(d) May extend to a member of the buyer's family.
(e) May extend to a guest in the buyer's home.

(25) The concept of passage of title
(a) No longer remains as important as it once was in determining rights of buyers and sellers.
(b) Governs who bears risk of loss.
(c) Always determines whether an action for the price may be maintained, as contrasted with an action for damages.
(d) Always determines the seller's right to reclaim goods sold.
(e) Always determines insurable interest.

(26) The term "F.O.B."
(a) Means "free on board."
(b) Means "freight on board."
(c) May control who bears the risk of loss of goods in transit.
(d) May control who bears the expense of shipping goods.
(e) Standing alone is an incomplete statement of a delivery term.

(27) The term "F.A.S."
(a) Means "freight and shipping."
(b) Means "free alongside."
(c) May control who bears the risk of loss of goods in transit.
(d) When used, may require the buyer to give needed instructions for making delivery of the goods.
(e) Should not be used together with the term "F.O.B.," as the terms used together would be contradictory.

(28) The term "C.I.F."

(a) Means that the price includes the cost of the goods and the insurance and freight to the named destination.
(b) Means cash is to be paid if the goods are to be forwarded.
(c) When used, requires the buyer, unless otherwise agreed, to obtain insurance to cover goods in transit.
(d) When used, still requires the buyer, unless otherwise agreed, to make payment against required documents of title for the goods which are held by the seller's agent.
(e) Should be used together with the statement of a named destination for goods to be shipped.

(29) Under a sale on approval, unless otherwise agreed,

(a) The risk of loss does not pass to the buyer until acceptance although the goods are identified to the contract.
(b) Title to the goods passes to the buyer on receipt by him of the goods if the goods are identified to the contract.
(c) Use of the goods consistent with the purpose of trial constitutes an acceptance of the goods by the buyer.
(d) Failure by the buyer to give timely notification to the seller of his election to return the goods constitutes an acceptance of the goods.
(e) Acceptance of any part of the goods is acceptance of the whole of the goods if the goods conform to the contract.

(30) When goods have been delivered by a seller to a buyer under a transaction of purchase, the buyer has power to effectively transfer a good title to the goods to a good faith purchaser for value

(a) Even though the seller was deceived as to the identity of the buyer.
(b) Even though the delivery of the goods by the seller was in exchange for a check which was later dishonored.
(c) Even though there was an agreement between the seller and the buyer that the transaction was to be a "cash sale" but cash was not received by the seller.
(d) Even though the delivery was procured through fraud.
(e) Only if the good faith purchaser for value is a merchant.

11/67

TOPIC EIGHT | # SECURED TRANSACTIONS

CONTENTS PAGE

*SECURED TRANSACTIONS. Article 9 (Secured Transactions) of the Uniform Commercial Code, which contains a new and comprehensive set of laws regulating security in personal property, is covered under this topic. The Article applies whenever personal property is used as security for a debt and to outright sales of accounts receivable and chattel paper. Creation, attachment, and perfection of a security interest, and the various priorities and rights of creditors and third parties are included.**

I. CHARACTERISTICS

A. Scope of Uniform Commercial Code, Article Nine (Secured Transactions):

1. Applies to any transaction (regardless of its form) which is intended to create a security interest in personal property or fixtures. Unlike prior law, the rights, obligations, and remedies of the parties to the secured transaction do not depend on title.
2. Supersedes existing legislation dealing with traditional security devices, such as chattel mortgages, conditional sales, trust receipts, factor's liens, and assignments of accounts receivable.
3. Provides basic uniformity throughout the United States for the first time in the history of security interests involving personal property.

B. Definitions

1. Security interest: an interest in personal property or fixtures

* Source: AICPA, *Information for CPA Candidates* (July 1970).

which secures payment or performance of an obligation. Such a security interest is either possessory or non-possessory.
2. Secured party: a lender, seller, or other person in whose favor there is a security interest, including a person to whom accounts, contract rights, or chattel paper have been sold.
3. Purchase-money security interest: a security interest is a "purchase-money security interest" to the extent that it is taken or retained by the seller of the collateral to secure payment of all or part of the purchase price or taken by a person who gives value to the debtor to enable him to acquire the collateral. As you will see, this is a most important definition.

II. CLASSIFICATION OF COLLATERAL

A. Tangible collateral

1. The Code divides tangible property into four different classes of goods.
   a. Consumer goods: goods used or bought primarily for personal, family, or household use.
   b. Equipment: goods used or bought for use primarily in business (including farming or a profession) or by a debtor who is a non-profit corporation or governmental sub-division or agency, or goods not included in the definitions of inventory, farm products, or consumer goods.
   c. Farm products: crops or livestock or supplies used or produced in a farming operation or products of crops or livestock in their unmanufactured state, if they are in possession of a debtor engaged in raising, fattening, grazing, or other farming operations.
   d. Inventory: goods that a person holds for sale or lease, or to be furnished under contracts of service or if he has so furnished them, or if they are raw materials, work in progress, or materials used or consumed in a business. A person's inventory is not classified as his equipment.
   e. The above classification of tangible collateral should be thoroughly mastered. Many of the rules that follow depend upon type of property involved.
2. The categorization is determined not necessarily by the physical characteristics of the property but by the characteristics of the owner-buyer or the owner-borrower (e.g., a refrigerator bought for use in the home would be a consumer good, but if bought for use in a physician's office would be equipment).
3. Where collateral has varying uses (e.g., an automobile used by a salesman for both professional and personal needs), the Code permits only one definition in a particular circumstance and the primary use governs (the one established either by declaration of

the debtor-owner at the time of acquisition of the collateral or by the physical facts existing at that time).

B. **Intangible collateral: the Code establishes three classifications for intangible property.**

1. Account: any right to payment for goods sold or leased or for services rendered—a right not evidenced by an instrument or chattel paper.
2. Contract right: any right to payment under a contract not yet earned by performance and not evidenced by an instrument or chattel paper.
3. General intangibles: any personal property (including things in action) other than goods, accounts, contract rights, chattel paper, documents, and instruments.

C. **Documentary collateral: the Code defines three kinds of documentary collateral.**

1. Instruments: includes a negotiable draft, check, certificate of deposit, or promissory note.
2. Documents: includes documents of title (such as a bill of lading, dock warrant, dock receipt, warehouse receipt, or order for delivery of goods) and any other document of title issued or addressed to a bailee (a keeper of goods) and giving instructions concerning goods in the bailee's possession.
3. Chattel paper: includes the usual conditional sales contract or a note and chattel mortgage. The Code has actually replaced these security devices but they remain in use and are effective under the Code so long as they meet its requirements.

III. THE PROBLEM

A. In order to understand this complex area of law, it is helpful to place yourself mentally in the shoes of a secured creditor. As such, you have to be concerned with the competing interests and claims of several people or classes of people. Your aim is to resort to the property to satisfy your loan; you must worry about the following people:

B. The debtor: essentially, a secured creditor's rights vis-à-vis his debtor are determined *by the contract* once the security interest attaches (see *infra*, p. 256, V). Formalities are minimal in relation to this party.

C. Lien and attaching creditors:

1. These competing creditors of the debtor are creditors who as a last resort have employed judicial process against the debtor in order to recover a debt.
2. A formal act is usually required known as *levy* to render process effective. This consists of finding property of the debtor and seizing it or fastening a notice to it.

3. A faulty security interest (one not complying with the Code's rules of secured transactions) will normally be defeated by a lien creditor's levy.
4. The lien creditor:
   a. *Attaches property* of a debtor prior to suit in order to preserve it to secure his claim.
   b. *Becomes a judgment creditor* when he wins a suit and obtains judgment against the debtor.
   c. *Executes his judgment* by selling the debtor's property either attached before judgment or levied upon after judgment.

D. The trustee in bankruptcy (see *infra*, p. 363):

1. A most worthy adversary, he represents the interests of the general creditors of the debtor in question.
2. His aim is to defeat any and all secured claims in order to maximize the dividend payable to the general creditors.

E. The good faith (*bona fide*) purchaser includes:

1. Generally one who buys, i.e., pays value, and is unaware of the existence of any security interest in the property. Such persons will normally defeat the rights of a faulty security interest.
2. Buyers in the ordinary course of business from one (the debtor) who regularly deals in goods of the kind involved. Such buyers will invariably defeat the rights of a secured creditor even if his security interest is perfected.

IV. CREATION OF A SECURITY INTEREST:

A. The Code has an affirmative policy that favors the effectiveness of a security interest.

B. To create a security interest:

1. Collateral must be in possession of the secured party; or
2. A security agreement must exist.
   a. The agreement must contain a description reasonably identifying the collateral.
   b. The agreement must satisfy the Statute of Frauds (i.e., it must be in writing and signed by the debtor).

V. ATTACHMENT OF A SECURITY INTEREST:

A. A security interest must attach to be enforceable.

B. The Code distinguishes between the attachment of an interest and its perfection.

1. Attachment is used to describe the rights of the secured party in the collateral upon creation of the security interest.
2. Perfection relates to some additional act that may be required to make the security interest effective against third parties.

C. Mechanics of attachment.

1. A security interest attaches when three elements are present:
   a. The parties agree that there should be such an interest.
   b. Value is given by the creditor.
   c. The debtor has rights in the collateral.
2. A security interest cannot attach in the absence of any of these three elements, and it comes into existence at the very moment all three co-exist, unless an explicit agreement postpones the attachment to a later date. The absence of an element is not fatal to the agreement but merely means that the security interest does not attach until the missing element comes into existence.

D. Future goods and after-acquired property as collateral.

1. The parties to the transaction may agree that goods not yet in existence or not yet owned by the debtor shall be subject to the secured party's interest.
2. A security agreement may provide that collateral, whenever acquired (i.e., after-acquired property), shall secure all obligations covered by the agreement.
3. In general, this after-acquired property clause is only applicable to commercial or business transactions, as contrasted to purchases by consumers or where the collateral is a farmer's crops.
4. The powers of the parties mentioned above, coupled with the recognition of the debtor's right to use or dispose of the collateral, in effect legalize a floating lien on a shifting stock of goods.

E. Priority of a security interest that has attached.

1. As between the secured party and debtor:
   a. Is effective even if not perfected.
   b. If a special security interest is lost, the creditor at least qualifies as a general creditor.
2. As between third parties and the creditor:
   a. An unperfected security interest is usually subordinate to interests of third parties who are unaware of the interest.
   b. An unperfected security interest may prevail over third parties who have a perfected security interest or a lien upon the collateral by levy or attachment if:
      (1) Such perfected interest or lien is subsequent in time to the unperfected interest, and
      (2) Is obtained with knowledge of the existence of the prior unperfected interest.

VI. PERFECTION OF A SECURITY INTEREST

A. Perfection is required to have a security interest that will be good against third parties, attaching creditors, and a trustee in bankruptcy.

B. Mechanics of perfection:

1. Perfection depends on:
   a. The nature of the collateral involved.
   b. The use of the collateral.
   c. The relationship between the debtor and the secured party.
2. Perfection may occur in three ways: by attachment of the security interest; by possession of the collateral; or by the filing of a financing statement.
   a. By attachment
      (1) Neither possession nor filing is required for perfection when creditor obtains *a purchase-money security interest* (see p. 254, I.B.3.) *in consumer goods or farm goods having a purchase price of $2,500 or less,* so long as the collateral is neither a fixture nor a motor vehicle.
      (2) Before the Code, the seller or other party financing the buyer could obtain a perfected security interest only by retaining possession (lay-away plan) or by filing the conditional sales contract or chattel mortgage. This is one of several major innovations introduced by the Code.
   b. Perfection by possession of the collateral.
      (1) Article 9 substantially preserves the common law possessory interest (as typified by the pledge) by requiring little or no formality to perfect a possessory security interest in property possessed by the secured party.
      (2) Possession is required to perfect a security interest in instruments. Interests in chattel paper and negotiable documents also generally require possession for perfection although the Code permits filing as an alternative method.
      (3) Under certain circumstances (e.g., when the debtor must have possession of the document of title in order to obtain the goods), the secured creditor must, from a practical standpoint, give up possession of instruments and documents used as collateral.
         (a) Where the secured party permits the debtor to have possession for a limited purpose (e.g., to label or bottle the goods), a perfected security interest may continue to be perfected for a maximum period of 21 days in negotiable instruments and documents even when the secured party is not in possession of such collateral and has not filed.
         (b) Even though the secured creditor must give up his possession in such a circumstance, the Code ensures

the priority of a holder in due course or *bona fide* purchaser over the secured creditor.

C. Perfection by filing.

1. With the exception of a security interest perfected by attachment (see p. 258, VI.B.2.a (1)), it is necessary to give public notice by filing a financing statement to perfect a security interest in all transactions involving a non-possessory security interest in accounts, contract rights, general intangibles, inventory, equipment, chattel paper, and documents of title.
2. The Code provides that a financing statement is legally sufficient if it:
   a. Is signed by the debtor and the secured party.
   b. Gives an address of the secured party from which information concerning the security interest may be obtained.
   c. Gives the mailing address of the debtor, and
   d. Contains a statement indicating the types or describing the items of collateral.
3. A financing statement filed in accordance with state law meets the filing requirements unless a federal statute requires a special method of filing (such as applies to a copyright or patent) to perfect a particular type of security interest.
4. Depending on the collateral involved and particular local preferences and variations in filing and recording techniques, the UCC prescribes a series of alternative rules that may be considered by each state.

VII. PRIORITY OF A PERFECTED SECURITY INTEREST

A. In general, a secured creditor will be permitted to enforce his perfected interest in the collateral against a creditor, or a trustee in bankruptcy in the absence of special circumstances.

B. A secured creditor is not always able to protect his perfected interest against all third parties.

1. When the perfection is by mere attachment (i.e., without filing as in the case of a purchase money security interest; see p. 258, VI.B.2.a.(1)), the secured party is not protected against improper disposition (i.e., sale) of the collateral by a consumer or farmer to a buyer who buys without knowledge of the security interest for his personal, family, or household purposes or for his own farming operations.
2. When the perfection is by possession (see p.258,VI.B.2.b.(2)),the secured party is protected against all third parties only as long as possession is maintained (see p. 258, VI.B.2.b.(3)).
3. For other than farm goods or consumer goods for which a

financing statement has been filed, a buyer who purchases goods in the ordinary course of business will prevail against a security interest in the goods, even if the buyer knew of the existence of the perfected security interest.

VIII. RIGHTS TO PROCEEDS

A. Where a security interest is effective in described collateral, the security interest continues to be effective in the proceeds received for such collateral upon a sale or other disposition of the collateral.
B. If the security interest in the original collateral was initially perfected, the security interest in the proceeds is also perfected at the subsequent time when the sale or disposition takes place.
C. The creditor's priority dates from the time of perfection of the original security interest.

IX. PRIORITIES OF SEVERAL CONFLICTING SECURITY INTERESTS IN THE SAME SECURITY

A. Generally speaking, the priority of conflicting security interests in the same collateral is determined as follows:

1. If the conflicting interests are each perfected by filing, priority is determined by the order of filing regardless of which security interest first attached and whether it attached before or after filing;
2. In the order of perfection, unless both are perfected by filing as above, regardless of which security interest attached first and in the case of a filed security interest, whether it attached before or after filing; and,
3. If none of the conflicting security interests is perfected, priority is determined by the order of attachment.

B. Knowledge of competing security interests. Security interests, perfected or unperfected, will normally have a priority over a third party who may have a perfected security interest or a lien upon the collateral by levy, attachment, or the like:

1. Which is subsequent in time and was obtained with knowledge of the existence of the prior security interest.
2. Essentially, the party taking with notice has not taken in good faith, without notice.

C. Where a negotiable document of title is involved (see p. 258, VI.B.2.b.(3)), conflicting claims will be resolved in favor of the party who holds the document.

D. Possession of documents: priority is granted to a secured party in possession of chattel paper or negotiable or non-negotiable instruments, documents, or securities as against the claim of a secured party with a non-possessory security interest in the same collateral.

X. RIGHTS OF PARTIES ON DEFAULT

A. Unless otherwise agreed, if the secured transaction is not at the outset a possessory one, a secured party has the right to take possession of the collateral after default.

B. When the collateral is accounts receivable, contract rights, general intangibles, chattel paper, or instruments, the secured party is entitled to notify the obligor to make payment directly to him (the secured party) where the assignor-debtor was theretofore making collections.

C. A secured party may dispose of collateral by sale or lease or in any other manner calculated to produce the greatest benefit for all parties concerned.

D. The debtor has a right to require the secured creditor to dispose of the goods:

1. If the debtor has paid 60% of the cash price in the case of a purchase-money security interest or 60% of the loan in the case of another security interest in consumer goods.
2. After satisfying disposition costs and repaying the balance of the debt, the debtor is entitled to the residuary, if any.
3. The purpose of this clause is to protect consumers against unfairness by secured creditors.

E. If it can be established that a secured creditor is not proceeding in accordance with the provisions of the Code or in good faith, an interested party may apply to the court for relief.

F. In addition to the above, the parties may agree to other remedies for the secured party, so long as they are not prohibited by the Code.

SECURED TRANSACTIONS: SUBJECTIVE QUESTIONS*

PERFECTION OF A SECURITY INTEREST

Q. Bill went to Ed's Motors and purchased a new automobile. Two weeks later, Bill was called by MNO Loan Company. The Company explained to Bill that it had been financing Ed's purchases of automobiles from the manufacturer and that to protect its interests it had obtained a perfected security interest in Ed's entire inventory of automobiles, including the car which Bill bought. MNO further explained that Ed had defaulted on a payment due to MNO, and

* See Introductory Note, p. 19.

MNO intended to assert its security interest in Bill's car and repossess it unless Bill was willing to make an additional payment of $500 for a release of MNO's security interest.
(1) If Bill refuses to make an additional payment, what rights under the Uniform Commercial Code, if any, can MNO Loan Company assert against the automobile? Explain.
(2) Discuss the scope of Article 9 of the Uniform Commercial Code, which deals with secured transactions.
(3) Explain what is meant by the terms "security interest," "purchase money" security interest, and "perfected" security interest.
(4) What steps were necessary for MNO Loan Company to obtain a perfected security interest in Ed's inventory of automobiles?

5/66; pp. 254, 258

Q. (1) Explain the meaning of the term "floating lien."
(2) Is such a lien valid? Explain.
(3) Describe the steps that are required to have the "floating lien" "attach" and become "perfected."

11/67; pp. 257, 259

SECURED TRANSACTIONS: OBJECTIVE QUESTIONS

Each of the following numbered sentences states a legal conclusion as it relates to the preceding related lettered fact situation. You are to determine whether each of the legal conclusions is true or false. Your grade will be determined from your total net score obtained by deducting your total of incorrect answers from your total of correct answers; an omitted answer will not be considered an incorrect answer.

(1) Charles purchased a power saw for use in his home from Herman's Hardware Store for $500, payable $100 "down" and the balance in specified monthly installments. This purchase was covered by a conditional sales contract (security agreement) which gave Herman a valid security interest in the saw to secure payment of the full purchase price. The contract further prohibited Charles from disposing of the saw so long as any part of the purchase price remained unpaid. No financing statement was filed for this transaction. Peter subsequently offered to purchase the saw from Charles.

(a) Herman has a perfected security interest in the saw.
(b) If Charles defaults after having paid $150 of the price, Herman must resell the saw within a stated period of time after repossessing it unless, after default, Charles waives his right to require such resale in writing.
(c) If Charles had purchased the saw for use in his cabinet making business, Herman would be required to file a financing statement to perfect his security interest.
(d) Unless Herman waives the prohibition contained in the contract, Charles may not transfer a valid title to the saw to Peter.

(e) If Charles sells the saw to Peter after Herman files a financing statement and Peter pays value without knowledge of Herman's security interest therein, Peter will take the saw free of the security interest.

(2) Baker Loan Company made secured loans to Smith, Jones and Roe. Smith gave Baker a security interest in his household furniture. Jones delivered to Baker his rare coin collection as a pledge. Roe's loan is evidenced by his promissory note, is repayable over three years in monthly payments, and is secured by a security interest in the inventory of Roe's Clothing Store, a sole proprietorship owned by Roe. Proper security agreements were made and financing statements were duly executed and filed with respect to all of these transactions on the dates of the transactions.

(a) The filing of a financing statement was required to perfect the security interest in Smith's household furniture.

(b) Baker's security interest in Jones' coin collection was perfected before a financing statement was filed.

(c) On filing a financing statement covering Roe's inventory, Baker's security interest therein was perfected, but only for a maximum period of two years.

(d) The financing statement for Roe's inventory must include a detailed itemization and valuation of the inventory if the financing statement is to be valid.

(e) Baker's security interest in Roe's inventory is superior to the rights of any customer of Roe's who purchases items therefrom in the ordinary course of business with actual knowledge of the security interest.

(3) Ace Motor Sales, a corporation engaged in selling motor vehicles at retail, borrowed money from Star Finance Company and gave Star a properly executed security agreement in its present and future inventory and in the proceeds thereof to secure the loan. Star's security interest was duly perfected under the laws of the state where Ace does business and maintains its entire inventory. However, through error, the financing statement filed by Star did not include the proceeds received from the sale of Ace's inventory. Thereafter, Ace sold a new pickup truck from its inventory to Albert and received Albert's certified check for the full price in payment therefor. Albert then resold the truck to Roger, a resident of the state, for use by Roger in a laundry business carried on by him in the state. Roger duly gave Albert a valid security interest in the truck to secure payment of the balance of the purchase price and the security interest was duly perfected under the laws of the state. Six months after purchasing the truck from Albert, Roger moved himself and his business and property to an adjoining state.

(a) Star must file an amendment to the financing statement every time Ace receives a substantial number of additional vehicles from the manufacturer if Star is to maintain a valid security interest.

(b) Star had a perfected security interest in Albert's certified check for 10 days after Ace's receipt of the check.
(c) The security agreement between Ace and Star could include a provision which would give Star a valid security interest in Ace's inventory without further filing if Star advanced additional money.
(d) Albert's security interest in the truck he sold to Roger would be perfected in the adjoining state by virtue of being perfected in Albert's home state, but only for a limited period of time.
(e) If Albert's security interest had not been perfected under the laws of his home state prior to removal of the truck to an adjoining state, the security interest may not thereafter be perfected in the adjoining state.

11/69

(4) The provisions of the Uniform Commercial Code dealing with secured transactions replace the following statutes in force in the jurisdictions adopting the Code:
(a) Uniform Conditional Sales Act.
(b) Chattel Mortgage Act.
(c) Factor's Lien Act.
(d) Uniform Trust Receipts Act.
(e) Retail Installment Sales Act.

(5) The Uniform Commercial Code
(a) Adopts a single lien theory.
(b) Does not distinguish between a possessory and a non-possessory security interest.
(c) Abolishes many distinctions based upon historical development and form.
(d) Emphasizes the importance of who holds title to goods.
(e) Narrows the availability of the different types of property which may serve as security.

(6) The Uniform Commercial Code governs a creditor's obtaining a security interest in
(a) Real estate.
(b) Inventory.
(c) Fixtures.
(d) After acquired property.
(e) Chattel paper.

(7) A security interest in goods may be created under the Uniform Commercial Code by a creditor's
(a) Obtaining an oral agreement under which he takes possession of the security.
(b) Obtaining an unsigned written security agreement.
(c) Obtaining a security agreement signed only by the debtor.
(d) Filing a financing statement which is not in itself a security agreement.

(e) Obtaining the debtor's written promise to execute a security agreement on demand of the creditor.

(8) If a creditor is able to perfect a security interest in goods, his security interest

(a) Assures him that his debt will be repaid.
(b) May have been perfected by possession.
(c) Entitles him to a position ahead of all other creditors.
(d) Has priority over all statutory liens.
(e) Will be entitled to the greatest protection available under the Uniform Commercial Code.

(9) The Uniform Commercial Code classifies personal property into groupings which include

(a) Consumer goods.
(b) Business goods.
(c) Equipment.
(d) Hard goods.
(e) Soft goods.

(10) If Adams sells a refrigerator to Baker on credit and obtains a proper security agreement so that the refrigerator may serve as collateral for the payment of the amount due

(a) Adams may perfect his interest in the refrigerator by filing a financing statement which evidences the existence of a security agreement.
(b) Adams has a "purchase money" security interest.
(c) If Adams files a financing statement within 10 days after he delivers the refrigerator to Baker, Adams' security interest will take priority over the rights of a lien creditor whose lien arose during that time.
(d) If Adams fails to file a financing statement, Adams' security interest will not be effective if Baker sells the refrigerator to his next-door neighbor, who buys it in good faith.
(e) If Adams fails to file a financing statement, Adams' security interest will not be effective if Baker sells the refrigerator to a second-hand dealer, who buys it in good faith.

5/67

TOPIC NINE

FEDERAL SECURITIES REGULATION

CONTENTS PAGE

FEDERAL SECURITIES REGULATION. Knowledge of the Securities Act of 1933 and the Securities Exchange Act of 1934 is tested under this topic. Included are the scope of the 1933 Act's registration requirements, exempt securities, exempt transactions, and the liability of the various parties involved in making a public *offering of securities. Included within the coverage of the 1934 Act are the application of the Act's rules to both listed and unlisted corporations, corporate reporting requirements, antifraud provisions and disclosure of insider information, and short-swing profits. As mentioned above, questions pertaining to the accountant's liability under both Acts will appear in Business Law.**

I. THE SECURITIES AND EXCHANGE COMMISSION

A. Purpose: The SEC was created by the Act of Congress entitled the Securities Exchange Act of 1934. It was created to administer the laws which relate in general to the field of securities and finance and to seek to provide protection for the public in their security transactions.

B. Acts administered:

1. Securities Act of 1933.
2. Securities Exchange Act of 1934.
3. The Public Utility Holding Company Act of 1935.
4. The Trust Indenture Act of 1939.
5. The Investment Company Act of 1940.
6. The Investment Advisers Act of 1940.

C. Composition: consists of five members, no more than three of whom may be of the same political party. It is a bipartisan, independent, quasi-judicial agency of the United States Government. The Commission's staff consists of lawyers, accountants, engineers, security analysts, examiners and other supporting employees.

D. Functions

1. Administrative interpretations: the SEC informally and formally issues rulings and opinions on the application of the laws it administers to proposed actions by parties subject to its jurisdiction. The most common administrative ruling by the SEC is known as the "no action letter" so-called because it indicates the SEC staff's intention to take no action regarding the petitioner's proposed action.
2. Quasi-judicial proceedings: the SEC holds hearings and makes determinations regarding violations of the laws it administers. Such determinations are subject to judicial review by appeal to the appropriate Federal Circuit Court.
3. Rule making: the SEC has been vested by Congress with the power to make rules implementing and explaining the 1933 and 1934 Acts. After soliciting comments and in rare cases the holding of public hearings on the proposed rules and when the rules

* Source: AICPA, *Information for CPA Candidates* (July 1970). This topic is new to the Business Law section; questions may be expected in the November 1972 and subsequent examinations.

become final they have almost the same validity as the Act they are based upon.

4. Investigations: the 1933 and 1934 Acts grant the SEC the authority to hold investigations into the practices of the investment industry and the application of the Acts it administers. In order to implement this investigatory power, Congress granted the SEC broad subpoena powers.

E. Enforcement

1. Injunctions: the SEC may seek and obtain preliminary and final injunctions to prevent violations of the Act.
2. Administrative proceedings: suspension or revocation of broker-dealer, stock exchange or security registration.
3. Criminal prosecutions:
   a. Where appropriate the SEC may institute criminal proceedings against violators of the Acts it administers. Such cases are tried in the Federal District Courts.
   b. The SEC assists United States Attorneys in appearing before Grand Juries, preparing cases for presentation to Grand Juries and obtaining indictments.

II. THE SECURITIES ACT OF 1933

A. Purpose:

1. The underlying purposes of the Act are to provide the investing public with the facts needed to evaluate the merit of the security being offered and to protect the investor from fraudulent or misleading statements by those seeking to sell the security.
2. The Act is popularly known as "the truth in securities law." It requires complete and honest disclosure to the public in marketing securities.
3. The SEC in no way passes on the merit or value of the securities being sold nor on the wisdom of investing in them. Instead, the SEC seeks to insure that the requisite information is available to the investors so that he can make his own determination of whether or not to invest in the securities being marketed.

B. The Act's basic prohibition.

1. The Act forbids a public sale without a registration statement being duly and properly filed with the SEC prior to an offer to sell, sale, distribution or solicitation to sell securities in interstate commerce.
2. In order to provide the investing public with the pertinent information contained in the registration statement, investors must

be furnished with a prospectus to enable them to make informed investment decisions.

3. The Act contains anti-fraud provisions which prohibit misrepresentation, deceit, and other fraud in the sale of securities generally (whether or not registration is required).
4. Where securities are marketed without complying with the registration and prospectus requirements of the Act, civil liability, administrative proceedings (i.e., stop orders) and criminal sanctions are provided. The parties responsible include, among others, the issuer, signers of the registration statement, directors, controlling persons, underwriters, accountants, lawyers, and other experts (see Accountant's Legal Responsibility, p. 15, III). The parties have a liability for misrepresentation which borders on that of an insurer.
5. Summary of the elements which may necessitate registration.
   a. Is interstate commerce involved, e.g., use of the mails?
   b. Are securities offered to the "public."
   c. Is an issuer, controlling person, underwriter, or dealer involved (see *infra*)?
   d. Is there an exemption available (see *infra*)?

C. Definitions

1. General: Much of the law in this area is either contained in or depends upon the definitions which follow.
2. Security: The Act states a broad listing of known types of securities (e.g., stocks, bonds, etc.) or in general any interest commonly known as a "security" (e.g., this would include a limited partnership interest) or any certificate of interest or participation in, temporary or interim certificate for, receipt for, guarantee of, or any warrant or right to subscribe to or purchase any of the foregoing.
3. Person: Again broadly defined to include corporations, partnerships, and other entities within the term.
4. Sale: Includes sell, offer to sell, offer for sale, etc. This broadly defined term contains one major exclusion, i.e., preliminary negotiations or dealings between an issuer and underwriter. (The SEC has issued a rule which exempts the typical merger or consolidation from registration by categorizing the transaction as an involuntary conversion rather than a sale.)
5. Issuer: Every person who issues or proposes to issue any security. This includes foreign as well as domestic issuers and foreign governments and their instrumentalities.
6. Interstate commerce: Means trade or commerce in securities or any transportation (e.g., use of the mails) or communication relating thereto, among the several states or territories of the

United States (including Puerto Rico, the Virgin Islands, and the Canal Zone).

7. Prospectus: Any prospectus, notice, circular, advertisement or letter of communication, written or by radio or television, which offers any security for sale or confirms the sale of any security. The prospectus is a liability document and consequently is couched in terms of hedges, limitations, and *caveats*.
8. Underwriter: Any person who has purchased from an issuer *with a view to* the distribution of a security, or who offers to or sells for an issuer. This definition is functional and includes a controlling person who makes a secondary offering or one in conjunction with the issuer. It is much broader than the conventional financial meaning.
9. Dealer: Any person who engages either full- or part-time directly or indirectly as an agent broker or principal, in the business of offering, buying or selling, or otherwise dealing or trading in securities issued by another person.
10. Controlling person: Not defined in the Act, but is used in connection with an Underwriter (see above 8.). The factors to be considered are:
    a. Stock ownership is looked to first; majority ownership naturally constitutes control.
    b. Actual or practical control, however, is the test. A 5% owner (or even less) may be a controlling person if he is on the board.
    c. In general, a controlling person has the power to influence the management and policies of the issuer.
    d. The power to exercise control is sufficient even if not exercised.
    e. Whether the person or group in question could procure the signing of a registration statement?
    f. If an officer and/or director or on the executive committee, a low percentage of stock would suffice.

D. Exempted securities: The Act provides a number of types of securities which are exempted for various policy reasons. The chief reasons for exemption are the issuer is regulated by another government agency, the issuer is such that the normal protection is not deemed necessary or in the case of commercial paper, common sense, convenience, and necessity. The following securities are exempt from registration:

1. Securities sold prior to July 17, 1933.
2. Securities of governments, banks, carriers, building and loan associations, and farm cooperatives.
3. Commercial paper, i.e., checks, notes, and similar paper arising out of a current transaction and which have a maturity not exceeding nine months.

4. Securities issued by charitable organizations.
5. Insurance and conventional annuity contracts although not necessarily variable annuities.
6. Any security exchanged by the issuer with its existing holders exclusively and where no commission or remuneration is paid or given directly or indirectly for soliciting such exchanges (e.g., a stock dividend or stock split).
7. Securities issued in reorganizations which are subject to court control (e.g., a Chapter X reorganization pursuant to the Bankruptcy Act).
8. Intrastate issues of securities: Where the issuing corporation and all prospective shareholders are located within one state or territory and the entire distribution is completed therein. As a warning, it must be pointed out that if a shareholder has changed his address to another state and materials addressed to him are forwarded to his new address the exemption is lost for the entire issue. The intrastate exemption is both complex and difficult to attain.
9. The SEC may, pursuant to its own regulations, exempt a transaction if it is deemed to be unnecessary for public protection and such issue does not exceed $300,000. In order to obtain such an exemption, the issuer must meet the requirements contained in Regulation A, issued pursuant to the 1933 Act. Although the requirements in Regulation A are not as onerous or as costly as a full registration, the investor is amply protected and liability is the same as that provided for violation of a full registration. Sales must be made via the use of an offering circular which is a substitute for the prospectus.
10. Securities issued by Small Business Investment Companies (SBIC's) may be exempted by the Commissioner if he deems protection of the public and investors to be unnecessary.
11. Despite the presence of a valid exemption, the securities exempted are subject to the Act's anti-fraud provisions.

E. Exempted transactions

1. Transactions by any person other than an issuer, underwriter or dealer: If a person is not within one of the above proscribed classes of people, he may sell his securities with impunity, i.e., he need not file a registration statement, nor is he required to sell via a prospectus. This broad exemption covers the overwhelming preponderance of sales by investors. It does not cover "a controlling person" of the issuer if he is categorized as an underwriter or sells through someone who would be deemed an underwriter. Transactions involving a "controlling person" represent the most controversial and legally significant part of this otherwise broad exemption.

a. A "controlling person" holds "restricted stock," i.e., stock which normally cannot be disposed of without registration (e.g., a secondary offering by a majority owner). This is the case whether the stock was bought from the issuer or in the open market or whether held for many years or was previously registered.

b. A controlling person may be categorized as an underwriter if he sells significant amounts of his restricted stock to the public. Thus, the exemption will be unavailable.

c. Similarly, if the controlling person sells restricted stock in the open market through his broker, the exemption will again be lost since the broker may be categorized an underwriter and the controlling person becomes an issuer. (See above definition of underwriter.) In order to permit limited sales by controlling persons, the SEC issued rule 154 which is discussed *infra* under Exemption 4—Brokers' Transactions.

2. Private offerings: non-public offerings by an issuer, i.e., private placement of securities to a limited number who are buying for investment. The dividing line between a private and a public offering is often difficult to ascertain. There is no hard-and-fast rule of thumb; instead, there are many factors to be weighed in determining whether the transaction qualifies as private. These are:

a. The number of people to whom the securities are offered. There is no warrant in the Act that states if a particular number is present or absent that the offering is public. However, SEC practice is partially based upon numbers, i.e., if the number is under 25 and they are relatively sophisticated investors, the offering, as a matter of SEC practice, will not be treated as a public offering.

b. The quality of the investors involved. Is the requisite knowledge available to them? Are they sufficiently informed about the issuer so that they do not need the registration protection? If they are, no registration would be required so long as the securities are not taken with a view to a subsequent reoffering to the public.

c. The securities are to be held for investment. Even if the offering of securities involved only one sophisticated "person" who had all the information a registration statement would contain, it will not qualify as a private placement if there is a prompt reoffering to the public. The practice is to obtain from the offerees a so-called investment letter which manifests an intent to take for investment and not for resale. In addition, it should contain a representation by each offeree that he intends to hold the securities for a given period of time, probably for at least two years.

3. Certain post registration transactions by a dealer (including an

underwriter no longer so acting). These include transactions which:

a. Occur at least forty days after the first date the security was *bona fide* (i.e., in compliance with the Act) offered to the public by the issuer or through an underwriter.
b. Occur at least forty days after a registration statement has become effective in respect to the security unless securities of the issuer have not been previously sold pursuant to an earlier effective registration statement (i.e., this is the issuer's first public offering). In such cases, i.e., an initial public offering, the applicable period is ninety days.
c. Transactions as to securities constituting the whole or a part of an unsold allotment or subscription by the dealer as a participant in the distribution of the securities by the issuer or the underwriter.

4. Brokers' transactions involving "controlling persons": The SEC pursuant to its rule-making function promulgated Rule 154 relating to a "controlling person's" sale of limited amounts of stock in the open market through a broker. The Act, as previously indicated, had exempted an individual's broker transactions where an issuer, including a "controlling person," underwriter, or dealer was not involved. However, no provision in the Act exempted sales by "controlling persons" without a registration statement being filed unless it constituted a private placement as discussed above. Rule 154 permits sales by "controlling persons" through a broker if the following requirements are met:
   a. The broker performs only the usual functions, i.e., executes the order on an agency basis as the seller's broker and receives only the "usual or customary" broker's commission.
   b. The broker's acting in a principal capacity is prohibited.
   c. The broker does not look for people to sell the security to.
   d. The selling principal, as far as known to the broker, must make no payment to any person other than to the broker in connection with the execution of the transaction.
   e. The amount that can be sold is limited as follows:

      (1) *Securities listed or admitted to trading on any securities exchange:* The amount of securities of any class which can be sold under Rule 154 for any person is that amount which, when added to all other sales of securities of such class by such person within the preceding period of six months, will not exceed the smaller of the following:

         (A) 1% of the outstanding securities of such class, or

         (B) the largest aggregate reported volume of trading of securities of such class on *all* securities exchanges during any one week within the four calendar weeks preceding the receipt of the order from such person.

(2) *Over-the-counter securities:* The amount of over-the-counter securities of any class which can be sold under Rule 154 for any person is that amount which, when added to all other sales of securities of such class by such person within the preceding period of six months, will not exceed a total of 1% of the outstanding securities of such class.

f. In effect, by meeting all of the above requirements *the broker is exempt*, i.e., he is not an underwriter, and this exemption insures to the benefit of the "controlling person."

F. The registration process

1. Information generally required to be disclosed:
   a. A description of the registrant's properties and business.
   b. A description of the significant provisions of the security to be offered for sale and the relationship to the registrant's other capital securities.
   c. Information about the management (director's and principal officers).
   d. Financial statements (see Accountant's Legal Responsibility, p. 15, III).
2. Upon filing the registration statement and prospectus with the SEC, they become public information. However, it is unlawful to sell prior to the effective date.
3. Registration statements become effective on the 20th day after filing or the 20th day after filing the last amendment. The SEC has the discretionary power to advance the effective date if it deems such action to be appropriate.
4. Registration statements are examined in detail by the Division of Corporate Finance to insure compliance with the disclosure requirements.
   a. In the event the statement appears to be materially incomplete or inaccurate, the registrant is notified by letter and normally afforded an opportunity to amend.
   b. The SEC has the power to refuse or suspend the effectiveness of any registration statement if it finds, after a hearing, the registration statement to be materially misleading, inaccurate, or incomplete. If the registration contains deliberate concealments or misrepresentations, a stop order will normally be issued suspending the effectiveness of the statement.

G. The anti-fraud provisions:

1. Are broader in scope than the registration provisions. They apply to *all persons* using interstate commerce, communication, or the mails to offer to sell or sell securities, if such persons:
   a. Employ any device, scheme, or artifice to defraud.

   b. Obtain money or other property by means of any untrue statement of a material fact or by the omission of a material fact deemed necessary to make the statements not misleading.
   c. Engage in any transaction, practice, or course of business which operates as a fraud or deceit upon the purchaser.
2. Are not subject to the same exemptions for certain securities discussed above (p. 270, II.D.).
3. Are generally similar to the 1934 Act's prohibitions (see *infra*, p. 281, III.F.).

H. Criminal penalties.

1. The Act contains criminal penalties of fine and imprisonment or both (maximum of $5,000 and five years) for any person who *willfully:*
   a. Violates the Act or the SEC's rules and regulations.
   b. Makes an untrue statement of any material fact in the registration statement or fails to state any material fact deemed necessary to make the statement not misleading.

I. Civil liabilities.

1. If the registration statement becomes effective and contains a false statement or omission of a material fact, any person who is unaware of the false statement or omission of material fact may:
   a. Sue every person who signed the registration statement.
   b. Sue every director of the issuer or a person named in the registration statement as about to become one.
   c. Sue every accountant, engineer appraiser or other expert for any authorized statement made by him in the prospectus or for any certification or valuation used in the registration statement.
   d. Sue every underwriter of the security.
   e. Assert his rights in any appropriate federal or state court; the SEC has no power to award damages.
2. The basis for the claim is an alleged false statement or omission of a material fact in the registration statement.
   a. Such a claim by the party suing (the plaintiff) establishes a *prima facie* case, i.e., one which will suffice unless contradicted by other evidence.
   b. Thus, the plaintiff does not have the added burden of proving that the defendants (issuers, directors, etc.) were negligent or fraudulent in certifying the financial statements.
   c. Plaintiff need not prove reliance upon the financial statement or that the loss suffered was the proximate result of the false statement or misleading omission.

   d. In effect, much of the burden of proof typically required of a plaintiff has been shifted to the defendant.
3. Defenses: No person, other than the insurer, shall be liable if he can sustain the following burden of proof:
   a. Signers, directors, and those other than experts in regard to their own statements that:
      (1) Regarding parts of the registration statement not purporting to be made by an expert, he had, *after reasonable investigation, reasonable ground to believe and did believe* the registration statements to be true and not to contain any omission of material fact.
      (2) Regarding parts of the registration statement purporting to be made on the authority of an expert (other than himself), he had no reasonable ground to believe and did not believe that the expert's statements were untrue or contained any omission of material fact.
   b. Experts: regarding authorized statements, reports, valuations or certifications by an expert in the registration statement, he will not be liable if he had, after reasonable investigation, reasonable grounds to believe and did believe that the statements he made were true and did not contain any omission of material fact. For further discussion of the liability of an expert, see Accountant's Legal Responsibility, p. 15, III.A.).
4. The standard of reasonableness is that required of a prudent man in the management of his own property. Judicial elaboration on this general test is contained in the *Bar Chris* case.
5. Generally, recovery, where a registration has been filed and becomes effective, is based upon the difference between the amount paid for the security (not exceeding the price at which the security was offered to the public) and:
   a. The value at the time of suit, or
   b. The value at the time the security was disposed of prior to suit, and
   c. In no event may recovery exceed the price at which the security was offered to the public.
6. In addition to the above liability, the Act provides:
   a. That any person who offers or sells a security in violation of the Act's registration requirement (e.g., fails to file a registration statement; see p. 268, II.B.) shall be liable to the person suing for:
      (1) The amount paid, plus interest, less the amount of income received upon tender of the security (rescission).
      (2) Damages if the party no longer owns the security.
   b. The same liability indicated above in a. applies to offers or sales of securities (whether or not exempted) in interstate commerce or by use of the mails, by the means of a prospectus or

oral communication, which contains an untrue statement or omission of a material fact.

7. The Act contains a two part statute of limitations, which bars actions under its provisions.
   a. First, any action must be brought within one year after discovery of the untrue statement or omission, or after such discovery should have been made by the exercise of reasonable diligence in cases where there is a failure to register within one year after the violation upon which the suit is based.
   b. Second, in no event can an action be brought more than three years after the security was offered in good faith to the public.

III. THE SECURITIES EXCHANGE ACT OF 1934

A. General: The 1934 Act, in addition to creating the SEC, is concerned with:

1. The integrity of the markets for outstanding securities including the national stock exchanges and over-the-counter markets.
2. The integrity of the proxy and tender offer machinery inherent in the operation of a growing corporate democracy.
3. The dealing by insiders in the stocks of their companies.
4. The regulation of broker–dealers, including the hypothecation (pledge) of customers' securities, the regulation of short selling, and the financial responsibility of broker–dealers.

B. Applicability: The Act's scope has been substantially increased as a result of the 1964 amendments. Some of the Act's provisions apply to any person using interstate commerce, e.g., the mails. Other provisions apply exclusively to those required to register.

C. Scope of the registration requirement:

1. National securities exchanges (e.g., the New York Stock Exchange) must register. This makes the Act applicable to members, brokers, and dealers of these exchanges.
2. Brokers and dealers engaged in interstate commerce must register.
3. Securities of issuers, traded on any national securities exchange must be registered.
4. Equity securities traded in interstate commerce (typically over-the-counter) and having in excess of $1 million in total assets and a class of equity securities held of record by 500 or more persons as of the last day of the issuer's fiscal year must be registered. This was the 1964 extension of applicability.

D. Corporate reporting requirement

1. Companies required to register (those issuers indicated in C.3 and

C.4, above) must file a registration application with the exchange on which the securities are traded and with the SEC.

a. The SEC's rules prescribe the nature and content of these registered statements, including certified financials.
b. The required data is generally comparable to, but less extensive than, the disclosure requirements required in the 1933 Securities Act registration.

2. Periodical and other reports.
   a. Annual reports. Every issuer whose securities are registered must file an annual report for each fiscal year after the last full fiscal year for which financial statements were filed in the registration statement. Normally, the report must be filed within 120 days after the close of the fiscal year and the financial statements must be certified by independent certified public accountants (CPA's).
   b. Semi-annual and quarterly reports. Financial statements (balance sheets, earning and profits, and other financial matters) must be filed. These need not be certified.
   c. Current reports. A current report of certain specified corporate and financial events must be filed within 10 days after the close of the month in which they occur.

E. Short-swing profits of officers, directors, and principal stockholders.

1. Purpose: to prevent certain "insiders" from unfairly using information about the company for their personal gain. Selling short (i.e., the sale of stock not owned by the "insider") is prohibited.
2. General: The Act (Section 16) provides that profits realized by persons required to report (i.e., "insiders") from the purchase and sale or sale and purchase of an equity security of the issuer within a period of less than six months inure to and are recoverable by or on behalf of the issuer.
   a. Any profit obtained by the "insider" belongs to the issuer (corporation). Either the corporation or any security holder may bring an action on behalf of the issuer (i.e., sue derivatively) to have the "insider's" profit recovered by the issuer. The security holder need not have been one at the time the "insider" profit was made.
   b. Liability for short-swing profits must be paid in full. They cannot be settled for less than the entire profit.
3. Reporting requirements: The Act requires an "insider" to file a report of his direct or indirect beneficial ownership of all equity securities of an issuer registered under the Act and subsequent changes of ownership:
   a. At the time the security is registered on a national securities exchange (e.g., The New York, American, or Pacific Stock Exchanges).

b. By the effective date of a registration statement filed by the issuer of an over-the-counter security.
c. Within 10 days after a person becomes an "insider."
d. Within 10 days of such change of ownership after the close of each calendar month.
e. Where reporting is not required, there is a corresponding exemption from liability.
f. Reportable transactions include the acquisition or disposition of:
(1) Any equity securities of the issuer.
(2) Any transferable options, puts, calls, spreads, and straddles. Restricted or qualified stock options are not included; however, their exercise would be a purchase and thus reportable.

4. "Insider" includes:
a. Directors: a trustee of a Massachusetts Trust would be considered a director.
b. Officers: the president, vice president(s), treasurer, secretary, and any other person who performs for an issuer functions corresponding to those performed by the foregoing officers.
c. Owners of more than 10% of a registered security: in determining what percent an individual owns, only outstanding stock is considered; treasury stock is subtracted from total issued stock to arrive at the number of shares outstanding.

5. Beneficial ownership includes:
a. Securities held in the name of a spouse or minor children.
b. Securities held by relatives who share the same house as the reporting person.
c. Securities held in trust to which the insider or his immediate family has a vested interest in either the income or trust corpus.
d. Securities held in a trust created by the insider which he retains the power to revoke; the trust must hold 20% or more of a security which would have to be reported.

6. Equity securities:
a. Includes all equity securities (i.e., common and preferred stock) of corporations listed on a national exchange and those traded over-the-counter which have total assets of $1 million and 500 stockholders of an equity security.
b. Does not include bonds, debentures, and other straight debts which are not equity securities.
c. Any security which is convertible into or exchangeable for stock is an equity security. This includes transferrable stock options, puts, calls, spreads, or straddles.

7. Less than six months:
a. A purchase on January 1 and a sale on June 30 is exactly six months and the short-swing profit provisions do not apply. A sale one day earlier would be a short-swing profit.
b. The shortest period of elapsed time which will make Section

16 applicable is six months minus one full period from midnight to midnight since the law does not take into account fractions of a day.

c. The less-than-six-months' test is strictly objective; the insider's motive and intent are irrelevant. Hence it may be a trap for the unwary. However, the prohibition may be readily avoided by waiting six months or longer. The holding period for long-term capital gain is more than six months and thus provides an added inducement to retain the stock for the requisite period.

8. What is a sale or purchase? Normally there is little difficulty in answering this question except in the case of:
   a. Conversions: the conversion of a convertible security is not a purchase of the underlying security or sale of the convertible security, provided there is:
      (1) No purchase of the convertible security (e.g. a convertible preferred) and sale of the underlying security (e.g. common stock) within six months.
      (2) No sale of the convertible security and the purchase of the underlying security within six months.
      (3) No receipt of cash in excess of 15% of the value of the underlying security upon conversion.
   b. Reorganizations: generally the exchange of securities in a merger or consolidation will be treated as a sale of the stock relinquished and the purchase of the stock received.
9. Exemptions from and limitations on the short-swing profit sections.
   a. Odd-lot transactions are exempt.
   b. Certain small transactions involving a market value not in excess of $3,000 are exempt.
   c. Transactions of six months or more in time are excluded.
   d. Losses taken on inside information but without a repurchase are excluded. But watch out for the anti-fraud provisions (Section 10b, *infra*).
   e. The passing on of inside information to a friend or business associate is not covered. But again the anti-fraud provisions may apply.
10. The Relationship of Short-Swing Profits to the Fraud Provisions.
   a. Those not within the definition of director, officer, or a more than 10% shareholder may be liable under Section 10b and Rule 10b-5. These would include any person having inside information, e.g., geologists, engineers, lawyers, tipees, accountants and some controlling persons who don't own more than 10% (see *infra* F.).
   b. A violation of the short-swing profit rule, may also result in liability under the anti-fraud provisions where the insider does in fact have and act upon "inside information." It is the

practice of the accounting profession when a member of the firm serves as a director not to own stock in the company. Many law firms have a similar policy.

11. Examples:
    a. A director of a registered corporation who buys 1,000 shares at $20 and three months later sells 1,000 shares at $30 has made a short-swing profit of $10,000 less expenses.
    b. An officer of a registered corporation who sells 1,000 shares at $30 and four months later buys 1,000 shares at $20 has made a short-swing profit of $10,000 less expenses.
    c. A more than 10% shareholder buys 1,000 shares on January 1 at $30, sells 1,000 shares at $20 three months later, and repurchases 1,000 shares at $10 on May 31 of the same year. The insider has made a short-swing profit of $10,000 less expenses (i.e., the sale at $20 and repurchase at $10). There is NO LIFO or FIFO application and losses are not offset. Always look back and look forward six months from the sale.

F. The anti-fraud provisions

1. Section 10b of the Act in conjunction with Rule 10b-5 represents the most controversial, dynamic, and ill-defined area of the Act. Without a doubt, the anti-fraud provisions have caused a virtual revolution in respect to corporate directors', officers', and others' responsibility to the shareholders of the corporation.
2. The Act provides: "It shall be unlawful for any person . . . by the use . . . of interstate commerce or the mails, or any facility of any national securities exchange, to use or employ (in respect to any security) any manipulative or deceptive device or contrivance in contravention of such rules and regulations as the SEC may prescribe as necessary and appropriate in the public interest or for the protection of investors.
3. Obviously, the above Section of the Act leaves much to be desired in the way of guidance and clarity. Therefore, pursuant to the SEC's rule-making authority, it promulgated the following rule involving the employment of manipulative and deceptive devices. "It shall be unlawful for any person to . . .:
   a. Employ any device, scheme, or artifice to defraud.
   b. Make any untrue statement of a material fact or omit to state a material fact necessary in order to make the statements made, in light of the circumstances under which they were made, not misleading or
   c. Engage in any act, practice, or course of business which operates or would operate as fraud or deceit on any person in connection with the purchase or sale of any security."
4. Purpose: These provisions seek to curb misrepresentations and

deceit, market manipulation and other fradulent acts and practices, and to establish and maintain just and equitable principles of trade conducive to the maintenance of open, fair, and orderly markets. Pursuant to this end the SEC's Rules and Regulations seek to:

a. Afford a remedy to a defrauded *seller* or buyer; other provisions of the regulatory pattern protected the buyer; this provision closed the previously existing loophole.
b. Define acts or practices which constitute a "manipulative or deceptive device or contrivance" prohibited by the Act.

5. Scope: The 1934 Act's anti-fraud provisions apply to all transactions involving interstate commerce, the mail or transactions on any national exchange involving the purchase *or* sale of securities. Thus, the securities need not be registered for the Act's prohibitions to apply and it covers *any person*, not just insiders, as defined in the short-swing profit provisions.
6. In order to prevail under the anti-fraud provisions, the plaintiff:
   a. Need not establish all the elements of common law fraud (see Contracts, p. 48), such as misrepresentation, materiality, scienter, intent to deceive, reliance, and causation. Some need not be proved at all and others have been substantially watered down. For example, a specific intent to deceive or injure need not be proved.
   b. Must show that a purchase or sale was made based upon material false, misleading, or undisclosed information.
   c. May seek recourse from any person who has made unfair use of material information which is undisclosed, or about which a false or misleading statement has been issued. Anyone (e.g., an employee such as a geologist who has discovered a significant find and is in possession of material information obtained in the course of his employment) is an insider within the meaning of the anti-fraud provisions.
   d. Is not obligated to show that the insider's purchase or sale was made on a face-to-face basis. Typically the transaction would be made on a national securities exchange or through a brokerage house in an over-the-counter market. No direct communication or lack thereof to the plaintiff is required.
7. Materiality: The determination of what is material inside information is crucial. Unfortunately, the Act does not define the term. The leading case in point (*Texas Gulf Sulphur*) defined the meaning of materiality in the following terms:
   a. "The basic test of materiality * * * is whether a reasonable man would attach importance * * * in determining his choice of action in the transaction in question. * * * This, of course, encompasses any fact * * * which in reasonable and objective contemplation might affect the value of the corporation's stock or securities. * * * Thus, material facts include not only in-

formation disclosing the earnings and distribution of a company, but also those facts which affect the probable future of the company and those which may affect the desire of investors to buy, sell, or hold the company's securities."

b. The court also indicated: "... whether facts are material within Rule 10b-5 when the facts relate to a particular event and are undisclosed by those persons who are knowledgeable thereof will depend at any given time upon a balancing of both the indicated probability that the event will occur and its impact in the light of the totality of the company activity. * * *"

c. New York Stock Exchange Standards: although the reporting standards apply only to those companies listed on the New York Stock Exchange, they provide the most comprehensive treatment of what kind of corporate information is material and which must be reported under the Exchange's requirements. It is, therefore, likely that those matters which the Exchange requires to be reported will be found to be material in respect to corporations in general, i.e., to those not listed on the Exchange. The Exchange treats the following types of fact situations as reportable and hence presumptively material.

(1) Dividend action and non-action. In the landmark *Cady Roberts* decision, the SEC indicated that information as to dividends will always be material.

(2) Unaudited sales and earnings figures must be filed quarterly with the Exchange and also must be divulged to the press.

(3) Any financial data, corporate action, or development which may affect securities. This would normally include information which relates to outstanding securities such as stock splits, rights offerings, a significant merger on acquisition tender offers, significant calls for redemption or senior financing, major changes in management, and finally, other significant developments such as a major ore find, a significant technological breakthrough, or major expansion plans.

(4) (a) The American Exchange has a similar policy and other exchanges require at a minimum prompt disclosure of dividend news.

(b) The National Association of Security Dealers also requires prompt public disclosure of financially significant developments by over-the-counter traded securities.

(5) In conclusion, although the various exchanges rules are not a part of the 1934 Act, they do apply to listed corporations and will undoubtedly be resorted to in determining what is "material."

d. Court cases: examples of the type of undisclosed information which has been deemed material include:

(1) A significant ore strike, categorized as one of the most important in modern times.
(2) The fact that there was a corporate contract for the sale of its assets to a third party at a higher price per share.
(3) A dividend cut.
(4) The fact that a merger was in the offing.

8. Nondisclosure: at present there is no specific statutory duty to affirmatively disclose material information by the corporation, directors, and other insiders with the exceptions indicated below. However, the law is in a state of flux; conceivably, such a duty might be imposed by the courts. A recent SEC release strongly urged disclosure of material information even if all parties forgo trading.
   a. Assuming the facts to be material and that they are not disclosed, all corporate insiders (any persons connected with the corporation and having such inside information) must forgo any trading in the stock of the corporation.
   b. This would obviously include directors, officers, shareholders, other corporate employees, lawyers, accountants, geologists, and engineers who are aware of the material information.
   c. It would also preclude tipping by such persons; i.e., although the insider does not trade personally, relatives and friends may be informed and trade with knowledge of the undisclosed material information. Furthermore, the tipees who received the information from the insider must forgo trading in the security or face potential liability under the Act.
   d. As discussed above, the stock exchanges have reporting requirements which apply to their listed corporations. It has been suggested that the New York Stock Exchange reporting requirements will be used by the courts in all cases involving nondisclosure under 10b-5, thereby making them generally applicable to all corporations whether listed or not. Although the law is in a state of flux at present, it seems clear that nondisclosure, even when the information is not used for trading by the corporate insiders and others, poses a serious legal problem and a potential liability. Furthermore, the 1934 Act, although it may not specifically require immediate disclosure of significant events as they occur, does require:
   (1) The annual filing of form 10-K which calls for full financial statements, but only limited disclosures in other areas.
   (2) Monthly and semi-annual reporting, but of a very limited nature.
   (3) A fairly limited disclosure pursuant to the proxy rules.
9. False or misleading press releases and disclosures: obviously if insiders must forgo trading in the stock of the corporation to which they have material inside information and fail to disclose it, it is even more apparent that the issuance of false or misleading information will result in liability to those profiting by it.

G. Proxy solicitations

1. Purpose: to insure that fairness is attained and democratic procedures are followed in the election of directors or the approval of other corporate action.
2. Scope: applies to the solicitation of proxies by any means of interstate commerce or the mails from the holders of *registered securities* whether listed on a national exchange or traded over-the-counter.
3. Any solicitation of votes either by management or minority groups must:
   a. Disclose all material facts on matters to be voted upon.
   b. Thus, shareholders are enabled to vote intelligently on corporate actions requiring their approval.
4. Shareholders must be afforded an opportunity to vote yes or no on each matter.
5. In proxy contests involving control of the management of a corporation, disclosure of the names and interests of all participants in the contest is required.
6. The SEC's rules require that proposed proxy material be filed in advance for examination by the SEC for compliance with the disclosure requirements.
7. Brokers must send out proxies for customers' shares held by them in the street name.
8. The SEC has promulgated rules which require management (the incumbents) to mail the proxy materials of the insurgents to the corporate shareholders if the insurgents so request and pay the expense incurred.

H. Tender offers

1. The Act was amended in 1968 to include tender offers by those seeking control of a company within its reporting and disclosure provisions.
2. The purpose is to inform shareholders of the subject corporation so that they may make informed decisions on take-over bids.
3. It applies to tenders or other planned acquisitions which will give the offeror over 10% of a company's equity securities.
4. Disclosure of pertinent information by the person(s) seeking control by direct purchase or by tender offer is required.

FEDERAL SECURITIES REGULATION: SUBJECTIVE QUESTIONS

THE SECURITIES ACT OF 1933

Q. (1) What is the measure of damages in civil liability suits under the Federal Securities Act of 1933, based on false registration statements?

(2) Under what conditions under the Federal Securities Act of

1933 may accountants be held liable for false registration statements?

11/62; p. 276

THE SECURITIES ACT OF 1934

Q. Andrews, a director of Omega Corporation, learned of a very valuable mineral discovery on certain land which could be acquired at a bargain price. Without revealing this information to Omega, Andrews, acting through his brother-in-law, acquired the mineral rights for the property and resold them to Omega at a large profit.
(1) Did Andrews incur any liability to Omega as a result of these transactions? Explain.
(2) If Andrews had owned the oil rights before he became a director of Omega, explain how he might properly have sold such rights to Omega at a profit thereafter.

11/69; p. 282

Q. (Continuing the facts in question above.) At the meeting of Omega's board of directors which approved purchase of these mineral rights, the board also decided to raise $1,500,000 in capital to exploit such rights by selling some of Omega's common stock (then held as treasury stock) to Smith for $500,000 and by a public sale in interstate commerce of newly authorized common stock. Smith attended the board meeting, was a sophisticated businessman who was thoroughly familiar with Omega's operations, and represented that he would acquire such stock on his own account for investment.

Immediately following the board meeting and before any public announcement of Omega's acquisition of the mineral rights was made, Baxter, one of Omega's directors, purchased a large block of Omega stock through his broker.

After a press release describing the acquisition of the mineral rights by Omega, Jones, another Omega director, purchased Omega stock through a broker and resold the stock five months thereafter at a large profit.

At all pertinent times, Omega was a large, publicly owned corporation whose stock was listed on a national securities exchange.
(1) Discuss the application of the Federal Securities Act to the sales of Omega's common stock to Smith and to the public.
(2) If Smith purchased the Omega stock intending to resell it immediately to the public in interstate commerce and Omega knew of this intention, is Omega obligated to register the stock with the Securities and Exchange Commission? Explain.
(3) Define the term "pre-emptive rights" and, assuming there were no restrictions on such rights in Omega's corporate charter or by-laws, state whether the existing common stockholders of Omega had such rights in the stock Omega sold to Smith and in the stock Omega sold to the public. Explain.

(4) Would Baxter be liable to members of the public whose stock he purchased under the circumstances described above? Explain.
(5) Could Omega recover from Jones the profit he made on the resale of the Omega stock he purchased? Explain.
(6) Assuming Omega has causes of action against Andrews and Jones and that the other officers and directors fail to cause the corporation to prosecute such action, how may these liabilities be enforced?

11/69; pp. 282, 284

FEDERAL SECURITIES REGULATION: OBJECTIVE QUESTIONS

Each of the following numbered statements states a legal conclusion as it completes the related lettered material. You are to determine whether each of the legal conclusions is true or false according to general principles of federal securities law. Your grade will be determined from your total net score obtained by deducting your total of incorrect answers from your total of correct answers; an omitted answer will not be considered an incorrect answer.

(1) The Securities Act of 1933:
 (a) Created the S.E.C.
 (b) Applies only to corporations whose stock is listed on a national exchange.
 (c) Does not apply to the securities of states or other domestic governmental instrumentalities.
 (d) Applies to private offerings of securities.
 (e) Is not applicable to a wholly intrastate offering of securities.

11/64

(2) The Securities Act of 1933:
 (a) Applies to all publicly offered securities.
 (b) Is known as the "truth in securities" act.
 (c) Is primarily based upon full disclosure of facts as the method of protecting the public.

5/62

TOPIC TEN | ANTITRUST

AICPA DESCRIPTION OF THE TOPIC

*ANTITRUST. Questions will appear in the Law section based upon the federal antitrust laws whose dominant concern is the preservation of competition. The Sherman, Clayton, Robinson-Patman, and Federal Trade Commission Acts are the major sources of law in this area. These questions will cover matters such as monopolization; price fixing and other cooperative activities among competitors; resale price maintenance; boycotts; exclusive dealing and tying restrictions; mergers; and price discrimination.**

I. INTRODUCTION

A. Purpose. The basic aim of the Federal Antitrust laws is to foster competition in the free enterprise sector of our economy by preserving competitive markets. In this way, it is believed that goods and services will be produced and distributed in the most efficient, economical, and technically proficient manner.

B. Federal antitrust legislation:

1. Sherman Act of 1890.
2. Federal Trade Commission Act of 1914.
3. Clayton Act of 1914.
4. Robinson-Patman Act of 1936.
5. Miller-Tydings Act of 1937.
6. Celler-Kefauver Act (amending Section 7, Clayton) of 1950.
7. McGuire Act of 1952.

C. Administration and enforcement.

1. The United States Justice Department was the sole government agency charged with the enforcement of the antitrust laws before the Federal Trade Commission was created in 1914. It retains exclusive dominion over criminal enforcement of the antitrust laws and may also proceed civilly on behalf of the United States to obtain injunctive relief (e.g., divestiture).
2. Private parties may bring suits under Sherman and Clayton to

* Source: AICPA, *Information for CPA Candidates* (July 1970). This topic is new to the Business Law section and questions about it may be expected in the November 1972 and subsequent examinations.

enforce the antitrust laws. They are encouraged to do so by the prospect of treble damages. Private litigants may also seek injunctive relief.

3. The Federal Trade Commission.
   a. An agency appointed by the President but with considerable independence from the executive branch due to the long terms in office. It was created to function as a specialist in trade practices, including antitrust.
   b. There are five commissioners with staggered seven-year terms with no more than three from any political party and not subject to removal by the President except for "inefficiency, neglect of duty, or malfeasance in office."
   c. The enforcement function has been broadened to empower the Commission to proceed against all violations of the Clayton Act, Sherman Act, and additional anti-competitive behavior that might be proscribed as an "unfair method of competition." It proceeds civilly after a hearing by a Federal Trade Commission examiner and a review by the full Commission if requested. If a violation is found, the Commission can issue a cease-and-desist order.

D. Collateral matters.

1. Patents and copyrights: in effect, both represent exceptions to the antitrust laws. A patent grants a 17-year, nonrenewable monopoly to the holder. So long as the patent is not used to carry out other anti-competitive activities (i.e., a patent misuse), it is insulated from the antitrust laws. Copyrights are for a 28-year period and are renewable for an additional 28 years. They are treated similarly for antitrust purposes.
2. Regulated industries: in a significant number of industries (e.g., utilities, railroads), competition is not feasible. Therefore, regulations and supervision by the government (state and federal) supersedes antitrust for the most part. However, the antitrust laws continue to apply to some aspects (particularly mergers) of even the most regulated enterprise.
3. Labor relations: although antitrust has been largely superseded by specific legislation covering labor relations, antitrust may still have application where labor unions act along with business firms to violate the antitrust laws.
4. International transactions: unique legal and political problems arise in the application of the federal antitrust laws to transactions occurring in whole or part beyond the borders of the United States. Although the law in general covers U.S. companies wherever they operate, some of the more specific prohibitions of antitrust laws are drawn to exclude transactions with international implications. Furthermore, some of the broader prohibitions of

antitrust are qualified by express exemptions applicable to international transactions, such as the limited dispensation accorded export trade associations by the Webb-Pomerene Act.

II. THE SHERMAN ACT

A. General. Post Civil War industrialization was marked by concentration of economic power in the hands of a few powerful corporations. It seemed that if the existing trends were left unchecked, monopoly or oligopoly would be the dominant theme in our American economy. The common law was apparently no match for the ingenuity of businessmen and their legal advisers. It was in this setting that the Sherman Act was passed by Congress. Despite its brevity, the Act is far-reaching because it is phrased as a declaration of rights. The Act was lacking in detail as drafted, so the job of creating much of the antitrust laws was left to the courts.

B. The statutory prohibitions of the Sherman Act are contained in the first two sections.

1. Contracts in restraint of trade: "Every contract, combination in the form of trust or otherwise, or conspiracy, in restraint of trade or commerce among the several states, or with foreign nations is hereby declared to be illegal." (Section 1)
2. Monopolization: "Every person who shall monopolize or attempt to monopolize or combine or conspire with any person or persons to monopolize any part of the trade or commerce among the several States, or with foreign nations shall be deemed guilty of a misdemeanor . . ." (Section 2).

C. The judicial standards.

1. The rule of reason: post 1911 the Supreme Court has applied a reasonableness test in ascertaining illegality under Section 1. The Court in effect rejected a literal interpretation of the Act which would have struck down each and every restraint. Instead, only unreasonable restraints are within the Act's proscription.
2. *Per se* illegality: despite the adoption by the Court of the rule of reason discussed above, certain types of restraints (e.g., price fixing) were held to be *per se* illegal or unreasonable. Under Section 1, this type of restraint is without legal justification because it has a pernicious effect upon competition with no counterbalancing justifying effects. Mere proof of having engaged in this type of activity is sufficient to constitute a violation; it is not necessary to show that the specific activity in fact represented an unreasonable restraint on competition.
3. Monopolization: here the Court primarily looks to the percentage share in the relevant market. If the defendant's percentage share

is sufficiently large to constitute monopoly power (e.g., the power to fix prices or to exclude competition), then unless the monopoly is thrust upon the defendant, he is guilty.

D. Sanctions: the Sherman Act contains both criminal and civil sanctions.

1. Criminal: the United States can proceed criminally against any person who has violated Section 1 or Section 2. Conviction can result in a fine of not more than $50,000 and/or imprisonment for not more than one year (a misdemeanor) or both.
2. Injunction: the United States and private parties can seek injunctive relief to prevent continued or threatened violations of the Sherman Act. The government frequently seeks injunctions to prevent mergers or to dissolve an illegal merger or monopoly.
3. Treble damages: private parties are empowered to seek treble (three times actual) damages against those violating the antitrust laws.
4. Seizure of property. The United States is authorized to seize property shipped in interstate commerce when it is the subject of an illegal restraint of trade (e.g., property shipped which is subject to an illegal price-fixing scheme). This remedy is rarely resorted to.

III. THE FEDERAL TRADE COMMISSION ACT

A. General: the Federal Trade Commission Act was passed by Congress in 1914. It added another instrumentality of antitrust enforcement, *viz.*, the Federal Trade Commission. It was empowered to proceed against all violations of the Sherman and Clayton Acts and also to identify additional anticompetitive behavior that might be proscribed as "an unfair method of competition."

B. The Federal Trade Commission:

1. Is a federal agency with considerable independence from the executive branch.
2. Was created as a specialist in trade practices, including antitrust matters.
3. Consists of five commissioners, appointed for staggered seven-year terms, with no more than three members from the same political party.
4. Has extensive investigative powers which may be used to study an entire industry or group of industries. Such studies may lead to recommendations for additional legislation or further FTC action.

C. The statutory standard and its applicability: the FTC Act as currently interpreted by the Courts encompasses:

1. Conduct violative of other antitrust laws.
2. Acts or practices still "in their incipiency . . . which when full blown would violate the antitrust laws."
3. Such additional acts or practices as come within the broad language of Section 5 which proscribes "unfair methods of competition."

D. Sanctions: the FTC, after review and consideration of any exceptions to an examiner's findings of fact and conclusions of law (assuming a violation to be found) may:

1. Issue an order directing the defendant to cease and desist from engaging in described conduct violative of the antitrust provisions involved. Judicial review of such a determination is available to the defendant.
2. Absence an appeal to the judiciary by the defendant or judicial affirmance of the Commission's order; monetary penalties of $5,000 for each violation become applicable. Each day of continued violation constitutes a separate offense.
3. On judicial review, a decree may be entered directing the defendant to comply with the FTC order and subjecting him to liability for contempt of court in the event of any future disobedience. In this connection, the FTC may seek court review.
4. FTC sanctions are wholly prospective; i.e., no penalties attach until a cease-and-desist order is entered and judicial review is exhausted or waived.

IV. THE CLAYTON ACT

A. General: the Clayton Act (1914) was intended to supplement and augment the broad prohibitions contained in the Sherman Act by specifically outlawing certain practices (i.e., tying arrangements, price discrimination, etc.). The Clayton Act as interpreted made *per se* violations out of some acts whose status under the Sherman Act was unclear. It was also intended to reach certain anti-competitive conduct in its incipiency even though it had not attained the threshold level required to violate the Sherman Act.

B. The Celler-Kefauver Amendment. This Act, passed in 1950, is undoubtedly the most important change in antitrust law in recent years. It:

1. Amended Section 7 of the Clayton Act, which applies to mergers, by making that Act applicable to the purchase of assets as well as stock acquisitions.
2. Manifested a congressional intent to create a more stringent test in the merger area.
3. Removed any doubt that the Clayton Act was intended to apply to conglomerate mergers.

C. The statutory prohibitions: omitting here various clauses relating to the requisite involvement of interstate or foreign commerce, the act made unlawful:

1. Price discrimination. Discrimination in "price between different purchasers of commodities," or not reflecting differences in the "grade, quality, or quantity of the commodity sold," or differences in the "cost of selling or transportation," or the necessity of meeting competition "where the effect of such discrimination may be to substantially lessen competition or tend to create a monopoly." (Section 2.) This section was amended by the Robinson-Patman Act, see Part V.
2. Exclusive dealings. Sales of "commodities" on the condition that the purchaser would not "use or deal in" the commodities of a competitor of the seller, where the effect of the transaction "may be to substantially lessen competition or tend to create a monopoly in any line of commerce." (Section 3.)
3. Mergers and acquisitions. Acquisition by a corporation of the stock or assets "where in any line of commerce in any section of the country, the effect of such acquisition may be substantially to lessen competition, or tend to create a monopoly." The Act also prohibits the use of a holding company to acquire competing corporations. (Section 7 as amended.)
4. Interlocking directorates. Membership on the boards of directors of two or more corporations, where one of the corporations had "capital, surplus, and undivided profits aggregating more than $1 million," and the several corporations were then or previously "competitors, so that the elimination of competition by agreement between them would constitute a violation" of the antitrust laws. (Section 8.)

D. The judicial standards: in applying the above statutory language ("to substantially lessen competition or tend to create a monopoly"), the courts have resorted to several differing approaches.

1. Qualitative substantiality: the court considers not only the volume or portion of interstate commerce affected but also all other relevant factors (e.g., the strength of the other competitors, the ease of entry by newcomers). Then, taking all these factors into account the court must decide whether competitive activity has actually diminished or probably will diminish.
2. Quantitative substantiality: the court relies almost exclusively on a numerical approach to the determination of whether the conduct is anticompetitive.
   a. Absolute quantitative substantiality is based upon the dollar volume of the product in interstate commerce or the number of outlets involved.
   b. Comparative quantitative substantiality is based upon the comparative or percentage share of the market in question.

E. Sanctions.

1. The United States is authorized to institute proceedings in equity to prevent or restrain violations of the Act.
2. Injured private persons may obtain treble damages.
3. Private plaintiffs may sue for injunctive relief based upon "threatened loss or damage by a violation of the antitrust laws."
4. Clayton Act violations are not criminal offenses and the Act does not provide for forfeiture of property.

V. THE ROBINSON-PATMAN ACT

A. General: the Act amended and greatly expanded the original prohibition against price discrimination contained in Section 2 of the Clayton Act. The principal changes the Act was responsible for were:

1. To make the anti-discrimination provisions applicable to buyers as well as sellers.
2. To provide a detailed, but somewhat confusing, enumeration of indirect violations of the Act (e.g., hidden or disguised rebates in the form of spurious brokerage commissions).
3. To provide criminal penalties for violation of the Act's provisions.

B. The statutory prohibitions: the Act makes it unlawful for any person engaged in interstate commerce either directly or indirectly:

1. To "discriminate in price between purchasers of commodities of like grade and quality . . . where the effect of such discrimination may be substantially to lessen competition or tend to create a monopoly in any line of commerce or to injure, destroy, or prevent competition with any person who either grants or knowingly receives the benefit of such discrimination, or with the customers of either of them." The exceptions and defenses to this broad proscription will be discussed *infra* Part VII.
2. To pay or grant or receive or accept brokerage commissions or any other compensation or allowance in lieu thereof for any such services rendered unless the party receiving said commissions is acting as a *bona fide* independent broker. In effect, brokerage commissions to customers are unlawful.
3. To pay or grant discounts or rebates to customers either in the form of actual allowances or the rendering of services for promotional or advertising expenses except when made available on proportionally equal terms.
4. To knowingly induce or receive a discrimination in price prohibited by the Act.

C. The judicial standards: essentially the courts have taken a hard-line position on defendents attempting to avoid violations of the Robinson-Patman Act. This is manifested by the court's:

1. Presumption that competition has been harmed when the price discrimination involves competing purchasers from the same seller.
2. Narrow and strict interpretation of the defenses such as the justification of price discrimination based upon quantity discounts, other cost justifications, or furnishing of services on an equal basis.

D. Sanctions.

1. Criminal: A fine of $5,000 and imprisonment for one year as the maximum penalty.
2. Injunction: The government may seek to obtain injunctive relief against a violator of the Act.
3. Civil: The court retains the civil sanction contained in the Clayton Act, see *supra*, Part IV.

VI. FAIR TRADE LEGISLATION

A. General: as a result of the Supreme Court's holding that price fixing is *per se* illegal, manufacturers of certain products sought legislation exempting resale price maintenance (i.e., the manufacturer determines the minimum price at which a retailer may sell) from the application of Section 1 of the Sherman Act. In effect the so called "fair trade" legislation discussed here amended the Sherman Act to permit this type of price fixing.

B. The Miller-Tydings Act: in essence this Act permitted resale price maintenance by manufacturers in interstate commerce where state law authorized it in respect to intrastate commerce. In a momentous decision the Supreme Court emasculated the Act by holding that it applied only in respect to those who agreed to resale prime maintenance. Thus, troublesome price cutters who refused to agree to sell at the manufacturer's price were free to sell at any price they wished.

C. The McGuire Act: Congress responded to the Supreme Court's decision *supra* by making resale price maintenance provisions applicable to non-signers as well as signers. Thus, resale price maintenance agreements are valid where:

1. There is a state law which permits the enforcement of resale price agreements between manufacturers and dealers.
2. The article or commodity sold bears the trademark, trade name, or brand name of the manufacturer.
3. Such commodity is in free and open competition with commodities of the same general class produced and distributed by others. The Act has no application to agreements among competitors; it represents a limited exception to the general rule under Section 1 of the Sherman Act that all forms of price-fixing are *per se* illegal.

VII. ANTITRUST APPLICATION TO VARIOUS RESTRAINTS OF TRADE

A. Price fixing: virtually all types of price fixing are *per se* illegal; i.e., they are without legal justification. This includes any agreement, combination or conspiracy aimed at raising, depressing, fixing, pegging, or stabilizing the price of a commodity in interstate commerce.

1. Agreements among manufacturers and retailers (vertical arrangements) are illegal unless otherwise validated by state and federal "fair trade" legislation. See *supra,* Part VI. Horizontal arrangements (i.e., among competitors) are illegal without further inquiry or proof upon it being shown that such an arrangement exists.
2. What constitutes a contract, combination, or conspiracy to fix prices? The law is clear; such arrangements are *per se* illegal, but proving their existence is another matter.
   a. Joint action solely between a corporation and its officers acting on its behalf is not illegal price fixing.
   b. An agreement between a parent and its subsidiary is not illegal if it fixes prices between the parent and subsidiary and goes no further, i.e., does not attempt to determine the prices at which the subsidiary's purchasers will sell.
3. Conscious parallelism (e.g., simultaneous price changes by competitors in an industry) may be resorted to in order to have the court infer that a conspiracy exists where it can't be directly proven.
   a. The usual pattern takes the form of an invitation to participate or a discussion of a plan which is then carried out although there is no proof of an actual agreement.
   b. Conscious parallel behavior does not in and of itself prove conspiracy; some additional plus factor is necessary (e.g., artificial elimination of quality differences or other types of abnormal marketing behavior).
4. Price leadership has little or no probative value in establishing a "contract, combination, or conspiracy" in restraint of trade.
5. Interstate commerce must be involved. However, no particular dollar volume in interstate commerce is required.
6. Attempted justifications based upon the reasonableness of the price charged or the avoidance of cutthroat competition are of no avail. An attempt to provide a floor under prices by selective buying in order to prevent ruinous price cuts is illegal.
7. The use of a trade association or an agent to determine prices is illegal. Reporting activities by a trade association may be found to constitute a conspiracy to fix prices even though such authority has not been actually agreed to by the members. The courts look to the effect of the association practices on prices.

B. Other cooperative activities among competitors: although price fixing is perhaps the best known type of cooperative activity engaged in by competitors, other types of joint activities have been placed in the *per se* illegal category. These include:

1. Territorial and other types of allocation of customers.
2. Agreements to limit production to certain designated levels.
3. Joint boycotts by competitors of a troublesome buyer.

C. Monopoly in a single firm: Section 2 of the Sherman Act makes it illegal for any person "to monopolize, or attempt to monopolize, or combine or conspire with any other person or persons to monopolize."

1. Monopoly is defined in terms of the *power* to control market prices or exclude competition.
2. The basic test applied is the percentage share of the market controlled. The higher the percentage, the greater the danger; e.g., 90% control certainly would constitute monopoly power; 10% would certainly not.
3. If monopolization is alleged, no specific intent need be shown. Thus, if the requisite monopoly power exists based upon the market percentage controlled, it is illegal—unless it was "thrust upon" the monopolist.
4. Plurality of actors is not necessary to violate the Sherman Act's proscription of monopolization or attempting to monopolize. Section 1 violations (e.g., price fixing), however, require plurality.
5. If an attempt to monopolize rather than actual monopolization is the alleged unlawful act, then a specific intent to monopolize must be shown.
6. Delineation of the relevant product and geographic market is of vital importance in determining the existence of a monopoly. The narrower the relevant market (product or territorial), the larger the defendant's share will be. Therefore, the defendant will usually argue:
   a. For the largest geographic area feasible.
   b. That the product is substantially interchangeable with other similar products—price, use, and qualities considered. For further consideration of market delineation, see *infra,* p. 301, Mergers.

D. Resale price maintenance: as previously indicated, the McGuire Act which amended the Miller-Tydings Act permits limited vertical price fixing (i.e., between a manufacturer and his distributors). The exemption from illegality is dependent on several factors, including state law permitting such arrangements. In the absence of such state legislation, resale price maintenance is treated the same as other types of price fixing, *viz, per se* illegal. See *supra,* Part VI.

E. Territorial and other limitations on resale:

1. Horizontal territorial limitations (i.e., among competitors) are *per se* illegal.

2. Vertical territorial limitations (i.e., between a manufacturer and his distributors) where typically the distributor receives an exclusive right to sell in a given territory but is precluded from selling outside that area (a franchising arrangement) are:
   a. *Per se* illegal if title to the product passes to the distributor. The restriction on the purchaser's right to sell where he wishes is an unlawful restraint of trade.
   b. Not *per se* illegal, but are to be tested under the rule of reason so long as the manufacturer–seller "retains all indicia of ownership including title, dominion, and risk, and so long as the dealers in question are indistinguishable from agents or salesmen of the seller.
3. Other limitations on resale, such as customer retention by the seller (i.e., the retailer–buyer is precluded from selling to cab companies, fleet operators, or the government), are *per se* illegal unless title is retained.
4. As a general rule, once the seller has sold his product to the buyer he cannot restrict the buyer's freedom to sell where and to whomever he chooses.

F. Boycotts.

1. A wholly unilateral or individual refusal to deal is normally not violative of antitrust law. The businessman can deal with whom he wishes. Only in the event the refusal is coupled with an attempt to monopolize do antitrust problems arise.
2. Joint boycotts, whether aimed at maintaining prices, excluding certain troublesome buyers from the market, or otherwise restraining trade are *per se* illegal.
3. Proof of joint action (conspiracy) may be inferred based upon consciously parallel behavior.

G. Tying restrictions: the classic type of tying arrangement involves a seller who has a highly desirable or unique machine or product and who forces his purchasers to take another nondescript product as a condition to acquiring the desired product. For example, a salt processing machine manufacturer requires his purchaser to buy all his salt from the manufacturers; or the maker of a business machine requires all punch cards be bought from it. Other varieties include full line forcing where a buyer must buy the whole line if he is to obtain any particular item.

1. Section 3 of the Clayton Act is the chief statutory provision where the "tie-in" involves goods, wares, or commodities. The test used is absolute quantitative substantiality, i.e., if the dollar volume is not insignificant or insubstantial then the arrangement is *per se* illegal. One case held that $500,000 was not insignificant or insubstantial.

2. Section 1 of the Sherman Act is also available but is used mainly when the "tie-in" does not involve goods, wares, or commodities. The test which has evolved is only slightly less strict than that used under the Clayton Act. The tying arrangement is *per se* illegal where it is found that the seller has "sufficient economic power to impose an appreciable restraint on free competitions in the tied product (assuming all the time, of course, that a not insubstantial amount of interstate commerce is affected)."
3. Reciprocity: although clearly not a tying arrangement, reciprocal arrangements are somewhat analogous. The typical case involves the big buyer who agrees to purchase the seller's product only if the seller agrees to purchase certain products sold by the big buyer. Such arrangements have recently been held illegal under Section 1 of the Sherman Act as unreasonable restraints of trade, and under section 7 of the Clayton Act. The law in this area is still in its formative stages.

H. Exclusive dealing arrangements and requirements contracts: These represent two very similar types of anti-competitive marketing devices.

1. The typical exclusive dealing arrangement prohibits the purchaser from selling a competing product. For example, a garage is required to sell only brand X gasoline for the duration of the contract.
2. Requirements contracts are phrased in terms of requiring the buyer to take all of his requirements of a given item (e.g., coal) from the seller for the duration of the contract.
3. The main statutory provision applicable to these types of arrangements is Section 3 of the Clayton Act; however, Section 1 of the Sherman Act and Section 5 of the Federal Trade Commission Act can also be resorted to, if necessary. For example, if goods, wares, or commodities are not involved, the Clayton Act is not applicable.
4. The test is primarily one of comparative quantitative substantiality, i.e., what percentage share of the market does the defendant control? If the requisite percentage share is substantial, there is little chance of the defendant's sustaining the arrangement. Where the share controlled is not great, other factors will be considered—a qualitative approach.

I. Mergers: Section 7 of the Clayton Act as amended in 1950 applies to vertical, horizontal, and conglomeral acquisitions whether accomplished by acquisition of stock or assets and regardless of whether the acquired company is operated as a separate company or merged into the acquirer. Although the Sherman Act is still applicable it is not as stringent as the Clayton Act and has fallen into disuse. Since 1950, the Supreme Court has almost invariably upheld the United States government in merger cases attacked via Section 7.

1. Relevant market: this includes "any line of commerce, in any section of the country."
   a. Product market definition: there may be coexisting markets. It is possible a merger may not substantially lessen competition in any of these markets. There may be:
      1. Broad markets, in which case the test is reasonable interchangeability of use and cross-elasticity of demand.
      2. Submarkets in which the test is "practical indicea" such as distinct customers, distinct prices, specialized vendors, products' peculiar characteristics and uses, and sensitivity to price changes; a relatively narrow market will qualify as submarket (e.g., florists' aluminum, household steel wool, household bleach).
   b. Geographic market definition: it must correspond to commercial realities of industry and be "economically significant," or the area to which a purchaser can practicably turn for supplies. Standards appear to be flexible; it appears to be easy for government to prove that area it has selected is relevant.
2. Basic test: Whether the merger "substantially lessens competition or tends to create a monopoly" (the Clayton Act). It is intended to cope with monopolistic trends in their incipiency, before a Sherman Act prosecution is justified.
   a. The government may proceed against a merger any time the merger threatens to restrain commerce. It needs not act at time of the merger. Thus, there is no statute of limitations applicable.
   b. Under the "failing company doctrine," a merger that is anticompetitive may be allowed if the acquired company is failing and there is no other purchaser whose acquisition of the company would be less anticompetitive.
   c. In a horizontal merger, the court will look at the market share resulting from the merger and the industry concentration trends.
      1. If the merger will give the new company 30% of the relevant market, there is a rebuttable presumption that the merger is unlawful. Section 7 prevents even slight increases in concentration in a concentrated market.
      2. A strong trend toward industry concentration from whatever cause may make a merger illegal even if the resulting company has only a 5 to 10% market share.
   d. Vertical mergers: the effect is to reduce either the available markets or supplies for others in the industry. It will be illegal if:
      1. The actual purpose is to foreclose competitors by forcing the acquired company to purchase its products only from the acquiring company and thereby preclude purchases from manufacturing competitors.

2. There is a significant concentration trend and a substantial portion of a substantial market may be foreclosed.
3. A large company goes into a *non*substantial market where there is no concentration trend, *if* it could finance a campaign by the acquired company to drive out competitors by price cutting or by keeping raw material prices high.
4. Raises barriers to entry.
5. Acquiring company was a potential competitor.

e. Conglomerate mergers: the acquisition of a company in a totally unrelated business, or one that sells related products that are not in the same market as the parents' products, or one that sells the parents' type of product in a different geographic market. In considering such a case, an analysis of the economic facts of each case is mandatory. Examples to date include:

1. Substitution of a powerful acquiring firm for a smaller, *already dominant* firm may raise entry barriers and reduce strong competition from existing firms who fear retaliation.
2. Situations where the acquiring company A is a potential entrant (e.g., product and market extension) into the field of the acquired company B. A will no longer be a potential entrant once it acquires B since it would not compete with B. The loss of A as a potential entrant may reduce competition in a concentrated market because other companies can raise prices without fearing that A will step in and undersell them. It is not necessary to show actual or planned entry by the acquiring corporation, just interest in and the capacity for entering.
3. A joint venture by two corporations to go into new field that neither party is in is illegal if both companies are probable entrants or one probably would enter and other would remain on the sidelines as a threatening potential entrant.

3. Sanctions

a. Preliminary injunctions can be obtained for violation of Section 7 by the Justice Department, the Federal Trade Commission, and private litigants if there is a good probability that a violation will be established on full hearing and if the injury to the public and plaintiff outweighs that to the defendant. The court may allow the acquisition but require the corporations to operate separately during litigation.

b. Divestiture of the acquisition: even after a number of years the court may order the dissolution of a long-standing merger as well as enjoining future acquisitions. No private litigant has obtained divestiture. However, the Justice Department has succeeded in several cases.

c. Other relief can be tailored to restore competition, especially technical and marketing assistance to a purchaser of divested assets.

d. Consent decrees.

J. Price discrimination: may be either direct (i.e., in the form of price differentials) or indirect (in the form of brokerage commissions or advertising expenditures). Both are severely proscribed by the Robinson–Patman Act.

1. The original version of Section 2 of the Clayton Act, which was amended by the Robinson–Patman Act, was aimed at local price cutting (primary line discriminations) which had as their purpose the elimination of the seller's competitors. The typical pattern involved a seller who sold in a large territorial market and cut prices in one segment of the market in order to eliminate competitors there while maintaining higher prices in the balance of the market.
2. The Robinson–Patman Act was primarily aimed at broadening the coverage of the price discrimination provisions to include price discriminations among the customers of the seller. The problem was the big buyer who demanded unjustified price differentials in order to drive out his competitors (a secondary line price discrimination). Here the big buyer—not the seller—is the real culprit.
3. Defenses: despite the broadness and harshness of the Robinson–Patman Act's proscriptions, there are certain defenses which are available:
   a. No harm to competition: this defense is only available in primary line price discriminations. If the alleged illegal price discrimination involves a resale by the customers of the seller (secondary line) rather than his competitors, injury is presumed and therefore need not be proved.
   b. The sale involves commodities, which are not of like grade and quality. However, private brand labels or sales to big buyers under their own name is not within this defense.
   c. Cost differentials: to the extent a seller can justify a differential based upon proof of actual cost savings due to volume purchases, this defense is available. The burden of proof is most difficult and the defendant bears it.
   d. Changing market conditions and seasonal variances: where in response to changing conditions affecting the market for or the marketability of the goods concerned, such as actual or imminent deterioration of perishable goods, or obsolescence of seasonal goods, a seller may validly discriminate in price.
   e. Meeting competition: to the extent that a seller has to meet existing *lawful* competition to retain his business, he may discriminate in price.

f. Indirect price discriminations have been treated most harshly by the courts. They have taken on the quality of *per se* offenses (see *supra*, Part V. B. 2 and 3).

ANTITRUST: EXAMINATION QUESTIONS*

Q. The Sherman Act, Section 1, provides: "Every contract, combination, in the form of trust or otherwise, in restraint of trade or commerce among the several states or foreign nations, is hereby declared to be illegal. . . ."

(1) What is the "rule of reason" and its effect upon the above statute? Explain.

(2) Is price-fixing subject to the "rule of reason"? Explain.

11/62; p. 291

Q. In our complex economic society, corporate integration has taken three forms–viz., horizontal, vertical, and conglomerate.

(1) Explain and illustrate the meaning of these terms.

(2) List the acts primarily concerned with the economic integration of businesses.

11/62; pp. 300-302

Q. The Jason Corporation sold various interrelated products which it manufactured. One of the items was manufactured almost exclusively by Jason Corporation. It was sold throughout most of the United States. The Corporation realized the importance of the product to its purchasers and decided to capitalize on the situation by requiring all purchasers to take at least two other Jason products in order to obtain the item over which it had almost complete market control.

At the spring sales meeting the president of Jason Corporation informed the entire sales force that they were to henceforth sell only to those customers who agreed to take the additional products. He indicated that this was a great opportunity to substantially increase sales of laggard items.

The plan was adopted and gross sales of the additional items more than doubled and were in excess of one million dollars.

You are the auditor examining the financial statements of Jason Corporation and upon inquiry as to the reason for the great spurt in sales of certain items the above facts came to light.

(1) Discuss the legal problems created by the above set of facts.

(2) What are the probable legal actions by customers, competitors and the United States government which Jason Corporation may face as a result of the above facts? Explain.

5/68 ; pp; 299-300

* See p. 19. for introductory note.

TOPIC ELEVEN | INSURANCE

CONTENTS PAGE

*INSURANCE. Under this topic primary emphasis is placed upon life and property (fire) insurance in relation to the successful management of a business. The topic embraces matters such as the insurable interest in the lives of owners and managers of the business entity and its debtors, and the insurable interest in property which the business owns, rents, or has sold under various financial arrangements.**

I. CHARACTERISTICS

A. Definition: a contract whereby, for a stipulated consideration, one party (the insurer) undertakes to compensate the other (the insured) for loss on a specified subject by specified perils.

1. Property insurance (e.g., fire, theft) is primarily an indemnity against risk of actual loss by distributing the loss over a group.
2. Life insurance is primarily a form of investment.
3. Insurance normally does not protect against willful intentional destruction by the insured, but it does protect against negligence by the insured.

B. Elements of the insurance contract:

1. Mutual assent (see Contracts, p. 33, III.A.).
   a. The application for insurance made by the prospective insured constitutes the offer.
   b. Acceptance is usually made by the company at its home office (see p. 307, I.B.5.b.).
2. Consideration (see Contracts, p. 39, III.B.).
   a. By the insured: payment, or promise of payment, of premium.
   b. By the insurer: promise to indemnify the policyholder for loss that may occur.
   c. By the beneficiary (the person to whom a policy of insurance is payable; normally the insured, except in life insurance). If the beneficiary is not the insured, he gives no consideration

* Source: AICPA, *Information for CPA Candidates* (July 1970).

and is not a party to the contract, but rather a third party beneficiary (see Contracts, p. 54, VI.C.).

3. Existence of the subject matter.
   a. Policy is void if the subject matter is not in existence at the time of issue and one of the parties knows this.
   b. Policy may be valid if the subject matter is not in existence at the time of issue and neither party knew this and the insurer assumed the risk of a prior fortuitous loss (e.g., a "lost or not lost" clause—see p. 318, IV.C.2.).
   c. Normally taking out insurance on a nonexisting subject matter will result in an unintentional misrepresentation of a material fact, making the insurance contract voidable at the option of the insurer.
4. Writing (see Contracts, p. 51, V.).
   a. The Statute of Frauds does not require a written contract because the event insured against may occur within one year from issue of the contract.
   b. Statutes in several states, however, require a writing:
      (1) For certain types of insurance, or
      (2) Because of general requirements that all contracts be filed with the state insurance commission.
5. Delivery.
   a. Neither by statute nor by common law is a physical or manual delivery of the contract a requisite for validity (compare this with the requirement of delivery of a deed in real property—see Property, p. 389, II.B.6.c.).
   b. Delivery is primarily a matter of intent in insurance law; any act or words by the insurer which clearly manifest an intent to be bound will constitute a constructive delivery.
   c. In the absence of any express provision in the policy, a contract of insurance is generally binding at the time of unconditional acceptance of the application and this fact is communicated to the insured.
6. Insurable interest.
   a. Definition: a relation between the insured and the event insured against, such that the occurrence of the event will cause substantial loss or injury of some kind to the insured.
   b Insurable interest in life:
      (1) Generally exists in the case of persons related by blood or law, or persons having a substantial interest engendered by love and affection, and in the case of other persons, a lawful

and substantial economic interest in having the life, health, or bodily safety of the insured continue.

(2) A corporation has an insurable interest in the lives of its officers on whose efforts its success depends.

(3) A partnership or an individual partner has an insurable interest in the lives of the partners.

(4) An unsecured or general creditor has an insurable interest in the life (but not in the specific property) of the debtor up to the amount of the debt.

(5) Any person of lawful age may effect a contract of life, accident, or health insurance upon his own person for the benefit of his estate or a named beneficiary although the beneficiary has no insurable interest in the insured's life.

(6) An insurable interest must exist when the policy was originally issued, but in most states it need not continue to exist until death or loss occurs. (E.g., W—wife—procures a policy on the life of H—husband—and W continues to pay all the premiums despite a subsequent divorce of H and W; W having had an insurable interest initially, may collect the full amount of the policy on the death of H.)

(A) The reason for this rule of law is that life insurance is an investment, and the policy owner builds up a valuable equity, which the law says he may maintain. This rule developed prior to the concept of a cash surrender value in life insurance policies.

(7) Generally speaking, in addition to a valid insurable interest, the insured must consent to having his life insured, except in the case of spouses, parents, and minors. (E.g., a wife could insure her husband's life without his consent.)

c. Insurable interest in property:

(1) Means any legally recognized or any substantial economic interest in the safety or preservation of the property insured against loss, destruction, or other pecuniary damage.

(A) The objectives of this requirement are (i) measurement of the insured's loss, (ii) prevention of wagering, and (iii) guarding against moral hazard (e.g., arson).

(2) Must actually exist at the time the loss occurs.

(3) A mortgagor has an insurable interest to the extent of the full value of the property mortgaged; the mortgagee has an insurable interest to the extent of the unpaid debt (see p. 315, III.E.1.).

(4) A tenant has an insurable interest in the property he leases.

(5) A stockholder has an insurable interest in the property owned by a corporation.

(6) A general creditor does not have an insurable interest in the property of his debtor while the debtor is alive; however, a secured creditor or judgment lienor does have an insurable interest in the specific property which secures the debtor or against which the judgment attaches.

(7) A Bailee has an insurable interest in the property held in his possession although he does not have a legal title thereto.

(8) A person has an insurable interest in the property of another if he has potential *liability* in the event of its destruction.

UCC RULE. The UCC has made some important changes in respect to the buyer's insurable interest in goods which are the subject matter of a contract of sale. These rules are in addition to those discussed above, and are intended to foster an early creation of the buyer's insurable interest in the goods. They are in no way intended to impair any insurable interest recognized by any other statute or rule of law.

(1) The buyer obtains a "special property and insurable interest" in goods by identification *of existing goods as those to which the contract refers. The rule applies even though the goods identified are non-conforming and the buyer would have the option of returning them.*

(2) Identification can be made at any time and any manner explicitly agreed to by the parties. In the absence of explicit agreement, identification occurs:

(a) When the contract is made if it is for the sale of goods already in existence and identified.

(b) In the case of future goods (other than growing crops and the unborn young of animals), when the goods are shipped, marked, or otherwise designated by the seller as the goods to which the contract refers.

(3) The seller retains an insurable interest in goods so long as title to or any security interest in the goods remains in him.

d. Against crimes: no "insurable interest" by the insured against crimes to be committed by him. But, there is an "insurable interest" against crimes to be committed against him (e.g., can insure against theft by another).

e. Insurance is distinguishable from a wager in that insurance is, and must be, based on a valid insurable interest, which the insured seeks to protect against risk of loss; moreover, insurance is entered into in common with others, resulting not only in an individual benefit, but also in a benefit to an entire group.

II. LIFE INSURANCE

A. Types:

1. Ordinary (straight) life: Premiums are to be paid so long as the insured lives; upon death a fixed sum is paid to the beneficiary.
2. Limited payment life (e.g., twenty-payment life): Premiums are paid for a specified number of years; the insured is protected throughout life, and payment is made to the beneficiary upon the death of the insured.
3. Endowment: Premiums are to be paid for a specified number of years; fixed sum to be paid to the insured at the end of this period or to his beneficiary if the insured dies prior to the end of this time.
4. Term policies: provide insurance for a fixed term of years only; the insurer pays only if death occurs within the term covered.

B. Standard provisions.

1. Grace period for overdue premiums: usually thirty days after premium is due.
2. Exclusion of risks: Usually only death due to military service, aviation, and suicide within two years of issuance of policy may be excluded.
3. Incontestability clause: Usually a policy cannot be contested for misstatements by the insured or for other reasons (e.g., concealments) after the policy has been in force for a given period, commonly two years, except for:
   a. Nonpayment of premiums.
   b. Risk not covered by the policy (e.g., the exclusion of death due to military service).
   c. Lack of an insurable interest.
   d. Failure to file proof of death within the required period.
4. The policy constitutes the entire agreement between the parties: This includes the application for insurance, if (as is usually the case) a copy is attached to the policy.
5. Adjustment of premium payments in accordance with the insured's true age, if the age was misstated.
6. A statement of options which the insured is entitled to in the event of default in premium payments after premiums have been paid for three full years; these options include:
   a. Cash surrender (this provision must be included).
   b. Extended insurance, usually in the form of term insurance, for the amount of the cash surrender value.
   c. Paid-up insurance for the amount of the cash surrender value.

7. A statement showing in figures the loan values available to the insured after premiums have been paid for three full years.
8. Dividend options:
   a. Payment in cash.
   b. Applied toward a reduction of premiums.
   c. Left with the company at interest.
   d. Applied toward the purchase of additional insurance, thereby increasing the face value of policy.
9. Reinstatement provision that the policy may be reinstated at any time within three years from the date of default in the payment of any premium (unless the cash surrender value has been exhausted or the period of extended insurance has expired), provided the insured:
   a. Procures evidence of insurability satisfactory to the insurer, and
   b. Pays all overdue premiums and any other indebtedness due the insurer, with interest.
10. Notice of premium due: usually must be sent from fifteen to forty-five days before it is due.
11. Sound health or delivery in good health clause: states that the policy shall not take effect unless and until the application has been approved at the home office and the policy has been delivered to the insured while he is in good health.
12. Assignability:
    a. The policy will invariably provide that the insured may assign (e.g., sell, pledge) the policy upon giving due notice to the insurer.
    b. If such a provision is not included, the beneficiary's rights in expectancy are vested, and an assignment even though consented to by the insurer will not affect the beneficiary's rights.
    c. Where there is a provision allowing assignment, consent of the insurer is not required, nor is the consent of the beneficiary required, despite the fact that his rights may be impaired; i.e., the assignee or pledgee of the policy takes a better claim to the proceeds than does the named beneficiary.

C. Rights of creditors and beneficiaries under policies of life insurance:

1. Rights of creditors of the insured:

a. Creditors cannot compel the insured to exercise his right to the cash surrender value of the policy.

b. If the policy is payable to the estate of the insured as the named beneficiary, the creditors can reach the proceeds upon death of the insured, since they are assets of the insured's estate.

c. Creditors can reach the proceeds even though not payable to the insured or his estate to the extent that it can be proved that the payment of premiums is a fraud on creditors.

d. If the policy is payable to a named beneficiary and the insured retains the right to change the beneficiary, the creditors in most jurisdictions have rights against the payment received by the beneficiary. (The minority rule is that the creditor has no rights against payments to the beneficiary.)

2. Beneficiary's right to proceeds as against his own creditors:

a. Generally, even if the beneficiary takes free of the insured's creditors, he does not take as against his own creditors.

b. However, some jurisdictions provide that if the beneficiary is the wife of the insured, she receives the proceeds free from the claims of her own creditors as well as those of her husband. This is the case even though the wife paid all the premiums.

D. Termination of life insurance coverage.

1. Expiration, i.e., of a term policy.
2. Lapse: default in payment of premiums.
3. Payment of loss upon death of the insured.
4. Forfeiture (see pp. 319–321, VIII., IX.).
5. Cancellation: Life insurance contracts cannot be cancelled by the insurer; however, other types of insurance may readily be cancelled.

III. FIRE INSURANCE

A. Nature and coverage:

1. Indemnifies the insured against property destroyed or damaged by fire within a specified period.
2. The person insuring must have an "insurable interest" at the time of the loss (see p. 308, I.B.6.c.).
3. Fire insurance, like most property insurance, is non-transferable in that the contract is a personal contract between the parties.

4. Covers loss due directly to a hostile fire, and also loss accompanying or resulting from a hostile fire (e.g., damage caused by smoke, water, or chemicals).
5. Does not normally include a loss caused by a friendly fire.
   a. Friendly fire: a fire burning in the place where it was intended to burn (e.g., an oil burner damaged by overheating would not be a loss covered by a standard fire policy).
   b. Hostile fire: one which breaks out from its confines where it was intended to be contained and becomes a hostile element.
6. Smoke damage and so on, caused by a friendly fire, may be insured against by adding the "extended coverage indorsement."

B. Types of fire insurance policies:

1. Blanket (compound) policy: a policy of fire insurance that contemplates that the risk is shifting or varying, and is applied to a class of property rather than to any particular article or thing.
2. Specific policy: covers a particular piece of property or property at a specific location (e.g., the building and machinery located at the X factory)
3. Floater policy: a policy intended to supplement specific insurance, the purpose of which is to provide indemnity for property which cannot, because of its frequent change in location and quantity, be covered by specific insurance.
4. Valued policy: one in which a definite valuation is, by agreement of both parties, put on the subject matter of the insurance and written on the face of the policy; such value, in the absence of fraud or mistake, is conclusive in the event of a total loss.
5. Open or unvalued policy: one in which the value of the property is not settled in the policy, merely a maximum for which the company will be liable; value recoverable will be determined at the time of the loss, based upon the fair market value of the loss at that date.

C. Amount recoverable:

1. Under either a valued or an open policy, if there is a partial destruction, only the actual loss sustained is recoverable.
2. In the event of a total loss:
   a. Under a valued policy, the insured will recover the amount stated in the policy without proof of actual value.
   b. Under an open policy, the insured will recover only the cash value of property destroyed as subsequently proved, i.e., to indemnify for the loss. (E.g., X insures with the I Insurance

Company, taking out an open policy with a maximum of \$25,000. The property is totally destroyed. X will receive the actual value of the property destroyed even though it is less than the \$25,000 maximum.)

D. Standard clauses:

1. An option to restore or rebuild is generally given to the insurance company.
   a. Protects the insurer against necessity of contesting inflated claims.
   b. Tends to discourage arson, which is generally motivated by a desire for a cash payment.
2. Co-insurance (*applies only to partial loss*):
   a. Co-insurance provides that if the owner insures his property up to a given percentage (usually 80%) of its value, he will recover any loss in full up to the face amount of the policy, but if he insures for less than the fixed percentage he must himself bear proportionately any loss.
   b. The formula for determining the amount of recovery is as follows:

$$\text{Recovery (\$6,000)} = \text{Actual loss (\$12,000)} \times \frac{\text{Amount of insurance (\$16,000)}}{\text{Co-insurance \% (80\%)} \times \text{Value of property (\$40,000)}}$$

3. Pro rata clause: Where the owner has insurance with several companies, and the aggregate exceeds the actual loss, he can collect from each company only that company's proportionate liability to the total amount of insurance. (E.g., X takes out two open-value fire insurance policies with two different insurance companies each having a \$10,000 maximum. In the event of total destruction of the property, which has a replacement value of \$15,000, X can only collect \$7,500 from each insurer.)
4. Occupancy of premises: Standard policy provides that if the premises become vacant or unoccupied for a given number of days (e.g., ten days), then the entire policy shall be suspended until the premises are reoccupied unless otherwise provided.
5. Assignment of policy:
   a. Normally non-assignable, since the relationship between insurer and insured is a personal one; therefore, policy usually provides that it will be void if assigned (prior to loss) without the company's consent indorsed on the policy.
   b. After loss caused by a fire, the insured may assign his claim against the insurance company.
   c. Fire insurance on property which is transferred does not ac-

company the property transferred; instead, the policy is void upon the transfer of the property due to the personal nature of fire insurance and the loss of an insurable interest.

6. Notice of loss within a specified period of time or immediate notice of loss:
   a. In the event of loss, the insured is required to give notice within a specified period of time, or the policy may require that notice of loss be "immediate"; failure to comply will permit the insurer to avoid liability.
   b. The word "immediate" has been universally construed by the courts to mean as soon as is reasonably possible under the circumstances, in accordance with due diligence.
7. Satisfactory proof of loss:
   a. The standard provision requires that "satisfactory" proof of loss (a verified written statement) be filed by the insured within a specified period of time (typically sixty days).
   b. "Satisfactory" proof of loss has been construed by the courts to require that the insured do all in his power to furnish the information requested in the policy.
8. Right of subrogation: The standard fire policy, covering only a mortgagee's interest, specifically provides that the insurance company shall be subrogated (see p. 321, XI.A.1.) to all rights and remedies the mortgagee has against the mortgagor. (E.g., X, a mortgagee, insures the property, securing the debt for his own exclusive benefit. As a result of a fire which destroys the premises the insurance company is obligated to pay X the full amount of the debt plus interest due on the mortgage. Upon payment the insurance company will be subrogated to mortgagee's rights against the mortgagor.)
9. Cancellation of the policy can be brought about by either the insured or insurer at will, usually on five days' notice.

E. Interest of those other than the named insured in the proceeds of fire insurance policies.

1. Mortgagor (debtor) and mortgagee's (creditor's) rights under a fire insurance policy:
   a. Each may take out a separate policy covering his own insurable interest—see p. 308, I.B.6.c.(3).

      (1) Mortgagor's interest in the policy procured by the mortgagee:

         (A) If the mortgagee insures independently and for his own benefit, the mortgagee may recover the full amount of his loss up to the maximum amount of the policy (i.e., the balance due) free from any claim of the mortgagor.

(B) The insurer will be subrogated to the mortgagee's claim against the mortgagor (see p. 315, III.D.8.).

(2) Mortgagee's interest in policy procured by the mortgagor.

(A) If the mortgage calls for the mortgagor to insure for the benefit of the mortgagee, the mortgagee shares in the proceeds to the extent of the unpaid balance on the mortgage.

(B) If the mortgagor procures the policy for his own benefit, then, in absence of the above agreement to insure for the benefit of the mortgagee, the mortgagor takes the full amount of the insurance payment free of any specific claim by the mortgagee (i.e., the mortgagee has no greater rights than a general creditor).

b. A single policy may be jointly procured by the parties to protect their respective interests.

(1) A standard or "union" clause may be included in the policy; in such a case there is a collateral independent agreement between the mortgagee and the insurer which protects the mortgagee's right to recover even though there be a default or breach on the part of the mortgagor. (E.g., where there is a standard or "union" clause, and the mortgagor deliberately sets fire to the property, the mortgagee can nevertheless collect as against the insurance company on his "independent contract.")

(2) The policy may contain a loss payable clause (i.e., "loss is payable to the mortgagee as his interest may appear"). In such a case the mortgagee can collect to the extent of his loss, but he is a beneficiary and, therefore, his rights may be defeated by a default on the part of the mortgagor.

2. Creditor's rights under a fire insurance policy:

a. Creditor has no rights prior to destruction of the property, nor may he force the debtor to surrender the policy in order to obtain a refund for the unused portion.

b. After loss the creditor may treat the proceeds as any other asset of the debtor; a secured creditor having a lien on property, in the absence of any agreement, has no lien on the proceeds of the insured debtor's policy.

3. Life tenant and remainderman's rights under a fire insurance policy:

a. If the policy is taken out for the benefit of both parties, the owner of the life estate is entitled to have:

(1) The proceeds applied to rebuilding of the estate destroyed, or

(2) The use of the proceeds during life, remainder to the remainderman.

b. If the life tenant, in the absence of any agreement to insure for the benefit of the remainderman, takes out insurance for his own benefit, he is entitled, as against the remainderman, to the full proceeds of the policies in the event of loss.

c. If the remainderman insures separately for his own benefit, the life tenant has no interest in the proceeds received by the remainderman.

4. Vendor (seller) and vendee's (buyer's) interest in a fire insurance policy:

a. The vendee has a right to the insurance proceeds of a policy on real property procured by the vendor where the premises have been destroyed after making of the contract of sale but prior to delivery of the deed, provided that the vendee pays the money due the vendor on the contract.

(1) Some states do not follow this rule because the common law rule, that the risk of loss is on the vendee during the period between the making of the contract of sale and transfer of the deed, has been changed by statute.

(2) The vendor is not entitled to all or part of the proceeds of a policy procured independently by the vendee which is taken out after the making of the contract of sale.

IV. MARINE INSURANCE

A. Nature of marine insurance:

1. Protects the ship, cargo, or freight against risks known as perils of the sea (fire, shipwreck, piracy, etc.).
2. Ordinary action of wind and wave, wear and tear, or loss due to delays occasioned thereby are not included in marine insurance.

B. Types of marine insurance:

1. Time policy: a policy of marine insurance in which the risk is limited not to a given voyage but to a certain fixed term or period of time.
2. Voyage policy: fixes the duration of risk in terms of a certain voyage.
3. Valued policy: a statement of value in the policy (unvalued policies in marine insurance are a rarity) which predetermines the worth of the property insured.

C. Standard clauses:

1. Seaworthiness: Insured must warrant that the vessel is competent to resist wind and weather and is competently equipped

and manned for the voyage, with sufficient crew and a captain of good character. If the warranty is not true, the insurer is not liable.

2. "Lost or not lost": If this clause is included in the policy, the insurer assumes a risk of loss that may already have occurred (as well as the risk of future loss), unless the insured knew the loss had occurred prior to issuance of the policy.
3. General average (gross average) consists of an expense, purposefully incurred, or a sacrifice made (e.g., throwing goods overboard to lighten the load) for the general safety of the vessel or cargo; the owners of merchandise on board and the owners of the vessel contribute toward this expense in proportion to their respective values exposed to the common danger and ultimately saved because of the expense incurred.
4. Particular average, as contradistinguished from general average, is a loss happening to the freight or cargo which is not to be shared by contribution among all those so interested, but borne only by the owner of the property to which it occurs.
5. By implication (i.e., without any express provision in the policy) a co-insurance clause is read into the contract as a matter of law (in all other types of insurance the co-insurance clause must be expressly included—see p. 314, III.D.2.).
6. Unless the policy specifically requires the consent of the insurer, it is assignable without such consent before or after loss upon warranty that the vessel will not deviate from the agreed voyage or engage in an illegal venture.

V. ACCIDENT INSURANCE

A. Definition: a form of insurance which undertakes to indemnify the insured against expense, loss of time, and suffering resulting from accidents causing him physical injury. Usually payment is at a fixed rate per week while the consequent disability lasts, and sometimes includes the payment of a fixed sum to his heirs in case of his death within the terms of the policy.

B. Within the meaning of accident insurance policies, "accidental injury or death" is an unintended and undesigned result arising from acts done, while injury or death by "accidental means" is a result arising from acts unintentionally done.

VI. AUTOMOBILE INSURANCE

A. Definition: insurance against loss or damage to a motor vehicle caused by fire, windstorm, theft, collision, or other insurable hazards, and also against legal liability for death or personal injuries or damage to property resulting from operation of the vehicle.

B. Types

1. Fire and theft: insures against damage to the car and its usual equipment, but not personal belongings.
2. Collision: insures against damage to insured's car caused by collision; most policies contain $50 or $100 deductible clauses.
3. Liability and property damage: indemnifies against liability on account of death or injuries caused to another.
   a. "Permissive user" clause: Policy covers anyone who drives the car with the owner's permission.
   b. "Drive any other car" clause: Insured is covered in any car in which he drives.
4. Comprehensive: a policy in which the scope of the insured event is stated to be any loss or damage to a subject matter insured (e.g., fire, theft, explosion), with the exception of collision or upset.

C. Binder: a memorandum of an agreement for insurance, intended to give temporary protection, pending investigation of the risk by the insurer in order to determine whether or not to issue a formal policy; although most commonly used in auto or fire insurance, a binder may be used in any type of insurance.

VII. TITLE INSURANCE (See Property, p. 387, II.B.2.b.)

VIII. WARRANTIES

A. Definition: a term of the insurance contract which prescribes as a condition precedent of the insurer's liability the existence of a fact which tends to diminish, or the nonexistence of a fact which tends to increase, the risk of the occurrence of *any* loss, damage, or injury.

B. Nature and characteristics:

1. A warranty is in the nature of a condition precedent.
2. The warranty *must* appear on the face of, be embodied in, or be attached to the policy itself.
3. Theoretically, a warranty is susceptible to no construction other than that the parties mutually intended that the policy should not be enforceable unless such statement or term be literally true.
   a. The legal consequence of a breach of a warranty is that the policy is voidable at the option of the insurer.
   b. Thus at common law, if the insured warrants that there will be a crew of fifty men on board his ship during a voyage and during a part thereof he has less than fifty, the insurance

company can avoid liability on the policy even though at the time of the loss the crew numbers fifty and the event causing the loss had no relation to that particular warranty.

4 Statutory changes in the common law:

a. Because of the harshness of the common law rule, most states have changed by statute all warranties made in life insurance policies to representations; thus, no effect is given to immaterial breaches (see below, IX.A.2.).

b. Statutory modification of the common law rule has been rare in other types of insurance.

5. Warranties may be (a) affirmative, or (b) continuing (promissory)

a. Affirmative: relates to the existence or nonexistence of fact at the time the contract is made.

b. Continuing: relates to the existence or nonexistence of fact throughout the term of the contract.

IX. REPRESENTATIONS AND CONCEALMENTS

A. Representations: statements as to past or present facts, either oral or in writing, by the applicant to the insurer preliminary to making of the contract, and which are not inserted in the policy.

1. Insured is said to be under a duty of utmost good faith and honesty in answering the insurer's questions, in that the facts are primarily within his knowledge. The same rule applies as to concealments.

2. If there has been a representation which was *material* to acceptance of the risk, the insurer can avoid liability on the policy. (E.g., X in applying for life insurance lied in stating that he had not been in a tuberculosis sanatorium within the last five years. As a result, the insurer can raise this as a defense upon X's death, in that it is material misrepresentation.)

3. In life insurance the incontestable clause (see p. 310, II.B.3.), after the policy has been in force for two years, will bar the insurer from avoiding liability based on the defense of misrepresentation. This incontestable clause is also applicable to concealments in the life insurance area.

B. Concealments: the mere failure of the applicant for insurance to communicate to the insurer his knowledge of a material fact that the insurer does not know.

1. In marine insurance the applicant is bound to disclose all material facts known to him *whether or not he regards them as material.*

2. In all other types of insurance it must be shown that the insured knew the concealment was material to the risk, in order to invalidate the policy.
   a. The test of materiality is whether or not the insurer would accept the risk knowing the fact in question.
   b. Knowledge of materiality by the insured is difficult to prove in that unless the insurer can show actual knowledge of materiality on the insured's part, he must prove that the nondisclosure was palpably material, i.e., a reasonable man must have known that it was material.

X. WAIVER, ESTOPPEL, AND ELECTION

A. Waiver: the intentional or voluntary relinquishment of a known right; it is generally used in the law of insurance to indicate any conduct by the insurer or his agents which has the legal effect of relinquishing a defense by the insurer based upon insured's failure to comply with a condition of the insurance contract. (E.g., the insured fails to give prompt notice of claim but nevertheless the insurer processes the claim without objecting to the delay.)

B. Estoppel: representation of fact made by the insurer to the insured which is reasonably relied on by the insured in changing his position to such an extent that it would be inequitable to allow the insured to deny the truth of its representation. (E.g., the X Insurance Company requests that Y—the insured—turn over all information concerning Y's auto accident so that X's legal staff can defend in the cause of action brought against Y. Y does so relying upon the insurance company to make the defense, and he, therefore, does nothing to obtain evidence necessary to make an independent defense. Even though the insurer—X—subsequently attempts to rely on a condition that may somehow avoid its liability to Y, the company may be estopped from doing so.)

C. Election: a voluntary act of choosing between two alternative rights or privileges. (E.g., the X Fire Insurance Company accepts and retains premiums after knowledge of a breach of a condition in the policy concerning storage of gasoline on the premises. In that the company would not be entitled to the premium unless the policy was valid, the insurer has made an election to excuse the breach and is bound despite the breach of the condition.)

XI. SUBROGATION

A. Definition: See Suretyship, p. 340, II.C.2.b.

1. As used in insurance law, the insurer is subrogated to the rights of or is substituted in the place of the insured for the purpose of claiming indemnity from a third person whose conduct caused the loss covered by insurance.

2. No right of subrogation is available under a life insurance policy even though the insured is killed intentionally or through the negligence of another. (E.g., X intentionally assaults Y—the insured—causing Y's death; the insurer, upon payment of the face amount of the policy to the beneficiary does not have any rights against X.)
3. Under an accident, automobile (collision), or fire insurance policy, the insurer who pays the claim is subrogated to any rights that the insured may have against a third party. (E.g., X takes out an auto insurance policy—collision—with the Y insurance company; X's car is badly damaged as a result of T's negligent driving into X's parked car. Upon payment the insurer is subrogated to X's rights against T.)
4. A general release of the third party tort-feasor by the insured, without the consent of the insurer, will release the insurer from its obligation in that the insured has cut off the insurance company's right to subrogation (see Suretyship, p. 326, II.A.6.).

INSURANCE: SUBJECTIVE QUESTIONS*

INSURABLE INTEREST

Q. Parker went to Able's insurance brokerage firm and indicated that he wished to take out a life insurance policy for $10,000. The broker recommended the Item Insurance Company. Parker filled out an application, took and passed a physical examination, and gave the broker a check for the first year's premium. The policy was issued by the Company. It contained the standard sound health clause, which states that the policy "shall not take effect unless and until the application has been approved at the home office and the policy has been delivered to the insured while he is in good health." Parker was killed in an automobile accident shortly after the policy had been mailed by the broker but before the policy arrived at his home. It had been sent to the broker, who at Parker's request forwarded it to Parker via mail. The Item Insurance Company denies liability on the policy. Will the insurance company prevail? Explain.

11/64; p.308

Q. Martin and Williams, two business partners, agreed that each would insure his life for the benefit of the other. On his application for insurance, Martin stated that he had never had any heart trouble when, in fact, he had had a mild heart attack some years before. Martin's policy contained a two year incontestability clause. Three years later, after the partnership had been dissolved but while the policy was still in force, Martin's car was struck by a car being negligently driven by

Peters. Although Martin's injuries were superficial, he suffered a fatal heart attack immediately after the accident which, it was established, was caused by the excitement. The insurer has refused to pay the policy proceeds to Williams, asserting that Williams at the time Martin died had no insurable interest in Martin's life and that, in any case, Martin's misrepresentation on his application about his heart condition voided the policy.

(1) Was the insurer's defense based on Martin's misrepresentation tenable? Explain.

(2) Was it necessary that Williams have an insurable interest in Martin's life to enforce the policy? Explain.

(3) If the policy on Martin's life had been taken out by Williams rather than by Martin, could the insurer defend against the claim on the ground that, at the time of Martin's death, Williams had no insurable interest in Martin's life?

(4) If the policy had been taken out by Williams and assuming he had no insurable interest in Martin's life at anytime, would the incontestability clause foreclose assertation of such a defense by the insurer? Explain.

(5) Assuming the insurer has no valid defense on the policy and pays Williams' claim, may the insurer in turn recover from Peters? Explain.

11/69; pp. 308, 310

Q. Fox Corporation took out an insurance policy on the life of Harrold, its vice president in charge of sales. After the policy had been in effect six years, Harrold left the Fox Corporation and accepted a similar job with the Frank Corporation, Fox's leading competitor. Fox Corporation has continued to pay the premiums on the policy and now that Harrold has died seeks to collect the face value of the policy from the insurance company. The insurance company denies liability on the policy and asserts that the policy is an illegal gambling venture by Fox Corporation. Who will prevail? Explain.

11/64; p. 308

Q. C Corporation owned two pieces of realty known respectively as Blackacre and Whiteacre. C Corporation concluded an oral contract for the sale of Blackacre with building to Byer. The closing date was set ninety (90) days after the agreement; at that time the purchase price and deed were to be exchanged. Immediately upon concluding the oral contract, Byer paid to G Fire Insurance Company the premium on a standard fire insurance policy covering the Blackacre building. Twenty days later the Blackacre building was completely destroyed in a fire of unknown origin. Byer duly notified the insurance company of the loss. Can Byer recover from the insurance company? Explain.

5/65; p. 308

Q. White owns an office building which he has leased to Bac Corporation for twenty years. White and Bac both procure fire insurance on the building for their own separate protection. The building is subsequently destroyed by fire caused by the negligence of an outsider.
(1) Can both White and Bac Corporation validly insure the building? Explain.
(2) Assume that both parties can validly insure the building against loss due to fire. How will the amount of recovery be determined in such a case? Explain.

11/66; p. 308

Q. C Corporation procured from E Life Insurance Company a $20,000 policy on the life of its president, Bilder, whose annual compensation averaged $30,000. Bilder stated in the application that his age was 40 years when in fact he was 47 years old. Three months later Bilder left the employment of the Corporation. Two months following his termination of employment, he died. Is the Corporation entitled to collect on the policy held on Bilder's life? Explain.

5/65; pp. 308, 320

Q. Arthur carried two policies with the X Insurance Company. One was upon his life; the other upon his home. His next-door neighbor was burning trash and negligently left the fire unattended and improperly safeguarded. The fire passed over to Arthur's property and destroyed his home. In trying to put out the fire, Arthur lost his life. The Insurance Company paid the decedent's estate the amount of the two policies and seeks to hold the neighbor liable for such payments on the ground of subrogation. Will it succeed? Explain.

5/65; pp. 321 -322

FIRE INSURANCE

Q. You are the accountant for Harry Scanlon, a farmer who owns land which borders on the right-of-way of the Western-Eastern Railroad. Harry explains to you that, due to the admitted negligence of the Railroad, hay on Harry's land worth $2,000 was set afire and burned. Harry filed a claim with the Railroad and with his fire insurance company and collected $2,000 from his fire insurance company. At the time the company paid, the representative mentioned that the company was considering suing the Railroad, but no suit has commenced. Six months has passed and Harry has now been contacted by the Railroad, which wishes to settle his claim. The Railroad is unaware that Harry has been indemnified by his fire insurance company. Harry has had a dispute with the Railroad for several years concerning the ownership of a small parcel of land, and the representative of the Railroad has offered to assign any rights which the

Railroad may have in the land to Harry in exchange for a release of his right to reimbursement for the loss he has sustained from the fire. Harry is inclined to accept the Railroad's offer, particularly since he has already been fully indemnified by his fire insurance company for the fire loss he sustained.

(1) On the basis of what legal or equitable theory, if any, would the fire insurance company have a right to institute an action against the Railroad? Explain.

(2) Could the fire insurance company institute an action against the Railroad prior to settling Harry's claim in full? Explain.

(3) May Harry Scanlon properly retain the payment made to him by his fire insurance company and also accept the Railroad's offer? Explain.

11/67; pp. 321-322

Q. Joseph Price bought a building valued at $100,000. Upon the purchase, Price's insurance agent suggested that he obtain fire insurance. The agent recommended a policy with an 80% co-insurance clause. Price agreed to such a policy but requested that the face value of the policy be limited to $60,000. Shortly after obtaining the insurance, a fire caused damage of $50,000 to the building.

(1) What is meant by the term "co-insurance"? Explain the effect of co-insurance on the recovery of a loss.

(2) Discuss the basis for computing Price's recovery from the insurance company because of the fire. Show the computation in your answer.

(3) Compute the amount Price would recover if the fire had completely destroyed the building.

11/67; p. 314

Q. Able and Baker are equal shareholders of the Alt Manufacturing Company, Inc., which owned a garage and storage facility that was used in its business. Title to this real property was recorded in the corporate name. Able and Baker purchased a fire insurance policy covering the building. They took out this policy in their own names as owners, rather than in the name of the Corporation, and personally paid the premiums due. The face value of the policy was $40,000, and it contained the standard 80% co-insurance clause. Filmore, an employee of the Corporation, negligently dropped his cigarette into a refuse receptacle and started a fire. The building was totally destroyed as a result of the fire. Subsequently Able and Baker assigned their rights under the policy to the Corporation. The fair market value of the property was admitted by all parties to be $100,000. The Corporation engaged a local CPA firm to examine its financial statements. During the audit a question has arisen as to how the insurance claim on the property should be treated. The Corporation asserts that on the basis of the facts, which are undisputed, the claim should be valued at the full face value of the policy, i.e., $40,000. The insurer denies all liability on the basis of (1) title being in the Corporation and not in the parties insuring and/or (2) the negligence of the Corporation's agent in causing the fire. As an alternative argument, the insurer asserts that even if it were found liable on the fire insurance policy, the amount recoverable is limited by the 80% co-insurance clause.

(1) In the absence of an assignment of their rights, were Able and Baker entitled to collect on the fire insurance policy? Explain.

(2) Does the insurer's defense of negligence on the part of the Corporation's agent preclude recovery by the Corporation? Explain.

(3) Assume that the insurance company is liable.

- (a) How does the co-insurance clause function and what is the purpose of this clause?
- (b) Will the co-insurance clause limit the amount of the Corporation's recovery? Explain.

(4) Assume that the insurance company has satisfied a judgment obtained against it on the above claim. Will the insurance company have any rights against anyone to recover the amount paid? Explain.

11/66; pp. 314, 321

Q. Roger owned the manuscript of a famous author's book that he insured with the Z Insurance Company against loss, including "all direct loss or damage by fire." In the course of rearranging his library, Roger negligently placed the manuscript with some magazines he intended to burn. The manuscript and magazines were thrown by Roger into a trash burner and were completely destroyed by the fire. Roger seeks to collect the proceeds from the insurance policy covering the manuscript. Will he succeed? Explain.

5/65; p. 313

Q. An employee of Carter Corporation negligently dropped a match into some waste material which was awaiting removal by the refuse collector from Carter's plant. The resulting fire spread to the plant and totally destroyed it. The plant and its contents were worth $180,000 at the time of the fire.

Carter's plant building and contents were insured for $200,000 against fire loss by Phoen Fire & Casualty Co. In a separate fire policy Phoen insured Carter's plant for $150,000 to Alpha Bank which had held a $150,000 first mortgage on Carter's plant. The unpaid principal on the mortgage was $100,000. The mortgage contained an acceleration clause which provided that substantial damage to the property by fire or other casualty would cause the entire unpaid principal to become due and payable.

Carter has filed a fire loss claim with Phoen under its fire insurance policy and Alpha Bank has filed a claim with Phoen under its policy.

Phoen has declined to pay Carter on its fire loss claim asserting that Carter's negligence voided the policy.

(1) Discuss the merits of Phoen's contentions as to its obligations under the policy with Carter.

(2) Assuming it has no defenses against the fire loss claims by Carter and Alpha, how much will Phoen ultimately have to pay on its policies to Carter and Alpha Bank? Explain.

(3) Would Phoen be liable on the policy to Alpha Bank if the mortgage on Carter's plant had been fully paid prior to the fire but Alpha Bank had nevertheless continued its policy with Phoen in effect?

11/69; pp. 315-316

INSURANCE: OBJECTIVE QUESTIONS

Each of the following numbered phrases or clauses states a legal conclusion, drawn from the facts given in the related lettered material. You are to determine whether **each** of the legal conclusions is true or false according to the **general principles of insurance law.** Your grade will be determined from your total net score obtained by deducting your total of incorrect answers from your total of correct answers; an omitted answer will not be considered an incorrect answer.

(1) Arthur owed Super Auto Sales Incorporated $2,000 as the balance due on the purchase of a new automobile from Super Auto Sales. Super obtained a perfected security interest in the auto pursuant to the provisions contained in Article 9 (Secured Transactions) of the Uniform Commercial Code. In addition Arthur owed $5,000 to the Goodwill Credit Union for a personal loan. Goodwill was an unsecured creditor.

Super Auto Sales and the Goodwill Credit Union each took out $2,000 of property insurance (fire, theft, collision, etc.) on the auto at the time it was purchased because this was one of the few assets Arthur owned. Goodwill also insured Arthur's life for $5,000 at the time they loaned him the money.

Arthur subsequently satisfied both loans fully. However, each party continued to pay the premiums on the original policies.

Later Arthur had an accident which resulted in his death and the total destruction of the automobile. The insurance policies were still in force.

(a) Super Auto Sales initially had a valid insurable interest in the automobile purchased by Arthur.

(b) The Goodwill Credit Union did not have an insurable interest in the automobile at any time.

(c) Super Auto Sales is entitled to recover $2,000 from the auto insurance policy.

(d) The Goodwill Credit Union is entitled to recover $5,000 from the life insurance policy.

(e) If the accident which caused Arthur's death and the destruction of the automobile was Arthur's fault, the respective insurance companies would be able to avoid liability on this basis.

(2) Wallace owned all the shares of stock of Marker Corporation. Marker Corporation owned a large factory building in which its product was manufactured. The building was worth $250,000.

Wallace insured the building for $250,000 against loss from fire. He inadvertently took out the policy in his own name, indicating that he rather than the corporation was the owner of the building. Fire subsequently totally destroyed the building.

(a) The Statute of Frauds requires that the insurance contract be in writing.

(b) Wallace, in his official capacity, could legally execute a quitclaim deed to the building and deliver the deed to a prospective purchaser.

(c) Wallace will be unable to recover the $250,000 loss covered by the fire insurance policy.

(d) If it is assumed that Wallace had no insurable interest in the building, he may nevertheless recover the premiums paid.

(e) If Wallace had sold all his shares in the Marker Corporation prior to the destruction of the building, he could not recover on the fire insurance policy.

(3) Horace obtained a $50,000 life insurance policy on his own life. He named his wife and a partner in his CPA firm as co-beneficiaries. He also had a $25,000 fire insurance policy on his home. These policies contain the standard provisions common to the type of insurance policy involved.

Both policies are three years old and are held for Horace's convenience by the insurance agent-broker who sold him the policies.

(a) Since there has been no delivery of the policies to Horace, they are not valid contracts.

(b) Horace's wife and his partner, as co-beneficiaries, own the life insurance policy.

(c) The life insurance policy is freely assignable without the consent of the insurance company.

(d) If Horace sells his home, he can assign the insurance policy to the purchaser even though the insurance company does not consent to the transfer of the policy.

(e) Because he lacks the requisite insurable interest in Horace's life, Horace's partner will be unable to collect on the policy.

(4) Franklin was the owner of a building valued at $80,000. Because he did not believe that a fire would result in a total loss, he procured a $40,000 standard fire insurance policy on the property from the Ace Fire Insurance Company. The policy contained an 80 per cent coinsurance clause.

Four years later, while the policy was still in effect and the value of the building was $100,000, a fire occurred which resulted in a $40,000 loss.

(a) The coinsurance clause requires Franklin to insure the building for 80 per cent of its value or he will receive nothing in the event of partial destruction.

(b) If the insurance company wished, it could have required a 100 per cent coinsurance clause in the policy.

(c) Franklin is obligated to the insurance company to spend the proceeds obtained from the insurance policy for repair of the building.

(d) Franklin will recover $20,000 from the insurance company.

(e) In the event of a total destruction of the property insured, the coinsurance clause would have no effect on the amount to be recovered.

(5) The Mecca Insurance Company sold a life insurance policy which contained the following clauses:

"This policy shall be incontestable during the lifetime of the insured after it has been in force for a period of two years from its date of issue except for nonpayment of premiums and except for violation of the policy relating to military or naval service in time of war.

"Death as a result of flight, travel or service in any species of aircraft, except as a fare-paying passenger, is a risk not assumed under this policy."

(a) Even if the insured dies in an airplane accident in which he was not a fare-paying passenger, the beneficiary will recover if the accident occurs two years or more after issuance of the policy.

(b) The incontestable clause will not preclude the Mecca Insurance Company from successfully asserting lack of an insurable interest on the purchaser's part even though the policy had been issued more than five years prior to the insured's death.

(c) Proof that the insured had initially misstated his age would be grounds for completely voiding the policy at the time of his death three years later.

(d) Many states require that an incontestable clause, such as the one printed above or one similar to it, be included in the policy.

(e) The incontestable clause will permit the insured's beneficiary to recover, despite the fact that the insured concealed certain material facts, if the insured lives for the requisite two years from issuance of the policy.

(6) The Superior Insurance Company sold Goodfellow a life insurance policy which contained the following clause:

"This policy shall constitute the entire contract between the parties, or if a copy of the application is indorsed upon or attached to the policy when issued, the policy and the application therefor shall constitute the entire contract between the parties."

This clause was required by state law to be included in the policy.

(a) The above clause indicates that the insurance policy and the application, if it is indorsed thereon, constitute an integration.
(b) The above clause would preclude the insurance company from showing that the insured fraudulently concealed material facts.
(c) The above clause would preclude the insurance company from proving an oral contemporaneous understanding which varies the terms of the policy.
(d) If Goodfellow agreed to it, the clause could be waived by indorsement at the time he obtained the policy.
(e) The insurance company will ordinarily indorse upon or attach a copy of the insured's application to the policy.

5/68

(7) Property insurance is
(a) A risk-bearing contract.
(b) A wager and thus subject to state gambling laws.
(c) A type of investment similar to a purchase made in the futures market.
(d) A kind of contract that is within the mandate of the Statute of Frauds.
(e) A protection which the policy holder can purchase against his own negligence.

(8) An ordinary life insurance contract
(a) Is an indemnity contract.
(b) Is an arrangement whereby the insured pays a premium and the insurer agrees to pay a specified sum of money at an uncertain time.
(c) Is an example of a third-party beneficiary contract.
(d) Is required by numerous state statutes to provide a 30-day grace period for the payment of premiums beyond the actual due date.
(e) Must be approved by the state in which it is sold.

(9) A person seeking to insure another's life
(a) Is generally considered as making an offer to enter into an insurance contract with the insurer.
(b) May not name himself as the beneficiary.
(c) Must have an insurable interest in the life of the insured.
(d) Must prove a blood relationship with the insured.
(e) Must get the insured's written consent as a condition precedent to the validity of the insurance contract.

(10) A corporation has an insurable interest in
(a) The lives of all of its employees.
(b) The life of the senior partner of the CPA firm which performs its annual audit.
(c) The life of a debtor to whom it has loaned money on general credit.

(d) The life of any stockholder owning more than 5% of the outstanding preferred stock.
(e) The lives of all of its key executives.

(11) An insurable interest in real property is held by
(a) The named heir of the owner.
(b) A general creditor of the debtor-owner of the realty.
(c) A person who has a mechanic's lien on the property.
(d) A stockholder of the corporation which owns the property.
(e) A person who has a reversionary interest in the property created by an *inter vivos* trust.

(12) As a general rule insurance law provides that
(a) The insured may assign a fire insurance policy as security for a debt.
(b) Life insurance policies are assignable.
(c) The parties to a life insurance policy cannot prevent or limit its assignment.
(d) The named beneficiary of a life insurance policy has a vested interest in the policy unless the insured has reserved the right to change the beneficiary.
(e) The purchaser of real property covered by a fire insurance policy automatically acquires an interest in the policy.

(13) An incontestable clause in a life insurance policy precludes the insurer from asserting the defense of
(a) Lack of insurable interest.
(b) Misstatement of fact.
(c) Nonpayment of premiums.
(d) Failure to file proof of death within the required period.
(e) Suicide by the insured.

(14) Property insurance usually protects the insured against
(a) A loss from a fire that is used for ordinary purposes, i.e., a friendly fire.
(b) A direct loss due to fire and loss resulting from a fire, such as smoke damage.
(c) A loss caused by his own negligence.
(d) A loss caused by the willful and wanton destruction of the property by a third person.
(e) A loss caused by the willful and wanton destruction of the property by the insured.

(15) The standard co-insurance clause
(a) Is usually provided for in both life and property insurance policies.
(b) Is designed to induce a property owner to insure his property at a higher percentage of its value than he might otherwise choose.
(c) Is not applicable in the event of the total destruction of the property.

(d) Is implied as a matter of law in fire insurance policies.
(e) Allows the insured to recover only such percentage of the loss as the actual amount of insurance bears to the stated percentage of the fair market value of the property.

11/65

TOPIC TWELVE | SURETYSHIP

CONTENTS PAGE

*SURETYSHIP. Included in this topic are the identification and characteristics of the surety relationship, the various rights of the parties to the relationship, the surety's defenses, and the co-surety relationship.**

* Source: AICPA, *Information for CPA Candidates* (July 1970).

I. CHARACTERISTICS

A. Definition: a promise by a person who binds himself to perform upon the default of another (i.e., he agrees with the creditor to satisfy the obligation if the debtor does not); includes all types of engagements to be responsible for the debt or default of another.

1. A tripartite transaction:
   a. The principal debtor: the primary obligor of the debt owed to the creditor; he bears the ultimate burden of performing.
   b. The creditor: the obligee of the debt owed by the principal debtor; the party to whom the surety is bound.
   c. Surety or guarantor: promises he will perform upon default of the principal debtor.
      (1) As between the principal debtor and the surety, the former should fulfill the duty or obligation.

B. Capacity to act as a surety or guarantor.

1. Individuals: the rules applicable to general capacity to contract apply (see Contracts, p. 43, III.D.).
2. Partners: See Partnerships, p. 157, II.C.1.b. (1).
3. Partnerships: ordinarily may enter into contracts of suretyship or guaranty unless the partnership agreement expressly prohibits it.
4. Corporations: Normally it is an *ultra vires* act for any ordinary corporation to enter into a contract of suretyship; however, a corporation specifically formed to carry on a suretyship business for compensation may so contract.

C. Suretyship and guaranty:

1. As used in the law generally, guaranty is treated as a synonym for suretyship.
   a. Nevertheless, technical distinctions may be discerned. (E.g., surety's liability is normally embodied in the same instrument as that of the principal debtor; the guarantor is not a party to the original undertaking, *but rather he contracts separately or collaterally*.)
2. Types of guaranty.
   a. Unconditional or absolute guaranty of payment: Since the guarantor unconditionally promises to pay, the guarantor is liable when the debt is due and the principal debtor does not pay (i.e., further action by the creditor versus the principal debtor is not necessary).

b. Conditional guaranty: Some condition must be met before guarantor will pay (e.g., guaranty of collection); the only type of guaranty that requires the creditor to exhaust his remedies against the principal debtor first (i.e., have a judgment returned unsatisfied).

c. Single guaranty: limited to one transaction.

d. Continuing guaranty: covers a succession of liabilities for which, as and when they accrue, the guarantor becomes liable.

3. *As used in this outline surety will include guaranty, except the conditional guaranty,* which is distinct and which will be specifically labeled where referred to hereinafter.

D. Common situations in which a suretyship relationship exists:

1. By express contract (e.g., where the surety promises to pay the debts of the principal debtor if credit is extended to said principal debtor).
2. Where one other than an accommodated party indorses a negotiable instrument; the indorser, by engaging to pay if the instrument is not paid after presentment, is, in effect, a surety.
3. Where a party sells mortgaged property and the purchaser expressly assumes the obligation (commonly called the assuming assignee), i.e., the purchaser or assignee personally promises to pay the mortgage debt. The seller is a surety and the purchaser is the principal debtor (see Property, p. 399, V.H.1.b.).

II. DEFENSES, RIGHTS, AND REMEDIES OF THE SURETY

A. Bases for the surety's defense.

1. The suretyship contract itself is void. (E.g., S guarantees P's promise to pay for narcotics.)
2. Fraud or duress.

   a. If the *creditor,* either by fraud or duress, obtains *the surety's promise,* the contract is voidable at the surety's option. (E.g., by threats upon S's life C obtains S's signature as a surety.)

   b. Fraud or duress by *the principal debtor on the surety* will not permit the surety to avoid liability to the creditor, if the creditor has extended credit in good faith, relying on the security of surety's promise. (E.g., P by fraud induces S to become a surety; P then obtains credit from C who relies on S's promise and who has no knowledge of the fraud used by P to obtain S's signature. S may not avoid liability to C.)

c. *If the creditor obtains the principal debtor's promise* by fraud or duress, the surety is not liable to the creditor unless the surety had knowledge of the fraud or duress. (E.g., C by fraud induces P to contract with him; S without knowledge of the fraud becomes a surety for P's performance. S has a good defense and may avoid liability.)

3. Impossibility or illegality of performance by the principal debtor. (E.g., S is surety for a debt owed by P to C; the debt agreement calls for payment of a usurious interest rate by P. S may use the defense of illegality and avoid liability.)
4. Mere tender of performance by the principal debtor or surety:
   a. Discharges the surety.
   b. May not discharge the principal debtor (e.g., the principal must still perform his obligation to pay money owed—see Contracts, p. 58, VII.B.1.f.).
5. Performance by the principal debtor discharges the surety.
6. Release of the principal debtor by the creditor, without the consent of the surety, discharges the surety; unless:
   a. The creditor expressly reserves his rights against the surety in the release. The creditor's reservation shows that he has no intention of releasing the surety; it is merely a covenant not to sue the principal and does not change the surety's rights of subrogation or reimbursement if he performs (see p. 339, II.C.2.a,b.).
   b. The release was obtained by fraud or duress. The surety is only discharged to the extent he has been prejudiced. (E.g., S is surety on a debt owed by P to C. P fraudulently obtains a release, and on the strength of this release, S returns collateral of P's which he was holding. C rescinds the release but not before P has absconded with the collateral. S's liability is reduced to the extent of the value of the collateral security.)
7. Material failure by the creditor to give the consideration agreed upon for the principal's obligation: If not due to the fault of the principal, the surety is not liable to the creditor.
8. For the effect of release of collateral held by the creditor, see p. 342, III.C.5.
9. The surety's right of set-off: The surety may normally set off any claims that he has against the creditor even though they did not arise out of the surety obligation.
10. Non-disclosure of facts by the creditor which materially increase the surety's risk: If the creditor knows or subsequently learns of facts of such a nature that the surety would not have

assumed the obligation had he been aware of these facts, and if the creditor, having had a reasonable opportunity, failed to notify the surety, the surety may assert this as a defense to avoid liability (e.g., failure to report to the surety the fact that an employee had previously stolen money from the company).

11. Statute of limitations:
    a. Generally measured from the date of default by the principal debtor, and will bar a cause of action against the surety after lapse of the appropriate period of time (e.g., six years from date of default by the principal debtor).
    b. If the principal prevents discovery by fraudulently concealing his default, the statute will begin to run in favor of an innocent surety from the time when the default should reasonably have been discovered by the creditor. The statute will not run in favor of the fraudulent principal debtor until actual discovery.
    c. Part payment or new promises by principal debtor after default will not prevent the statute from running in favor of the surety.
12. Varying the surety's risk by modifying the principal debtor's duty:
    a. It is generally held in the law of suretyship that a special standard or principle is applicable to the obligation of the surety.

       (1) This special standard requires that the surety's obligation be limited to the letter of the law; any variance, no matter how minor, will be interpreted as increasing the obligation of the surety, thereby permitting the surety to be discharged.

       (2) This standard or principle is known as *strictissimi juris.*

       (3) However, if the creditor modifies the principal's duty and such modification can only be beneficial to the surety, he is not discharged (e.g., a creditor reduces the interest rate from 4% to 2%).
    b. Some of the more common variations which have been held to release the surety are:

       (1) A change in the identity of the principal debtor or debtors. (E.g., the creditor permits the principal debtor to substitute another for performance of his debt or duty; or in the case of a partnership, one of the partners withdraws or retires and the creditor grants further credit on a continuing guaranty.)

(2) A legally enforceable variance in the amount, place, time, or manner of principal debtor's payments (such variance *must be binding* on the creditor).

(3) A change in the duties of the principal. (E.g., a surety company bonds the performance of a principal as assistant cashier of X bank, and he is subsequently promoted to head cashier.)

(4) The creditor's surrender or impairment of security held by him for the performance by the principal debtor. [E.g., creditor returns to principal debtor bonds held as part security; surety is released *pro tanto* (see p. 342, III.C.5.).]

c. In order to release the surety, there must be an actual variation in the terms rather than an option or election which the principal debtor can exercise under the express terms of the agreement which the surety has guaranteed. (E.g., P elects to continue his lease for two years, exercising an option which was a part of the original contract between P and C and upon which S assumed the obligation as a surety.)

d. Regarding all variations, if the creditor obtains the consent of the surety to make the variance, the surety is not discharged.

e. The *Restatement of Security* makes a further distinction or limitation on the discharge of the surety:

(1) If the surety is a *compensated surety* (a commercial surety which is in the business of acting as a surety for a premium), the surety is generally discharged only if the modification materially increases the risk.

(2) If the modification does not increase the risk materially, the obligation is reduced only by the extent of loss due to the modification. This rule applies to extensions of time (i.e., the compensated surety is only entitled to have the obligation reduced by the extent of loss due to the extension of time).

B. Defenses which are not available to the surety:

1. Death or insolvency (including discharge in bankruptcy) of the principal does not release the surety, nor does insolvency of the surety discharge his estate.
2. Lack of capacity of the principal debtor is not a defense available to the surety. (E.g., a surety for an infant principal cannot use this as a defense to avoid liability.)

3. The surety, except in the case of a conditional guarantee (see p. 335, I.C.2.b.), is not discharged because the creditor takes no action to enforce his claim against the principal debtor.
4. The creditor's failure to give notice of default is not a defense available to the surety, unless the rules of the Negotiable Instruments Law apply, or unless the surety's obligation is affected by the creditor's failure to give notice.
5. Failure of the creditor to resort to the collateral security which he holds.
   a. The surety is not discharged so long as the creditor does not surrender it; however, if the creditor does not make timely resort to the collateral, he may be accountable to the surety for any depreciation in its value.
   b. The surety may not compel the creditor to first proceed against the collateral security, unless he can show undue hardship or that there has been a conditional guarantee.

C. Rights and remedies available to the surety.

1. If the surety cannot avoid liability, he may, nevertheless, attempt to shift the ultimate burden in whole or in part.
2. In this connection, the following are the most common rights or remedies available to the surety:
   a. Reimbursement or indemnity: The duty of the principal to repay or reimburse the surety where the surety, upon default of the principal, performed the obligation owed by the principal debtor to the creditor:

      (1) Where the surety was obtained by or with the consent of the principal, the surety is entitled to his reasonable outlay.

      (A) The surety may only recover for the amount that he paid the creditor in satisfaction of the debt—e.g., if the surety settles with the creditor for less than the full amount of the debt, the surety can only recover the lesser amount.

      (B) The statute of limitations begins to run (in favor of the principal debtor) against this right from the date surety satisfies the creditor, not from the date of default by the principal debtor.

      (2) Where the surety is obtained without the consent of the principal (e.g., the creditor on his own initiative obtains a surety), the surety is entitled to a reimbursement to the extent that the principal has been unjustly enriched.

(3) Where the surety is a mere volunteer (i.e., not obtained by or with the consent of the principal and not legally bound to render performance to the creditor) he is not entitled to a reimbursement.

b. Subrogation: Where the surety pursuant to his contractual undertaking fully satisfies the obligation of the creditor, the surety, to the extent he has contributed to the satisfaction, has the same rights as the creditor (i.e., succeeds to the creditor's rights):

(1) In security held for the principal's performance. (E.g., P owes C $500 secured by five $100 bonds held by C as collateral security. P defaults and S, upon payment of the $500 which he is contractually obligated to pay, is entitled to the bonds.)

(2) Against the principal debtor. (E.g., S was legally bound as the surety on P's bond for payment of employees' wages. P defaulted and became a bankrupt. S paid the wage earners' claims. As a result S would be subrogated to the wage earners' rights to a priority or preference in bankruptcy.)

c. Exoneration: a suit in equity, after maturity of the debt, to compel the principal debtor to pay the creditor.

d. Contribution: arises only where there is a co-surety relationship (see p. 342, V.).

III. THE CREDITOR'S AND SURETY'S RIGHTS IN COLLATERAL PLEDGED BY THE PRINCIPAL DEBTOR

A. In addition to the surety's obligation, collateral to secure performance of the principal debtor's duty is often pledged with either the surety or creditor.

B. Collateral pledged with the surety.

1. The creditor's rights in the collateral *prior to default:*

a. Collateral pledged for the creditor's protection.

(1) The surety must retain the collateral as trustee for the benefit of the creditor.

(2) Equitable relief may be obtained by the creditor to prevent the surety from releasing or otherwise impairing the collateral.

b. Collateral pledged with the intent that it only benefit the surety.

(1) Even if both the surety and the principal debtor are solvent the creditor has an interest in the collateral pledged.

(2) Equitable relief may be obtained to prevent the surety from releasing or otherwise impairing the collateral pledged as security.

2. The creditor's rights in the collateral *after* the principal debtor's default:
   a. Unless the debt owed to the creditor is fully satisfied, the security must be utilized to satisfy the principal debtor's duty to the creditor.
   b. However, creditor may choose to disregard the collateral held by the surety and go immediately against the surety on his promise.
3. Surety's rights in the collateral:
   a. In general, the surety holds any collateral as trustee for the creditor's benefit, and as such he is a custodian subject to equitable duties to retain and preserve the collateral.
   b. The surety has the right of reimbursement (see p. 339, II.C.2.a.), but only upon satisfaction of the creditor. (E.g., S holds $1,000 in bonds as collateral to secure P's $1,000 debt to C; P defaults and S satisfies P fully by paying him $1,000. S has a right of reimbursement and may resort to the collateral he holds.)

C. Collateral pledged with the creditor.

1. The creditor must return the collateral upon payment by the principal debtor prior to default.
2. The creditor need not resort to the collateral pledged even though it is in excess of the amount due; instead, he may, immediately upon default, proceed against the surety on his promise.
3. Upon default, the creditor may resort to the collateral he holds if he so desires.
   a. Excess, if any, must be returned to the principal debtor.
   b. If the collateral is insufficient to satisfy the debt, the creditor retains his rights to the balance as against the surety and the principal debtor.
   c. In general, if both the principal and the surety provide collateral and the creditor elects to resort to the collateral, he must first exhaust the principal debtor's collateral before resorting to the surety's collateral.
4. The surety, upon satisfaction of the principal debtor's obligation to the creditor, is subrogated (see p. 340, II.C.2.b.) to the creditor's rights to the collateral.

5. Surrender, or willful or intentional destruction, of the collateral held by the creditor reduces the surety's obligation by that amount.

IV. STATUTE OF FRAUDS

A. In general (see Contracts, p. 44, III.E.):

1. Contracts of suretyship and guaranty are "promises to answer for the debt, default, or miscarriage of another," within the meaning of the statute of frauds.

B. Transactions resembling suretyship but which are not included:

1. Warranty: As used, for example, in the sale of personal property or in contracts of sale, warranty signifies a representation or promise as to title, quality, or fitness made by the seller to the buyer: a two-party transaction.
2. Novation: Where it involves a tripartite transaction, in which one obligor is substituted for another, no suretyship relationship exists, in that there is always only one obligor liable at any one instant of time.
3. Indemnity: The promisor agrees to hold a person harmless from loss, irrespective of liability of a third person (e.g., insurance).
   a. Indemnity is a two-party transaction, whereas a surety relationship is tripartite.
   b. The indemnitor (e.g., an insurance company) pays because it has assumed the risk of loss, not because of any default by the principal debtor as in suretyship.
4. *Del credere* agent: See Agency, p. 127, I.C.3.f.

V. CO-SURETYSHIP

A. Characteristics:

1. *Restatement of Security* defines co-suretyship "as the relation between two or more sureties who are bound to answer for the same duty of the principal, and who, as between themselves, should share the loss caused by the default of the principal."
2. Elements:
   a. Each surety is bound to answer for *the same duty,* and *shares in the burden* upon default of the principal.
   b. Co-sureties need not know of each other's existence at the time of undertaking their obligations.
   c. Both are usually bound for the same amount, but they still may be co-sureties even if they are bound for different amounts, so long as they share the same burden.

d. Generally co-sureties are jointly and severally liable; creditor may sue them jointly or proceed against each individually to the extent he has assumed liability.

e. Right of contribution among co-sureties: See p. 343, V.B.

f. Rights and duties are normally fixed by contract among the co-sureties; in absence of such a contract, the rules of equity apply.

g. Judicial preference is to find a co-surety relationship where there are two or more sureties and no express agreement to the contrary.

3. Co-suretyship distinguished from subsuretyship:

a. In subsuretyship, the subsurety is entitled to have the principal surety bear the entire burden, i.e., the subsurety is in effect a surety for the principal surety. (E.g., X owes Y $1,000. S is the surety on this obligation. He secures SS to act as surety for him, i.e., to perform the surety obligation in the event he cannot perform. S is the principal surety and SS the subsurety.)

b. In subsuretyship the principal surety has the primary duty of performance in the event of default by the principal debtor.

c. It is usually necessary to have an express agreement to create a subsurety relationship because of the judicial preference for co-suretyship.

B. The right of contribution among co-sureties: a right which arises when a co-surety, in performance of his obligation, pays more than his proportionate share, and which entitles the co-surety to compel the other co-sureties to compensate him for the excess amount paid. (E.g., X and Y are equal co-sureties on a $10,000 obligation, i.e., each guarantees the $10,000 debt. The principal debtor defaults; X pays the entire $10,000 and has a right of contribution against Y for $5,000. Had Y guaranteed only $5,000 of the debt while X guaranteed $10,000, X upon paying the full amount would have a right of contribution against Y for $3,333.33.)

1. Statute of limitations: begins to run against the co-surety's right of contribution as of the time the payment is made by the co-surety to the creditor, provided payment is after maturity of the debt.

2. Collateral and its effect on co-sureties:

a. Collateral held by the creditor does not prevent creditor from proceeding immediately against one or all of the co-sureties.

b. Collateral pledged with a co-surety does not affect the right of contribution.

c. However, in the final settlement of their liability to each other, each co-surety is entitled to share in any collateral in proportion to his liability for the principal debtor's debt. (E.g., X and Y are co-sureties on a $20,000 debt and they hold collateral of $15,000. X is surety for $20,000 and Y is surety for only $10,000. Upon default of the principal debtor and payment of the debt by the sureties, X has a right to $10,000 of the collateral and Y to $5,000.)

C. Release of co-surety by creditor.

1. Unless there is a reservation of right against the co-sureties, release of one co-surety reduces the other's obligation to the extent the released co-surety could have been compelled to make a contribution. (E.g., X, Y, and Z are co-sureties, each guaranteeing fully a $12,000 debt owed by P to C. If C releases X, C can collect only $8,000 from the remaining sureties, since either Y or Z could have compelled X to contribute $4,000.)

VI. SURETY BONDS

A. Definition: acknowledgement of an obligation to make good the performance by another of some act or duty. It is:

1. A bond with a condition, e.g., faithful performance. The performance of the condition by the principal debtor discharges the obligation.
2. Issued by a surety company engaged in business of assuming risks for compensation—see p. 338, II.A.12.e.(1).

B. Types.

1. Fidelity bonds:
   a. Guarantee faithful performance of duties on the part of an employee.
   b. The employee's duties may not be significantly varied without the surety company's consent; to do so without consent releases the surety.
2. Performance bonds:
   a. Guarantee faithful performance of a contract.
   b. Most frequently concern construction and supply contracts.
3. Official bonds assure proper performance of office by public officials.
4. Judicial bonds are given in connection with a judicial proceeding.

SURETYSHIP: SUBJECTIVE QUESTIONS*

CHARACTERISTICS

Q. Mason Supply Company required its customers to provide guarantors of collection if a customer's credit standing was not satisfactory. While auditing Mason's books a CPA discovered that several of the customers were in arears on their accounts. Mason wishes to proceed against the various guarantors.
(1) How does a guaranty of collection differ from the usual surety undertaking? Explain.
(2) What steps must be taken by Mason in order to collect from each guarantor? Explain.

11/68; pp. 334-335

Q. C is a seller of merchandise. S guaranteed the collectibility of C's accounts in connection with sales made to P. P defaulted and C wants to be certain that he will be able to hold S liable on the guaranty. What steps must C take to avoid losing or impairing his rights against S? Explain.

5/63; pp. 335, 337

DEFENSES

Q. Easy Credit Corporation made a personal loan to Whitworth after Acme Surety Company agreed to serve as his surety for an appropriate fee. Subsequently, Whitworth defaulted on the loan and disappeared. After his disappearance it was discovered that Whitworth had fraudulently misrepresented the extent of his assets to both Easy Credit and Acme Surety. Easy Credit seeks to collect from Acme Surety on the surety undertaking. Acme Surety asserts the defense of fraud and refuses to pay.

Will the defense of fraud prevail against Easy Credit? Explain.

11/68; p.335

Q. The Friendly Finance Company is engaged in the personal loan business. Some loans made by the company are secured by a pledge of collateral such as diamonds, rare coins, works of art, etc. The Company has a surety bond with Safety Surety Company covering its employees.

Charles Johnson was employed by Friendly Finance as a collection agent and was covered in this capacity by Safety's surety bond. Subsequently Johnson was promoted to the position of assistant cashier. In this position he received payments on loans and also had access to the vault in which the collateral was kept. Surety was not advised of Johnson's promotion. Several months after his promotion Johnson began substituting imitations for the pledged diamonds and

* See Introductory Note, p. 19.

rare coins. His thefts have been detected and the loss amounts to $15,000. Friendly Finance seeks recovery from Safety Surety Company. In your audit of Friendly Finance you find that the Company has recorded an account receivable of $15,000 from Safety in anticipation of collection of its claim.

Is Friendly justified in recording the account receivable? Explain.

5/70; pp. 337-338

Q. P wanted to purchase certain goods on credit from C. The terms of payment were 2/10, net 30. C requested that P obtain a surety on the obligation before he would agree to the credit terms. P went to S, a well-known financier and friend of P, and asked him, as a personal favor, to assume the role as surety on the contract with C. S did so, and the goods were duly shipped to P on open book account with the terms indicated as 2/10, net 30. C, not having received payment after 20 days had expired, went to P and requested that P execute a promissory note, which covered the amount owed and specified that payment would not be due until two months from the date of execution. P agreed and signed the note. P subsequently defaulted on the note, and C sued S on his surety promise. Can C recover against S? Explain.

5/63; pp. 337-338

Q. Paul obtained a loan of $1,000 from Charles on January 1, 1962, payable on April 15, 1962. At the time of the making of the loan, Stanley became a non-compensated surety thereon by written agreement. On April 15, 1962, Paul was unable to pay and wrote to Charles requesting an extension of time. Charles made no reply, but did not take any immediate action to recover. On June 30, 1962, Charles demanded payment from Paul and, failing to collect from him, proceeded against the surety, Stanley. Stanley claims that as Charles had allowed Paul more time than the agreement had called for, he has been discharged as surety thereby. Is Stanley's claim valid? Explain.

11/64; p. 338

Q. Thomas Fredrickson became a non-compensated surety on a debt owned by Martin Cuff to Walter Hutchins. Cuff defaulted on the loan and sought an extension of time in which to repay. Hutchins refused to extend the time of repayment and after waiting more than a month demanded payment by Fredrickson. Fredrickson refused to pay claiming he had not been notified promptly of Cuff's default and that in any event he was not liable until Hutchins exhausted his remedies against the principal debtor, Cuff. He suggested that Hutchins sue Cuff.

(1) What is the effect on the surety's undertaking of a failure to give prompt notice of default? Explain.
(2) Must a creditor exhaust his remedies against the debtor before proceeding against the surety? Explain.
(3) What would have been the effect upon Fredrickson's liability if Hutchins had granted Cuff's request for a binding extension of time? Explain.

5/70; pp. 338-339

Q. James Harper borrowed $20,000 from Franklin Jackson. William Samson & Company, a customer of Harper's was the surety on the loan. Harper became insolvent and defaulted on several debts owed to his creditors. Jackson joined with several other creditors in petitioning for an involuntary bankruptcy proceeding against Harper. Harper was duly adjudicated a bankrupt and his assets distributed to creditors. Jackson seeks to hold Samson & Company on the surety undertaking to the extent he was not satisfied on the loan. Samson & Company wants to be reimbursed by Harper to the extent it is liable to Jackson. You are the accountant for Samson & Company and are concerned with the effect of the above facts upon Samson & Company's balance sheet.
(1) How should Jackson's rights against Samson & Company be treated? Explain.
(2) What effect will Harper's discharge in bankruptcy have against any claim to reimbursement that Samson & Company may have? Explain.

5/70; p. 340

RIGHTS AND REMEDIES

Q. Saxon was the surety on a building contract between Palmer Construction Company and Carleton. Saxon had the privilege of completing the building if Palmer should default. The contract also stipulated that any payments after default would be made directly to Saxon when the building was completed.

Palmer incurred losses in the construction and defaulted. Saxon then spent $100,000 to complete the building and received $115,000 in payments from Carleton. Palmer asserts a claim to the profit.

Is Saxon entitled to the entire $115,000? Explain.

11/68; p. 340

Q. The S Surety Company has written a general fidelity bond covering defalcations by employees of the Able Corporation. Upon being informed of shortages caused by the wrongful activities of an employee of Able Corporation, the S Surety Company paid the Able Corporation the full amount of its loss. The S Surety Company now seeks to hold the CPA firm that gave an opinion upon the corporation's statements liable for the shortages. The shortages were the result of clever forgeries, collusive fraud, and unrecorded transactions which would not be uncovered by an examination made in accordance with generally accepted auditing standards. Upon what right, well recognized in the law of suretyship, does the S Surety Company rely in attempting to impose liability upon the CPA firm?

5/63; p. 340

COLLATERAL

Q. Simon was the surety on a $1,000 debt owed by Phillips to Charles. To insure that Phillips would satisfy the obligation, Simon held $800 of Phillips' securities as collateral. Phillips became insolvent and fraudulently obtained a written release from Charles which he used to obtain the securities from Simon. Charles learned of the fraud, rescinded the release and notified Simon of the fraud. Phillips has disappeared and Charles is attempting to enforce the surety undertaking against Simon.

What is the effect of the fraudulently obtained release on Simon's surety undertaking? Explain.

11/68; pp. 340-341

Q. On January 1, 1963, Leonard loaned Bert $1,000. Upon receipt of the $1,000, Bert gave Leonard a signed non-negotiable promissory note which acknowledged the debt and included a promise to repay the $1,000 plus 4% interest one year from date. As part of this transaction, Bert gave to Leonard, as security for the loan, certain stocks, properly indorsed, then having a market value of $1,300. On June 10, 1963, the market value of the stock had fallen to $800, and Leonard demanded of Bert further security for the loan. Pursuant to this demand Bert requested his friend Stewart to sign the non-negotiable note of January 1 as surety. When Stewart signed the notes as surety, he received no consideration therefor and was unaware that Leonard was then holding the stocks as security for Leonard's loan to Bert. On January 1, 1964, Leonard demanded payment of the note from Bert and, failing to collect from him, he demanded payment from Stewart, who paid $1,000 to Leonard. A few days later, Stewart learned that Leonard was holding Bert's stocks as security for the loan and demanded these stocks from Leonard.
(1) State and explain the right upon which Stewart as a surety is basing his demand on Leonard that he be given Bert's stocks.
(2) On the facts as stated above, is Stewart entitled to the stocks? Explain.

11/64; p. 341

CO-SURETYSHIP

Q. David desired to establish credit with Carl, but the latter required a surety to protect himself from loss. At David's request, Sam and

Seth wrote letters to Carl in which Sam guaranteed David's credit up to $10,000, and Seth guaranteed it up to $20,000, both guaranties being continuous. Sam and Seth were aware of each other's guaranty.
(1) David became insolvent when he was indebted to Carl to the extent of $9,000. Sam was compelled to pay the full amount. To what extent may Sam obtain contribution from Seth? Explain.
(2) If Sam is in possession of collateral worth $3,000 given by David to protect Sam against loss from his guaranty, how would this affect your answer to (1) above? Explain.

11/64; p. 343

Q. George owed money to Marsh, and Wilson was the surety on George's debt. Still feeling insecure, Marsh obtained Fairfax as a subsurety on Wilson's undertaking. George defaulted and Marsh seeks recovery on the surety undertakings.
(1) What rights does Marsh have against Wilson? Explain.
(2) What rights does Marsh have against Fairfax? Explain.
(3) Assuming Fairfax pays Marsh in full, what rights does Fairfax have against Wilson? Explain.

11/68; p. 343

SURETY BONDS

Q. Paul was hired as a file clerk by the Cattleman's Bank. As it did for all employees, the Bank paid a bonding company to furnish a bond indemnifying the Bank against loss arising from Paul's performance of his clerical duties. After six months with the Bank, Paul was promoted to a teller's position. Within one month after he became a teller the Bank learned that Paul had embezzled $25,000.
(1) Describe the meaning of the term "suretyship relationship."
(2) Describe the relationship between
 (a) Paul and the Bank,
 (b) The Bank and the bonding company, and
 (c) Paul and the bonding company.
(3) On what grounds, if any, may the bonding company refuse to indemnify the Bank? Explain.
(4) If the bonding company indemnifies the Bank, on what theory, or theories, may the bonding company proceed to recover against Paul? Explain.

5/66; pp. 337-338, 340

Q. Excelsior Bank hired Ronda as a secretary and obtained a surety bond from King covering the Bank against losses up to $50,000 resulting from Ronda's improper conduct in the performance of her secretarial duties.

Both Ronda and the Bank signed the application for the bond. After one year of service Ronda was promoted to the position of teller in the Bank and the original surety bond remained in effect.

Shortly after Ronda's promotion a surprise audit revealed that Ronda had taken advantage of her new position and stolen $25,000 from the Bank. She was arrested and charged with embezzlement.

Ronda had assets of only $10,000 at the time of her arrest.

(1) Identify and describe the legal relationship among Excelsior Bank, Ronda and King. Discuss in full the nature of the rights and duties of each of the parties.

(2) If the Bank demands a payment of $25,000 from King, what defense, if any, might King raise to deny an obligation to the Bank?

(3) If King fully reimburses the Bank for its loss, under what theory or theories, if any, may King attempt to recover from Ronda.

5/68; pp. 337-338, 340

SURETYSHIP: OBJECTIVE QUESTIONS

Each of the following numbered statements states a legal conclusion. You are to determine whether each legal conclusion is true or false according to general principles of suretyship law. Your grade will be determined by deducting your total of incorrect answers from your total of correct answers; if you omit an answer it will not affect either total.

(1) Humbolt Hardware Company (a partnership which manufactures hardware), Charles, and Williams have each duly become co-sureties of a $12,000 loan made to Francis by Richards.

(a) If Humbolt were a corporation formed for the same purposes as the partnership, the making of the above described agreement would, ordinarily, be *ultra vires*.

(b) If none of the co-sureties had known of the others at the time they made their respective suretyship agreements, the relationship of co-suretyship would not exist among them.

(c) If Richards should fully release Francis without reserving his rights against Humbolt, Charles and Williams, they would also be fully released.

(d) If Francis should default on repayment of the loan, Richards may recover only $4,000 from Humbolt.

(e) If, on Francis' default, Williams should pay Richards the full $12,000, Williams would be entitled to recover $4,000 each from Charles and Humbolt.

(2) Davidson purchased Backacre (improved real property) with funds obtained by a first mortgage loan made to him by Zeno Bank. Davidson thereafter sold Backacre to Harvey subject to Zeno's first mortgage which Harvey duly assumed. To finance the purchase from Davidson, Harvey obtained a loan from Yellowstone Bank and gave Yellowstone a second mortgage on Backacre to secure the mortgage. Irving guaranteed repayment of Harvey's loan from Yellowstone.

(a) Davidson is a surety on the first mortgage debt assumed by Harvey.

(b) Davidson and Irving are co-sureties for Harvey's obligations for the purchase of Backacre.
(c) If Harvey should default on the second mortgage, Yellowstone Bank may not collect the debt from Irving if Harvey has filed a voluntary bankruptcy petition in Federal Court.
(d) If Harvey should default on both mortgages, the banks must first foreclose the mortgages on Backacre before proceeding against Davidson or Irving.
(e) If Harvey had previously defaulted on several other loans made to him by Yellowstone and Yellowstone willfully failed to advise Irving of this at the time it obtained his guaranty, Irving may assert such failure as a defense in an action against him on the guaranty by Yellowstone.

(3) Franklin Corporation borrowed money from the Lifetime Insurance Company and gave Lifetime a non-negotiable promissory note for the amount of the loan. Lifetime insisted that Walter Williams, the president of Franklin, sign the note as co-maker. In addition, Lifetime insisted that Franklin pledge 1,000 shares of stock that Franklin owned in a subsidiary corporation.
(a) Williams is liable as a surety on the loan by Lifetime to Franklin.
(b) If Lifetime should assign the notes and collateral to a third party, Williams would be released.
(c) If Franklin should default and Williams should pay the loan, Williams would be entitled to Lifetime's rights in the pledged stock.
(d) Lifetime must file a financing statement to perfect its security interest since collateral was received.
(e) If Franklin should default and Lifetime should thereafter sell the pledged stock for an amount in excess of the debt, Lifetime may retain the profit.

11/69

(4) A person who is planning to make a loan to an individual may lawfully ask, as a condition to obtaining the loan, that the individual
(a) Pledge personal property having a value far in excess of the amount of the loan in order to provide the creditor with security.
(b) Execute a negotiable promissory note for the amount of the loan.
(c) Agree to overstate the amount of the loan in order to permit the interest rate to appear to be allowable under the usury law.
(d) Procure a certified public accountant's report which does not fairly present the financial condition of the individual.
(e) Obtain another person's promise to answer for his debt.

(5) A suretyship relationship
(a) May be a two-party transaction.
(b) Is usually founded on a contract.
(c) Requires a written offer and acceptance.

(d) Requires a formal contract between all of the parties.
(e) May arise by operation of law.

(6) A surety
(a) Does not have a right to reimbursement for a greater amount than he has paid.
(b) May seek exoneration before satisfying any of the outstanding obligations.
(c) May assert his right to contribution against the creditor after the creditor has been paid.
(d) May become subrogated to the rights of the creditor after the creditor has been paid.
(e) Must assert all available bona fide defenses of which he is aware in a suit brought by the creditor, if he is going to recover subsequently in an action for reimbursement against the principal debtor.

(7) A surety may successfully assert as a defense against the creditor who sues him
(a) The death of the principal debtor.
(b) The insolvency of the principal debtor.
(c) A private agreement affecting the surety's liability made by the principal debtor and the surety.
(d) The non-disclosure by the creditor of facts which materially increase the surety's risk.
(e) A substantial modification of the principal debtor's obligation which is not agreed to by the surety.

(8) If a surety has agreed to be responsible for the debt of the principal debtor under a conditional guarantee
(a) The creditor can immediately sue the surety upon the maturity of the obligation.
(b) The creditor must join the principal debtor in a suit brought against the surety.
(c) The creditor can institute an action against the surety once he has commenced an action against the principal debtor.
(d) The creditor must first exhaust all of the legal remedies he has against the principal debtor before he can sue the surety.
(e) The creditor may lose his rights against the surety if he delays suing the principal debtor.

5/67

(9) A suretyship relation
(a) Imposes upon the surety a primary obligation to the creditor.
(b) Can arise by operation of law.
(c) Is usually considered a type of contract within the Statute of Frauds.
(d) Allows the surety to set off against the creditor a personal claim that he has against the creditor even though it did not arise out of the suretyship relation.

(e) Allows the surety to set off against the creditor a personal claim that the surety has against the principal debtor.

(10) A defense available to a surety against the creditor is
- (a) The minority of the principal debtor.
- (b) The insanity of the principal debtor.
- (c) The bankruptcy of the principal debtor.
- (d) Inducement of the contract by duress on the part of the creditor upon the principal debtor.
- (e) Material breach on the part of the creditor.

(11) In a co-suretyship relation
- (a) The co-sureties must be bound to answer for the same obligation of the principal debtor.
- (b) The co-sureties must be financially acceptable to each other.
- (c) The statute of limitations will begin to run in favor of the co-sureties from the time of default by the principal debtor.
- (d) The right of subrogation is denied to the co-sureties.
- (e) The co-sureties will be able to avoid liability if there is a tender of performance by the principal debtor.

(12) Seth is a non-compensated surety on Peter's debt. Seth can avoid liability on this debt if he can show that
- (a) His promise was obtained through fraud upon him by the creditor.
- (b) His promise was made at the time the loan was made but he received no consideration for his promise.
- (c) Peter died after Seth became a non-compensated surety.
- (d) A modification was made in the suretyship contract that can only be beneficial to him.
- (e) His promise was obtained through fraud upon him by Peter.

(13) Star is a compensated surety on Paul's debt to Charles. Star and Paul will be able to avoid liability if
- (a) Paul obtains a discharge in bankruptcy.
- (b) Charles unconditionally releases Paul.
- (c) Paul is a minor.
- (d) Paul dies before the debt becomes due.
- (e) Star can prove that his promise was obtained through the fraud of Paul.

(14) Stan agrees to act as a surety for Pat.
- (a) The general rules regarding Stan's capacity to contract are applicable.
- (b) If Stan is a trading corporation the agreement is *ultra vires*.
- (c) Stan may legally act as a surety if Stan is a partnership.
- (d) Stan may not legally bind as a surety a non-trading partnership of which he is a member.
- (e) If the creditor knows that Pat is a minor, Stan will be released.

(15) Arthur and Baker are co-sureties on a debt owed by Peter.
- (a) They must be bound to answer for the same debt.

(b) They must be aware of each other's existence at the time of contracting.
(c) They must be financially acceptable to each other.
(d) Arthur's right to contribution will not be affected by a release of Baker by the creditor with a reservation of rights against Arthur.
(e) Baker's right to contribution will become available only when he has satisfied the creditor in full.

5/65

TOPIC THIRTEEN | BANKRUPTCY

CONTENTS PAGE

*BANKRUPTCY. The Federal Bankruptcy Act is the basis for questions dealing with bankruptcy. This topic includes methods of dealing with financial failure in lieu of bankruptcy, acts of bankruptcy, voluntary and involuntary petitions in bankruptcy, administration of the bankrupt's estate, preferences, priorities, exemptions, duties of a bankrupt, bankruptcy offenses, and the effect of a discharge on the bankrupt's debts.**

I. METHODS OF DEALING WITH FINANCIAL FAILURE (OTHER THAN BANKRUPTCY)

A. Inaction by the creditors.

1. Causes:
   a. Large exemptions under state laws (see p. 368, IV.A.2.).
   b. Existing property is pledged or mortgaged for more than can be realized upon a forced sale.
   c. The expense of collection is in excess of any probable return.

B. Aggressive collection.

1. Procedures:
   a. Procure judgments against the debtor and have the debtor's property seized and sold as a means of collection (subject to restriction in the exemption laws).
   b. Attach the debtor's property to insure collection of judgments the creditors are currently seeking.
   c. Levy upon property conveyed by the debtor to a third person in fraud of the creditors.
   d. Garnish monies owed to the debtor and apply the proceeds to the creditor's claims.
   e. Employ statutory proceedings, or seek equitable relief to discover debtor's hidden assets.
2. Results:
   a. Commonly gives rise to a race to obtain general or specific liens upon the debtor's property. (Liens usually have priority in accordance with the various dates at which they arise or are recorded—see Property, p. 398, V.G.2.f.).

      (1) Encourages a "race of diligence" among creditors which is expensive, inequitable, and tends to disrupt any business the debtor may have.
   b. Some liens may be avoided in bankruptcy proceedings (see p. 364, III.D.3.a.).

* Source: AICPA, *Information for CPA Candidates* (July 1970).

C. Adjustments: The need for action combined with the disadvantages of aggressive collection may influence creditors to institute:

1. Compositions.

   a. Definition: an agreement made upon a sufficient consideration, between an insolvent or embarrassed debtor and his creditors, whereby the latter for the sake of an immediate or early payment agree to accept an amount which is less than the full value of their claims. This amount is distributed pro rata in discharge and satisfaction of their claims.

      (1) Composition agreements are to be distinguished from extension agreements, which are simply agreements to postpone collecting debts.

   b. Elements of an enforceable agreement.

      (1) Consideration:

         (A) By the creditors: mutual promises by creditors not to press their claims against debtor.

         (B) By the debtor: an immediate pro rata payment, or a series of stipulated future payments.

      (2) Following agreement and pending its performance, debtor continues in control of his assets and business.

      (3) There must be an agreement to the composition between all or several of the creditors.

         (A) Upon the unqualified acceptance of the composition, the creditors bind themselves to accept a given percentage of the debt owed them, and any attempt to withdraw before rejection by the debtor would be a breach of the agreement.

         (B) At common law, non-participating creditors will not be bound without their acquiescence; however, under state statutes and the Bankruptcy Act—see p. 358, I.C.1.d.(1)—when a majority of the creditors agree, they bind the non-assenting creditors.

   c. Breach of agreement:

      (1) Fraud: misrepresentation by the debtor will enable the creditors to avoid the agreement.

      (2) Secret preference: an agreement by the debtor to give preferential treatment to a creditor's claim.

         (A) Such an agreement is void and other creditors can rescind the composition agreement on discovering such a preference.

(B) The actual payment made by the debtor, as a preference, may be recovered for the benefit of the other creditors, but the latter cannot then rescind the composition.

(3) Breach by debtor:

(A) If the composition is executory (i.e., the debtor is not to be released by the composition until final payments are made) the agreement is voided and the original debt, or amount which remains unpaid, is revived.

(B) If the composition is executed (i.e., the debtor was released by the composition from his prior obligations and stipulated future payments were substituted therefor), creditors' only remedy for a default would be damages equal to the unpaid balance of the composition.

d. Arrangements.

(1) Composition and extension agreements are embodied in provisions for arrangements in Chapter XI of the Bankruptcy Act.

(2) The court in approving any arrangement entered into must be satisfied that:

(A) The arrangement has been accepted by all creditors affected, or at least by a majority (see p. 363, III.C.3.).

(B) The debtor has deposited any funds required.

(C) The arrangement is for the best interest of creditors.

(D) The arrangement is fair and equitable and made and executed in good faith.

(E) The debtor has not committed any acts which would bar his discharge.

2. Creditors' committees:

a. Definition: the submission of business and financial affairs by the debtor to the control of a committee of creditors.

(1) This may involve investing the committee with:

(A) Control of stock in the debtor's corporation.

(B) Power to hire and fire employees.

(C) Managerial control (without taking title to the assets).

3. Receiverships.

a. Definition: the general administration of a debtor's assets by a court appointee for the benefit of all parties as their interests may appear; or, the administration of assets in a particular case (such as a foreclosure of a mortgage) for the benefit of particular creditors having secured claims antedating their bills in equity.

(1) Receivers are appointed by a court of equity upon proper application and proof by one or a number of creditors who are in agreement.

(A) Traditionally, creditors must show an inadequate legal remedy by procuring a judgment and having an execution returned unsatisfied before they can institute a "creditors' bill in equity" for the appointment of a receiver.

(B) General receiverships can be superseded by a few creditors (see p. 361, II.C.2.) petitioning for bankruptcy so that at least an informal understanding between creditors is likely.

4. Assignment for the benefit of creditors.

a. Definition: usually made pursuant to a state statute; consists of a voluntary transfer by an insolvent debtor of all his assets to a trustee or assignee, to be sold or otherwise liquidated for the benefit of such creditors as wish to participate.

(1) There need be no agreement among all the creditors prior to the assignment.

(2) The debtor ceases to have control over his business or assets after the assignment.

(3) The assignment must completely and irrevocably transfer title to the debtor's assets to the trustee or assignee.

b. Rights of non-assenting creditors:

(1) Cannot reach assets which have been assigned for the benefit of the assenting creditors.

(2) Can attach any surplus remaining after the assenting creditors have been paid.

(3) Can reach property acquired by the debtor after the assignment.

(4) Can have an irregular assignment set aside and proceed against the debtor as if no assignment had been made.

(5) Can petition the debtor into bankruptcy.

c. Statutory assignments:

(1) Most states have statutes which regulate assignments for the benefit of creditors; in some of these states all such assignments must be made in accordance with the statute.

(2) Provisions common to most statutes:

(A) Prohibition of all preferences.

(B) The debtor must assign all assets except those exempted by law.

(C) The debtor may retain no control or custody over the assets assigned.

(3) Some statutes provide that an assignment for the benefit of creditors operates as a release of the unpaid balance, provided the creditors consent thereto.

5. Corporate reorganization.

a. Definition: see Corporations, p. 200, XI.

b. Reorganization is provided for in Chapter X of the Bankruptcy Act.

(1) Corporations eligible or amenable to such reorganization are also eligible for and amenable to ordinary bankruptcy.

(2) A petition for corporate reorganization may be filed before or after the adjudication of bankruptcy.

(3) Petitions for reorganization must set forth:

(A) The fact that the corporation is insolvent (see p. 360, II.A.3.) or unable to pay its debts.

(B) Jurisdiction of the court as to this matter.

(C) The nature of the corporation and its financial condition.

(D) Any pending proceeding against the corporation.

(E) The status of any plan for reorganization, adjustment, or liquidation.

(F) A need for relief that cannot be obtained through an arrangement (see p. 358, I.C.1.d.).

(G) Request that a plan be effected.

II. BANKRUPTCY

A. Definitions.

1. Bankrupt: a person who has committed an act of bankruptcy and who under the law is liable to be proceeded against by his creditors for the seizure and distribution among them of all his non-exempt property.

2. Adjudication of bankruptcy: the state, condition, or status of a person after an adjudication of bankruptcy has been made in a court having bankruptcy jurisdiction.

3. Insolvency: a financial status.

a. In the equity sense, the inability to meet debts as they mature.

b. In the bankruptcy sense, the aggregate value of assets, at a fair valuation, is not sufficient to pay outstanding liabilities.

B. Purpose of National Bankruptcy Act: to provide a means whereby an honest but insolvent debtor may secure relief from his debts and to give all creditors an equal chance to share in the debtor's assets in proportion to their claims.

C. Petitions in bankruptcy: filed with the court, accompanied by a schedule of the debtor's assets and liabilities, and a request for discharge.

1. Voluntary petitions.
   a. The debtor asks that he be adjudicated a bankrupt.
   b. They may be filed by any person, partnership, or corporation except a municipal, railroad, insurance, or banking corporation or a building and loan association.
2. Involuntary petitions.
   a. A creditor or creditors file a petition requesting that debtor be adjudged a bankrupt; the debtor must owe $1,000, or more.
      (1) A single creditor may file if there are less than twelve creditors, and if his provable claim (see p. 367, III.F.1.), fixed as to liability and liquidated as to amount, aggregates $500 in excess of the value of any security he may hold.
      (2) Three or more creditors are required to join in filing if the debtor's creditors are twelve or more in number, and they may file a petition if their provable claims aggregate $500 in excess of the value of any security held by them.
   b. Petitions may be filed against any natural person (except a farmer or a wage earner whose annual compensation does not exceed $1,500) and may be filed against any "moneyed, business or commercial corporation" except municipals, railroads, insurance companies, or banking corporations or building and loan associations which are reorganized or liquidated by other procedures.
   c. The procedure involves filing of petitions by the appropriate persons stating that during the preceding four months the alleged bankrupt has committed one or more of the six acts of bankruptcy.

D. Acts of bankruptcy: must occur within four months of filing of the petition.

1. Fraudulent conveyance:
   a. The transfer or concealment of any part of the debtor's assets, or permitting another to transfer or conceal a debtor's assets with "intent to hinder, delay or defraud creditors" or with the effect of creating a "constructively fraudulent transfer" (the Bankruptcy Act adopts the Uniform Fraudulent Conveyance Act).

b. Solvency (in the bankruptcy sense) is a complete defense to this act; however, fraudulently transferred or concealed property is excluded in a determination of solvency.

2. Making or suffering a preferential transfer: the transfer of any part of the bankrupt's property while insolvent and within four months of the petition to one or more creditors for or on account of an antecedent debt. Such transfers enable the transferee to be preferred over the other creditors of the same class. A preference may be an act of bankruptcy without being voidable (see p. 365, III.D.3.c.).

3. Failure to discharge a lien by legal proceedings while insolvent: suffering a creditor to obtain a lien through legal proceedings and failing to vacate or discharge the lien within thirty days, or at least within five days prior to the date set for any rule or other disposition of the property affected by the lien, while the debtor is insolvent.

4. Assignment for the benefit of creditors:

   a. The non-assenting creditors dissatisfied with the assignment can petition for bankruptcy of the debtor.

   b. The assignor's solvency in this situation is immaterial.

5. Appointment of a receiver or trustee: The debtor permits or procures, voluntarily or involuntarily, such an appointment while insolvent and unable to pay debts as they mature.

6. Written admission: regardless of insolvency if the alleged bankrupt admits in writing both his inability to pay his debts and his willingness to be adjudicated a bankrupt.

III. ADMINISTRATION OF A BANKRUPTCY ESTATE

A. Referee: an official appointed by the judge of a bankruptcy court (i.e., a Federal District Court). He is given specific power to handle the common bankruptcy procedures and is generally vested with the power to issue such process, make such orders, and enter such judgments as may be necessary to enforce the act.

B. Appointment of receiver (or marshal): Upon application of the interested parties, the appointment may be made by the court to protect interests of creditors and prevent any danger or loss to the estate up to the time the trustee is appointed and supersedes the receiver. The appointment may be requested whether the petition is voluntary or involuntary.

C. First creditors' meeting: The bankrupt furnishes a list of creditors, who must be given at least ten days' notice by mail.

1. A referee ordinarily presides. (A judge may lawfully do so.)
2. Claims are allowed for the purpose of determining who may vote, although they may be more closely examined at a later date.
3. Creditors pass upon matters presented by a majority vote both in number and amount of allowed claims.
   a. If the two majorities do not agree, the court administers the estate without instruction from creditors on that point.
   b. Claims of $50 or less are not counted in computing the number of creditors voting or present, but are counted in computing the amount of allowed claims.
   c. Relations of individual bankrupts, stockholders, officers, directors of a corporate bankrupt, and fully secured creditors are excluded from voting.
4. Creditors may elect trustee.
   a. This may be impractical in non-asset cases.
   b. The referee may appoint a trustee where one has not been elected.

D. Trustee.

1. Duties:
   a. The administration of assets. To collect, liquidate, and distribute the estate:
      (1) Trustee must:
         (A) Examine all proofs of claim.
         (B) Object to the allowance of improper claims.
         (C) Decide whether to sue upon contested claims.
      (2) Trustee may, within sixty days after adjudication of bankruptcy, elect to assume or reject any executory contract, or lease of the bankrupt (unless in the case of a contract it contains a clause prohibiting assignment, or in the case of a lease it automatically terminates or gives an option to the landlord to re-enter upon the event of bankruptcy).
         (A) Any contract not assumed is deemed rejected as a matter of law.
      (3) Trustee may continue or discontinue a legal action brought by the bankrupt for benefit of the bankrupt estate.
   b. Investigation of the bankrupt at the first creditors' meeting and at any other of the following meetings:
      (1) Examination of a bankrupt includes investigation for any property that may have been withheld.

(2) The trustee may order a bankrupt or others holding property for the bankrupt to "turn over" said property, and may bring a hearing to require such turnover.

(3) The trustee may examine the bankrupt at any hearing upon objections to his discharge unless the court directs otherwise.

c. Abandonment of property in cases where it is worthless.

(1) Where doubtful, an order from the court may be obtained.

2. Powers:

a. Title of the trustee, as of the date of bankruptcy, to all the bankrupt's non-exempt property which could, by any means, have been transferred or which might have been sold under judicial process against him or otherwise sequestered, although personal rights (such as a cause of action for injury to the bankrupt's person) remain in the bankrupt.

(1) The bankrupt may reclaim title to his non-exempt insurance policies from the trustee upon payment of their cash surrender value.

b. Powers exercisable by the bankrupt pass to the trustee, except rights of expectancies which do not pass.

(1) However, all property the title to which vests in the bankrupt within six months after bankruptcy, by bequest, devise, or inheritance, passes to the trustee.

c. The trustee may interpose any defense available to the bankrupt against third persons, and he is not bound by any attempt of the bankrupt, after bankruptcy, to waive defenses such as the statute of limitations, Statute of Frauds, and usury.

3. May set aside:

a. Liens on assets of the estate; if the liens were obtained by legal or equitable proceedings while the bankrupt was insolvent and within a period of four months before the petition in bankruptcy, they may be invalidated by the trustee even if such liens would have been good if the bankruptcy proceedings had not started.

(1) However, statutory liens in favor of employees, contractors, mechanics, and landlords, and statutory liens for taxes due to the United States or any state subdivision are valid even when arising or when perfected within the four months and even though the debtor is insolvent.

(2) Trustee may elect to preserve a *defeasible lien for the benefit of the estate.*

(A) Thus, if a lien may be set aside, but is the sole incumbrance on a bankrupt's otherwise exempt assets, the trustee may use it *himself* to make such assets available for distribution as a part of the estate.

b. Fraudulent conveyances. The trustee has title to property transferred by a bankrupt in fraud of his creditors.

(1) He is likely to assert his right by use of section 70c or 70e (see p. 365, III.D.3.d.) and in this way invalidate fraudulent conveyances (see p. 361, II.D.1.) and fraudulent retentions of possession (requirements are governed by local law).

c. Preferences (see p. 362, II.D.2.) may only be invalidated by proving that the creditor receiving the preference had reasonable cause to believe that the debtor was insolvent.

(1) A transfer to finance, or in promotion of a preference, may also be voidable.

(2) Amounts owed for new payments or deliveries to the bankrupt by a creditor already preferred may be "set off" against any voidable preferences.

d. Transfers.

(1) Section 70c gives the trustee the standing of a hypothetical lien creditor as of the date of bankruptcy, and permits him in this role to attack transfers which were imperfect against a holder of a lien by legal or equitable proceedings at the date of bankruptcy.

(A) This right is independent of the existence or nonexistence of any actual creditor at this time.

(2) Section 70e declares that a transfer by the bankrupt which is voidable under any applicable state or federal law by any actual creditor having a provable claim shall be null and void as against the trustee in bankruptcy.

(A) Once a transfer is vulnerable in part, it is completely vulnerable to the trustee. (E.g., a trustee may invalidate a large mortgage entirely by asserting a valid claim of a small creditor.)

E. Claims.

1. General creditors are subordinate to reclamations, trust claims, rights of secured creditors, and set-offs.

a. Reclamation: a proceeding brought by a person who claims specific property in bankrupt's estate as his own.

b. Trust claim: the beneficiary of property which the bankrupt held in trust is entitled to the specific property or its proceeds.

c. General creditor: one who has no security or priority.

d. Preferred creditor: one who has been given a preference.

e. Secured creditor: a creditor who holds some special assurance for payment of his debt, such as a mortgage or lien.

(1) Creditors who are fully secured may resort to their security in satisfaction of their claims (if not fully secured see p. 367, III.F.2.i.).

f. Set-offs are allowed for mutual debts or credits between creditor and bankrupt estate.

(1) Business custom and accepted standards determine which debts may be set off.

(2) Claims to be mutual must at least be between the same two parties, and to be available for set-offs they must be provable.

(3) Surplus security, if any, goes to the trustee in bankruptcy and becomes a part of bankrupt's estate.

2. Priorities are prescribed for certain claims which are paid in full before the general creditors' share.

a. Priorities are to be distinguished from property rights of secured creditors. Priority creditors have a statutory advantage effective upon distribution of the bankrupt's estate, which does not include any property validly claimed as security by a secured creditor. In this sense, secured claims outrank claims entitled to priority.

b. The order of priorities is:

(1) Administration costs, including expense of preserving the estate and attorneys' and accountants' fees.

(2) Wage priority is restricted to $600 per claim earned within three months before bankruptcy; to the extent that the wage earner's claim exceeds $600, his claim is a general one.

(3) Expenses of successful opposition to an arrangement or discharge.

(4) Taxes: federal, state, and local, excluding taxes which exceed the value of the bankrupt's interest in the property taxed.

(5) Claims of the United States other than taxes and any state priority for rent accrued within three months before bankruptcy on account of actual occupancy.

c. Debts, contracted after the granting of a discharge where the discharge is subsequently set aside for fraud or a similar reason, take precedent over reinstated debts.

3. Deferred claims may arise by reason of contract, fraud, or estoppel.

a. The commonest subject for deferral is a claim by a creditor in a proprietary relation to a business which has become bankrupt.

F. Proof and allowance of creditors' claims.

1. Proof of claims:
   a. All claims must be filed within six months after the date set for the first creditors' meeting.
   b. Claims must be under oath and signed by the creditor, setting forth a statement of the claim, the consideration therefor, security held, if any, payments made on the claim, and a statement that the claim is justly owing.
2. Debts or claims which may be proved:
   a. Claims upon contracts, express or implied, including tort claims if the creditor at his election may recover upon a contractual or quasi-contractual theory.
   b. Judgments obtained by the date of bankruptcy are provable whether or not founded on provable claims.
   c. Anticipatory breaches.
   d. Leases, but in no event are they allowable in an amount exceeding one year's rent.
   e. Contingent claims are not provable unless they are presented and can be valued.
   f. Tort claims are provable only under a. or b., or if an action has been commenced prior to and is pending at the time of filing a petition.
   g. Court costs incurred by a creditor before filing of the petition.
   h. Claims arising after an involuntary petition but before the adjudication and before appointment of a referee, for property transferred or services rendered for the benefit of the estate to the extent of the value of the property or services.
   i. Secured creditors have a provable claim only to the extent, if any, of the deficiency of their security.
3. Non-allowable claims, not discharged by bankruptcy:
   a. If a creditor has received a transfer voidable in bankruptcy, none of his claims are allowable, unless he surrenders the property transferred.
   b. Penalties in agreements as such are not allowable, except for the amount of any pecuniary loss sustained by the act, transaction, or proceeding out of which the penalty or forfeiture arose.
   c. Interest is not allowable on general claims or taxes, unless there is a surplus after paying the principal of all claims, but

a secured creditor may include interest in enforcing his security.

G. Dividends: payments made to creditors; the rate must be uniform as to all unsecured creditors.

IV. RIGHTS, DUTIES, AND LIABILITIES OF A BANKRUPT

A. Rights and exemptions of a bankrupt.

1. Right to counsel.
2. The Bankruptcy Act allows the bankrupt to claim exemptions provided for by federal and state laws. These include:
   a. Wearing apparel, wages, jewelry, growing crops, and tools.
   b. Two of the most important exemptions, insurance and homestead, have been greatly liberalized in several states.

B. Duties of a bankrupt:

1. First and foremost duty is to surrender all his non-exempt property.
2. Attend the first creditors' meeting, and later meetings if so ordered by the court.
3. Verify proofs of claim submitted to the trustee.
4. Execute and deliver papers as ordered by the court.
5. Prepare and file a schedule of his assets, indicating where they may be located.
6. Prepare a preliminary statement of his affairs to be submitted at least five days prior to the first creditors' meeting.
7. Submit to examination concerning his affairs upon a court order to do so.
8. File an inventory of the cost of his goods upon court order.

C. Bankruptcy offenses:

1. Bankrupt will be denied a discharge from his debts if bankruptcy offenses are committed.
2. Bankrupt or any other party will be liable to fine and imprisonment for commission of bankruptcy offenses, which include knowingly and fraudulently:
   a. Concealing property, or documents affecting property of the bankrupt's estate from an officer or creditors entitled to them.
   b. Concealing, mutilating, falsifying, or making a false entry in any document or book of account relating to the bankrupt's affairs after or in contemplation of a bankruptcy proceeding.
   c. Presenting false claims against the estate.

d. Receiving property from the bankrupt after the filing of a petition with intent to defeat the law.
e. Receiving, or attempting to receive, money or other compensation for acting or forbearing to act in a bankruptcy proceeding.

V. DISCHARGE OF A BANKRUPT

A. In order to obtain a discharge a person must be adjudged an "honest debtor." An "honest debtor" must not have committed any of the following acts, which will bar discharge:

1. Commission of a bankruptcy offense: These acts normally occur during bankruptcy proceedings as indicated above.
2. Destruction, falsification, concealment of, or failure to keep, books of account or records from which his financial condition and business transactions can be ascertained, unless the court finds the bankrupt's acts to have been justified.
3. False statements as to his financial condition, used to obtain or extend credit.
4. Removal, destruction, or concealment of property within twelve months prior to filing of the petition in bankruptcy.
5. Discharge or composition which relieved bankrupt, and was confirmed under the Bankruptcy Act, within six years prior to the present bankruptcy.
6. Refusal to obey court orders.
7. Failure to explain satisfactorily any losses of assets, or an amount of assets insufficient to meet his liabilities.

B. Debts not affected by a discharge:

1. Only debts provable in bankruptcy (see p. 367, III.F.2.) are dischargeable.
2. Some debts, although provable, are not dischargeable; these include:
   a. Taxes (federal or any state, county, district, or municipality).
   b. Alimony and undischargeable torts. Included in this category are liabilities for obtaining money by false pretenses or false representations, or for malicious injuries.
   c. Unscheduled debts: debts which have not been scheduled in time for proof, unless the creditor had notice or actual knowledge of the proceedings in bankruptcy.
   d. Breach of fiduciary duty created by the debtor's fraud while acting as an officer or in any fiduciary capacity.

e. Wages due to workmen, servants, clerks, or salesmen which have been earned within three months before commencement of the proceedings.

f. Monies to secure the performance of an employment contract; sums retained by the employer to secure faithful performance of a contract of employment.

C. Revival of debts discharged in bankruptcy (see Contracts, p. 41, III.B.4.c.(1)).

D. Revocation of discharge.

1. Court may revoke a discharge when it has been shown that there was fraud in procuring it.

BANKRUPTCY: SUBJECTIVE QUESTIONS*

ACTS OF BANKRUPTCY

Q. Zeta Corporation is insolvent. It has twenty unsecured creditors and three creditors who have liens on its assets. Zeta, while insolvent, paid $20,000 to Jones, one of its unsecured creditors, in partial payment of goods sold and delivered by Jones to Zeta six months earlier. Adams, one of the secured creditors, loaned Zeta funds ten months ago and two months ago, when he knew Zeta was insolvent, obtained from Zeta a security interest in the company's accounts receivable which he duly perfected under applicable state law. Collins, another of the secured creditors, sold Zeta some machinery six months ago and obtained a security interest therein which he has neglected to perfect. Barton, the remaining secured creditor, holds a mortgage on Zeta's plant which he obtained two years ago and which is duly filed and recorded under applicable state law.

(1) Has Zeta committed an act of bankruptcy? Explain.

(2) Assuming Zeta has committed an act of bankruptcy, how many of its creditors must join in an involuntary petition in bankruptcy? How much in provable claims must such petitioning creditors have? Explain.

(3) Assume an involuntary petition has been filed against Zeta and Zeta has been adjudicated bankrupt, all other facts recited above remaining the same. Discuss the rights of Adams, Collins and Barton in relation to Zeta's trustee in bankruptcy.

(4) Assuming Jones received a preference, might the trustee be able to recover the $20,000 from Jones? Explain.

5/70; pp.361, 362

* See Introductory Note, p. 19.

Q. For several years Martin supplied raw materials to Brown, who processed the goods into a finished product for sale to retail customers. Martin supplied goods to Brown on credit terms, and to secure his claim for unpaid goods, Martin obtained and properly perfected a "floating lien" on all of the goods sold to Brown. Six months ago Martin heard that Brown was in financial difficulty and stopped selling goods to him. Martin was not paid by Brown for several shipments of goods and heard that recently Brown made a general assignment for the benefit of his creditors. Also Martin heard that a group of Brown's creditors may attempt to place Brown into bankruptcy.

(1) Has Brown committed an "act of bankruptcy"? Explain.

(2) Is the commission of an "act of bankruptcy" necessary to become a voluntary bankrupt? Explain.

(3) Under what circumstances may Brown's creditors proceed to have Brown adjudicated an involuntary bankrupt?

(4) Assume that Brown's creditors may proceed to have him adjudicated an involuntary bankrupt. What action would they have to take in order to commence a bankruptcy proceeding?

(5) Will the number of creditors required to commence an involuntary bankruptcy proceeding vary depending upon the number of Brown's creditors? Explain.

11/67; p. 362

PREFERENCES

Q. On January 2, 1961, Richard Retailer purchased twenty television sets on credit, executing trust receipts which stated that title remained in the finance company to secure payment of the price. The Uniform Trust Receipts Act was in force, and it required the filing of a statement that trust receipt financing was contemplated. That provision of the Act was complied with on January 3, 1961. On August 15, 1961, Richard Retailer became bankrupt and the finance company claimed the remaining television sets on hand. The trustee in bankruptcy also claimed the television sets and claimed that the finance company had a "voidable preference."

(1) What is meant by the term "preference" under the Bankruptcy Act? Explain.

(2) Who will prevail in the above case, the finance company or the trustee? Explain.

(3) Suppose, instead of selling on credit via trust receipts financing, the manufacturer had sold the twenty sets for fair market value to Richard Retailer one week before bankruptcy. Could this transaction be set aside as a preference? Explain.

11/61; pp. 362, 364-365

BANKRUPTCY: OBJECTIVE QUESTIONS

Each of the following numbered statements states a legal conclusion. You are to determine whether each legal conclusion is true or false according to general principles of bankruptcy law. Your grade will be determined by deducting your total of incorrect answers from your total of correct answers; an omitted answer will not be considered an incorrect answer.

(1) Richardson owns all of the stock of Richardson Corporation. Recently the firm has been unprofitable. A supplier who in the past sold to the Corporation on credit now demands cash on delivery because he believes the Corporation is becoming insolvent.

(a) The Corporation is insolvent in the equity sense if it is unable to meet its debts as they mature.
(b) The Corporation is insolvent in the bankruptcy sense if its assets valued on the basis of a voluntary sale are less than its liabilities.
(c) The Corporation cannot be considered insolvent so long as Richardson has adequate funds which he can donate to the Corporation.
(d) Proof of insolvency is itself an act of bankruptcy.
(e) If an involuntary petition in bankruptcy should be filed against Richardson charging him with concealing his assets with intent to defraud his creditors, proof by Richardson that he was solvent at the time the petition was filed would be a complete defense to the action.

(2) Harris, while he was insolvent and within four months of filing a petition in bankruptcy, transferred property to Michael, a creditor of his for an antecedent debt. The effect of the transfer was to enable Michael to obtain a greater percentage of his debt than Harris's other creditors of the same class.

(a) Harris's action will not bar him from obtaining a discharge in bankruptcy.
(b) Michael need not return the payment he received if he did not know that Harris was insolvent when the transfer was made.
(c) The transfer of property from Harris to Michael constitutes a preference.
(d) Harris's action will bar him from filing a voluntary petition in bankruptcy.
(e) Harris's action constitutes an act of bankruptcy.

(3) Anderson conveyed all of his property to Barker to escape the unfair demands of Collins. Anderson instructed Barker to sell the property and pay the proceeds to all of Anderson's creditors except Collins.

(a) Anderson committed an act of bankruptcy.
(b) Solvency would not be a valid defense to an involuntary petition filed in bankruptcy by Collins.

(c) The conveyance of the assets to Barker was a preferential transfer.
(d) A trustee in bankruptcy would seek to set aside such a conveyance.
(e) If Anderson had not excluded Collins from participation in the distribution of the proceeds from the sale of the property by Barker, Collins would be barred from filing an involuntary petition in bankruptcy.

(4) John Mitchell, an employee of the Sampson Aircraft Company, earns $120 per week. He has amassed $5,000 of unpaid bills which are payable to nine creditors who wish to have him declared a bankrupt.
(a) To place Mitchell into involuntary bankruptcy at least three of his creditors with claims aggregating at least $500 over the value of any security they hold must file a petition for involuntary bankruptcy against him.
(b) To place Mitchell into involuntary bankruptcy he must have committed an act of bankruptcy within four months of the filing of a petition against him.
(c) If Mitchell is adjudged a bankrupt he will be assured of obtaining a discharge.
(d) If Mitchell obtains a discharge in bankruptcy he will be automatically and unqualifiedly relieved of all his debts.
(e) If Mitchell is declared a bankrupt and obtains a discharge he may not incur any credit obligations for six months after his discharge unless he informs his potential creditor that he was recently a bankrupt.

(5) Thomas Serota owns a shop in which he repairs electrical appliances. Jones Company left a machine with Serota for repair. Electrical Supply Company sold Serota a machine on credit three months ago for testing electrical appliances and has a perfected security interest as security for payment of the unpaid balance due. Serota's creditors have now filed an involuntary petition in bankruptcy against him.
(a) Jones Company should file a creditor's claim with the trustee in bankruptcy to obtain the return of their machine.
(b) Jones Company will be entitled to share in any *pro rata* distribution of assets made to the creditors of Thomas Serota.
(c) Electrical Supply Company must turn its perfected security interest over to the trustee in bankruptcy and share as a general creditor of the bankrupt's estate.
(d) If the trustee desires to do so he may successfully claim that Electrical Supply Company's perfected security interest constitutes a preference which is voidable.
(e) Electrical Supply Company is a secured creditor which is free to repossess the electrical testing machine sold to Serota and satisfy the obligation by properly disposing of the collateral.

(6) Wood and Small are partners who wish to file for voluntary bankruptcy.

(a) Wood and Small may be adjudged bankrupt as individuals separately from the partnership.
(b) The partnership cannot be adjudged a bankrupt.
(c) A voluntary bankrupt may not be adjudicated a bankrupt until a trustee in bankruptcy is appointed.
(d) A creditor who wishes to file a claim against the bankrupts must be present or represented at the first creditors' meeting.
(e) The marshalling of assets doctrine will apply if the partnership and both partners are insolvent.

5/69

(7) D, debtor, owes $61,000 to A, $4,000 to B, and $2,000 to C. D is in financial difficulty and unable to meet his debts as they mature. He offers to pay A, B, and C 50 cents on the dollar in satisfaction of these debts, and the parties accept this offer.

(a) The parties have agreed to a composition agreement.
(b) There is a lack of consideration to enforce the contract.
(c) X, another unpaid creditor, can attach the assets which D has set aside for satisfying A, B, and C's debts.
(d) D can satisfy a debt owed to Y in full without violating his agreement with A, B, and C.
(e) D is insolvent in the bankruptcy sense from the above facts.

(8) In order for a person to be adjudged a bankrupt under the Bankruptcy Act

(a) He must owe debts totaling more than $2,000.
(b) There must be at least three creditors.
(c) A petition in bankruptcy must be filed by a majority of creditors.
(d) The creditor must agree to the commencement of bankruptcy proceedings.
(e) A petition in bankruptcy must be filed.

(9) Acts of bankruptcy include a debtor's

(a) Making a fraudulent conveyance.
(b) Intentionally making a preference.
(c) Making a general assignment for the benefit of creditors.
(d) Orally admitting his willingness to be adjudged a bankrupt.
(e) Requesting the appointment of a receiver immediately before becoming insolvent.

(10) Bankruptcy proceedings may be instituted against any person or corporation, including

(a) A married woman.
(b) A municipal corporation.
(c) A banking corporation.
(d) A building and loan corporation.
(e) A partnership.

(11) At the first meeting of creditors after bankruptcy proceedings have commenced

(a) A judge or referee presides.
(b) Creditors may not examine the debtor unless he agrees.
(c) Creditors may appoint up to four persons to act as trustees.
(d) Important policy decisions must be agreed to by all creditors.
(e) An attorney who represents a general creditor may be chosen to represent the trustee.

(12) Duties of a bankrupt include

(a) Organizing the first meeting of creditors.
(b) Preparing a schedule of his property.
(c) Determining which of his creditors' claims are provable.
(d) Executing transfers to the trustee of his property in foreign countries.
(e) Collecting and reducing his estate to money under direction of the court.

(13) The trustee in bankruptcy is vested by operation of law with the bankrupt's title to all kinds of property, including

(a) Patents.
(b) Property transferred in fraud of creditors.
(c) Exempt property.
(d) Contingent remainders.
(e) Interests in real property.

(14) In order for a debtor to make a preference constituting an act of bankruptcy, he must, among other things, transfer property

(a) While he is insolvent.
(b) Within six months before the filing of a petition in bankruptcy.
(c) To a creditor on account of a present debt.
(d) To a creditor on account of an antecedent debt.
(e) To a creditor and thereby enable him to obtain full payment of his debt.

(15) If bankruptcy proceedings are instituted, a secured creditor

(a) Must turn over the security he holds to the trustee in bankruptcy.
(b) May waive his security, prove his claim for the full amount, and participate in sharing the debtor's assets on an equal footing with other priority creditors.
(c) May satisfy the obligation owed to him from the security he holds.
(d) May prove his claim as an unsecured creditor to the extent his security is inadequate.
(e) May be paid in full although priority creditors may receive only part of what is due to them.

(16) Classes of claims which have priority under the provisions of the Bankruptcy Act include

(a) Expenses of bankruptcy administration.

(b) Wages earned within one year before the date of bankruptcy.
(c) Debts of less than $50.
(d) Taxes.
(e) Claims of creditors which are outstanding for more than three years.

(17) A bankrupt can be denied a discharge in bankruptcy if
(a) Creditors receive less than 25 cents for every dollar owed to them.
(b) He fails to explain satisfactorily a deficiency in assets.
(c) He refuses to obey an order or writ.
(d) He negligently fails to keep adequate books of accounts.
(e) He was a bankrupt before and discharged 10 years ago.

(18) Debts discharged by completion of bankruptcy proceedings and discharge of the debtor include
(a) Contract obligations.
(b) Alimony.
(c) Taxes.
(d) Debts incurred within one month after the bankrupt's discharge.
(e) A debt arising from the commission of a willful injury.

11/66

(19) A common law or non-statutory assignment for the benefit of creditors
(a) Requires the debtor to transfer irrevocably the title to and control over the assets transferred.
(b) Requires the consent of the creditors.
(c) Requires the assignee to make a ratable distribution of the property among all the creditors.
(d) Immunizes the debtor's assets from attachment and execution.
(e) Releases the debtor from liability on any unpaid part of his debts after the distribution to creditors.

(20) Under the Bankruptcy Act a priority
(a) Is given to certain statutorily designated classes of creditors.
(b) Is given to certain classes of creditors at the discretion of the referee.
(c) Is given to administration costs, which include attorneys' and accountants' fees.
(d) Is given to landlords for rent due without qualification as to amounts.
(e) Creditor will be paid in full before the general creditors receive their shares of the insolvent's property.

(21) The Federal Bankruptcy Act
(a) Was enacted by Congress pursuant to power granted under the commerce clause.
(b) Allows the individual states to enact their own bankruptcy laws provided such laws meet certain minimum requirements.

(c) Gives creditors who have the same priority the right to share in the bankrupt's property in proportion to their claims.
(d) By specific provision invests the Federal District Courts with exclusive original jurisdiction over bankruptcy proceedings.
(e) Affords the bankrupt a release from all debts incurred before adjudication if he has fully complied with the law.

(22) The following natural persons or business entities may voluntarily petition themselves into bankruptcy:
(a) A solvent person.
(b) An insolvent person who owes a specified minimum amount of debt.
(c) An individual engaged in farming.
(d) An insolvent person who is the majority stockholder of a solvent corporation.
(e) A building and loan association which has transferred a part of its property to a creditor with intent to prefer him over other creditors.

(23) The Federal Bankruptcy Act
(a) Treats a partnership as an entity separate from the partners.
(b) Allows an involuntary petition to be filed against the partnership and any, but not necessarily all, of the general partners.
(c) Allows an involuntary petition to be filed against the partnership after a final settlement of partnership affairs.
(d) Provides that if all the partners are adjudged bankrupt the partnership shall also be adjudged bankrupt.
(e) Provides that the discharge in bankruptcy of a partnership automatically discharges the individual general partners from the unpaid balance of partnership debts.

(24) An involuntary petition in bankruptcy may be filed
(a) Against a wage earner with an annual compensation of $1,400.
(b) Against a corporation engaged solely in dairy farming.
(c) Only if the debtor owes a minimum of $1,000.
(d) Only if the debtor has committed an act of bankruptcy.
(e) Only if the debtor has at least three creditors.

(25) Solvency in the bankruptcy sense is a complete defense by the debtor who has committed the following act of bankruptcy:
(a) An assignment for the benefit of creditors.
(b) A fraudulent conveyance.
(c) Written admission by the debtor of his inability to pay his debts and of his willingness to be adjudged a bankrupt.
(d) A preferential transfer.
(e) Permitting a creditor to obtain a lien.

(26) A referee in a bankruptcy proceeding
(a) Is elected by a majority of the creditors having provable claims.
(b) Is, in effect, the court of bankruptcy, limited only by statutory provisions for judicial review.
(c) Is charged with the duty of declaring liquidating dividends.

(d) Is elected only when necessary to preserve assets of the estate.
(e) Is charged with taking any steps necessary to set aside any unlawful preference, transfer, or lien.

(27) A trustee in a bankruptcy proceeding
(a) Is elected or appointed only if the debtor is adjudicated a bankrupt.
(b) Is vested by operation of law with whatever title the debtor has as of the date of the filing of the petition.
(c) May resort to a state court to compel third persons to deliver to him property belonging to the estate of the bankrupt.
(d) May set aside a preferential transfer made by the debtor even though the preferred creditor did not know or have reasonable cause to believe that the debtor was insolvent at the time of the transfer.
(e) Acts on behalf of the debtor under the general supervision of the referee.

(28) Debts of the bankrupt may be proved and allowed against his estate if they are based upon
(a) A workman's compensation award if the injury occurred before the adjudication of bankruptcy.
(b) An open account.
(c) Contingent claims whether or not capable of liquidation or of reasonable estimate.
(d) Fixed liabilities evidenced by a written instrument absolutely owing but not due at the time of the filing of a petition.
(e) Negligence claims not reduced to judgment at the time the petition is filed.

(29) Commission of a bankruptcy offense
(a) Can only occur during the bankruptcy proceedings.
(b) Includes the action by an officer of a corporation, in contemplation of a corporate bankruptcy proceeding, of concealing any property of the corporation.
(c) Makes the offender liable to fine and imprisonment.
(d) May only be committed by the bankrupt.
(e) May result in barring a discharge in bankruptcy.

(30) The following provable debts are not discharged by bankruptcy:
(a) All federal and state taxes.
(b) Liabilities for support and maintenance of children.
(c) Claims resulting from the negligence of the bankrupt.
(d) Debts due for wages which have been earned by corporate officers within three months before the filing of the petition.
(e) Any monies deposited with the bankrupt by an employee as security for faithful performance.

5/65

TOPIC FOURTEEN | PROPERTY

CONTENTS PAGE

*PROPERTY. This topic is concerned primarily with real property law, although the distinction between real and personal property is also included. Among the subjects covered are the various estates in land, conveyances of real property, adverse possession, the landlord-tenant relationship, and real property mortgages.**

I. CHARACTERISTICS

A. Definitions.

1. Property: in the strict legal sense, an aggregate of rights relating to ownership and resultant control of things tangible and intangible, guaranteed and protected by the government.
2. Real property: land, and generally whatever is erected or growing upon or affixed permanently to land.
   a. Realty includes the surface and contents of land.
   b. Natural products of land are realty while attached to it (e.g., growing trees), but personalty when severed from the land (e.g., timber).
3. Fixture: something which was originally a chattel (i.e., personalty), but which was annexed to land so as to become "a part thereof."
   a. Chattel: an article of personal property, a movable thing. A chattel real is any interest in real estate less than a freehold (see below, I.B.1.a.).
   b. Requisites for conversion of a chattel (personalty) to a fixture (realty):

      (1) Actual annexation to the realty, or to something appurtenant (belonging) thereto, and

      (2) Use of the personal property for the purpose for which the real property is used (e.g., heavy machinery necessary for the operation of a factory may become part of the realty).

      (3) Intention (the key requisite) to make the article a permanent addition to the freehold, as gathered from the intention of the parties expressed in the agreement, the nature of articles affixed, the relation and situation of the person making annexation, the structure and mode of annexation, and the purpose or use for which it has been made.
   c. Trade "fixtures" remain personal property. They include readily detachable items such as refrigerators, removable equipment, and so on.

* Source: AICPA, *Information for CPA Candidates* (July 1970).

B. Interests which persons have in land (estates in land):

1. Estates are classified as to duration (freehold and non-freehold).
   a. Freehold: estate for life or greater duration. The owner is seised (i.e., he possesses a freehold interest in land).
      (1) Estate in fee simple: estate of potentially infinite duration.
         (A) Fee simple absolute: an estate in fee simple which is not subject to a restriction–see (B) below. (E.g., A conveys Blackacre "to B and his heirs.")
         (B) Fee simple defeasible: estate in fee simple subject to one or more restrictions which may defeat the estate; for example:
         (i) Special limitation: causes the created interest automatically to expire upon the occurrence of a stated event. (E.g., A conveys Blackacre "to B and his heirs, so long as it is used for educational purposes.")
         (ii) Condition subsequent: causes the conveyor or his successor in interest to have the power to terminate the interest upon the occurrence of a stated event. (E.g., A conveys Blackacre "to B and his heirs, but if gambling is permitted on the premises then A has the right to re-enter and repossess the land.")
         (C) Transfer of fee simple:
         (i) *Inter vivos:* from one living person to another by deed.
         (ii) Intestate succession: where the owner dies without leaving a will.
         (iii) Devise: where the owner dies making provision for passage of property in his will.
      (2) Estates in fee tail (abolished by statute):
         (A) An estate of potentially infinite duration.
         (B) Subject to a restriction that it is inheritable only by descendants of the first taker (grantee). (E.g., A conveys Blackacre "to B and the heirs of his body.")
      (3) Life estate.
         (A) Not an inheritable estate (cannot be transferred by will).
         (B) Estate specifically described as to duration in terms of the life or lives of one or more human beings.
         (C) May not be terminable at any fixed or computable period of time. (E.g., A conveys Blackacre "to B for the term of his natural life.")

(i) Life tenants may not misuse or allow the land to deteriorate during their tenancy and must keep it in repair.

(ii) Life tenants may alienate (transfer by sale or gift) or mortgage their interests in the land unless this has been prohibited.

b. Non-freehold (chattels real; no seisin, only possession).

(1) Estates for years. Even if the estate is for 10,000 years it is not considered a life estate—see above, I.B.1.a.(3)(C). (E.g., L leases Blackacre "to T for the period of two years.")

(2) Estate at will: land held subject to the will of the transferor or transferee.

(A) An estate which is terminable at will of the transferor or transferee, upon giving notice, and which has no other designated period of duration. (E.g., L leases Blackacre to T for "as long as L wishes.")

(B) Estate from period to period: an estate at will which will continue for successive periods of a year, or successive periods of a fraction of a year, until it is terminated. Notice of termination only takes effect at the end of the current period. (E.g., L leases Blackacre to T for a two-year period from April 1, 1956, to April 1, 1958, at a rental of $50 per month, payable in advance, on or before the tenth day of the month. T holds possession beyond April 1, 1958, and on April 9, 1958, tenders $50 to L which L accepts. Notice of termination could only take effect at the end of the month.)

(3) Estates at sufferance: When a person who had a possessory interest in land by virtue of an effective conveyance wrongfully continues in the possession of the land after the termination of such interest, but without asserting a claim of superior title; actually there is no tenancy at all, merely a wrongful possession. This is neither an estate nor property. (E.g., L leases Blackacre to T for a period and T continues to occupy the land after that period without L's consent.)

(4) Statutory tenancies: estates in land created by statute; these vary, depending upon state law (e.g., a tenancy created during the war as a result of emergency legislation to deal with housing shortages).

2. Estates classified as to time of possession.

a. Present estate: an estate now existing, vested in a holder who has present use or possession of the property.

b. Future estate: the right of use or possession by the owner is deferred to a future time.

(1) Reversion: the balance of fee which reverts to the grantor after a lapse of a particular precedent estate granted by him. (E.g., A, having a fee simple interest in property, gives B a deed to the property "for life.")

(2) Remainder: the balance of a larger estate which passes to a third party other than the grantor after a particular precedent estate expires.

3. Concurrent estates.

a. Joint tenancy: estates acquired by two or more persons.

(1) Every joint tenancy requires the four unities of:

(A) Time: All tenants take their interests in the premises at the same instant of time.

(B) Title: All tenants take their interests from the same source (the same deed or the same will).

(C) Interest: Every tenant has the same identical interest in the property as every other tenant.

(D) Possession: Every joint tenant owns the undivided whole of the property. He does not own a fractional interest; he is part and parcel of the group which owns the whole. (E.g., A conveys "to B and C absolutely in joint tenancy.")

(2) At common law when the type of tenancy was unclear, a finding of the existence of a joint tenancy was preferred over the finding of a tenancy in common (see below, I.B.3.c.). Today, by statute, a tenancy in common is preferred over a joint tenancy.

(3) Survivorship: Upon the death of one joint tenant, the survivor or survivors own the whole of the property and nothing passes to the heirs of the decedent.

(A) A severance of the joint tenancy can only be made by *inter vivos* conveyance, never by will, because survivorship is prior to and defeats the effect of the will.

(B) If all the tenants except one die without having severed their interests, the lone survivor owns the whole property.

b. Tenancy by the entirety: joint tenancy held by a husband and wife.

(1) Neither spouse can dispose of any interest in the estate by the entireties; both must join in the conveyance, nor can

they destroy the tenancy without mutual consent.

(A) A creditor of one spouse cannot levy upon the estate owned by the entirety, nor is a judgment against one spouse a lien against the estate held by entirety.

(2) Divorce eliminates the unity of person and destroys the tenancy by entirety. The divorced persons become tenants in common of the property.

c. Tenancy in common:

(1) Owned concurrently by two or more persons.

(2) Each person owns an undivided interest in the whole.

(A) Each tenant can dispose of his undivided fractional part by deed or by will.

(B) No right of survivorship; upon death the interest descends to heirs.

(C) May be destroyed by merger, when the entire title vests in one person. (E.g., X, a tenant in common with Y, purchases Y's undivided interest.)

d. Community property: In several states, property owned by each spouse before marriage remains his or her separate property; however, property acquired during the marriage, excepting that which is acquired by gift, descent, or devise, as the separate property of one, becomes joint property of the husband and wife.

e. Tenancy by severalty: an estate which a person owns by himself.

C. Intangible rights relating to land.

1. Profit *a prendre*.

a. Definition: right to go upon the land of another and take part of the soil or produce (e.g., wood, minerals, game).

b. Creation:

(1) Express or implied grant.

(2) Express reservation.

(3) Prescription.

2. Easement.

a. Definition: right to use the land of another or to have the land of another used in a particular way.

b. Classification by type:

(1) In gross: a mere personal right to use the land of another,

existing for the convenience of, and not in connection with any land owned by, the holder of the easement. (E.g., X sells all his land to Y, reserving the right to hunt upon it.)

(2) Appurtenant: exists in conjunction with the land of the holder of the easement; it is held by virtue of ownership of an estate in land.

(A) Servient land: land subject to the easement.

(B) Dominant land: land served by the easement. (E.g., X sells part of his land to Y giving Y a right to hunt on all the land. Y has an appurtenant easement; the dominant estate is Y, the servient estate X.)

(3) An easement appurtenant is preferred over an easement in gross; hence, if there is doubt as to whether an easement is appurtenant or in gross, it is construed as an easement appurtenant.

c. Classification by use:

(1) Affirmative: entitles the easement owner to do affirmative acts on the land in the possession of another.

(2) Negative: takes from the owner of the servient tenement the right to do some things on his land which he would have a right to do were it not for the easement.

d. Creation by:

(1) Grant or reservation. (E.g., A conveys to B one-half of Blackacre, granting a right of way on A's remaining land, while reserving to this remaining land a right of way on B's land.)

(2) Natural right: A landowner has the natural right to have his land supported by the adjoining landowner's land. (E.g., A may not excavate on his land at a point so close to B's land as to cause a cave-in upon B's property.)

(3) Necessity. (E.g., A purchases land in the middle of a large tract with no right of way included in the deed; a right of way will be implied in this situation because of the necessity of entrance and exit.)

(4) Prescription: arises when land is used for the period of the statute of limitations (which limits the owner's right to take action against the user after a specific period of time) if the use is:

(A) Wrongful.

(B) Open and notorious.

(C) Continuous and without interruption. An easement

by prescription may be prevented by active opposition by the landowner.

(5) Custom: public use of land, meeting the requirements for an easement by prescription leading to the acquisition of a public easement by the general public.

e. Extinguishment, expiration, and regulation.

(1) Extinguishment:

(A) Release of rights by the holder of the easement.

(B) Abandonment (express) amounting to more than mere non-use.

(C) Adverse obstruction of the easement by the owner of the servient land for a period longer than the statutory period—see p. 385, I.C.2.d.(4).

(D) Union of dominant and servient estates (merger).

(2) Expiration:

(A) Of time; determined at the time of its creation.

(B) By operation of statutes in some states.

(3) Regulation: Servient tenant can enjoin the dominant tenant's excessive use of the easement.

3. License: permits one person to come onto land in the possession of another without being a trespasser (e.g., a movie ticket).

a. Arises from consent given by the one in possession of land; consent being given, no prescriptive right can arise through a license.

b. Distinguished from a lease in that a licensee can never have possession of land, whereas a leasee always has possession.

c. Distinguished from an easement in that an easement is a substantial interest in land of another, whereas a license is not an interest in land and requires no formalities for its creation.

II. CONVEYANCE OF TITLE TO REAL PROPERTY

A. Marketable title.

1. Title free from:

a. Encumbrances.

b. Encroachments.

c. Restrictions.

d. Doubt as to validity.

2. It is not a perfect title, because subordinate rights as to temporary use and possession may be legally in existence, but it is one

for which a court of equity would grant specific performance of the contract of sale and compel the vendee to accept.

B. Conveyance of title.

1. Contract for sale of real property:
   a. Usually entered into before a deed is given in exchange for payment.
   b. Generally must be in writing and signed by the party to be charged in order to fulfill the requirements of the statute of frauds (see Contracts, p. 44, III.E.).
   c. Contains an implied covenant that title will be marketable, unless otherwise stated.
   d. Seller's remedies for breach of contract by the buyer.
      (1) May retain any part payment made by the buyer.
      (2) May take action for damages for breach of contract.
      (3) May take action at law for recovery of the balance of the purchase price.
   e. Buyer's remedies for breach of contract by the seller:
      (1) Rescission and recovery of any part payment made to the seller.
      (2) Action for damages for breach of contract.
      (3) Foreclosure of the buyer's lien, equal to the amount of any part payment made by the buyer.
      (4) Suit for specific performance.
2. Search of title:
   a. Abstract of title: a condensed history of the title of the land containing a summary of conveyance, mortgages, liens, and liabilities affecting the land.
   b. Title insurance: insurance against loss or damage caused by unknown defects, or failure of title to a particular parcel of realty.
      (1) A guaranty of title given by a title insurance company undertakes to make good any and all loss resulting from a defect or failure of the title, whereas title insurance contains a fixed maximum limit on liability.
      (2) A certificate of title furnished by a title insurance company is merely the company's opinion on the status of title, and the company is liable only for want of care or skill on the part of its examiner.
3. Closing of title: The purchaser makes payment and executes

such instruments as are required in contract of sale, and the seller delivers a valid deed duly executed.

a. Escrow: grantor delivers the deed to a third person (escrow agent) to be held by him until performance of a condition.

4. Parts of a deed:

a. Premises clause: includes the date, names of grantor and grantee, any recitals that may be employed to explain the purpose of the conveyance, and a statement of consideration.

b. Granting clause: includes the words of conveyance, and frequently the limitation of the estate, and the description of the land conveyed.

c. Habendum or "to have" clause: sets forth the estate transferred. Tenendum or "to hold" clause is joined with the habendum clause, forming the "to have and to hold" clause.

d. Reddendum: contains any reservations or conditions attached.

e. Covenants: contains the warranties of the grantor as to the title.

f. Conclusion: contains the signature, seal, and attestation (signature of witnesses).

(1) In many states today there is a simple statutory short form of deed.

5. Kinds of deeds:

a. Full covenant and warranty. Grantor warrants that:

(1) He owns property and has right to convey it.

(2) Purchaser will be protected against an eviction by the grantor or a person asserting a paramount right.

(3) Premises are free from encumbrances, except those specified.

(4) He will execute and procure any further documents or assurances necessary to perfect the title.

(5) He will defend grantee's title against adverse claimants.

b Bargain and sale: conveyance of title without the above warranties; however, the grantor does warrant that he has done nothing during his term of ownership that would impair title.

c. Quitclaim: seller does not purport to convey title, but rather releases any claim he has to the property.

6 Execution of deed; it must be:

a. Signed by the grantor.

(1) In many states the deed must also be sealed; this is the common law rule.

(2) An agent may sign for the grantor where the agency was created in writing and signed by the grantor.

(3) Printed signatures are usually allowable but unwise in that they might be attacked on the grounds of non-execution.

b. Witnessed or acknowledged.

(1) Attestation: the signing by witnesses who attest to the grantor's execution of the deed.

(2) Acknowledgement: the act of the grantor acknowledging his signature before a notary or other public official.

(3) States require either (1) or (2) or both.

c. Actually delivered: final and actual passing of possession of a deed in such a manner that it cannot be recalled.

(1) Where there is a recitation of consideration within the deed it is immaterial if this payment is actually made; delivery itself passes title.

(2) Failure to attach Federal Revenue Stamps (transfer tax) to a deed would not invalidate it.

(3) May be delivered to anyone, including an infant.

7. Recording:

a. A deed when delivered is effective between immediate parties without recording.

b. Statutes providing for recording of deeds:

(1) Recording protects the holder of a recorded deed against third parties acquiring another deed to the same land which would take precedence over his; the second buyer is charged with notice of A's recordation.

(2) Unrecorded deeds are not good against innocent purchasers in that no notice has been given. One cannot qualify as an innocent purchaser if a stranger is openly occupying the land.

8. Reformation: Where there is a misspelling in the deed or an obvious mistake made in the deed, the court will reform it upon petition of the holder.

III. OTHER METHODS OF ACQUISITION OF TITLE TO REAL PROPERTY

A. Adverse possession: Occupancy must be:

1. Hostile to the owner and under some claim of right.
2. Actual.

3. Open and notorious.
4. Exclusive.
5. Continuous for the prescribed period (e.g., fifteen years).
   a. Whether each of these elements exists is primarily a question of fact.
   b. Unless required by statute, good faith on the part of the adverse possessor is immaterial. He may mature his title with no rightful claim at all if the above elements exist.
   c. The possessor cannot acquire a larger estate in the land than that which he has claimed throughout the entire period of adverse possession.
   d. The recording statutes have no application to title obtained by adverse possession.
   e. One who holds by adverse possession may validly convey the property by deed to another.

B. Eminent domain: the right of the state and its subdivisions to take private property for public use upon just compensation.

1. Taking must be for the public good or safety.
2. Taking may be temporary or permanent in nature.

C. Inheritance: See Wills and Trusts, p. 413, I.H.

D. Marriage:

1. Under common law:
   a. Dower: life interest of the wife in one-third of the lands of which the husband was seised in fee at any time during the coverture (marriage to the husband).
   b. Curtesy: Upon his wife's death a husband is entitled, for the term of his natural life, to his wife's freehold estates (consisting of the lands or tenements of which she was seised in possession in fee simple or in tail—see p. 381, I.B.1.a.—during coverture), provided they have had lawful issue born alive which might have been capable of inheriting the estate.
2. Under legislation in most states (see Wills and Trusts, p. 413, I.I.).

IV. LANDLORD AND TENANT

A. Characteristics

1. Definition: the relationship which arises from a contract for the possession and control of real property, usually for a fixed duration of time.
   a. Landlord retains a reversionary interest.

b. Contract is called a lease.
   (1) Landlord is the lessor.
   (2) Tenant is the lessee.
c. Consideration for the contract is called rent.

2. Elements of the landlord-tenant relationship.
   a. Contract: express or implied, which fulfills the following requirements:
      (1) Parties capable of making a contract (capacity).
      (2) Consideration. When consideration is not specified, the law will imply an obligation to pay a reasonable value for use and occupation.
      (3) Mutual consent.
      (4) Valid subject matter.
      (5) Writing: when the statute of frauds so requires (e.g., when the duration of the lease is greater than one year—see Contracts, p. 44, III.E.). However, where there is actual possession and partial payment the contract will be enforceable even without a writing.
   b. Exclusive possession by the tenant: The tenant has the right to exclusive possession and may maintain an action in ejectment to recover possession. He is distinguished from a mere licensee (persons who have permission to use land, but do not have the right of exclusive possession, e.g., the owner of a coin-operated washing machine installed in the basement of an apartment building would be a licensee and not a tenant).
   c. Tenant's right are subordinate to the landlord's title.
   d. Reversion in the landlord (i.e., land or space reverts to the landlord at the termination of the lease).

3. Types of tenancies:
   a. Tenancy for a definite period of time, including tenancy for years; usually created by a lease.
   b. Tenancy from period to period: one which will continue for successive periods of a year or successive periods of a fraction of a year unless it is terminated and which is typically created by an express agreement.
   c. Tenancy at will: one which can be terminated at will by either party, usually on thirty days' notice.
   d. Tenancy by sufferance:
      (1) Exists when a tenant comes into possession rightfully, but holds over wrongfully.
      (2) Tenant can usually be evicted as a trespasser upon the landlord's giving due notice.
      (3) Landlord may instead elect to treat the tenant as having renewed the lease in accordance with the prior terms.
   e. Statutory tenancies: Emergency rent laws prevent the landlord from removing the tenant so long as he pays a reasonable rent.

B. Leases, rights, duties, and liabilities

1. Landlord impliedly covenants (compare with a deed where no covenants will be implied):
   a. To give the tenant the legal right to possession.
   b. To give the tenant the right to quiet possession.
   c. That the tenant will not be evicted.
      (1) This covenant is only breached when there has been an eviction.
      (2) Eviction may be either actual or constructive.
         (A) Actual: an actual physical ouster of the tenant from all or part of the premises granted.
         (B) Constructive: an injurious interference with the tenant's beneficial use and enjoyment of the premises (e.g., failure to supply heat during the winter); tenant may elect to treat this as an eviction and surrender possession.
2. Major provisions of the lease.
   a. Term or duration of the lease.
   b. Rent: payable in advance only when so specified in the lease.
   c. Description of the premises.
   d. Use of the premises.
   e. Fitness for use. The tenant should require that the landlord covenant that the premises will be fit for a particular purpose, or the landlord will be under no obligation, unless he has made fraudulent statements concerning this matter.
   f. Repairs. The common law duty to make repairs is on the tenant, except when:
      (1) Landlord assumes the duty by lease.
      (2) Duty is imposed on the landlord by state statute.
      (3) Landlord has exclusive possession of portions of the premises used in common (e.g., stairways).
      (4) Repairs are of a structural nature.
   g. Destruction or substantial injury to the premises. In most states tenants may surrender possession without further obligation to pay rent, unless:
      a. Damage or destruction is due to the tenant's fault, or
      b. The lease provides otherwise.
   h. Removal of fixtures and improvements made by the lessee. There can be removal if terms are personality, but not if they are realty (see Property, p. 380, I.A.3.).
   i. Insurance and taxes. In absence of any provision in the lease, the tenant is under no duty to insure premises or to pay taxes.
   j. Condemnation of leased premises. In absence of a provision in the lease, the amount taken under eminent domain must be apportioned between the landlord and tenant.
   k. Assignment or subletting.

(1) Definitions:

(A) Assignment is the transfer by the lessee of his entire interest without reserving *any* reversion therein in himself. Assignor will remain liable on the express terms of the lease despite the assignment. (E.g., if the assignee defaults in payment of the rent, the assignor will nevertheless be liable.)

(B) Subletting is the transfer of only part of the sublessor's interest, leaving a reversion in him as to the premises sublet. (E.g., L leases an apartment to T for one year and a day; T immediately sublets the apartment to S, but only for one year. L is a lessor, T is a tenant and sublessor, and S is a sublessee.)

(i) A new landlord-tenant relationship is created between the sublessor and his sublessee, and the sublessee will not be liable to the original lessor on any of the covenants contained in the original lease.

(ii) Sublessor will remain liable to the lessor for performance of all the terms of his original lease.

(2) Most leases contain a clause prohibiting assignments and subletting unless the landlord gives his consent in writing.

(A) A provision in a lease prohibiting either one of these does not thereby prohibit the other.

(B) Consent (in writing) by the landlord to one assignment is deemed to be a consent to all subsequent assignments, but the rule as to subletting is otherwise.

(C) There exists a division of authority on whether or not the landlord may arbitrarily withhold his consent.

l. Compliance by the tenant with laws and ordinances.

(1) Most leases require this compliance.

(2) Generally, this provision in a lease does not extend to the making of substantial improvements or building changes.

m. Quiet enjoyment.

(1) Landlord implicitly covenants that:

(A) He has paramount title to let the premises, and

(B) Neither he, nor any person claiming a paramount title, nor any condition subject to his control, shall disturb the tenant's right to absolute possession of premises.

(2) An express covenant of quiet enjoyment by the landlord, and its limitations, will override this implied covenant.

3. Liability to third parties.

a. Tenant is liable to third parties for injuries due to dangerous conditions where he has exclusive possession of the premises.

b. Tenant is not liable for injuries caused on the premises not under his exclusive possession.

c. Landlord is liable when he leases the premises with a nuisance on them and injury results therefrom.

(1) Tenant is also liable in such case if he discovers the nuisance and fails to report it.

(2) Lease can contain a provision that the tenant will hold the landlord harmless. Thus, the tenant must pay the landlord if the latter has to pay an injured party in cases where both the landlord and tenant are liable.

4. Alterations of the lease (see Contracts, p. 59, VII.C.4.).

C. Termination of the tenancy

1. Expiration of the lease.
   a. If the tenant "holds over" the landlord may:
      (1) Treat the tenant as a trespasser.
      (2) Sue him for damages and remove him by legal proceedings, or
      (3) Treat him as obligated for additional rent, according to the terms of the prior lease, for the period of the holdover.
      (4) Neither a. nor b. above applies when the tenant "holds over" because of sickness or when emergency rent laws provide otherwise.
2. Forfeiture of the tenant's right to possession of the premises.
   a. May result from:
      (1) Nonpayment of rent.
      (2) Using the premises for an unauthorized purpose.
      (3) Unauthorized assignment or subletting.
   b. Remedies for nonpayment of rent:
      (1) Suit for rent.
      (2) Summary proceedings to dispossess the tenant.
      (3) In some states both can be done in one proceeding.
3. Eviction: breach of landlord's covenant of quiet enjoyment.
   a. Actual eviction: ousting a tenant from possession of all or part of the premises by some direct act of the landlord.
   b. Constructive eviction: The tenant is forced to quit the premises not by some direct act of the landlord, but because of an act or condition under the landlord's control which he permits to exist.
      (1) Conditions not under the landlord's control cannot constitute constructive eviction.
      (2) Tenant must quit the premises promptly if he is to claim a constructive eviction.
   c. Eviction by paramount title: The tenant is ousted by someone who has title superior to the landlord's.
   d. There is no breach of the covenant of quiet enjoyment when the eviction is by government exercise of eminent domain (see Property, p. 390, III.B.).
4. Surrender:
   a. Tenant yields the remainder of his term to the landlord, and

b. Landlord accepts and repossesses the premises. If the landlord does not "accept" the tenant's surrender, the tenant remains liable for damages.

5. Destruction or substantial injury to the premises (see p. 392, IV.B.2.9.).
6. Termination by operation of law.
   a. Tenant:
      (1) Death of the tenant does not terminate a tenancy for years, unless the lease so provides.
      (2) Bankruptcy of the tenant terminates the lease.
   b. Landlord:
      (1) Death of the landlord has no effect on tenancy for years or at will.
      (2) Bankruptcy of the landlord has no effect on tenancy.

V. REAL ESTATE MORTGAGES

A. Definition: any conveyance or transfer of land intended by the parties, at the time of making, to be solely as security for the payment of money or the doing of some prescribed act.

1. Under common law ("title theory") the transfer, while giving no right of possession to the mortgagee, did transfer title and create an estate.
2. In most states ("lien theory") the transfer creates a mere lien and title remains with the mortgagor.

B. Purchase money mortgage: a special type of real estate mortgage given concurrently with a sale of land by the vendee (buyer) to the vendor (seller) to secure the unpaid balance of the purchase price; it creates a non-possessory lien which attaches against the land purchased.

C. A real estate mortgage differs from:

1. A chattel mortgage in that a chattel mortgage has as the subject matter of the lien personal property.
2. A trust deed on real estate, which is a mortgage on property executed by the mortgagor to a third person who acts for the benefit of several mortgagees. A "trustee" is usually used only where there are multiple mortgagees or creditors of the same mortgagor. It is a species of mortgage, but should be distinguished from the usual mortgage relationship between a debtor and a single creditor.
3. A conditional sale, which is a *sale* of personal property (typically the sale of consumer goods), wherein the transfer of title is made to depend upon the performance of a condition, usually the payment of the price.

D. Elements of a mortgage.

1. Parties:
   a. Mortgagor: the one executing the mortgage to secure his obligation (the debtor).
   b. Mortgagee: the one to whom the mortgage is executed and delivered to secure the obligation due him (the lender).
2. The property: any transferable interest in land may be mortgaged.
3. The obligation secured: any obligation capable of reduction to a monetary equivalent may be secured by a mortgage.
4. Personal liability of the mortgagor:
   a. The mortgagor personally assumes the mortgage debt either by promising to pay, as a part of the provisions of the mortgage agreement, or by executing a collateral promise, called a bond.
   b. Where there is a mortgage on the property and a promise within the mortgage or a bond is executed:
      (1) The real property is the primary security for the mortgage debt.
      (2) However, the mortgagor is personally liable either on his promise in the mortgage or via the bond, and if there is a deficit after the sale of the land, the mortgagor is liable for the difference.
         (A) In some states a mortgagor has the right to have property appraised and have the appraised figure, instead of the price realized on the foreclosure sale, taken as the value of the property in determining the amount of the deficiency.

E. Contents of a mortgage. A mortgage usually contains at least the following items:

1. Names of the parties (mortgagor and mortgagee).
2. The principal amount of indebtedness secured, the due date, and the rate of interest payable thereon.
3. A complete description of the property mortgaged.
4. The mortgagor usually covenants that:
   a. He will pay the indebtedness.
   b. He will insure the property for the mutual benefit of the mortgagor and mortgagee.
   c. He will not remove, demolish, or otherwise destroy the buildings without the mortgagee's consent.
   d. The entire indebtedness will become payable forthwith upon default for a certain period of time (the acceleration clause).

e. The mortgagee shall not be required to accept prepayment of the mortgage obligation unless there is a prepayment clause or the mortgagee so desires.

f. The mortgagee may appoint a receiver to collect rent in the event of default and foreclosure proceedings.

5. The possession of the property mortgaged shall remain or vest in the mortgagor.

F. Formalities in the execution of mortgages.

1. A mortgage is considered "an interest in real property" within the meaning of the Statute of Frauds and therefore must be in writing and signed by the mortgagor (see p. 44, III.E.).
2. Generally speaking, a mortgage must conform to the same formalities as are necessary for the execution of a deed (see Property, p. 388, II.B.6.).

G. Rights of the mortgagor and mortgagee.

1. The mortgagor:
   a. Retains possession of the land.
   b. In a majority of states retains legal title to the land mortgaged (lien theory, see p. 395, II.A.2.).
   c. May lease the land, and is entitled to the rents and profits thereon.
   d. Has an equity of redemption, which is defined as the right of the mortgagor to redeem the property after it has been forfeited at law (by breach of the condition of the mortgage), upon paying the amount of debt, interest, and costs.
      (1) It cannot be waived or bargained away at the inception of the mortgage.
      (2) It exists until cut off by foreclosure.
      (3) It rests upon equity principles.
   e. Has a *right* of redemption after the foreclosure sale.
      (1) Commences when the equity of redemption ends.
      (2) It is strictly statutory and varies from state to state.
2. Mortgagee:
   a. Usually has a lien on the land; however, under the title theory (see p. 395, II.A.1.), the mortgagee gets title subject to defeasance. (I.e., a title is actually conveyed to the mortgagee which is defeated or extinguished upon payment of the debt due.)
   b. May assign the mortgage to a third party who succeeds to the rights of the mortgagee.

c. Obtains a lien against the land which is superior to subsequent purchasers, lessors, or mortgagors of the land, unless there is a failure to record the mortgage and a sale to an innocent purchaser by the mortgagor. However, foreclosure of the lien will cut off all subsequently created interests.

d. Should record the mortgage so that all persons who subsequently acquire an interest in the mortgaged property will take subject to it.

e. Can foreclose his mortgage upon default in payment of the debt due.

(1) Suit to foreclose is brought in a court of equity.

(2) Successful foreclosure results in a judgment which directs that the property be sold at a foreclosure sale.

(3) Surplus, after expenses, goes to the mortgagor; similarly, mortgagor is liable for any resulting deficit—see p. 396, II. D.4.b.(2).

f. Priorities among mortgagees:

(1) If there are mortgages on the same property, properly executed and duly recorded, the first in time will have priority over subsequent ones.

(2) Upon foreclosure the first mortgage, in order of priority, will be fully satisfied before any payment is allocated to subsequent mortgages.

(3) The doctrine of marshaling of assets may help the second mortgagee obtain a share. (I.e., if the first mortgagor holds a mortgage on property other than that to which the second mortgagee's lien attaches, the second mortgagee may compel the first mortgagee to first foreclose the other property available as security.)

H. Sale of the mortgaged property.

1. The grantee (buyer) may take the land subject to the mortgage or may personally assume the mortgage, depending upon his bargain with the mortgagor-grantor.

a. Grantee taking subject to the mortgage (non-assuming grantee) or a grantee who takes in ignorance of a duly recorded mortgage:

(1) Grantee is not personally liable for the mortgage debt.

(2) Mortgaged property is a "surety" for the mortgage debt; i.e., it may be foreclosed and sold to satisfy the debt.

(3) If the property does not satisfy the debt upon foreclosure, the grantee is not personally liable; however, the original mortgagor will be liable on his promise to pay the debt.

b. Grantee who assumes the mortgage (assuming grantee) is personally liable, as the principal debtor, for the mortgage debt and the mortgagor-grantor is the surety for the mortgage debt; i.e., mortgagee may hold either the grantee or grantor for the full amount of the mortgage debt, but the grantee will be liable to the grantor if he pays, since the grantee has assumed the debt.

c. Suretyship rules control the mortgagor's release upon the grantee's securing a change in the mortgage terms, e.g., an extension of time—see Suretyship, p. 338, II.A.12.b.(2).

I. **Defenses to the mortgage obligation:** to the extent that the secured obligation is invalid, or subject to a defense, so also is the mortgage securing it (e.g., usurious interest rates, gambling debts).

J. **Termination of the mortgage lien.**

1. Merger occurs when the mortgagor and the mortgagee are in effect one and the same and therefore the mortgage interest is merged into the greater estate.
2. Payment: Upon due payment of the debt the mortgagor is entitled to a satisfaction piece or surrender of the bond or note and the mortgage.
3. Tender: If the mortgagor, on or after maturity of the debt, tenders the amount due and the mortgagee refuses the tender, the mortgage will be terminated, i.e., the lien ends, but the debt is not extinguished.
4. By operation of the statute of limitations: If there are no payments made after maturity for the prescribed period as set forth in the state statutes, then the mortgage lien and debt will be unenforceable where the statute is pleaded as a defense.

VI. PERSONAL PROPERTY: CHARACTERISTICS

A. **Definition:** everything that is the subject of ownership not coming under the denomination of real property (see Property p. 380 I.A.2.).

1. Personal property is divisible into:

   a. Corporeal personal property (choses in possession)—property of a personal, tangible, and movable nature (e.g., cattle, tools, furniture).

   b. Incorporeal personal property (choses in action)—intangible personal rights not reduced to possession, but recoverable by a suit at law (e.g., accounts receivable, tort claims, patents, copyrights).

B. Acquisition of property. Title to personal property may be acquired by:

1. Finding lost property. Finder acquires a title which is good against everyone but the true owner.
   a. Reasonable effort must be made to locate owner, though no expense need be incurred in so doing.
   b. Owner may reclaim his property from anyone, including innocent purchasers for value, unless statutory time limit has expired.
   c. Finder does not have to assume possession of the lost property, but if he does take possession, he becomes a bailee for the owner, although his responsibility is limited to exercising slight care for the property.
2. Acquisition of unowned property. Intentional exercise of exclusive domain over an unowned object of personal property creates a property right in the object by appropriation (e.g., capture of wild animals or catching of fish).
3. Creation of products by personal labor, physical or mental (e.g., manufacture, artistic productions).
4. Accession—owner's right to additions to his property brought about naturally or artificially, e.g., natural increase in herd of animals. (Automobile sold on conditional sales contract gives seller title which will embrace additions that the buyer adds if they may not be readily removed without damage.)
5. Confusion (merger, blending, or intermingling)—goods of a similar character belonging to two persons are so mingled that separation of the precise goods is impossible. The title of neither party is lost and the law recognizes a tenancy in common (in unequal shares if such be the facts) in the commingled whole, and either party may sue for severance.
   a. If in a severance case, the plaintiff fraudulently, knowingly, and wrongfully caused the mingling, he will be held to have forfeited his title. This rule (forfeiture) does not apply if the plaintiff was merely negligent.
6. Gift: a voluntary transfer of personal property without consideration.
   a. Gift *inter vivos*: a gift between two living people; irrevocable where there is:
      (1) Competency of parties.
      (2) Voluntary transaction.
      (3) Transfer of possession—there must be delivery and acceptance.
         (A) A delivery may be actual (e.g., manual delivery of

ring) or constructive (e.g., delivery of bill of sale, savings bankbook).

(4) Intent to pass title.

b. Gift *causa mortis*: gift in contemplation and fear of approaching death where elements of a gift *inter vivos* are present (see above, VI.), and

(1) There is contemplation of impending death by donor, and

(2) Donor died shortly after making the gift before recovering from illness which induced him to contemplate death, and

(3) Donor has not revoked the gift prior to his death, and

(4) Donee has not died before donor.

(A) If death does not occur, the condition of the gift fails and the donor recovers the gift.

7. By inheritance.

REAL PROPERTY: SUBJECTIVE QUESTIONS*

DEFINITIONS

Q. Rollo owned certain land which he developed into a successful and valuable cranberry farm. The farm included an elaborate water and sprinkling system. Needing additional capital, Rollo borrowed $25,000 from the Mortgage Savings and Loan Bank. He executed a note for the $25,000 secured by a real estate mortgage on the farm. This mortgage was recorded the next day. After describing the land, the mortgage provided:

> Together with all and singular tenements, hereditaments thereunto belonging or in anywise appertaining and any and all fixtures upon said premises at the time of execution or at any time during the term of this mortgage.

Subsequently Rollo borrowed $5,000 from the Cranberry Credit Association, giving a note for $5,000 secured by certain chattel mortgages covering the watering and sprinkling system. Rollo defaulted on the debt owed to Mortgage Savings and Loan and they foreclosed the real estate mortgage. The Cranberry Credit Association intervened and claimed a lien superior to that of the Mortgage Savings and Loan Bank insofar as the water and sprinkling system was concerned. The property in dispute, i.e., the water and sprinkling system, included pipe lines consisting of trunk lines and lateral pipe lines, sprinkler heads, pumps, motors, frames, power poles, wiring, and transformers. The above property constituted an integrated system

* See Introductory Note, p. 19.

installed with the intent of making a permanent improvement, actually annexed to the realty, and designed and constructed to make the particular land a commercial cranberry farm.

(1) Define the term *fixture* as used in real property.

(2) List *and* explain the rules or tests followed in deciding whether personal property attached to land has become real property.

(3) In the above situation does the Cranberry Credit Association or the Mortgage Savings and Loan Bank have the superior right to the property in dispute? Explain.

11/60; p. 380

INTERESTS IN LAND

Q. Alan transferred his farm, Greenacre, by proper deed to his son Blair for life, with remainder to Blair's son Curt. Curt was alive at the time of the transfer. The property was subject to a mortgage note having twenty years to run with 5% interest payable semiannually.

(1) State and define the kinds of estates held by Blair and Curt under this transfer.

(2) State *three* implied duties imposed upon Blair in connection with his acceptance of the deed transferring Greenacre to him.

11/63; pp. 381-382

CONVEYANCE OF TITLE

Q. On January 15, 1965, Stone and Black concluded an oral agreement concerning the sale of Stone's apple orchard to Black. Payment of the $10,000 purchase price and delivery of the deed was to take place on March 15, 1965.

(1) Assume that on February 1, 1965, Black made a $5,000 down payment which Stone accepted. On March 15, 1965, Black tendered the $5,000 balance to Stone, who refused to accept it and offered a return of the $5,000 previously paid to him. Will Black succeed in a suit for breach of contract against Stone? Explain.

(2) Assume that on February 10, 1965, Stone wrote Black a signed letter which set forth all material facts and confirmed their oral agreement. On March 15, 1965, when Black tendered to Stone the $10,000 purchase price, Stone refused to accept it and refused to deliver the deed.

- (a) Will Black succeed in a suit for breach of contract against Stone? Explain.
- (b) Assuming that Black has a cause of action against Stone, is the remedy of specific performance available? Explain.

(3) Assume that on March 15, 1965, Black paid Stone the $10,000

purchase price and received a deed to the property. On April 1, 1965, oil was discovered on the land. Stone seeks to return the $10,000 to Black and obtain a reconveyance of the land on the ground that there had been a mutual mistake of fact concerning the presence of oil on the property. Will Stone succeed? Explain.

11/65; p. 387

ACQUISITION OF TITLE

Q. Hershey, an accountant, performed professional services for Martin for several years without receiving any compensation. Hershey pressed Martin for payment. Martin explained that at the moment he was unable to pay Hershey in cash. However, as payment he offered to deed to Hershey part of his property which he had purchased in an isolated area in another state many years before. Hershey and Martin agreed that Hershey should take a trip to inspect the property before deciding whether or not Hershey would agree to Martin's offer. Expecting that Hershey would accept the property once he saw it, Martin drew and signed a deed for the property and asked Hershey to hold the deed for the property conditionally until his return. Hershey visited the property and found that Ahrens had moved on to the property several years before and that Ahrens considered it his own. Hershey also discovered that Saffer, who bought a strip of adjacent land from Martin, had for a long time regularly crossed the property to visit his land. Hershey returned home still unsure of whether or not he should accept Martin's proposition. On arrival, however, Hershey learned that Martin had died insolvent and, fearing the loss of his fee, Hershey produced the deed and announced to the executor of the estate that he considered the property his own. Martin's executor questions Hershey's title.

(1) As between Hershey and the executor of Martin's estate, who is entitled to the land? Explain.

(2) Under what theory might Ahrens claim title to the land? What facts would Ahrens have to show to claim title to the land?

(3) Under what theory or theories might Saffer claim the right to cross the land? What facts would Saffer have to prove in order to claim an interest in the land?

5/67; pp. 389-390

LANDLORD AND TENANT

Q. In your audit of the financial statements of Kirby Real Estate Company you must evaluate an account receivable for rent due on a three-year lease for office space executed one year before by John Lane. The lease provides for a rental of $200 per month and Mr. Lane posted three months' rent as security pursuant to the terms of the lease. Three months ago Mr. Lane died.

Your examination of the lease reveals that it gives the tenant the right to sublet the space but makes no provision for what is to happen if the tenant should die. Since Mr. Lane's death the Company has attempted to relet the premises and placed a "for rent" sign on the door in an attempt to lessen the damages. Mr. Lane's executor contacted the Company and indicated that he does not believe the estate is liable on the lease and stated that he intends to remove all of the decedent's furniture from the office. The executor contends:

a. In absence of a contrary provision in the lease, leases automatically terminate on the death of the tenant.
b. Kirby Real Estate Company's action in attempting to relet the premises and placing a "for rent" sign on the office door constituted an acceptance of a surrender of the lease by operation of law.
c. The most to which Kirby Real Estate Company is entitled is the amount of the security posted when the lease was signed.

(1) Discuss and evaluate each of the executor's arguments that the estate should not be responsible on the lease.

(2) Under what common law remedy would a landlord be able to assert a right to retain control over the decedent's furniture until his claim for rent is satisfied.

(3) Assume the executor is able to sublet the office to a desirable tenant who is willing to pay $250 per month rent for the remainder of the lease and informs the landlord that he intends to be bound by the lease and to sublet. Summarize the rights and duties of the executor and the subleting tenant. As a part of your answer distinguish between a sublease and an assignment of a lease.

5/69; pp. 393-395

Q. You are the accountant for the Ajax Washing Machine Company. The Company installs and operates coin-metered washing machines in the basements of apartment houses for the use and convenience of the tenants. While auditing the records of Ajax, you found the following: Ajax recently entered into an agreement with the owner of a building, under which the building owner granted Ajax permission to install and maintain a coin-metered washing machine for three years from the date of installation. Ajax retains ownership of the machine and is to keep all proceeds derived from its use, paying the owner a fixed monthly amount for the privilege of having the machine in the building. The agreement further provides that the building owner will furnish Ajax space which the owner chooses and the power required for the operation of the machine. In addition, the owner agrees that he will allow Ajax to enter the building to service the machine. Recently the building owner sold his property to a new owner, who has disconnected the machine and who refuses to comply with the agreement. He alleges that the agreement is not binding on him.

(1) List and describe the essential elements required for a lease.
(2) List and describe the essential elements required for a license.
(3) Did the agreement between the parties create a lease or a license? Explain.
(4) Must the new owner of the building honor the agreement entered into between the former owner and Ajax? Explain.
(5) If the agreement had been called a "Lease" and if Ajax had been referred to as the "Tenant" and the former owner as the "Landlord," would your answer to (4) change? Explain.

5/67; p. 391

REAL ESTATE MORTGAGES

Q. O borrowed $60,000 from M and secured it by a mortgage on a business building owned by O. If you were buying the building from O for $90,000, but paying only the $30,000 excess over and above the mortgage, would you prefer to buy it "subject to" or "assuming" the mortgage debt? Give the reasons for your answer.

11/60; pp. 398-399

Q. Jack, who owned Blackacre, obtained a $10,000 loan from a bank, giving the bank his bond (promise to pay) secured by a real property mortgage on Blackacre. The mortgage was duly recorded. Jack subsequently sold Blackacre to Roger, expressly warranting that there were no mortgages on the property. Roger was unaware of the bank's interest in the property. Jack has disappeared, and the bank has demanded payment from Roger. Roger has refused, and the bank is seeking to foreclose its mortgage.

(1) Does Roger have any personal liability on the debt? Explain.

(2) May the bank foreclose its mortgage? Explain.

(3) Will the bank's rights be superior or inferior to Roger's? Explain.

(4) If the bank had not recorded the mortgage but Roger was aware of the bank's mortgage, would the result be different? Explain.

(5) What is meant by the mortgagor's equity of redemption in connection with real property mortgages?

5/62; p. 397

Q. Arnold purchased land from Barton for $100,000, made an initial payment of $25,000 and gave Barton a mortgage for the remainder of the purchase price to be paid in monthly installments. The mortgage required that any sale of the land while it was encumbered by the mortgage must have Barton's approval.

After Arnold obtained title, Carlton offered to purchase the land and assume the mortgage. Both Arnold and Barton agreed to the terms of the purchase and title was transferred to Carlton. Subsequently Carlton was unable to make the payments to Barton.

(1) Contrast the legal significance of "assuming" a mortgage on property as compared with taking property "subject to" a mortgage.

(2) Describe the legal relationship and the rights and duties of Carlton and Arnold resulting from Carlton's assumption of the mortgage.

(3) Upon default, how can Barton assert a right to payment against Carlton when in fact Carlton never promised Barton anything?

11/68; pp. 398-399

PERSONAL PROPERTY

Q. You were requested by Charles to prepare a net worth statement for him as of December 31, 1967 which will be furnished to his bank. You must determine whether or not a truck having a fair market value of $20,000 should be included in Charles's net worth. Charles was in the trucking business as a sole proprietor during 1967. Filmore, Charles's uncle, looked upon Charles as his favorite nephew and wished to help Charles in business. Filmore decided to present Charles with a new truck which Charles needed but lacked the funds to purchase.

Filmore invited Charles to lunch and told him about the intent to make a gift of the truck to him. In fact, he told Charles he had hoped to give him the truck right after lunch, but delivery was not to be made to Filmore until the following week. To evidence his intent Filmore wrote the following on a piece of paper:

> "I hereby acknowledge my intent to make a gift of a new truck to my favorite nephew, Charles. Therefore, for good and value consideration, consisting of my love and respect for him, I irrevocably promise to deliver said truck to Charles as soon as I receive it.
>
> Daniel Filmore."

Filmore had two waiters sign the paper as witnesses and gave it to Charles.

Filmore later learned that sometime before the luncheon Charles had been complaining to other relatives that "Uncle Filmore is a tightwad and a cheapskate." Consequently, Filmore refused to turn the new truck over to Charles.

Charles asserts that a valid *inter vivos* gift was made at the luncheon or, in the alternative, that his uncle was equally bound by the promise he made.

(1) What are the requirements necessary to establish a valid *inter vivos* gift?

(2) Did Filmore make a gift to Charles at the luncheon? Explain.

(3) Did Filmore make a legally binding contract with Charles for delivery of the truck? Explain.

(4) Assuming that the truck had actually been delivered to Filmore prior to the luncheon, that he turned the keys over to Charles at the luncheon and that Charles drove the truck back to his own place of business after the luncheon, would Charles be entitled to the truck? Explain.

5/68; pp. 400-401

Q. Pierre, owner of Ritz Restaurant, Inc., had in his possession several valuable items which wealthy patrons had lost or left in the restaurant. The total value of these items was in excess of $5,000.

Ritz Restaurant's financial position was poor. Consequently, Pierre decided to pledge the items in question as collateral for a loan. He took the items to Friendly Finance Company and obtained a loan of $3,500 on the property pledged.

(1) What is the legal relationship and duty of Pierre of Ritz Restaurant, Inc. to the original owners of the property in question? Explain.

(2) As between the original owners of the property and Friendly Finance Company, who is entitled to the property? Explain.

5/68; p. 400

PROPERTY: OBJECTIVE QUESTIONS

Each of the following numbered phrases or clauses states a legal conclusion as it completes the related lettered material. You are to determine whether each of the legal conclusions is true or false according to the general principles of property law. Your grade will be determined from your total net score obtained by deducting your total of incorrect answers from your total of correct answers; an omitted answer will not be considered an incorrect answer.

(1) X now owns Blackacre. Ultimately he wants this land to belong to the Y charity.

- (a) X may presently give Blackacre to the Y charity and reserve to himself a life estate with a general power of appointment over the property.
- (b) If X makes an unrestricted outright gift of Blackacre to the Y charity, Y charity may then sell the property even if X does not approve of the sale.
- (c) In his will, X may devise Blackacre to the Y charity but provide that the property will revert to his estate if it is not used for educational purposes.
- (d) In his will, X may not effectively devise Blackacre to his wife for life if she survives him, then to the Y charity.
- (e) If Y charity is no longer in existence at the time it is to receive Blackacre, the *cypres* doctrine may be applied.

(2) If X decides to give Blackacre to the Y charity during his life, and if

the charity agrees to accept the property, X may effectively transfer title
(a) Even though he lacks capacity to contract.
(b) By delivering a quitclaim deed.
(c) By sending a letter clearly manifesting his intent to make a present gift of the property to the Y charity.
(d) And reserve to himself an easement allowing him to hunt on the property.
(e) And require the Y charity to maintain the property and pay all expenses in connection with its upkeep.

(3) If X makes a completed unrestricted gift of Blackacre to Y charity, Y charity
(a) May find its title is subject to a dower claim by X's wife.
(b) May abandon its title to the property.
(c) May be required to give up the property to the state if the state exercises its power of eminent domain for a private purpose.
(d) May sue X, the former owner of the property, for wasting the property during the time he held it.
(e) May force X, the former owner of the property, to retake the property if it is found to be unsuitable for Y charity's purposes.

5/66

(4) Ownership of personal property may be acquired by
(a) Ownership of real property.
(b) Finding lost property.
(c) Being a bailee.
(d) Purchase or barter.
(e) Accession.

(5) The following items constitute personal property:
(a) The right to income on land.
(b) A brick wall built around an undeveloped plot of land.
(c) A liquidated account.
(d) A quantity of nursery trees for planting but not as yet planted.
(e) Lumber salvaged from a wrecked building.

(6) The validity of a gift *causa mortis,* i.e., made in contemplation of impending death, depends upon
(a) The intent to pass present title to the property.
(b) The death of the donor occurring before the death of the donee.
(c) The actual or constructive delivery of the property which is the subject matter of the gift.
(d) The death of the donor from the existing cause which induced him to contemplate the gift.
(e) The gift being made in contemplation of the approaching end of one's life in the normal course of things.

(7) The owner of a brief case lost it.
(a) Losing property is the same as abandoning it.
(b) Title to the brief case remains with the owner.

(c) A finder of the brief case will acquire good title if the owner lost the case as a result of gross negligence.
(d) The person in charge of the property upon which the case was found has rights to the case superior to those of the finder.
(e) A finder of the case who takes it into his possession becomes a bailee by operation of law.

(8) Under certain circumstances personalty may be deemed to be part of real estate. Such a conversion of personal property into real property requires

(a) Actual annexation of the personalty to the realty.
(b) The consent of both landlord and tenant.
(c) That the personal property be adapted to the purpose for which the realty is used.
(d) That the person affixing the property, at the time it is affixed, intends the installation to be permanent.
(e) That personal property be of material benefit to the realty.

11/65

TOPIC FIFTEEN

WILLS AND ESTATES AND TRUSTS

CONTENTS PAGE

*WILLS AND ESTATES AND TRUSTS. This topic includes the execution and validity of a will, the administration of a decedent's estate, and the creation and administration of a trust.**

* Source: AICPA, *Information for CPA Candidates* (July 1970).

I. WILLS

A. Definition: the legal declaration of a man's wishes as to the disposition of his property, to be performed after his death; may include provisions for the guardianship of his children, or the administration of his estate.

B. Testamentary capacity.

1. To dispose of realty: All persons have testamentary capacity, except infants and those of unsound mind.
2. To dispose of personalty: All persons have the capacity except those under statutory age (e.g., eighteen years) and those of unsound mind.

C. Execution of wills: formalities:

1. Will must be signed by the testator at its physical end.
2. There must be at least two (three in some states) attesting witnesses, each of whom must sign his name as a witness at the end of the will, at the request of the testator.
3. Testator must sign in the presence of, or acknowledge his signature to, the attesting witnesses.
4. Testator, at the time of his signing or the acknowledging, must declare the instrument to be his last will and testament.
5. Nuncupative (oral) will; invalid unless:
   a. Made by a soldier or sailor while in actual military service, or a mariner while at sea, and
   b. Within the hearing of two persons (i.e., contents of statement must be proved by at least two witnesses).
6. Holographic (handwritten) will:
   a. Usually requires the same formalities as any other will; must be written entirely in the testator's handwriting.
   b. Requires no witnesses when written by a soldier or sailor on active duty or a mariner at sea.
   c. Some states provide that a nuncupative will, or a holographic will made without witnesses, will only be valid for a limited period of time after the serviceman has returned from active military duty.

D. Nature of the interest created in the beneficiary.

1. A will only becomes effective upon the death of the maker; if anything is presently transferred to a beneficiary, it is not a will.
2. A will is ambulatory, i.e., the testator has the power to alter the will during his lifetime.

3. A will is capable of passing property not owned by the maker at the time the will was made.
4. A will does not affect the rights of joint tenants to succeed to the deceased's interest in jointly-owned property which has as its principal feature the right of survivorship. Thus, real property, stocks, bonds and savings accounts held in joint tenancy pass to the survivor according to the terms of the joint ownership and not by will.

E. Revocation.

1. Requires testamentary capacity.
2. A will may be revoked:
   a. By a writing: a new will or other document executed with same formalities as the original will.
      (1) A new will does not necessarily revoke a prior will, but may do so expressly or by implication.
      (2) A document other than a will must expressly revoke the will for revocation to be effective and be executed with the same formalities.
   b. By act: torn, cancelled, or destroyed by testator with deliberate intent, or by another person in the presence of the testator and at least two witnesses and with the testator's consent. There can be no partial revocation by a physical act of the testator or another.

F. Republication and revival of revoked wills.

1. By repeating formalities necessary to execute a will.
2. By codicil: a writing executed with the same formalities as a will, which alters or confirms a will; codicils are revocable and ambulatory.
3. The will is generally considered executed as of the date of republication.

G. Legacy: a disposition of personalty under a will.

1. A *general* legacy is a gift of personal property payable out of the general assets of the testator (e.g., a gift of $1,000).
2. A *specific* legacy is a gift of personal property particularly specified (e.g., grandfather's gold watch).
3. The importance of the distinction is that:
   a. A specific legacy adeems (is extinguished) unless it exists unchanged in substance at the death of the testator. (I.e., if the specific property is destroyed prior to the testator's death, the gift would be revoked.)

b. A general legacy is not subject to ademption.

H. Inheritance: in its restricted sense, something obtained through the laws of descent and distribution from an intestate (one who died without a will). In its popular sense, it includes property obtained by devise (will) or descent.

I. Rules of intestate succession, i.e., how the property is to be disposed of if the deceased died without a will (the rules vary from state to state).

1. Surviving spouse.
   a. Common law rule: The husband is entitled to curtesy and the wife is entitled to dower (see Property, p. 390, III.D.1.).
   b. Many states have enacted statutes permitting either surviving spouse:
      (1) To receive a given portion of the estate. Even where there is a will the spouse may elect to receive what is known as a statutory share of the spouse's estate, despite the fact that the decedent has cut the survivor out of the will or specified only a nominal amount.
      (2) Size of the share depends on whether descendants or parents also survive decedent.
2. Order of distribution after spouse has received a share (prevailing law):
   a. To descendents (e.g., children, grandchildren of deceased), and if none survive:
   b. To ascendants (e.g., parents, grandparents of deceased), and if none survive:
   c. To collaterals (e.g., brothers and sisters of deceased), and their children.
   d. *Per stirpes:* a method of dividing an intestate share or a share stipulated in a will. A class or group of distributees takes the share which their deceased ancestor would have been entitled to. The representatives of the ancestor divide his share among themselves rather than taking it as individuals. For example, X, a widower, died intestate or provided in his will that his estate is to be divided among his surviving descendants in equal shares *per stirpes.* At his death, his son and two children of a deceased daughter survive him. The son gets one half and the two grandchildren divide the other half.

II. ESTATE ADMINISTRATION

A. Purposes:

1. To carry out decedent's wishes as expressed in a will.

2. To discover and collect the assets of the decedent.
3. To pay all claims and taxes against the estate.
   a. In order to pay the debts of the estate the personal representative (executor or administrator) may sell the assets of the estate.
   b. He must sell the personalty first, and if this does not meet the claims, he may, with court authorization, sell the realty.
   c. Testator can, by will, empower the executor to sell realty for any and all purposes.
   d. Generally a creditor who might have asserted a claim against the administrator or executor has no remedy against heirs, devisees, legatees, or distributees after the completion of the administration of the estate.
4. Distribute the estate to those entitled to it.

B. Executors and administrators.

1. Definitions:
   a. Executor: the person named in the will to carry out its terms.
   b. Administrator: the person appointed by the probate court to administer an estate when the decedent died intestate.
   c. Administrator with the will attached: the person appointed by the probate court to administer the estate when the decedent left a will but failed to name an executor or where the decedent named an executor but the named executor for some reason fails to qualify.
2. Distinctions:
   a. Executor.
      (1) Authority derived from the testator.
      (2) Duties defined by the will.
      (3) Must pay debts and distribute the assets of the estate as directed by the will.
      (4) May be exempted by the will from filing a bond.
      (5) Receives letters testamentary.
      (6) After appointment the executor's title to personalty relates back to the date of death of the testator.
   b. Administrator.
      (1) Authority derived from the probate court.
      (2) Duties defined by law.
      (3) Must pay debts and distribute assets as required by the intestate succession law.

(4) Required by law to file a bond.

(5) Receives letters of administration.

c. Administrator with will attached.

(1) Generally bound by the same rules that apply to an ordinary administrator; however, he will distribute the assets in accordance with the terms of the will and not according to the intestate succession laws.

(2) The will may define the executor's duties and provide for a waiver of bond even though an executor is not named.

3. Competency of a person to act as an executor or administrator

a. Generally any person competent to make a will.

b. Usual statutory exceptions:

(1) Persons indebted to the estate.

(2) Persons with interests hostile to the estate.

(3) Insolvent or bankrupt persons.

(4) Illiterate or incompetent persons.

(5) Non-resident aliens.

(6) Felons.

4. General duties of executors and administrators:

a. Required to use reasonable diligence and act in entire gooc faith in that this is a fiduciary relationship, i.e., a position o highest trust.

b. May contract on behalf of the estate, subject to probat court approval.

c. May engage necessary legal, accounting, and other services.

d. Must use reasonable care to promptly collect and preserve the assets of the estate; failure to exercise due care will impose tort liability on the negligent party. (E.g., he is liable for any shrinkage of assets due to negligence or violation of his duty.)

e. Must not commingle the estate funds with his own.

(1) Commingling is a misdemeanor in some states.

(2) He is liable for shrinkage in assets if funds have been commingled.

f. Represent the estate in suits brought against it.

g. Must keep adequate accounting records to show disposition of the assets of the estate.

h. At conclusion of his duties toward the estate, an accounting is generally rendered and a judicial settlement is secured in the probate court, thereby closing the estate. The financial accounting rendered should contain:

(1) An inventory of all assets of the estate.

(2) A statement of all debts of the estate.

(3) The disposition of the assets according to the will or according to law.

(4) Expenses, costs, and commission of the executor or administrator.

i. In all matters, in addition to those above, relating to settlement of the estate, the executor or administrator is subject to probate court control.

C. Probate: proof of the will before a suitable court and approval thereof by that tribunal.

1. Determination generally is good against the world.
2. A beneficiary may not establish his title to the property unless the will is probated, except in a few states where a devisee of land may establish the devise in another proceeding.
3. A will admitted to probate is not subject to collateral attack (an incidental proceeding, not provided by law, for the express purpose of attacking a matter that has been judicially decided) on the ground of forgery, improper execution, lack of testamentary capacity, or revocation.
4. If a subsequent will is discovered, it may be probated and carried out; but parties relying on the earlier decree (such as bona fide purchasers from the devisees) will be protected.

D. Construction proceeding: where the validity, effect, or construction of the particular provisions of the will are questioned.

III. TRUSTS

A. Private express trust.

1. Definition: a fiduciary relationship in which one person holds legal title to property subject to an equitable obligation to keep or use it for the benefit of another.
2. Elements.

   a. Settlor: one who creates a trust.

   (1) In addition to being the settlor, may also be either a trustee or beneficiary, but not both.

   (2) May revoke a trust only if the trust instrument so provides.

   (3) Must have legal capacity to make an *inter vivos* transfer of property.

b. Trustee: Generally, any person capable of taking title to property is competent. If a named trustee declines to serve by refusing to accept the trust property and the responsibility of serving as a trustee, the settlor cannot force him to do so.

(1) An infant may be a trustee; however, as contracts of an infant and conveyances by an infant are voidable, he cannot properly administer a trust. An infant trustee will normally be removed by the court, at least until he becomes of age.

(2) A mental incompetent may be a trustee, subject to the same incapacities and disabilities as if acting with reference to his own property.

(3) Trustee has the legal, but not the beneficial, interest in the trust property.

(4) Sole beneficiary cannot be the sole trustee of the trust; merger of the equitable and legal interests occurs and hence there is no trust.

c. Trust property: may consist of any interest in property which may be the subject of a present transfer.

(1) An attempt to create a trust in future property is not a present trust, but a contract to create a trust in the property when it is acquired.

(A) If there is no consideration, it is an unenforceable promise to create a trust. (E.g., if a man declares himself trustee of an express trust for his wife of profits he may earn from the stock market for the coming year, it is not a present trust. Moreover, since there is no consideration, it is unenforceable as a contract to create a trust.)

(B) If there is consideration, the property automatically becomes trust property when it is acquired by the settlor.

d. Beneficiary: has the equitable interest; it may be any ascertained or ascertainable person or group of persons, natural or artificial, including the settlor.

3. Creation: Settlor must manifest an intention either orally, in writing, or by conduct, to create a trust; however, knowledge and acceptance of the trust by the trustee or beneficiary are not required; it may be created by:

a. *Inter vivos* transfer to the trustee; if personalty is the subject of the trust there need not be a writing. This may provide for the ultimate disposition of the property in trust upon the death of the settlor without the necessity of submitting the trust instrument for probate. This is so since the property has been transferred to the trustee and no longer is a part of the settlor's estate upon death.

b. Testamentary transfer to the trustee (i.e., a trust to take effect on the death of the settlor); must comply with the requirements for a valid will (i.e., be in writing and subscribed by witnesses—see p. 411, I.C.).

c. Settlor declaring himself the trustee of property without any transfer.

4. Creation of a trust of real property must be evidenced by a writing signed by the settlor in order to satisfy the Statute of Frauds (see Contracts, p. 44, III.E.).

   a. Writing need be signed only by the donor.

   b. Must sufficiently designate the property, beneficiary, and the purpose of trust.

   c. Oral trust is valid if the trust has been fully or partly executed, or if there is a resulting trust (see p. 420, III.C.) or a constructive trust (see p. 420, III.D.).

5. No consideration is necessary for the present creation of any trust; however, a contract to create a trust in the future requires the same consideration as any other contract.

6. Restrictions.

   a. Trust must be "active," i.e., the trustee must actually have some duties to perform. (E.g., trustee has possession of property and has power to manage it.)

      (1) In most states passive trusts (i.e., trustee has no discretionary duties) have been abolished and title to the property rests in the beneficiaries.

   b. Trusts of personal property may be created for any lawful purpose. The law of the domicile of the settlor governs the validity of trusts of personal property.

   c. In some states trusts of real property are limited to a few purposes. (E.g., a trust to receive the rents and profits of real property and apply them to the use of the beneficiaries. This type of trust is known as a spendthrift trust, in that it is often used to protect improvident persons; the equitable interest of the beneficiary is inalienable. The law of the situs of the realty governs the validity of trusts of realty.)

   d. Duration is limited by the rule against perpetuities. The rule states that a trust cannot have a greater duration than lives in being plus twenty-one years. This rule exists because, when a trust is created, the absolute power of alienation of the property held in trust is suspended. The law wishes to prevent the tying up of title to property for an unreasonable length of time; it prefers to measure the period it will allow this suspension to continue in terms of human lives rather than fixed years. (E.g., a trust for one hundred years with X as trustee for the benefit of Y would fail.)

e. Trust cannot be used for a purpose which is illegal, fraudulent, or contrary to public policy (e.g., if the purpose of the trust is to force the beneficiary to adopt another religion, the trust is illegal).

(1) Effect of an illegal trust:

(A) If attacked by the persons injured by the illegal trust, the court will set it aside.

(B) If the persons injured do not attack the trust, and the beneficiaries are innocent parties, the court will grant performance. (E.g., the settlor creates a trust of his assets with his children as beneficiaries, so as to defraud creditors. If the creditors do not attack the trust and the children are innocent parties, the children may enforce the trust.)

B. Charitable trust.

1. Essential differences from a private trust:

a. Trust has as its object some social benefit.

b. The duration may be unlimited, i.e., not subject to the rule against perpetuities.

c. Beneficiaries are an *indefinite and unascertainable* number of persons. (E.g., a trust to help the poor of New York City forever is valid even though the beneficiaries cannot be completely ascertained and the duration is unlimited.)

(1) Beneficiaries may be identifiable and the charitable trust may nevertheless be valid if the group is large enough to gain sufficient social advantages. (E.g., a trust to help those who suffered during a particular hurricane is a valid charitable trust even though the persons eligible are identifiable. But a trust to help John and Mary Doe is invalid as a charitable trust, in that the group is too small for sufficient social benefit.)

2. *Cy pres* ("as nearly as possible") doctrine is applicable. If the settlor manifests a particular charitable intent the court will apply the trust fund to a closely related charity when and if the designated purpose has been fulfilled or the named charity is unable to take it. (E.g., a trust to aid in the abolition of slavery was sustained after the Civil War as indicating the general purpose of helping the Negro race. The trust fund was applied to the education of free Negroes in the South.)

3. The following purposes are considered to be charitable:

a. Relief of the poor.

b. Advancement of education.

c. Advancement of religion.

d. Promotion of health.

e. Other purposes which have a sufficient social utility.

4. Honorary trusts are not generally recognized by American courts, in that they lack a proper beneficiary. (E.g., a trust to provide oats and a stable for a favorite horse is invalid, in that a horse is not a proper beneficiary.)

C. Resulting trust (an implied trust).

1. Definition: exists when one person transfers property to another and it is presumed that the transferor did not intend the transferee to have any beneficial interest in the property; a trust will result in favor of the transferor or his estate. The sole duty of the trustee is to wind up the resulting trust by returning the property to the transferor.

2. May arise in the following situations:

   a. Failure of an express trust (e.g., because the beneficiary is dead at time of the creation of the trust).

   b. Trust is fully performed without exhausting the trust property.

   c. Property is paid for by one person, but title is in another; creates a presumption of a resulting trust in favor of the party who paid the purchase price. However, there is presumption of a gift if the grantee is the wife or child of the payor.

D. Constructive trust (an implied trust).

1. Definition: a remedial device in the form of a trust created by operation of law in order to prevent unjust enrichment.

   a. Arises regardless of the intention of the parties.

   b. Otherwise, characteristics are the same as those of resulting trusts.

2. May arise when property has been acquired by:

   a. Fraud, mistake, undue influence, duress.

   b. Homicide.

   c. Breach of a fiduciary obligation.

E. Totten trust (savings bank trust).

1. Definition: Depositor deposits his own money in a bank "in trust" for another person and indicates his intent to create a trust by other acts.

   a. Mere deposit is not sufficient to show irrevocability of a totten trust.

   b. Factors which indicate that an irrevocable trust exists (none is conclusive of itself):

(1) Express statement by depositor of his intent.

(2) Notice to the beneficiary of the deposit in trust form.

(3) Delivery of the bank book to the beneficiary.

(4) Failure of depositor to withdraw balance before death.

(5) Close relationship of depositor to beneficiary.

c. Factors showing revocation of totten trust:

(1) Withdrawal of all the funds by depositor.

(2) Beneficiary predeceases depositor.

(3) Depositor's will cannot be carried out without invading the trust.

(4) Revoked to the extent necessary to pay funeral expenses or creditors of depositor.

F. Administration of trusts.

1. Duties of trustee:

a. Those imposed by terms of the trust; however, deviation from those duties may be permitted in emergencies.

b. Those imposed by law.

(1) Take possession of the trust property.

(2) Defend the trust against attack by settlor or third parties if there are reasonable grounds for such a defense.

(3) Reasonably protect trust property from loss or destruction and make the trust property productive.

(4) Must not commingle trust funds with his personal funds; if a loss occurs, trustee will be liable, even if he is acting innocently and in good faith.

c. Trustee, in absence of provision to the contrary, may:

(1) Sell trust property if necessary to carry out the trust purpose.

(2) Lease real estate even if the trust instrument prohibits its sale.

(3) Compromise claims in connection with the trust estate.

d. If more than one trustee is named for a non-charitable trust, all must agree before any action may be validly taken.

2. Liabilities of trustee:

a. In contract: as a general rule, personally liable on contracts made on behalf of the trust (unless the contract provides otherwise), but may reimburse himself from trust income.

b. In tort: personally liable for torts committed by himself or his agents, but may reimburse himself if he was not personally at fault (e.g., in cases of liability without fault).

3. Income v. corpus (principal).
   a. Proceeds received from use of the trust property are treated as income for the income beneficiary. They include the following:
      (1) Interest on notes and bonds owned by the trust.
      (2) Net rents (gross rents less cost of collection, insurance, and repairs).
      (3) Royalties from property which is subject to depletion.
   b. Ordinary expenses are chargeable to the trust income and include the following:
      (1) Cost of insurance on the trust property.
      (2) Interest on mortgage on the trust property.
      (3) Repair of the buildings on the trust property.
   c. Changes in form of the trust *res* (property) are treated as *corpus* for the remainderman and include the following:
      (1) Stock dividends in the form of the corporation's own stock. Dividends in the form of stock in another corporation are treated as income. Stock splits are, of course, corpus.
      (2) Proceeds from the sale of a stock subscription right by the trustee.
      (3) Sums received in settlement of claims arising out of damage to the corpus (e.g., insurance proceeds from the destruction of a house owned by the trust estate). However, any payment based on loss of the trust income is treated as income.
   d. Extraordinary expenses are chargeable to trust corpus and include the following:
      (1) Cost incurred in sale or purchase of trust property.
      (2) Cost of improvements made by the trustee where the improvement will last longer than the income beneficiary's interest; the value of the income beneficiary's yearly interest in the improvement is calculated by dividing the cost of the improvement by the number of years of its expected duration. This amount is reserved annually by the trustee and added to the corpus.
4. Accounting: periodic submission of accounts of trust property for court approval; it may be voluntary or by court order.
5. Settlement: Account is settled when the court approves the trustee's handling of trust property as set forth in his account.

6. Resignation of a trustee.
   a. May not resign as a matter of course; he must obtain:
      (1) Order of the court, or
      (2) Consent of all the beneficiaries, or
      (3) Discharge in accordance with the trust instrument.
   b. May resign as a matter of personal convenience if serving without compensation, or without agreement as to duration.

G. Termination.

1. Natural termination at end of the designated trust period.
   a. Death of settlor or trustee during the trust period does not ordinarily terminate the trust.
   b. Refusal of named trustee to serve will not ordinarily terminate the trust.
2. Achievement of the trust purposes before natural termination of the trust period.
   a. If the settlor and all the beneficiaries agree to a termination, it will be granted, although the trust purposes have not been accomplished.
   b. If only the beneficiaries consent to the termination without consent of the settlor, and if any of the trust purposes have not been accomplished, the termination will not be granted.
3. Merger: The legal and equitable estates are vested in the same person (e.g., the sole trustee is the sole beneficiary).
4. Failure of the trust purpose.
   a. If a private trust becomes impossible of performance or illegal, it terminates.
   b. If a charitable trust becomes impossible or illegal and the *cy pres* doctrine is not applicable, the trust terminates. (E.g., a trust to provide a home for Confederate veterans of the Civil War terminates when the last such veteran dies.)
5. Upon termination of the trust, the trustee has the duty to transfer with reasonable dispatch the trust property to those entitled to it. His legal interest is terminated when this has been accomplished.

WILLS AND ESTATES AND TRUSTS: SUBJECTIVE QUESTIONS*

WILLS

Q. You have been the CPA for Arnold Smith, who has died. Mr. Smith, a widower, left surviving his mother, age 86, and a son, Donald, age

* See Introductory Note, p. 19.

26. Arnold Smith's daughter, Rita, died one year before he did, and is survived by her husband, Bob, and two children, Alice and Marie. At the time of Mr. Smith's death, Bob was still a widower and Alice and Marie were minors. Mr. Smith's will, which was duly probated, provides, in part:

"All the property which I shall own at the time of my death or which shall be subject to disposition under my will is hereinafter referred to as my Residuary Estate.

"If any descendant of mine shall survive me, my Residuary Estate shall be divided and set apart for my descendants who shall survive me, in equal shares *per stirpes.* The shares so set apart shall be dealt with as hereinafter provided in this Article, and I bequeath and devise them accordingly.

"(1) In the case of each share set apart for a descendant of mine who shall be under age of twenty-five (25) years and who shall have been in being at the time of my death, my trustee shall hold such share as the principal of a separate trust for the primary benefit of such descendant, shall invest and reinvest such principal and shall pay the net income therefrom to such descendant. Such trust shall continue until such descendant shall attain the age of twenty-five (25) years or shall sooner die. Thereupon my trustee shall distribute the entire principal of such trust to such descendant, or if he shall not be living, shall distribute or otherwise deal with such principal as such descendant, by his last will duly admitted to probate and not otherwise shall direct (except that the power so granted to such descendant shall not be exercisable, to any extent, in favor of such descendant, his estate, his creditors or the creditors of his estate), and, to the extent, if any, that such principal shall not be disposed of effectively through the exercise by such descendant of the power granted to him, my trustee shall distribute such principal to the XYZ charity, a home for foster children.

"(2) In the case of each share set apart for any other descendant of mine, such share shall be distributed to such descendant.

"If no descendant of mine shall survive me, I bequeath and devise my Residuary Estate to the XYZ charity."

Mr. Smith's Residuary Estate equals $100,000. The executor and the attorney for the estate have asked you to assist in preparing financial reports for the estate.

(1) Under the above terms of the will, who are the beneficiaries and what is the amount and nature of each of their legacies? Explain.

(2) Assume that a beneficiary's share has been placed in trust under the terms of the will:

(a) If the trustee believes that the beneficiary is not in need of income currently, under the above terms of the will may he accumulate income for the beneficiary so that it can be paid to the beneficiary at a later time when he is in need? Explain.

(b) Describe the power which a beneficiary of a trust is given over the disposition of the principal of his trust.

(3) Assume that a beneficiary of a trust dies before attaining the age of 25 years and did not effectively exercise his power under the trust, so that XYZ charity becomes entitled to receive the principal of the trust. If at that time XYZ charity is no longer in existence, explain what would happen to the trust fund if the *cy pres* doctrine is applied.

(4) Do the trust provisions of the will possibly violate the rules against perpetuities? Explain.

11/66; pp. 413, 419, 421

Q. Wellington purchased several thousand dollars worth of corporate securities in the joint names of "Wellington and Potter or the survivor."

Later, Wellington decided that Potter should not receive the corporate securities at Wellington's death because Potter had become wealthy. Wellington, therefore, went to his attorney and executed a codicil to his Last Will and Testament naming his brother as the party to receive the securities upon his death.

Wellington is now dead.

Who is entitled to the securities in question? Explain.

5/68; p.412

PRIVATE EXPRESS TRUSTS

Q. Frugal, for whom you perform accounting services, told you that he plans to create his own *inter vivos* trust (living trust) and that he plans to name you the trustee.

Frugal showed you the following provision in a draft of the disposition he plans for the trust principal at his death.

"On my death the then principal of the trust shall be distributed to my then living descendants, in equal shares *per stirpes.*"

(1) Would such a trust instrument have to be probated as a will at Frugal's death since the trust instrument provides for disposition of the property at death? Explain.

(2) If you do not wish to serve as trustee is there any way of your avoiding the responsibility even if Frugal insists that he will name you as trustee over your objection? Explain.

(3) State the percentage of trust principal which each party would receive at Frugal's death if during his life Frugal had only two children, Rita and Selma, and was survived by

(i) John, his brother,
(ii) Susan, his sister,
(iii) Rita, his daughter,
(iv) Thomas and Mary, his grandchildren whose mother is Rita, and
(v) Albert, his grandchild (whose mother, Selma, predeceased Frugal).

5/68; pp. 413, 417, 423

TRUST ADMINISTRATION

Q. X, as trustee for the benefit of Y, the life beneficiary, received the $1,000 annual cash dividends on the stock which made up the corpus of the trust. Y was abroad at the time of receipt and X in good faith and with complete honesty deposited the money in his own (X's) bank account. Before Y returned X's bank failed and the dividend in bankruptcy will only amount to fifty cents on the dollar. Y claims that X must make up the difference. Is X liable? Explain.

11/61; p. 421

Q. Thomas has transferred his transistor manufacturing business to the X Trust Company in trust for the benefit of his son, Peter, for life, with the remainder to go to Peter's son James. The X Trust Company insured the business with the Y Insurance Company by taking out two policies. The first policy was a standard fire insurance policy covering the building, equipment, etc. The other policy was secured to cover the loss of income during any period that the business was inoperable as a result of tornado, earthquake, or fire. The buildings and equipment were subsequently destroyed by fire and the Y Insurance Company paid the proceeds to the X Trust Company. Both Peter and James claim the entire proceeds of the insurance policies. What disposition should the X Trust Company make of the entire proceeds under the terms of the trust? Explain.

11/61; p. 422

Q. (1) In December, 1958, Howard transferred 1,000 shares of Z Company stock to the X Trust Company in trust for the benefit of his wife for life with the remainder to go to his son. The Z Company declared a noncash dividend in 1960 of 10 shares of stock of the M Company for each 100 shares of Z Company stock. The M Company stock had been bought by Z Company as an investment. The son claims that this dividend should be added to the corpus (principal) whereas the wife claims that she is entitled to the dividend. How should the trust company treat the dividend? Explain.

(2) Same facts as above except that in 1960 the Z Company split up its stock 2-for-1. Subsequently, the trustee sold one-half of the 2,000 shares of the Z Company stock at a profit and the son and wife both

claim the proceeds. How should the trust company treat the stock split-up and the proceeds from the sale? Explain.

11/61; p. 422

WILLS AND ESTATES AND TRUSTS: OBJECTIVE QUESTIONS*

Each of the following numbered phrases or clauses states a legal conclusion as it completes the related lettered material. You are to determine whether each of the legal conclusions is true or false according to the general principles of wills and estates and trusts law. Your grade will be determined from your total net score obtained by deducting your total of incorrect answers from your total of correct answers; an omitted answer will not be considered an incorrect answer.

(1) The creation of an express trust consisting of real property
- (a) Must be evidenced by a writing to satisfy the Statute of Frauds.
- (b) Requires consideration to be effective.
- (c) Can be done by a minor.
- (d) Is subject to the rule against perpetuities.
- (e) Requires that the subject matter be definite and specific.

(2) The trustee of a legally effective trust
- (a) Can be anyone legally capable of dealing with property.
- (b) Must exercise a high degree of loyalty toward the creator of the trust.
- (c) Must be specifically named by the creator of the trust.
- (d) Is an insurer against loss of trust property.
- (e) Is, in effect, the agent of the beneficiary.

(3) The beneficiary of a legally effective trust
- (a) Must be specifically identified by name or by designation of the class to which he belongs.
- (b) May be a judicially declared incompetent.
- (c) May ordinarily transfer or assign his interest in the trust.
- (d) May be legally protected from having his creditors reach his interest in the trust by the donor's creation of a spendthrift trust.
- (e) Will be presumed to have accepted the trust in the absence of an express disclaimer.

(4) A charitable trust
- (a) May be created solely for philanthropic purposes.
- (b) May be created to aid individual but unascertained students.
- (c) Is not affected by the rule against perpetuities.
- (d) May have its purpose changed by application of the *cy pres* doctrine.
- (e) Must have as trustee some corporate body to assure continuity of existence.

(5) An implied trust
- (a) Is created by equity to prevent injustice.
- (b) Can take the form of a constructive or charitable trust.

(c) May be expressly created by the parties involved or may be inferred from their conduct.
(d) That takes the form of a resulting trust imposes no duties of performance upon the trustee.
(e) Is not subject to the Statute of Frauds.

(6) A spendthrift trust
(a) Is one which provides a fund for the maintenance of an improvident person.
(b) Cannot prohibit the beneficiary from selling his interest in the trust.
(c) Can prohibit the beneficiary from subjecting the distributed trust income to the claims of his creditors.
(d) Can be created by a person for his own benefit to immunize himself against the claims of his creditors.
(e) Is often prohibited as contrary to public policy in thwarting the just claims of creditors.

5/65

(7) X may effectively dispose of his interest in the following property by will:
(a) Property he owns as a joint tenant.
(b) Property he owns as a tenant by the entirety.
(c) Property he owns as a tenant in common.
(d) Insurance proceeds payable to his estate.
(e) X's life estate in real property.

(8) X may effectively
(a) Make a contract to make a particular provision in his will.
(b) Make a holographic will with his wife.
(c) Orally revoke his will.
(d) Execute a new will which does not revoke a prior will.
(e) Amend a prior will by executing an unwitnessed codicil.

(9) In his will X may not effectively
(a) Revoke his prior will if he does not have capacity to execute a new will.
(b) Revive an old will after it has been revoked.
(c) Designate a particular fund in his will from which transfer and estate taxes are to be paid.
(d) Appoint a guardian for his minor children.
(e) Establish a trust to run as long as any of his descendants are living.

(10) X may effectively condition a bequest made in his will by requiring the legatee
(a) To survive X for six months.
(b) To attend X's funeral service.
(c) To refrain from attacking X's will.
(d) To commit a crime.
(e) To be under the age of 21 at X's death.

(11) After X's death, the executor named in X's will
- (a) Must, under all circumstances, offer the will for probate.
- (b) May refuse to serve because he is too busy.
- (c) Will receive letters of administration to evidence his appointment.
- (d) Must offer X's will for probate in the state in which the will was drawn.
- (e) Will be required to post a bond if the will does not relieve him of this obligation.

(12) After X's death, his personal representative will have the implied power
- (a) To pay X's funeral expenses and debts.
- (b) To erect a suitable gravestone on his grave.
- (c) To use estate funds to continue to maintain and expand X's business.
- (d) To use estate funds to invest in a new business.
- (e) To continue to administer the estate for as long a time as the majority of beneficiaries wish him to do so.

(13) If during his lifetime X decides to establish a trust, he may
- (a) Provide that the income from the trust is to be paid to himself during his life and that on his death the principal of the trust is to be distributed to his estate.
- (b) Appoint himself as one of the trustees of the trust.
- (c) Reserve the right to revoke the trust.
- (d) Bequeath part of his estate to the trust by his will.
- (e) Provide that the income from the trust is to be paid to Y charity for 500 years.

(14) If during his life X establishes a trust, he may not authorize his trustee
- (a) To keep all trust assets invested in a particular stock.
- (b) To allocate stock dividends received to principal rather than to income.
- (c) To lend money to the trust.
- (d) To withhold income from one beneficiary and pay it to another.
- (e) To accumulate income for a minor.

(15) If X establishes a trust, the provisions of the trust will not be effective to the extent that the trust
- (a) Encourages the furtherance of an unlawful purpose.
- (b) Is established to hold insurance policies on X's life.
- (c) Violates the rule against perpetuities.
- (d) Prohibits the beneficiary from assigning his income from the trust.
- (e) Stipulates the particular state law which is to govern the trust.

5/66

TOPIC SIXTEEN

REGULATION OF THE EMPLOYER–EMPLOYEE RELATIONSHIP

CONTENTS PAGE

*REGULATION OF THE EMPLOYER–EMPLOYEE RELATIONSHIP. Questions on this topic are based upon the Fair Labor Standards Act, the Social Security Act, and typical state workmen's compensation laws. The emphasis of these questions is on the impact that these laws have on the employer–employee relationship.**

* Source: AICPA, *Information for the CPA Candidate* (July 1970).

I. THE FAIR LABOR STANDARDS ACT (ALSO KNOWN AS THE "WAGES AND HOURS LAW") INCLUDES PROVISIONS REGULATING:

A. Minimum wages and equal pay.

1. Currently (1971), the minimum wage is $1.60 per hour for employees engaged in interstate commerce or the production of goods for interstate commerce or for employees of such enterprises.
2. This figure has been changed several times by Congress in the past decade and will undoubtedly be increased again in the near future.
3. The hourly rate is not required if there is an alternative method, such as a piece-rate method of payment which satisfies the Act.
4. Discrimination in wages based upon the sex of the employee is prohibited. This applies to both employers and labor unions.

B. Maximum hours and overtime.

1. Time and one-half the regular hourly rate of pay is mandatory for hours worked in excess of 8 in a given day or 40 per work week.
2. The provisions apply only to employees engaged in interstate commerce or in production for interstate commerce.
3. The averaging of days or weeks is not permitted; each day or week is treated separately.
4. Exemptions from this part of the act are provided for as follows:
   a. Employers in industries of a seasonal nature; such employees are paid overtime at the rate of one and one-half times the regular rate for hours in excess of 10 per day or 50 per week.
   b. Employees who are guaranteed a weekly pay for variable hours and hospital employees.

C. Special exemptions from both the minimum wage and maximum hour provisions of the Act are granted to several classes of employees and employers. These include, for example:

1. Executive, administrative and professional employees.
2. Retail and service establishments.
3. Amusement and recreational establishments.
4. Forestry, fishing, and offshore seafood processing.
5. Agricultural employees.
6. Learners, apprentices, students, handicapped workers, and messengers.
7. Railroads, express companies, and water, motor and air carriers.

D. Prohibition: it is unlawful for any person to transport or sell goods in

interstate commerce with the knowledge that such goods were produced in violation of the minimum wage or maximum hour provisions of the Act.

E. The Secretary of Labor has power to compel attendance of witnesses and production of books, papers, and documents and to make investigations regarding practices subject to this Act. Court review is available for any person aggrieved by a wage order of the Secretary of Labor.

F. Sanctions: violators of the Act are subject to criminal proceedings, wage suits by employees for unpaid wages, and wage collections by the government. The Federal District courts have jurisdiction to restrain violations of the Act.

G. Child labor provisions:

1. "Oppressive child labor" is defined as:
   a. Employment of a child under 16, subject to exceptions determined by Secretary of Labor.
   b. Employment of minors between 16 and 18 years of age in occupations determined by the Secretary of Labor to be hazardous to their health or well-being.
2. The Act prohibits the employment of "oppressive child labor."
3. Child labor exemptions:
   a. Children employed in agriculture outside of school hours.
   b. Children employed as actors.
   c. Children under 16 years of age employed by their parents in a nonhazardous occupation.
   d. Children delivering newspapers to the consumer.
4. Provisions similar to those indicated in D, E, and F, above, also apply to violations of the child labor part of the Act.

II. SOCIAL SECURITY

A. Basic statute is the Federal Social Security Act. This Act covers three basic programs:

1. Social insurance.
2. Public assistance to the needy.
3. Children's services.

B. The social insurance provisions are those which bear upon the employer–employee relationship. They consist of:

1. Old-age, survivor's, and disability insurance.
2. Hospital insurance (Medicare).
3. Unemployment insurance.

C. Financing social insurance:

1. Old-age, survivor's, disability, and hospital insurance are financed

out of taxes paid by employers, employees, and the self-employed under provisions of the Federal Insurance Contributions Act and the Self-Employment Contributions Act.

2. Unemployment Insurance. Taxes paid by employers are:
   a. Taxes imposed under state unemployment insurance laws.
   b. Taxes imposed under federal unemployment insurance laws.

D. Employment taxes:

1. Rates
   a. Taxes under Federal Insurance Contributions Act are the same rate for both employer and employee.
   b. The rates are scheduled to rise to 5.2% in 1971 (4.6% for old-age, survivor's, and disability benefits and 0.6% for hospital insurance) 5.65% in 1973, 5.7% in 1976, 5.85% in 1980, and 6.05% in 1987.
   c. Only the first $7,800 of wages are taxable for 1971.
   d. If, by working for two employers during the year, an employee pays tax on more than $9,000, he is entitled to a refund or credit. The employer is not entitled to an equivalent refund since all wages paid to every employee are taxable up to $9,000.
   e. The above figures are as of June, 1971.
2. Employee tax
   a. Employer must withhold employee tax by deducting amount of tax from employee's wages as and when paid.
   b. Employer must furnish each employee with a written statement as to wages paid during calendar year.
3. Self-employment tax: a maximum of $7,800 during 1971 and $9,000 after 1971 is taxed at rate a about 1½ times that of employees' income.
4. Unemployment insurance tax
   a. Employer must pay a federal unemployment tax if he employs four or more in employment covered by the Federal Unemployment Tax Act. Only the first $4,200 (1971) in wages is taxable.
   b. Employers are entitled to a credit against federal unemployment tax for contributions paid under state unemployment compensation laws.
   c. Experience rating: employers' contribution payments under state laws may be adjusted based on the employer's employment experience. An additional credit is allowed against federal unemployment tax if the state payments are reduced.

E. What are wages?

1. Not limited to money; include other forms of compensation.
2. Do not include employee benefits (e.g., hospitalization, insurance premiums).
3. Serviceman's basic pay is subject to tax.

4. Special rules for farm workers, domestic workers, and casual workers.
5. Payments on account of sickness, medical, or hospitalization expenses are not considered wages and are not taxable for old-age, survivor's, and disability insurance.
   a. Employer's plan must make such provision for all employees.
   b. Exemption also runs to payments by an employer for insurance or into a fund.
6. Payments to an employee or a plan on account of employee's retirement is also not taxable. The same conditions apply to health benefits.
7. Bonuses and commissions paid as compensations are considered wages.
8. Travel expenses are not wages.
9. Supplemental unemployment benefit plan payments are:
   a. Considered wages if the individual employee has a beneficial interest in the fund.
   b. Not wages if no interest is established until the employee is eligible to receive benefits from the fund.
10. Vacation and dismissal allowances constitute wages.

F. Coverage.

1. To pay tax and receive benefits:
   a. One must be an "employee."
   b. Services rendered must be "employment."
   c. Compensation received must be "wages."
2. Definition of employee:
   a. This relationship exists when a person for whom services are performed has the right to control not only the result to be accomplished, but also how that result is to be accomplished (otherwise, one is an independent contractor—See Agency *supra* p. 128, I.C.4.a).
   b. Partners, self-employed persons and independent contractors are not covered by unemployment provisions. They are covered as self-employed persons for old-age, survivors, and liability insurance purposes,
   c. Officers and directors of corporations are "employees" within the meaning of the definition if they perform services and receive remuneration for them from the corporation.
3. Definition of employer:
   a. Old-age, survivors, and disability insurance provisions contain no explicit definition of employer. He or it can be an individual, corporation, partnership, trust, or other unincorporated group or entity.
   b. For Federal Unemployment Tax Act: one who employs one employee for a total of at least 20 calendar days during

a year, each such day being in a different week. State definitions may differ.

4. Definition of employment:
   a. Any service performed by an employee for a person employing him irrespective of citizenship or residence of either (only problems arise when service is outside U.S. for an employer not sufficiently connected with the U.S.).
   b. Only services not covered by the social security system are those specifically exempted.
   c. Special rules and tests as to coverage for agricultural labor, casual labor, domestic workers, and government employees.

G. Election of coverage.

1. The Federal Unemployment Tax Act makes no provision for coverage of services which are exempt from statutory coverage.
2. Old-age, survivors, and disability insurance coverage may be extended to certain classes of services otherwise excluded, e.g., state and local government employees.

H. Benefits.

1. Various kinds of benefits are payable under the social security system, depending upon the average monthly earnings and the relationship of the beneficiary to the retired, deceased, or disabled worker. The individual upon whose earnings record the benefits are based must have attained a certain "insured status" by acquiring "quarters of coverage."
2. Quarters of coverage for wages: an individual must be paid $50 or more during a quarter to be credited with a quarter of coverage. The quarters of coverage are used in determining whether the worker is fully insured.
3. Fully insured workers:
   a. When a worker has 40 quarters of coverage he is fully insured for life, regardless of b. below.
   b. To be fully insured, a worker needs one quarter of coverage for each year after 1950 (or after the year in which he attained age 21 if that was later than 1950) and before the year in which he died or the year he attained retirement age.
   c. Retirement age for full benefits is 65 for men and 62 for women.
4. An individual is insured for disability insurance benefits if he meets a statutory insured status test based upon quarters of coverage.
5. Currently insured: to be currently insured, a worker must have not less than 6 quarters of coverage during the 13-quarter period ending with the quarter in which he dies, becomes entitled to

old-age benefits, or most recently became entitled to disability benefits.

6. If a worker is both fully insured and currently insured, then the following benefits are available:
   a. Benefits for dependents of retired or disabled workers.
   b. Survivors benefits for dependents.
   c. Lump-sum death payment.
7. Benefits are subject to an earnings test such that benefits are reduced with increased earnings of the beneficiary. The maximum retirement benefit for a man retiring at age 65 is $250.70 (1971).
8. Medical care for the aged, i.e., for persons 65 and over, requires:
   a. A hospital insurance plan.
   b. A voluntary medical insurance plan.
   c. Both plans are financed from individual premium payments. The medical insurance premiums are matched dollar for dollar by government contributions.

III. WORKMEN'S COMPENSATION

A. Compulsory and elective acts. The states are split, some have:

1. A compulsory law that requires all employers within its scope to provide those benefits specified.
2. An elective system whereby the employer may accept or reject the Act; if he rejects it, he loses the three common law defenses against an employee's suit for damages: assumption of risk, negligence of fellow employees, and contributory negligence (see *infra*, p. 438, III.E.1.).

B. Scope of Workmen's Compensation legislation.

1. Every state has a workmen's compensation law. Additionally there are federal workmen's compensation laws such as the Workmen's Compensation Law of the District of Columbia and the Federal Employee's Compensation Act.
2. In no jurisdiction does the law apply to all employments. Generally those not covered include: agricultural workers, domestic workers, exceptions below a fixed number of employees, public employees, and casual workers.
3. To constitute employment, the following rights must be found to be retained by the employer:
   a. The exercise of control over the details of work.
   b. The payment of compensation—not required to be in money.
   c. The power to hire and fire.
4. Numerical exceptions: generally employers are exempt if they employ less than a certain number of people. Most Acts permit voluntary acceptance.

5. Charitable institutions generally are excluded by Compensation Acts unless the Acts are voluntarily accepted.
6. Contractors and subcontractors are generally not covered.
7. Occupational diseases: the trend is to include this danger within the scope of the Compensation Acts.
8. Second injuries: since it is unfair to impose the total cost of compensation on the latest employer, second injury funds have been created by almost all states. Consequently the employer pays only for compensation resulting from the second injury, while the employee receives total compensation.
9. Actions against third parties: acceptance of the Workmen's Compensation Act by the employee is in lieu of an action for damages against the employer and bars such suit.
   a. There is no prohibition against an action for damages against a third party whose negligence has caused an injury.
   b. If an employee accepts workmen's compensation benefits in preference to suing a third party, he must transfer his claim to his employer.
10. Coverage of minors under the Workmen's Compensation laws: most Acts cover minors and many provide double compensation or additional penalties if the minor is illegally employed.
11. Workers injured outside the jurisdiction: the question arises as to which state's law applies. Basically the answer to this question is determined by a consideration and weighing of the following factors:
    a. The place of employment.
    b. The nature of the employment.
    c. The place where the employment contract was made.
    d. The residence of the employee.
    e. The place of the employer's business.
12. Public employees: many states provide a compensation for public employees, or at least certain classes of them.

C. Insurance requirements for workmen's compensation:

1. Nearly all states require the employee to obtain adequate insurance or to submit proof of financial ability to carry his own risk, i.e., to "self-insure."
2. Several states have state funds which the employer must insure with; others have state funds but the employer may use a private insurance company in lieu thereof if he wishes.

D. Administration of claims.

1. There are two general methods:
   a. By the state judicial system (only used in a few states).
   b. By a compensation board or commission created by state law

to specifically administer the Workmen's Compensation Laws.

2. The employer is required under penalty of law to report all injuries. In many jurisdictions the insurance companies take this burden off the employer after he has submitted the preliminary report to them.
3. The employee is required to give prompt notice of injury to the employer (not the insurance company) usually within 30 days.
4. The employee is also required to file his claim with the board or other appropriate authority within from 60 days to 2 years depending upon the jurisdiction.
   a. Failure to file a timely claim may bar recovery unless the board waives the requirement.
   b. In other states the employee who fails to file a timely notice will be barred only if the failure to file is prejudicial to the employer.
5. Time at which the period begins to run in respect to 2, 3, and 4, above, is subject to a split of authority. Most commonly, the time the accident is first noticed is used instead of the time it occurred.

E. Law suits for damages:

1. Employers who are required or accept coverage of the Workmen's Compensation Laws are generally exempt from damage suits by employees. Those who reject Workmen's Compensation in elective jurisdictions are not obliged to pay compensation but are subject to suits for damages. In such cases the three common law defenses are not available to the employer. These are:
   a. Contributory negligence; i.e., the worker's own negligence caused the accident in whole or part.
   b. The fellow servant (employee) doctrine; i.e., a fellow worker caused the injury.
   c. Assumption of the risk; i.e., by taking a hazardous job the employee assumed the risk of being hurt.
2. Covers "on the job" injuries; i.e., those injuries to workmen connected with and arising out of their work. Negligence, even if gross, is not a bar to recovery. However, intentionally self-inflicted injuries are not covered nor are injuries due to self-intoxication. The liability of the employer is a form of strict liability, i.e., liability without fault.
3. Employees are not covered by workmen's compensation while in transit to or from the employer's place of business. However, once the employee has arrived upon the employer's property, he is usually covered.
4. In the event the employee rejects Workmen's Compensation coverage and the employer is required to or has accepted it, the law generally allows the employer to resort to the above three common law defenses.

5. In about two-thirds of the states, the employee may sue for damages if the employer has failed to adequately provide a self-insured compensation plan or has not paid for insurance coverage. The defenses are not available.

F. Types of benefits.

1. Disability benefits: employee receives a percentage of his weekly wage. The benefits are:
   a. Subject to maximum and minimum weekly amounts.
   b. Payable for a stated maximum number of weeks unless there is a permanent total disability; in such a case, a few states provide for payments for life.
2. Death benefits: schedules are usually provided containing a maximum and minimum benefit; in some states payment is provided to a widow for life or until remarriage and to children until a specified age, normally 18.
3. Medical benefits: necessary medical aid and care is required to be furnished to an injured employee. This is in addition to compensation or other benefits. Many states require this to be furnished without limit as to time or amount so long as the board finds it to be necessary.
4. Rehabilitation: if the employee is unable to engage in his previous occupation after the accident and recovery period, some states provide that he shall receive training, paid for by the state, to prepare him for another occupation.
5. Specified injuries: a schedule of compensation is normally provided which covers the loss of certain members of the body. This benefit is based solely upon the loss of the member and is not dependent upon the loss of earning power.
6. Waiting period: most Workmen's Compensation Laws provide for a specified waiting period after injury before disability benefits are paid.
   a. This waiting period has no application to medical benefits, to which the employee is immediately entitled.
   b. If disability continues for a certain number of weeks, most states provide that weekly disability benefits are to be computed retroactively to the date of injury.

REGULATION OF THE EMPLOYER–EMPLOYEE RELATIONSHIP: EXAMINATION QUESTIONS*

WORKMEN'S COMPENSATION

Q. Henry was engaged by the Acme Corporation as a lathe operator. One day, during regular working hours, he sustained a serious injury while

* See Introductory Note, p. 19.

trying to adjust a faulty mechanism on his lathe. Henry claims benefits under the workmen's compensation law of the state in which he works.

(1) The Acme Corporation contests the claim on the grounds that Henry is an independent contractor and therefore not subject to the benefits available under the workmen's compensation law. Henry contends that he is an employee of Acme Corporation. Discuss fully those factors which would be relevant in establishing that Henry is an employee rather than an independent contractor.

(2) Assume that Henry is an employee. Acme Corporation, as employer, contests the claim on the grounds that Henry was grossly negligent in attempting to fix the faulty mechanism while the motor of the lathe was running. Will Henry recover? Explain.

11/64; pp. 436, 438

PART TWO

A RECENT EXAMINATION AND ANSWERS

A RECENT EXAMINATION IN BUSINESS LAW

8:30 A.M. TO 12 NOON

Prepared by the Board of Examiners of the American Institute of Certified Public Accountants and adopted by the examining boards of all states, territories and the District of Columbia.

NOTE TO CANDIDATES: Suggested time allotments are as follows:

	Estimated Minutes	
	Minimum	*Maximum*
All questions are required:		
No. 1	20	25
No. 2	20	25
No. 3	20	25
No. 4	25	30
No. 5	20	25
No. 6	25	30
No. 7	20	25
No. 8	20	25
Total for examination	170	210

You must arrange the papers in numerical order of the questions. If more than one page is required for an answer, write "continued" at the bottom of the page. Number pages consecutively. For instance, if twelve pages are used for your answers they should be numbered from 1 through 12.

A CPA is continually confronted with the necessity of expressing his opinions and conclusions in written reports in clear, unequivocal language. Although the primary purpose of the examination is to test the candidate's knowledge and application of the subject matter, the ability to organize and present such knowledge in acceptable written language will be considered by the examiners. DISREGARD OF THESE INSTRUCTIONS MAY BE CONSIDERED AS INDICATING INEFFICIENCY IN ACCOUNTING WORK.

NUMBER 1 (ESTIMATED TIME—20 TO 25 MINUTES)

Each of the following numbered statements states a legal conclusion relating to the lettered material. You are to determine whether each of the legal conclusions is true or false according to general principles of insurance and property law. Your grade will be determined from your total net score obtained by deducting a weighted total for your incorrect answers from your total of correct answers; an omitted answer will not be considered an incorrect answer.

EXAMPLE QUESTION

XX. Albert orally ordered a $600 standard model television console for his home from Mastercraft Appliances. Mastercraft accepted the order and later sent Albert a purchase memorandum in duplicate with a request that Albert sign and return one copy. Albert did not sign or return the purchase memorandum and he refused to accept the television console. Mastercraft sued and Albert asserted the Statute of Frauds as a Defense.

1. The purchase memorandum sent by Mastercraft would be sufficient to defeat Albert's reliance on the Statute of Frauds.
2. If Albert admits in court to making the oral contract, the contract would be enforceable.
3. A purchase memorandum is insufficient to satisfy the Statute of Frauds if it omits any of the terms agreed to by the parties.
4. A writing sufficient to satisfy the Statute of Frauds would not be necessary if Albert had received and accepted the television console.
5. Specific performance is the only remedy Mastercraft can obtain in its suit against Albert.

Answer Sheet

1.T......	F ▬▬▬
2.T ▬▬▬	F......
3.T......	F ▬▬▬
4.T ▬▬▬	F......
5.T......	F ▬▬▬

A. Mortimer, a CPA, was a sole public accounting practitioner. He applied for and obtained a $100,000 malpractice insurance policy from the Faithful Insurance Company.

1. If Mortimer sells his practice, he may transfer to the buyer the insurance policy in exchange for the premium applicable to the unexpired portion of the policy.
2. If Mortimer intentionally issues an unqualified auditor's opinion on financial statements he knows to be false, the insurance company will not be liable under the policy.
3. If Mortimer admits a junior partner, the policy will automatically cover the new partnership.
4. In the event the insurance company has to pay a claim to one of Mortimer's clients for Mortimer's negligence, the insurance company will be subrogated to the client's rights against Mortimer.

B. Williamson, Johnson and Fox were partners in a public accounting firm. The firm purchased a $50,000 life insurance policy on the life of each of its partners to provide funds to purchase the partnership interest of a deceased partner. The partnership was named as the beneficiary and paid all premiums.

5. Each partner owns the individual policy covering his life.
6. The partnership has a valid insurable interest in the lives of its partners.
7. The individual partners have an insurable interest in the lives of their partners.
8. The voluntary withdrawal of one of the partners would require the partnership to surrender the policy for its cash surrender value.
9. In the event of financial stress, the partnership could assign its interest in the policies to its creditors.
10. If the firm went bankrupt, its creditors would have a prior claim to the insurance policies over the claims of creditors of the individual partners.

C. A CPA's client, Granite Flexible Tube Corporation, entered into a sale-and-leaseback agreement with the Greenleaf Foundation. The CPA's examination revealed the following: Under the terms of the contract Greenleaf purchased Granite's plant and warehouse for $750,000. Granite received $450,000 in cash, and

Greenleaf assumed a $300,000 mortgage on the plant and warehouse held by the First State Bank. In addition, Granite obtained a 30-year lease on the property at an annual rental of $25,000.

11. Granite has an insurable interest in the plant and warehouse.
12. Greenleaf has an insurable interest in the plant and warehouse.
13. First State Bank has an insurable interest in the plant and warehouse.
14. If Granite retained the same amount of fire insurance (full coverage) that it had prior to the sale of the plant and warehouse, it would not be entitled to recover more than the fair market value of its interest in the property at the time of destruction.
15. Greenleaf's purchase of the plant and warehouse and assumption of the mortgage completely released Granite from its obligation to pay First State Bank.

D. On January 1, 1967, Wilson Packing Company insured its plant, which had a fair market value of $220,000, with the Miracle Insurance Company for $200,000 on a standard fire insurance policy that included a 90% coinsurance clause. On the night of December 28, 1969 a fire started in an adjoining building, which was owned by the Star Chemical Company. The fire spread to Wilson Packing and partially destroyed the plant. The extent of the damage was determined to be $80,000 and the fair market value of the plant at the time of the loss was $240,000. In his examination of Wilson's financial statements for the year ended December 31, 1969, a CPA is considering the effects of the fire and various related insurance aspects.

16. The coinsurance clause will not prevent Wilson from recovering the full amount of the loss ($80,000).
17. Assuming the building had been totally destroyed, Wilson could have recovered $180,000 from Miracle Insurance.
18. Assuming Wilson does not fully recover its loss from Miracle Insurance, it can recover from Star Chemical if Star's negligence caused the fire.
19. Wilson may not assign its right of recovery under the Miracle policy to its creditors.
20. Miracle, to the extent it pays Wilson under the Wilson policy, will be subrogated to Wilson's rights against any third party who may have wrongfully caused the fire.
21. If the fire had been caused by the negligent maintenance of Wilson's heating and electrical equipment, Miracle would not have been obligated to pay on the policy.
22. If Wilson negotiated a partial settlement with Star Chemical and gave Star a complete release from liability, Miracle would not be obligated to pay on the policy.

23. To avoid the operation of the coinsurance clause, periodic valuations of the insured property should be made and the insurance coverage increased accordingly.

E. Warren applied for $50,000 of life insurance with the Gem Life Insurance Company. He filled in the application and arranged for a physical examination. The application contained a clause which stated:

 Coverage of the insured will begin only upon delivery of the policy to the applicant in good health.

24. Even without the above clause, physical delivery of the policy is a prerequisite to the making of a contract of insurance.
25. Such clauses have been held invalid as against public policy by the majority of states.
26. Receipt of the policy by Warren while suffering from a common cold would not bar recovery, even though the cold developed into pneumonia which caused Warren's death.
27. If Warren died in an auto accident before delivery of the policy, there would be no recovery against Gem on the policy.

F. Marshall owned a seven story office building. He occupied one floor and rented the remaining floors. He originally insured the property against fire with the Superior Fire and Casualty Company for $200,000. Subsequently he took out another policy with the Freedom Fire Insurance Company for the same amount. The property was totally destroyed by fire and it has been agreed by all parties that at the time of the loss the fair market value of the building was $300,000. Both policies contained the standard pro rata liability clause. Marshall's CPA is studying the policies in order to prepare himself for a discussion with his client and his client's attorney.

28. Marshall will collect a total of $300,000.
29. Superior will be liable for $200,000 since it was the original insurer.
30. In the event that Superior was insolvent and unable to pay more than $100,000 on the Marshall policy, Freedom would be obligated to pay $200,000.

NUMBER 2 (ESTIMATED TIME—20 TO 25 MINUTES)

Each of the following numbered phrases, clauses and sentences states a legal conclusion relating to the lettered material. You are to determine whether the legal conclusion is true or false according to the Uniform Commercial Code and the general principles of contract law. Your grade will be determined from your total of correct answers less a penalty for your incorrect answers; an omitted answer will not be considered an incorrect answer.

A. Davis, a CPA, has a one-year retainer agreement with Franklin Corporation. Davis is to examine the financial statements, prepare tax returns and be available for consultation on financial matters. The retainer provides for an annual fee of $12,000. Davis has a claim for $3,000 for services rendered to the Corporation prior to the execution of the retainer agreement. Davis performs the required services for the first four months and is paid therefor. Davis then is required to retire completely from practice because of a severe heart attack and assigns to Leeds, another CPA, his $3,000 claim against the Franklin Corporation and his rights and duties under the retainer agreement.

31. Davis' assignment of his $3,000 claim against the Franklin Corporation is valid, even without Franklin's consent to such assignment.
32. Franklin Corporation is not legally obligated under the retainer agreement to accept Leeds as its CPA for the remaining period.
33. Franklin Corporation may recover a judgment against Davis for breach of contract.
34. If Leeds sues Franklin Corporation, the latter may assert against Leeds all defenses it had against Davis before Davis assigned the claim to Leeds.
35. The assignment to be valid must be in writing.

B. The following telegrams are exchanged among Gordon, a watch merchant, Andrews, another watch merchant, and Speculator.

a. September 1, 1970. To Andrews: Offer you my collection of 25 original 1928 Mickey Mouse watches for $1,500. Offer will be held open until September 10.

Gordon

b. September 2, 1970. To Gordon: Mickey Mouse market is bearish now. I am still considering your offer, will advise shortly.

Andrews

c. September 2, 1970. To Gordon: Understand you are offering for sale 25 original 1928 Mickey Mouse watches for $1,500. I accept your offer.

Speculator

d. September 3, 1970. To Andrews: Your judgment of market condition is wrong. Offer withdrawn.

Gordon

e. September 3, 1970. To Speculator: You know value

when you hear about it. It's a deal.

Gordon

f. September 7, 1970. To Gordon: You're a hard man to deal with. Accept your offer.

Andrews

36. Gordon's withdrawal of his offer to Andrews was effective when Andrews received Gordon's telegram dated September 3.
37. Andrews' telegram dated September 7 operates as an acceptance only when Gordon receives that telegram.
38. Speculator's telegram dated September 2 created a contract between Gordon and Speculator when received by Gordon.
39. Gordon has entered into a contract with both Andrews and Speculator.
40. Assuming Gordon died on September 6, his offer to Andrews terminates on that date even if Andrews had no notice until September 15.

C. Ott owes Casey $6,000 which is past due. Casey offers to discharge this debt if Ott promises to pay $3,000 to Casey's wife, pay $2,000 to Milton, a creditor of Casey, and give Casey his stamp collection which has a market value of $500. Ott accepts the offer.

41. This contract is an example of a bilateral contract.
42. After Ott fully performs, Casey may recover a judgment against Ott for $500.
43. Assuming Ott defaults, Casey's wife and Milton may recover judgments against Ott for $3,000 and $2,000 respectively.
44. Casey's wife and Milton are both incidental beneficiaries.
45. If Ott fully performs, there is an accord and satisfaction.

D. In the presence of three witnesses, Boyd enters into an oral agreement with Stanley to purchase Stanley's house for $30,000 cash. Thereafter, Stanley refuses to sell the house to Boyd. Boyd sues Stanley for breach of contract and seeks a decree of specific performance from the court to compel Stanley to deliver a deed to the house. Stanley pleads the Statute of Frauds as a defense.

46. The oral agreement is void.
47. The oral agreement is valid and enforceable if the three witnesses testify in court that the oral agreement was entered into.
48. Assuming that the agreement has been signed only by Stanley, Boyd need not also sign it to satisfy the Statute of Frauds.
49. Assuming that the agreement is enforceable, Boyd is entitled only to an award of money damages.
50. Assuming that Boyd gave Stanley a cash deposit, the oral

agreement is unenforceable.

E. Norton, a minor, purchased a car for his personal use for $1,000 cash from Adams, a car dealer. Norton also purchased an acre of unimproved land for $3,000 cash from Holmes. Adams and Holmes knew that Norton was a minor.

51. Norton may disaffirm both contracts at any time during his minority by tendering the car and the land to Adams and Holmes respectively.
52. A disaffirmation by Norton must be in writing and signed to be legally effective.
53. Norton's ratification of the two contracts during his minority would not legally bar him from disaffirming both contracts at any subsequent time.
54. Norton may ratify his contracts only by giving Adams and Holmes written notice to that effect when he reaches his majority or within a reasonable time thereafter.
55. Neither Adams nor Holmes may disaffirm his contract with Norton if Norton wants to affirm.

F. Peters, a car dealer, makes the following representations to Evans in selling a car to Evans for $900.

a. The car has been driven 50,000 miles.
b. The market value of the car is $1,000.
c. The manufacturer's warranty on the car does not expire for one year.

The facts are:

a. Peters turned back the odometer from 70,000 miles.
b. The market value of the car is $800.
c. Unknown to Peters the warranty has expired.

56. Peters' statement as to the value of the car constitutes fraud.
57. Peters' statement as to the warranty constitutes fraud.
58. Evans may rescind the contract at any time after he discovers that Peters turned back the odometer.
59. If Evans affirms the contract after discovering that Peters turned back the odometer, he is barred from recovering a judgment for damages against Peters.
60. There is a legal difference between innocent misrepresentation and fraud.

NUMBER 3 (ESTIMATED TIME—20 TO 25 MINUTES)

Each of the following numbered phrases, clauses and sentences states a legal conclusion relating to the lettered material. You are to determine whether the legal conclusion is true or false according to the Uniform Commercial Code and general principles of sales law. Your grade will be determined from your total of correct answers less a penalty for your incorrect answers; an omitted answer will not be considered an incorrect answer.

A. Archer, a farmer, wrote Nevins, a tractor dealer, as follows:

> Confirming telephone conversation of today, please ship me one Centipede Model 2 tractor at $3,500, COD.
>
> Archer

Nevins failed to deliver the tractor to Archer who therefore bought one elsewhere for $5,000.

61. Archer has a valid cause of action on a contract of sale against Nevins.
62. The answer to the preceding question would be different if Archer's letter had been accompanied by a $3,500 check which Nevins cashed.
63. Assume that 15 days after receiving and reading Archer's letter, Nevins wrote Archer advising that the price for the tractor was $4,000 and that he would not sell for $3,500. In such a case, Archer would have a valid cause of action against Nevins for breach of contract.
64. The answer to the preceding question would be the same if both Archer and Nevins were tractor dealers.
65. Assume that promptly upon receipt of Archer's letter, Nevins shipped the tractor and Archer refused to pay $3,500 on delivery. In such a case, Archer may successfully defend Nevins' action for breach of contract on the basis that no enforceable contract existed.

B. In connection with his examination of the financial statements of the Commonwealth Boiler Company for the year ended March 31, 1970, a CPA is concerned about the legal implications of the following situation: Commonwealth Boiler Company agreed in a contract of sale made on January 2, 1970 to sell and deliver nine boilers to Osgood Contracting Corporation, three boilers to be delivered on or about February 1, three on or about March 1 and the remaining three on or about April 1. Payment of the price, plus interest, was to be made by Osgood in six monthly installments commencing May 1. In negotiating the contract on January 2 Osgood falsely represented its solvency to Commonwealth in writing. On March 15, after timely delivery of the first six boilers, Commonwealth learns of Osgood's insolvency. No payment of any part of the price of the boilers has been made by Osgood.

66. Commonwealth may legally refuse to deliver the remaining three boilers unless Osgood pays the price therefor in cash on delivery.
67. Before it is obligated to deliver the remaining three boilers, Commonwealth may demand immediate cash payment for the six boilers previously delivered.
68. If the remaining three boilers have been shipped but not

yet delivered, Commonwealth may stop delivery in transit.

69. If, immediately upon discovery of Osgood's insolvency, Commonwealth demands return of all boilers previously delivered, its rights therein would be superior to those of other general creditors of Osgood even though it had no perfected security interest in the boilers.
70. On the basis of the facts set forth in item 69, Commonwealth could reclaim the six boilers from Dunkins, even though Dunkins had acquired them from Osgood in good faith and for value.

C. Ace Equipment Company delivered a printing press to Green Printers, Inc. The written agreement between Ace and Green provided that the press could be returned after a reasonable trial period if it did not satisfy Green's needs. Payment was to be made upon Green's acceptance. One week after delivery of the press, Green is adjudicated a bankrupt. Ace Equipment's CPA is discussing with the credit manager the amounts, if any, to be included in the financial statements for this transaction.

71. This was a sale-or-return transaction.
72. The answer to item 71 would be different if Green was in the business of selling printing presses for its own account.
73. Risk of loss on the press was upon Ace after the delivery to Green.
74. Ace could successfully repossess the printing press from Green's trustee in bankruptcy.
75. Assuming that the agreement between Ace and Green providing for the return of the press was not written, Ace could not repossess the press from Green's trustee in bankruptcy.

D. Pursuant to a written contract of sale Falmouth Ltd., a British manufacturer, agreed to sell and deliver 15 electric generators to Harris & Co., an American equipment dealer located in St. Louis, terms $150,000, C.I.F. New York. In connection with his effort to secure a proper cut-off of inventory transactions at the balance sheet date, several legal questions have come to the attention of Harris' CPA regarding the contract with Falmouth.

76. The price to Harris included the cost of the goods, freight to New York and insurance for Harris' account.
77. Harris is required to pay the price upon tender to it of proper documents although the goods have not yet arrived in New York.
78. Assuming Falmouth properly discharges all of its obligations under the contract, risk of loss of the goods at sea is upon Harris.
79. If Falmouth had neglected to effect insurance for Harris' account, the answer to the preceding questions would be the same.

80. If the contract had specified "C & F" terms, risk of loss at sea would be upon Falmouth.

E. Ingram, a do-it-yourself type, decided to paint the exterior of his house with the new Excello All Purpose brand of paint which was advertised to be "no-chipping or peeling and absolutely weatherproof" for five years. Ingram purchased the Excello paint from Collins' paint store. Shortly after painting the house, Ingram discovered that the paint had blistered and was peeling in several places and that his paint job had not stood up well in a mild rain storm.

81. Since Ingram bought the paint from Collins by trade name, no implied warranty by Collins attached to the sale.
82. In selling the paint to Ingram, Collins impliedly warranted its merchantability.
83. Advertising claims such as those made by Excello have been held to be express warranties.
84. If Ingram advised Collins of his intended use for the paint and Collins suggested the Excello All Purpose brand, Collins warranted the fitness for use by Ingram.
85. If Collins sold the paint to Ingram with a written warranty that it was suitable for exterior use, there could be no implied warranties in connection with the sale.

F. Dexter Company, a clothing manufacturer, purchased goods from Johnson Fabrics, Inc. The contract specified 100 bolts of a 50% wool, and 50% acetate fabric in a particular color. Only 75 bolts were delivered by Johnson and 25 of these were not of the color specified in the contract.

86. Dexter may reject the entire shipment.
87. Dexter may accept the 50 bolts of the proper color and reject the remainder of the shipment.
88. Assume Dexter accepted the entire shipment and later discovered, on testing, that the goods were only 25% wool. In such a case, Dexter is bound by its acceptance.
89. If the goods were shipped FOB Johnson's plant, risk of loss was upon Dexter and it could not reject the goods.
90. Assume that Johnson became insolvent before delivery but after identification to the contract and that Dexter paid for the goods upon execution of the contract and seven days before Johnson's insolvency. In such a case, Dexter could recover the goods from Johnson's creditors.

NUMBER 4 (ESTIMATED TIME—25 TO 30 MINUTES)

a. During your examination of the financial statements of the Fantastic Fan and Air Conditioning Corporation, you wish to ascertain the validity of a certain account receivable.

The account resulted from an $8,000 sale of air conditioning equipment to Arista Apartments by Joe Wells, a free lance jobber. Wells had been retained previously to sell certain products for Fantastic Fan; the relationship had deteriorated and for more than six months Wells had not been commissioned to make such sales. Nevertheless Wells, representing himself as the sales agent for Fantastic Fan, made the aforementioned $8,000 sale. Upon receiving the Arista order from Wells, Fantastic Fan promptly notified Arista that it accepted the order and would ship within 10 days.

Prior to delivery Arista, learning of Wells' lack of authority and realizing that it had made a bad bargain, promptly repudiated its order by notifying Fantastic Fan that it was not bound on the purchase contract because of Wells' lack of authority.

1. Has a valid and enforceable account receivable been created? Explain.

b. Your examination of Fantastic Fan's financial statements also discloses a problem relating to accounts payable.

James Williamson was one of Fantastic Fan's general purchasing agents. On August 11th the president of Fantastic Fan sent Williamson a lengthy memorandum indicating that storage space had become so costly that the Company was no longer prepared to purchase and store a large inventory of fans during the winter. The president stated that no further purchases were to be made. The Company had previously made such purchases when it could buy manufacturer close-outs at bargain prices.

Williamson glanced hurriedly at the memo but did not pay serious attention to it at the time. Unfortunately, he called upon one of the Company's leading suppliers of fans later on the same day and was offered 500 large fans at a substantial reduction. Williamson promptly accepted and signed an order for the 500 fans on Fantastic Fan's behalf. Williamson had made such purchases in prior years. Fantastic Fan upon learning of the purchase promptly notified the manufacturer that it cancelled the order and denied liability since Williamson had no authority to make the purchase.

1. Is Fantastic Fan correct in its denial of liability? Explain.

c. During your examination of the financial statements of the White Bakery Company you discover that a tort liability claim of $100,000 has been asserted against the Company. Frank Anthony was one of the Company's delivery truck drivers. One afternoon while making deliveries Anthony decided to watch a few innings of the home team's baseball game on television. Fearing detection if he remained in the neighborhood where his route was located, he drove to another part of town where the Company did not have any customers. He parked the delivery truck on a side street and proceeded to the Lucky Horse Bar and Grill. While watching the game there he became embroiled in a heated argument with William

Watson, another customer of the bar. In a rage, Anthony pushed Watson off his bar stool. Watson suffered a broken hip and is suing White Bakery for $100,000.

1. Is White Bakery liable to Watson as a result of Anthony's tortious conduct? Explain.

d. During your examination of the financial statements of the Ace Equipment Company you discover a problem relating to a sale.

Charles Jackson was one of Ace's best salesmen. The company had placed him on a special incentive payment plan whereby he could double his salary if he doubled his sales volume. Jackson was very aggressive and used hard sell techniques. He had an opportunity to sell 15 fork lifts to a cargo handling company, a sale that would put him over the top of his incentive plan. The cargo company insisted upon an express warranty that the particular fork lifts would handle 8,000 pounds safely. Jackson, without authority and knowing the lifts were only guaranteed to handle 7,000 pounds, represented that the equipment had an 8,000 pound capacity. He thought that the lifts probably were adequate. Ace Equipment neither authorized this express warranty nor was aware of Jackson's misrepresentation.

Two weeks after delivery of the fork lifts one of them gave way and dropped a carton containing computer equipment weighing 7,800 pounds. The cargo company seeks to return the fork lifts to Ace and to recover for the damage caused to the computer equipment. Ace refuses to refund the money for the fork lifts and denies liability for Jackson's misrepresentation.

1. What are the rights of the cargo company against Ace Equipment? Explain.

NUMBER 5 (ESTIMATED TIME—20 TO 25 MINUTES)

a. The Chriswell Corporation decided to raise additional long-term capital by issuing $3,000,000 of 8% subordinated debentures to the public. May, Clark & Co., CPAs, the company's auditors, were engaged to examine the June 30, 1970 financial statements which were included in the bond registration statement.

May, Clark & Co. completed its examination and submitted an unqualified auditor's report dated July 15, 1970. The registration statement was filed and became effective on September 1, 1970. Two weeks prior to the effective date one of the partners of May, Clark & Co. called on Chriswell Corporation and had lunch with the financial vice president and the controller. He questioned both officials on the company's operations since June 30 and inquired whether there had been any material changes in the company's financial position since that date. Both officers assured him that everything had proceeded normally and that the financial condition of the company had not changed materially.

Unfortunately the officers' representation was not true. On July 30, a substantial debtor of the company failed to pay the $400,000 due on its account receivable and indicated to Chriswell that it would probably be forced into bankruptcy. This receivable was shown as a collateralized loan on the June 30 financial statements. It was secured by stock of the debtor corporation which had a value in excess of the loan at the time the financial statements were prepared but was virtually worthless at the effective date of the registration statement. This $400,000 account receivable was material to the financial condition of Chriswell Corporation, and the market price of the subordinated debentures decreased by nearly 50% after the foregoing facts were disclosed.

The debenture holders of Chriswell are seeking recovery of their loss against all parties connected with the debenture registration.

1. Is May, Clark & Co. liable to the Chriswell debenture holders? Explain.

b. Meglow Corporation manufactured ladies' dresses and blouses. Because its cash position was deteriorating, Meglow sought a loan from Busch Factors. Busch had previously extended $25,000 credit to Meglow but refused to lend any additional money without obtaining copies of Meglow's audited financial statements.

Meglow contacted the CPA firm of Watkins, Winslow & Watkins to perform the audit. In arranging for the examination, Meglow clearly indicated that its purpose was to satisfy Busch Factors as to the Corporation's sound financial condition and thus to obtain an additional loan of $50,000. Watkins, Winslow & Watkins accepted the engagement, performed the examination in a negligent manner and rendered an unqualified auditor's opinion. If an adequate examination had been performed, the financial statements would have been found to be misleading.

Meglow submitted the audited financial statements to Busch Factors and obtained an additional loan of $35,000. Busch refused to lend more than that amount. After several other factors also refused, Meglow finally was able to persuade Maxwell Department Stores, one of its customers, to lend the additional $15,000. Maxwell relied upon the financial statements examined by Watkins, Winslow & Watkins.

Meglow is now in bankruptcy and Busch seeks to collect from Watkins, Winslow & Watkins the $60,000 it loaned Meglow. Maxwell seeks to recover from Watkins, Winslow & Watkins the $15,000 it loaned Meglow.

1. Will Busch recover? Explain.
2. Will Maxwell recover? Explain.

NUMBER 6 (ESTIMATED TIME—20 TO 25 MINUTES)

Simpson and Walker are partners in a chain of grocery stores.

Simpson dies on February 1. A week later, Mrs. Simpson advises Walker that she has decided that she will take her late husband's place as a partner in the business. Walker refuses to allow her to do so. Mrs. Simpson tells Walker that she will not insist if Walker turns over to her one half of the grocery stores in the chain; her late husband owned a one-half interest in the partnership. Walker refuses and insists on buying her out although the partnership agreement contains no provisions for such a transaction. In the meantime Norris, a creditor of the partnership before Simpson's death, sues the partnership, Walker and the Estate of Simpson individually, while Overton, a personal judgment creditor of Walker, seeks to attach partnership property to satisfy the judgment that he obtained against Walker.

a. What effect does Simpson's death have on the partnership?
b. What are Walker's rights with respect to the partnership upon Simpson's death?
c. What are Mrs. Simpson's rights with respect to the partnership upon her husband's death? Explain.
d. What are Norris' rights against the partnership, Walker and and the Estate of Simpson?
e. What are Overton's rights against the partnership property? Explain.

NUMBER 7 (ESTIMATED TIME—25 TO 30 MINUTES)

a. In your examination of the financial statements of the Terminal Ice Company for the year ended September 30, 1970 you discover correspondence relating to a dispute concerning the transferability to Igloo Ice Cream Company of Terminal's contract with The Polar Bear Ice Cream Company. Polar Bear had been purchased by Igloo. A synopsis of the facts follows.

Terminal made a contract to deliver ice to Polar Bear. Before the contract expired, Polar Bear assigned the contract to Igloo. Terminal refused to deliver ice to the assignee and was threatened by Igloo with legal action for recovery of damages for the alleged breach.

The contract obliged Terminal to sell and deliver to the loading platform of Polar Bear up to 250 tons of ice per week for $23.25 a ton. The contractual rights of Terminal were (a) to be paid every Tuesday for all ice purchased by Polar Bear during the week ending at midnight of the preceding Saturday; (b) to require Polar Bear neither to buy nor accept ice from any source other than Terminal, except for amounts needed in excess of the weekly maximum of 250 tons. The contract was for a period of three years with an option that permitted Polar Bear to renew for an additional three years. Polar Bear renewed for three years.

Before the first year of the renewal contract had expired, without the consent or knowledge of Terminal and for a valuable consideration, Polar Bear executed and delivered to Igloo on August 15, 1970 a written assignment of its agreement with Terminal. The assignment was part of the purchase transaction by which Igloo acquired "the plant, equipment, rights, credits, choses in action, goodwill, contracts, and trade, custom and patronage rights" and any other assets of Polar Bear's ice cream business. The purchaser took full possession and continued the former business carried on by Polar Bear which was to be operated as a separate division engaged in the ice cream business serving the same area as before the purchase. Igloo was prepared to pay cash for all ice delivered under the contract.

Igloo is a much larger company than Polar Bear and serves an area contiguous to Polar Bear's. Igloo's plants are more efficient and have sufficient capacity to supply the markets of both companies during most of the year; thus, Igloo would probably buy ice from Terminal only when there was a price advantage in doing so.

As soon as Terminal learned of this purported assignment and the acquisition of Polar Bear by Igloo, it notified Polar Bear that the contract was terminated and declined to deliver any ice to Igloo. Obligations between the original parties were fully performed and discharged to the date of assignment.

1. What are the legal problems and implications of the above facts? Discuss.
2. What is the effect of these legal problems and implications on the financial statements of Terminal Ice Company for the year ended September 30, 1970? Discuss.

b. In the course of the examination of the financial statements of Williams Watch Company for the year ended October 31, 1970, the following situation was discovered during a review of correspondence included in the purchase orders outstanding file.

[A letter addressed to Williams]

October 12, 1970. Gentlemen: We offer a once in a lifetime sale of gold filled expansion watch bands, catalogue #426, at $7.26 each. Minimum order 500, maximum order 1,000. Acceptance by October 15, 1970. Delivery F.O.B. Buffalo by the end of the month, 2/10, net/30.

Very truly yours,
Jackson Watch Band Co.

[To this Williams replied by mail]

October 15, 1970. Gentlemen: We accept. Please rush shipment of 500. We can use them immediately. Ship draft against bill of lading inspection allowed.

Williams Watch Co.

[Jackson sent Williams the following letter]

October 17, 1970. Gentlemen: Sorry your acceptance did

not arrive until October 16 and was improper in several respects. We regret we cannot accept your counter offer because the price on the item has risen to $8.75 each. We will be happy to receive an order at this price.

Very truly yours,
Jackson Watch Band Co.

Further review disclosed that on October 15, 1970, Williams Watch made a firm contract to sell Promotions, Inc. 500 gold filled expansion watch bands identified as #426 at $8.00 each. Williams Watch has been unable to find another supplier who would provide 500 watch bands of a quality comparable to #426 at a unit price of less than $8.75.

1. What are the legal problems and implications of the above facts? Discuss.
2. What is the effect of these legal problems and implications on the financial statements of Williams Watch Company for the year ended October 31, 1970? Discuss.

NUMBER 8 (ESTIMATED TIME—20 TO 25 MINUTES)

a. Joseph Martin persuaded his employer, Robert Franklin, to issue a check payable to the order of Milton Small in the amount of $1,000. Martin represented to Franklin that Small was entitled to a refund of $1,000 for merchandise returned that day by Small. Franklin delivered the check to Martin and instructed him to mail it to Small.

Martin's statement was false. He did not know any person called Milton Small. When Martin received the check intended for Small, he endorsed the check in the name of Milton Small and delivered it to Arthur Smith, a holder in due course. Martin absconded and when Franklin discovered what had happened he stopped payment on the check. Smith sues Franklin.

1. Was the check bearer paper or order paper at the time of issue? Explain.
2. Was Martin's endorsement effective to negotiate the check? Explain.
3. May Smith recover from Franklin? Explain.

b. Lawrence executed and delivered a check for $1,000 payable to the order of Evans. Lawrence used due care in preparing the check. However, Evans (by methods best known to forgers) raised the amount to $10,000 and negotiated the check for value to Mark who took the check in good faith without notice of the alteration. When Mark presented the check for payment it was returned marked "insufficient funds." Mark then sued Lawrence. In connection with his examination of Lawrence's financial statements, a CPA is attempting to determine the liability and related loss on this item, if any.

1. Can Mark recover? Explain.
2. If so, how much? Explain.

c. In the course of his examination of Smith's financial statements, a CPA learns that Smith drew a check on the State Bank payable to the order of Paul N. Hodys in the sum of $500 and delivered it to Hodys for goods sold and delivered. Morris stole the check from Hodys, endorsed Hodys' name and delivered the check to Parks who took the check for value in good faith and deposited the check in his account in the National Bank. National Bank collected the amount of the check from State Bank who in turn charged Smith's account in the sum of $500.

1. What are the rights of Smith against State Bank? Explain.
2. What are the rights of Hodys against State Bank? Explain.
3. What are the rights of State Bank against National Bank? Explain.

SUGGESTED ANSWERS*

(These answers are not in any sense official. They represent merely the opinion of the director of education of the American Institute of Certified Public Accountants.)

ANSWER TO QUESTION NUMBER 1

1. F	6. T	11. T	16. F	21. F	26. T
2. T	7. T	12. T	17. F	22. T	27. T
3. F	8. F	13. T	18. T	23. T	28. T
4. F	9. T	14. T	19. F	24. F	29. F
5. F	10. T	15. F	20. T	25. F	30. F

ANSWER TO QUESTION NUMBER 2

31. T	36. F	41. T	46. F	51. F	56. F
32. T	37. F	42. F	47. F	52. F	57. F
33. F	38. F	43. T	48. T	53. T	58. F
34. T	39. T	44. F	49. F	54. F	59. F
35. F	40. F	45. T	50. T	55. T	60. T

ANSWER TO QUESTION NUMBER 3

61. F	66. T	71. F	76. T	81. F	86. T
62. T	67. T	72. T	77. T	82. T	87. T
63. F	68. T	73. T	78. T	83. T	88. F
64. F	69. T	74. T	79. F	84. T	89. F
65. F	70. F	75. F	80. F	85. F	90. T

ANSWER TO QUESTION NUMBER 4

a. Yes. Despite Wells' total lack of authority the contract he made with Arista may be ratified by Fantastic Fan. The elements necessary in order for Fantastic Fan to invoke the ratification doctrine are as follows:

1. The unauthorized agent must purport to act for and on behalf of the principal. Wells did so in his dealings with Arista.
2. There must be a principal in existence at the time the contract was made who had the capacity to appoint an agent to enter into the contract. Fantastic Fan was in existence and could have appointed Wells to make the contract.
3. The principal must ratify the contract prior to the third party

* *Supplement to the Journal of Accountancy,* Uniform CPA Examination Questions and Unofficial Answers (Nov. 6–8, 1970).

withdrawing from or repudiating the contract. Fantastic Fan did so. Thus, Arista is bound on the contract made by Wells on Fantastic Fan's behalf.

b. No. Although Williamson had no actual authority to make the contract, Fantastic Fan is liable on the basis of Williamson's apparent authority. This authority is based upon Williamson's position as a general purchasing agent and the fact that similar purchases had been made by Williamson in prior years. Limitations on an agent's usual authority are not binding on third parties who deal with the agent without knowledge or notice of such limitations.

c. No. The law imposes broad liability upon the principal for the torts of his agent, but there is an exception which would apparently apply here, the "independent frolic" rule. When the agent has abandoned his employer's calling and independently engages in an activity unrelated and entirely outside the scope of his employment, the law does not hold the principal liable. Anthony's behavior seems to be clearly within this exception.

d. The cargo company can rescind the contract for a breach of warranty and/or fraud and obtain damages for injury to the computer equipment. A principal is liable for the misrepresentations made by his agent either on a warranty theory, in which case knowledge of falsity need not be proved, or on the tort of fraud where the agent has the requisite knowledge that his representation is false. Under both theories the cargo company may recover damages and rescind the contract.

ANSWER TO QUESTION NUMBER 5

a. Yes. The situation is covered by the Securities Act of 1933. That Act made significant changes in the legal liability of accountants. First, it eliminated privity as a defense in cases involving third party investors suing accountants for negligence. Any person acquiring securities described in the registration statement may sue if the financial statements contain a false statement or misleading omission of a material fact. Clearly the financial statements in question contained either a false statement or material omission. However, the CPA may avoid liability if he can show freedom from negligence or fraud by showing that he had, after reasonable investigation, grounds to believe and did believe the financial statements were true. The Act requires, however, that the CPA be able to sustain this freedom from fault not only as of the date of the financial statements, but beyond that, as of the time when the registration statement became effective. In this case it would appear that the CPA cannot avoid liability. He failed to make any reasonable effort to check the validity of the statements as of the effective date. Merely taking the word of the Company's executives would not be sufficient. Thus liability may be imposed upon the accountants, May, Clark & Company. The Corporation and its officers will also be liable.

b. 1. Yes, but only to the extent of $35,000. The original $25,000 loan by Busch Factors was in no way related to the negligently prepared financial statements. This $25,000 loan was made prior to the issuance of the unqualified auditor's report. Hence, there is no causal relationship between the negligence of the CPAs and this portion of the loss.

As to the $35,000 advance, the requisite causal relationship was clearly present. The problem here lies in the ancient privity of contract requirement which holds that a CPA is not liable for mere negligence to third parties with whom he has not contracted. However, there are several exceptions to the privity rule which permit recovery despite the absence of a direct contractual relationship between the accountant and the third party plaintiff. The exception which would apply in this case is the primary benefit or third party beneficiary rule. This rule is invoked when the accountant is informed of the specific person or persons for whose primary benefit the audit is being performed. Under these circumstances privity is not required, and a third party such as Busch can recover for mere negligence as a third party beneficiary.

2. No. Unless the privity requirement is subjected to further substantial inroads or is abolished altogether, Maxwell will not recover. As indicated above, in the absence of a direct contractual relationship or an exception to the privity rule, recovery by a third party plaintiff against the accountant for mere negligence is not permitted. The primary benefit rule would not seem applicable as applied to the facts of the Maxwell situation. Therefore, recovery would be denied.

ANSWER TO QUESTION NUMBER 6

a. Simpson's death causes the dissolution of the partnership. However, upon dissolution the partnership is not terminated but continues until the winding up of partnership affairs is completed.

b. Walker has the right to wind up partnership affairs or to complete transactions begun but not finished at the time of Simpson's death. Walker is entitled to reasonable compensation for his services in winding up the partnership affairs.

c. Mrs. Simpson has no interest in specific partnership property. Mr. Simpson's coownership in partnership property did not pass to Mrs. Simpson upon his death. His coownership of partnership property ceased to exist upon his death and the ownership of the partnership property remains exclusively with the surviving partner. What passes to Mrs. Simpson is the interest of the deceased in the partnership and she has a right to insist that the partnership be wound up. However, she has no right to participate in either the winding up of the business or the management of the partnership. She is entitled to an accounting from the surviving partner, a right which accrues from the date of Mr. Simpson's death unless there is an agreement to the contrary, and to share in the distribution of the proceeds of liquidation.

d. The partnership is liable; all partners are liable jointly for all debts and obligations of the partnership and all partners are jointly and severally liable for certain specified wrongful acts not applicable here. The individual properties of the deceased partner and Walker are liable for all obligations of the partnership incurred while each was a partner but subject to the prior payment of their separate debts. Thus, the estate and Walker must satisfy all personal claims before Norris' claim against the partnership can be satisfied against them. When a partner pays a partnership debt he has a right to contribution from his copartner.

e. Overton may not attach the partnership property to satisfy his personal judgment against Walker. A partner's right in specific partnership property is not subject to attachment or execution, except on a claim against the partnership. The court, however, may charge the partnership interest of the debtor partner with payment of the unsatisfied amount of such judgment.

ANSWER TO QUESTION NUMBER 7

a. 1. The legal implications of these facts relate to whether the original contract between Terminal and Polar Bear was assignable. The answer to this question depends on whether there was a material change in Terminal's obligation as a result of the purported assignment.

As a general proposition, most contractual rights to receive a commonplace item, such as ice, are assignable. However, the courts are reluctant to uphold the assignment of rights where there is a requirements contract which obligates the seller to supply a purchaser's particular requirement for a product and the buyer promises to buy exclusively from a particular seller.

In the past, rights such as these were not considered to be assignable because of their being too personal. The modern view, which has been codified in the Uniform Commercial Code, looks at the effect that the assignment will have on the performance of the obligor's (Terminal's) duty. If the court concludes that the obligor's performance will be materially altered, the assignment is invalid.

In the case at hand, Polar Bear and Terminal had been doing business for three years prior to the renewal of the contract. The prior dealings, Polar Bear's geographic market, the size of Polar Bear's plant and other factors surrounding the relationship made the average quantity of ice to be taken over the term of the contract fairly certain. Now Igloo, a much larger ice cream company, will be the buyer. It is unlikely that Igloo's demands will be the same as those of its predecessor. It could take no ice from Terminal for given periods and still supply the Polar Bear Market by manufacturing ice cream at one of its other nearby plants. This would tend to be most profitable to Igloo if the market price of ice were to decrease below that of the assigned contract. On the other hand, if the price of ice in the area of either company were to rise above that in the assigned contract, Igloo would take the maximum, 250 tons, every week of the contract and ship ice cream to its other markets. Based upon these considerations, the change in parties would represent a material change in the seller's (Terminal's) obligation and hence would not be assignable.

The legal problem raised by the delegation of the duty by Polar Bear to Igloo to pay for the ice would apparently be overcome in that Igloo offered to pay cash on delivery thereby eliminating any extension of credit. Delegations which involve extension of unsecured credit are normally not permitted.

2. Terminal apparently will not have to perform and can avoid the obligation on the grounds discussed above. An opinion letter from counsel should be obtained and a footnote to the financial statements should be prepared in conformity with the opinion letter.

b. 1. The following issues are raised by these facts:

(a) Was the acceptance made within the time stipulated for acceptance in the offer?

(b) Did the variations contained in the acceptance constitute a rejection of the offer and, hence, a counter-offer?

(c) Having decided or assuming that a contract between Williams Watch and Jackson Watch Bank did arise, what remedies are available to Williams Watch?

(d) Must Williams Watch perform its contract with Promotions, Inc.?

The acceptance was made by mail, an authorized means which was reasonable in the circumstances. When an authorized means is used, the Uniform Commercial Code provides that acceptance takes place at the time the acceptance is dispatched. Since the acceptance was posted on the 15th of October and acceptance was permitted to be made at that time, it was a timely acceptance.

The minor variations do not prevent the creation of the contract under the Code. They are treated as mere proposals to the offeror which he may accept or reject. The letter of October 17 may be construed as rejecting the proposed modifications but the variations do not prevent a valid acceptance from taking place on October 15 upon posting of the letter.

The conduct of Jackson Watch appears to constitute an anticipatory repudiation of the contract, i.e., it has repudiated with respect to a performance not yet due. The Code provides the aggrieved party (Williams) with a variety of remedies. It may:

(1) For a commercially reasonable time await performance.

(2) "Cover," i.e., purchase substitute goods in the market and recover from Jackson the difference between the price paid to cover (presumably $8.75) and the contract price ($7.26).

(3) Recover damages if "cover" is not resorted to. The damages will be based on the difference between the market price at the time the buyer learns of the breach (again presumably $8.75) and the contract price.

(4) In any case, suspend its own performance.

The remedy of specific performance would not be available to Williams Watch.

Williams Watch has a binding contract with Promotions, Inc. and will be liable for breach of contract if it fails to perform. Neither the fact that it was counting on Jackson Watch Bank to perform nor the fact that the price has risen sharply will permit Williams Watch to avoid its obligation.

2. The implications of these problems must be considered by Williams Watch in preparing its financial statements for the year ended October 31, 1970. The treatment to be given them will depend upon the legal approach taken by Williams Watch and the outcome anticipated by legal counsel. As a minimum, details of the contracts and expected legal steps should be shown in a footnote. If the loss anticipated in fulfilling the Promotions, Inc. contract is expected to exceed the net recovery to be made from Jackson Watch, provision should be made for the excess.

ANSWER TO QUESTION NUMBER 8

a. 1. The check is order paper because it is payable to the order of a named payee, even though the payee is a fictitious or nonexisting person. The Uniform Commercial Code changes the rule under the Uniform Negotiable Instruments Law which held that such a check was bearer paper.

2. Yes. When the check was made payable to the order of a payee whose name was supplied by an employee of the drawer and the employee intended that the named payee have no interest in the check, then anyone can endorse the payee's name to make the endorsement effective.

3. Yes. Because Martin's endorsement was effective to negotiate the check to Smith, Smith acquired valid title to the check. Since he is a holder in due course he may recover against Franklin. This does not, of course, affect the criminal or civil liability of Martin, the person wrongfully endorsing the name of another.

b. 1. Yes. There was a material alteration by Evans, a holder, which discharges prior parties except a subsequent holder in due course. Since Mark is a holder in due course, Lawrence is not discharged as to him, and Mark may recover against Lawrence.

2. Mark, as a holder in due course, can recover according to the original tenor of the check, $1,000. If Lawrence had by his negligence substantially contributed to the alteration he would be precluded from asserting the defense of material alteration and would be liable for

$10,000. However, since he used due care in preparing the check he is liable only according to its original tenor.

c. 1. Smith can compel State Bank to credit his account for $500 since the State Bank, as drawee, did not pay Hodys as Smith had directed.

2. Hodys, as rightful owner of the check has a claim in conversion against State Bank which, as drawee bank, paid the check on a forged endorsement.

3. State Bank has paid the collecting bank, National Bank. State Bank may recover $500 from National Bank for breach of warranty since National Bank warranted that all prior signatures were genuine and valid.

APPENDIX

Beginning in May 1960 a substantial number of objective questions have been utilized on the examination in commercial law, thereby reducing the number of essay questions. This major shift of position by the Institute is not likely to change. Note, however, that in May 1968 the format of the objective questions changed. The current approach is to give fewer (i.e., 30 instead of 60) parts to each question but to build the questions around short fact situations. This approach requires more skill in analysis than was previously the case.

As a result, the student has the opportunity of studying almost fifteen hundred objective questions used on the prior exams. It is safe to state that a good percentage of the objective questions will be used in slightly altered form on future exams. In fact, some are already repeats from previous exams. In addition, in many areas the objective questions have served as the basis for subsequent subjective questions. Finally, due to the great number of questions, many of the areas have been covered in great detail; consequently, by mastering the answers to the objective questions, you can test your grasp of the area and secure an excellent final review.

We therefore have included the unofficial solutions to all the objective questions contained in the book. We urge you to take at least one or two of the objective exam questions from each area and test yourself. In light of the change in format discussed above, it would be best to select the questions post-May 1968 where possible. The most recent objective questions appear first in each of the topics. In addition, you should familiarize yourself with the solutions to all the questions, since you may thereby add valuable points to your score. The objective questions in Sales, Commercial Paper and Banking and Secured Transactions are exclusively based upon the Uniform Commercial Code. All prior questions on these topics have been deleted.

ACCOUNTANT'S LEGAL RESPONSIBILITY: OBJECTIVE QUESTIONS (pp. 26-29)

	a	b	c	d	e	f	g	h	i	j
1.	F	T	T	T	F					
2.	F	T	T	F	F					
3.	T	T	F	T	T	T	T	T	T	F
4.	F	T	F	F	T	T	T	F	F	F

CONTRACTS: OBJECTIVE QUESTIONS (pp. 74-86)

	a	b	c	d	e
1.	T	F	T	T	F
2.	F	F	T	F	T
3.	T	F	T	F	T
4.	F	T	T	T	T
5.	T	T	T	F	F
6.	F	T	T	T	F
7.	T	F	T	F	F
8.	F	T	F	T	F
9.	T	F	T	F	T
10.	T	F	F	T	F
11.	T	F	F	T	F
12.	T	F	F	T	T
13.	T	T	F	T	T
14.	F	T	F	F	F
15.	T	F	T	F	T
16.	T	F	F	F	F
17.	T	T	T	T	F
18.	F	F	T	T	F
19.	T	T	T	F	T
20.	T	T	F	F	F
21.	T	T	F	F	F
22.	T	T	T	F	F
23.	F	F	F	T	F
24.	F	F	T	F	T
25.	T	F	T	T	T
26.	T	F	F	F	T
27.	F	T	F	T	F
28.	T	T	T	T	T
29.	F	F	T	T	T
30.	F	F	T	F	F
31.	T	F	F	F	T
32.	T	F	F	F	T
33.	F	T	T	F	T
34.	T	F	F	F	T
35.	T	T	F	F	F
36.	T	T	F	T	F

COMMERCIAL PAPER AND BANKING: OBJECTIVE QUESTIONS (pp.116-123)

	a	b	c	d	e
1.	F	F	T	F	F
2.	T	T	F	T	F
3.	F	F	F	F	F
4.	T	T	F	F	T
5.	F	F	F	T	T
6.	T	F	F	T	T
7.	T	F	F	T	T
8.	F	F	F	T	T
9.	F	F	F	T	F
10.	T	F	T	T	T
11.	F	T	F	T	T
12.	F	F	T	T	F

	a	b	c	d	e
13.	T	F	T	F	T
14.	F	T	T	T	F
15.	T	F	F	F	T
16.	F	T	T	T	F
17.	F	T	T	T	T
18.	T	T	T	T	T
19.	T	F	T	F	T
20.	F	T	F	F	F
21.	T	T	F	T	T
22.	F	F	F	T	T
23.	F	T	T	F	T
24.	T	F	F	F	F

AGENCY: OBJECTIVE QUESTIONS (pp. 139-148)

	a	b	c	d	e
1.	F	F	T	F	F
2.	F	T	F	F	T
3.	F	T	T	F	F
4.	T	T	T	F	F
5.	T	F	F	T	F
6.	T	F	T	T	F
7.	F	T	T	T	T
8.	T	F	F	F	T
9.	T	F	F	F	T
10.	F	T	T	F	F
11.	T	F	F	T	T
12.	T	T	T	F	F
13.	T	F	F	F	T
14.	T	T	F	F	F
15.	F	F	T	F	F
16.	T	T	F	T	F
17.	T	F	F	F	F
18.	F	T	T	T	F
19.	F	F	F	T	T
20.	F	T	T	T	F
21.	F	T	T	F	T
22.	T	T	F	F	T
23.	F	F	F	F	T
24.	T	F	F	T	F
25.	T	F	T	T	F
26.	T	T	T	F	F
27.	T	F	T	T	F
28.	F	T	T	T	T
29.	F	F	T	F	T
30.	T	F	T	T	T

PARTNERSHIPS: OBJECTIVE QUESTIONS (pp. 166-176)

	a	b	c	d	e	f	g	h	i	j
1.	T	F	T	F	F	F	F	F	F	T
2.	T	T	T	T	F					
3.	T	T	T	F	T					
4.	T	T	T	F	T					
5.	T	T	F	T	T					

	a	b	c	d	e
6.	F	F	T	T	F
7.	F	T	T	T	T
8.	F	T	F	F	F
9.	T	F	T	F	T
10.	F	F	T	F	F
11.	F	T	T	T	F
12.	F	F	F	F	F
13.	T	T	T	F	F
14.	T	T	F	T	F
15.	T	F	F	T	F
16.	T	T	F	F	F
17.	T	T	T	F	T
18.	F	F	T	T	T
19.	F	T	T	F	T
20.	T	F	T	F	T
21.	F	T	T	F	F
22.	T	F	F	F	F
23.	T	F	T	T	F
24.	T	T	F	F	F
25.	T	F	T	F	F
26.	F	F	F	F	T
27.	T	F	T	F	F
28.	T	T	F	T	T
29.	T	T	F	F	T
30.	T	T	F	T	F
31.	T	F	F	T	T
32.	T	F	F	F	T
33.	T	F	F	T	T
34.	T	T	F	F	T
35.	F	F	T	F	T

CORPORATIONS: OBJECTIVE QUESTIONS (pp. 206-217)

	a	b	c	d	e
1.	F	T	F	T	T
2.	F	F	F	T	F
3.	F	F	T	T	T
4.	T	T	F	T	T
5.	T	F	F	T	F
6.	T	T	T	T	F
7.	F	F	T	T	T
8.	F	T	T	F	F
9.	F	T	F	F	T
10.	T	T	T	F	F
11.	T	T	F	F	F
12.	T	T	T	T	F
13.	F	F	F	F	F
14.	T	T	T	T	F
15.	F	T	T	T	F
16.	F	F	T	F	F
17.	F	T	F	F	T
18.	F	F	T	F	F
19.	F	T	T	T	F
20.	T	T	T	T	T
21.	T	T	F	F	T
22.	T	F	F	T	T
23.	F	T	F	F	F
24.	T	T	F	F	F
25.	T	T	T	F	F
26.	F	F	T	T	F
27.	F	T	F	T	F
28.	F	T	F	T	F
29.	F	T	F	T	F
30.	T	T	F	F	F
31.	T	T	F	T	T
32.	F	T	T	T	T
33.	T	F	T	F	T
34.	T	T	T	F	T
35.	F	F	T	T	T
36.	T	F	F	F	F
37.	F	T	F	T	F
38.	T	F	T	F	F
39.	F	T	F	T	T
40.	T	T	T	T	T

SALES: OBJECTIVE QUESTIONS (pp. 243-251)

	a	b	c	d	e
1.	F	F	F	F	F
2.	T	T	T	F	T
3.	T	F	T	T	T
4.	F	F	F	F	T
5.	T	T	T	T	T
6.	F	T	T	F	F
7.	T	F	T	T	F
8.	F	T	F	F	T
9.	F	F	F	T	F
10.	F	F	T	F	F
11.	F	F	T	T	T
12.	F	F	F	T	T
13.	F	F	T	F	T
14.	F	T	T	T	F
15.	F	F	T	T	T
16.	F	T	F	F	F
17.	T	T	T	F	F
18.	T	T	F	T	F
19.	F	T	F	F	T
20.	F	F	T	T	F
21.	F	F	T	F	F
22.	T	F	F	F	T
23.	F	F	T	F	T
24.	F	F	F	T	T
25.	T	F	F	F	F
26.	T	F	T	T	T
27.	F	T	T	T	T
28.	T	F	F	T	T
29.	T	F	F	T	T
30.	T	T	T	T	F

SECURED TRANSACTIONS: OBJECTIVE QUESTIONS (pp. 262-265)

	a	b	c	d	e
1.	T	F	T	F	F
2.	T	T	F	F	F
3.	F	T	T	T	F
4.	T	T	T	T	F
5.	T	F	T	F	F
6.	F	T	T	T	T
7.	T	F	T	F	F
8.	F	T	F	F	T
9.	T	F	T	F	F
10.	T	T	T	T	F

FEDERAL SECURITIES REGULATION: OBJECTIVE QUESTIONS (p. 287)

	a	b	c	d	e
1.	F	F	T	F	T
2.	T	T	T		

INSURANCE: OBJECTIVE QUESTIONS (pp. 327-331)

	a	b	c	d	e
1.	T	T	F	T	F
2.	F	T	F	T	T
3.	F	F	T	F	F
4.	F	T	F	T	T
5.	F	T	F	T	T
6.	T	F	T	F	T
7.	T	F	F	F	T
8.	F	T	T	T	T
9.	T	F	T	F	F
10.	F	F	T	F	T
11.	F	F	T	T	T
12.	T	T	F	T	F
13.	F	T	F	F	F
14.	F	T	T	T	F
15.	F	T	T	F	T

SURETYSHIP: OBJECTIVE QUESTIONS (pp. 350-353)

	a	b	c	d	e		a	b	c	d	e
1.	T	F	T	F	T	9.	T	F	T	T	F
2.	T	F	F	F	T	10.	F	F	F	T	T
3.	T	F	T	F	F	11.	T	F	T	F	T
4.	T	T	F	F	T	12.	T	F	F	T	F
5.	F	T	F	F	T	13.	F	T	F	F	F
6.	T	T	F	T	T	14.	T	T	T	T	F
7.	F	F	F	T	T	15.	T	F	F	T	F
8.	F	F	F	T	T						

BANKRUPTCY: OBJECTIVE QUESTIONS (pp. 372-378)

	a	b	c	d	e		a	b	c	d	e
1.	T	T	F	F	T	16.	T	F	F	T	F
2.	T	T	T	F	T	17.	F	T	T	T	F
3.	T	F	T	T	F	18.	T	F	F	F	F
4.	F	T	F	F	F	19.	T	F	T	T	F
5.	F	F	F	F	T	20.	T	F	T	F	T
6.	T	F	F	F	T	21.	F	F	T	T	F
7.	T	F	T	T	F	22.	T	T	T	T	F
8.	F	F	F	F	T	23.	T	T	F	T	F
9.	T	T	T	F	F	24.	F	T	T	T	F
10.	T	F	F	F	T	25.	F	T	F	T	T
11.	T	F	F	F	T	26.	F	T	T	F	F
12.	F	T	F	T	F	27.	T	T	T	F	F
13.	T	T	F	T	T	28.	T	T	F	T	T
14.	T	F	F	T	F	29.	F	T	T	F	T
15.	F	F	T	T	T	30.	T	T	F	F	T

PROPERTY: OBJECTIVE QUESTIONS (pp. 407-409)

	a	b	c	d	e		a	b	c	d	e
1.	F	T	T	F	T	5.	T	F	T	T	T
2.	F	T	T	T	T	6.	F	T	T	T	F
3.	T	F	F	F	F	7.	F	T	F	F	T
4.	T	T	F	T	T	8.	T	F	T	T	T

WILLS AND ESTATES AND TRUSTS: OBJECTIVE QUESTIONS (pp. 427-429)

	a	b	c	d	e
1.	T	F	F	T	T
2.	T	F	F	F	F
3.	T	T	T	T	T
4.	F	T	T	T	F
5.	T	F	F	T	T
6.	T	F	F	F	T
7.	F	F	T	T	F
8.	T	T	F	T	F
9.	T	F	F	F	T
10.	T	T	T	F	T
11.	F	T	F	F	T
12.	T	T	F	F	F
13.	T	T	T	T	T
14.	F	F	F	F	F
15.	T	F	T	F	F